Ireland in crisis

Manchester University Press

Series editors
DAVID EDWARDS & MICHEÁL Ó SIOCHRÚ

The study of Early Modern Irish History has experienced something of a renaissance in the last decade. However, studies tend to group around traditional topics in political or military history and significant gaps remain. The idea behind this series is to identify key themes and set the agenda for future research.

Each volume in this series comes from leading scholars from Ireland, Britain, North America and elsewhere, addressing a particular subject. We aim to bring the best of Irish historical research to a wider audience, by engaging with international themes of empire, colonisation, religious change and social transformation.

Already published

The plantation of Ulster: Ideology and practice
Micheál Ó Siochrú and Éamonn Ó Ciardha (eds)

Ireland, 1641: Contexts and reactions
Micheál Ó Siochrú and Jane Ohlmeyer (eds)

The Scots in early Stuart Ireland: Union and separation in two kingdoms
David Edwards and Simon Egan (eds)

Debating Tudor policy in sixteenth-century Ireland: 'Reform' treatises and political discourse
David Heffernan

The Irish parliament, 1613–89: The evolution of a colonial institution
Coleman A. Dennehy

Ireland in crisis

War, politics and religion, 1641–50

EDITED BY PATRICK LITTLE

Manchester University Press

Copyright © Manchester University Press 2020

While copyright in the volume as a whole is vested in Manchester University Press, copyright in individual chapters belongs to their respective authors, and no chapter may be reproduced wholly or in part without the express permission in writing of both author and publisher.

Published by Manchester University Press
Oxford Road, Manchester M13 9PL

www.manchesteruniversitypress.co.uk

British Library Cataloguing-in-Publication Data
A catalogue record for this book is available from the British Library

ISBN 978 1 5261 2670 2 hardback
ISBN 978 1 5261 8248 7 paperback

First published 2020
Paperback published 2024

The publisher has no responsibility for the persistence or accuracy of URLs for any external or third-party internet websites referred to in this book, and does not guarantee that any content on such websites is, or will remain, accurate or appropriate.

Typeset in 10.5/12.5 Minion Pro by
Servis Filmsetting Ltd, Stockport, Cheshire

*For A.L.L.
and in memory of P.W.S.*

Contents

List of figures and tables	page ix
Notes on contributors	x
Series editors' preface	xii
Preface	xiii
Abbreviations	xiv

Introduction: the confederate wars revisited   1
Patrick Little

1 Holding on: the earl of Cork's Blackwater army and the defence of Protestant Munster, 1641–43   20
David Edwards

2 The Sea Adventure to Munster and Connacht, July and August 1642   43
David Brown

3 'To hold a good opinion of my loyalty and zealous affections': the earl of Clanricarde and the royalist cause in Connacht, 1643–46   61
Aoife Duignan

4 'Clotworthy is a zealous man, yet hath his purse well lined': Sir John Clotworthy, John Davies and the politics of supply, 1644–45   79
Andrew Robinson

5	The Irish Parliament after the rebellion, 1642–48 *Coleman A. Dennehy*	100
6	The recruiter returns to the Irish Parliament, 1642–48 *Bríd McGrath*	119
7	The politics of preferment: the marquess of Ormond, Archbishop Ussher and the appointment of Irish bishops, 1643–47 *Patrick Little*	138
8	The marquess of Ormond, Lord Montgomery of the Ards and the problem of authority in Ulster, 1649 *Kevin Forkan*	155
9	The confederate Catholics of Ireland and popular politics *Eamon Darcy*	172
10	Oliver Cromwell, priestcraft and the 'deluded and seduced' people of Ireland *John Morrill*	193

Index   211

Figures and tables

FIGURES

1	Map of the Blackwater Valley, 1641–43 (drawn by Colin Rynne)	*page* 31
2	Known returns by year of first mention	122
3	Social status of recruiter MPs	127
4	Ethnic origin of recruiter MPs	129

TABLES

1	Cork's command: castles and garrisons in the southern Blackwater Valley, 1642	30
2	The length of sessions of the House of Commons	104
3	Attendance levels of members of the House of Commons	107
4	Attendance levels of members of the House of Lords	108
5	Petitions presented to Parliament in the seventeenth century	111

Notes on contributors

David Brown is Archival Discovery lead for the Beyond 2022 Project, Trinity College Dublin. His monograph, *Empire and Enterprise: Money, power and the Adventure for Irish Land, 1642–1660*, will be published by Manchester University Press in 2020. He previously worked on the *Down Survey of Ireland* project, under Micheál Ó Siochrú, and is co-editor of a five-volume scholarly edition of the *Books of Survey and Distribution* for the Irish Manuscripts Commission.

Eamon Darcy teaches at Maynooth University. His publications include *The Irish Rebellion of 1641 and the Wars of the Three Kingdoms* (Woodbridge, Suffolk, 2013) and *The World of Thomas Ward: sex and scandal in late seventeenth-century Co Antrim* (Dublin, 2016).

Coleman A. Dennehy is a legal historian who has taught at University College Dublin and University College London (as IRC Marie Skłodowska-Curie Fellow), and at the University of Limerick. His monograph, a legal and administrative history of *The Irish Parliament, 1613–89: the evolution of a colonial institution*, was published by Manchester University Press in 2019.

Aoife Duignan is Student Complaints Officer at University College Dublin. Her doctoral thesis was a study of politics and war in Connacht during the 1640s. She has contributed chapters to Robert Armstrong and Tadhg Ó hAnnracháin (eds), *Communities in Early Modern Ireland* (Dublin, 2006) and David Edwards and Simon Egan (eds), *The Scots in Early Stuart Ireland* (Manchester, 2016).

David Edwards is Senior Lecturer in History at University College Cork, and was Principal Investigator of the Irish Research Council Senior Collaborative project 'The Colonial landscapes of Richard Boyle, 1st Earl of Cork, c.1602–1643'. He is the author of *The Ormond Lordship in County Kilkenny, 1515–1642* (Dublin, 2003), and joint-editor of *Age of Atrocity:*

violence and political conflict in early modern Ireland (Dublin, 2007) and *The Colonial World of Richard Boyle, first earl of Cork* (Dublin, 2018).

Kevin Forkan is Head of Archives and Library at M+, the new museum for visual culture in Hong Kong. He previously held research positions at NUI Galway and Trinity College Dublin, working under Nicholas Canny and Jane Ohlmeyer, and his publications include 'The Ulster Scots and the Engagement, 1647–8', *Irish Historical Studies* 35 (2007), and 'Ormond's alternative: the lord-lieutenant's secret contacts with Protestant Ulster, 1645–6', *Historical Research* 81 (2008).

Patrick Little is a Senior Research Fellow at the History of Parliament Trust in London. He is the author of *Lord Broghill and the Cromwellian Union with Ireland and Scotland* (Woodbridge, Suffolk, 2004) and a number of articles on Ireland in the 1640s and 1650s.

Bríd McGrath is Adjunct Assistant Professor in the Department of History, Trinity College Dublin, where she teaches palaeography. She has edited the *Minute Book of the Corporation of Clonmel, 1608–1649* (Dublin, 2006) and *Acts of the Corporation of Coleraine, 1623–1669* (Dublin, 2017), and has published a large number of articles and papers on early modern Irish parliaments and towns.

John Morrill FBA, HonMRIA is Emeritus Professor of British and Irish History at the University of Cambridge and a Life Fellow of Selwyn College. His 130 publications include fifteen books and essays on the life and thought of Oliver Cromwell and he is the general editor of a five-volume edition of Oliver Cromwell's letters, speeches and writings, to be published by Oxford University Press.

Andrew Robinson works as a researcher in the public sector in relation to policing and criminal justice in Northern Ireland. He completed his PhD entitled '"Not otherwise worthy to be named, but as a firebrand brought from Ireland to inflame this Kingdom": the political and cultural milieu of Sir John Clotworthy during the Stuart Civil Wars' at Ulster University in 2013, and has subsequently published articles on Clotworthy, Owen O'Connolly and the 1641 Rising in Co. Monaghan.

Series editors' preface

The study of early modern Irish history has experienced something of a renaissance in recent years, with the publication of a number of major monographs examining developments in Ireland during the sixteenth and seventeenth centuries from a variety of different perspectives. The idea behind this new series is to identify themes for further exploration and thereby set the agenda for future research. Manchester University Press, a leading academic press with a strong record of publishing Irish related material, is the ideal home for this venture.

This latest volume in the series explores one of the most controversial episodes of early modern Irish history. After decades of neglect, the late 1990s witnessed an outpouring of studies on different aspects of the war in Ireland during the 1640s. Since then, however, historians have focused more on the outbreak of the conflict in 1641 and the subsequent Cromwellian conquest and land settlement of the 1650s. The time is right, therefore, for a major reappraisal of key developments during the entire decade of the 1640s but one that eschews the traditional focus on high politics and major military campaigns. The essays published here, by a select panel of established and up-and-coming scholars, explore a disparate range of topics from regional warfare to popular politics and officially sanctioned piracy. Each chapter provides fresh insights and perspectives in select areas, while collectively addressing (directly or indirectly) the crisis of authority caused by the collapse of a colonial system of governance that had functioned more or less effectively since 1603. Throughout the 1640s all sides struggled to assert their legitimacy in the face of numerous and repeated challenges from their (sometimes fluctuating) opponents. Ultimately, the English Parliament prevailed, primarily through sheer military might and the effective deployment of the massive financial resources of the English state. This volume will help explain why.

David Edwards and Micheál Ó Siochrú

Preface

Edited volumes are a team effort, and I am indebted to the contributors for their cheerful cooperation, which has made this volume a pleasure to edit. For similar reasons I would like to acknowledge the help of the series editors, David Edwards and Micheál Ó Siochrú, and the editors at Manchester University Press, Emma Brennan and Meredith Carroll. I am also grateful to Jane Ohlmeyer for hosting a workshop on the volume at Trinity College Dublin in September 2016, and for all who attended, especially Robert Armstrong, Padraig Lenihan and Tadhg Ó hAnnracháin, whose wise counsel was much appreciated. Finally, I would like to thank all my friends in Dublin for their generosity and hospitality over nearly three decades. My oldest connections with that city, and its ancient university, are acknowledged in the dedication.

In general, spelling and punctuation of original sources have been modernised, but at the request of Professor Morrill the final chapter is an exception to this rule, as it involves detailed discussion of documents derived from his forthcoming edition of Cromwell's letters, speeches and writings. I have attempted a compromise between different usages by adopting 'Derry' for the city and 'Londonderry' for the county, while 'Connacht', 'King's County' and 'Queen's County' (as opposed to Offaly and Laois) are used throughout. As is customary, dates are given old style, but with the New Year beginning on 1 January, and for printed sources London is the place of publication unless otherwise specified.

P.J.S.L.
December 2018

Abbreviations

A & O	C.H. Firth and R.S. Rait (eds), *Acts and Ordinances of the Interregnum, 1642–1660* (London, 1911)
Armstrong, *Protestant War*	Robert Armstrong, *Protestant War: the 'British' of Ireland and the Wars of the Three Kingdoms* (Manchester, 2005)
Baillie Letters and Journals	David Laing (ed.), *The Letters and Journals of Robert Baillie* (3 vols, Edinburgh, 1842)
BL	British Library, London
Bodl.	Bodleian Library, Oxford
Carte, *Life of Ormonde*	Thomas Carte, *The Life of James, Duke of Ormond* (6 vols, Oxford, 1851)
Clanricarde Letter-Book	John Lowe (ed.), *Letter-Book of the Earl of Clanricarde, 1643–47* (Dublin, 1983)
Clanricarde Memoirs	Ulick De Burgh (ed.), *The memoirs and Letters of Ulick, Marquis of Clanricarde and Earl of St Albans* (London, 1757)
Clarendon, *Rebellion*	Edward Hyde, earl of Clarendon, *The History of the Rebellion and Civil Wars in England*, ed. W.D. Macray (6 vols, Oxford, 1888)
Gilbert, *Contemporary History*	J.T. Gilbert (ed.), *A Contemporary History of affairs in Ireland from AD 1641 to 1652* (3 vols, Dublin, 1879)
Gilbert, *Irish Confederation*	J.T. Gilbert (ed.), *History of the Irish Confederation and the war in Ireland* (7 vols, Dublin, 1882–91)
CJ	*Journals of the House of Commons*

CJI	*Journals of the House of Commons of Ireland*
CSP Dom.	*Calendar of State Papers, Domestic*
CSP Ire.	*Calendar of State Papers, Ireland*
CSP Ven.	*Calendar of State Papers, Venetian*
DIB	*Dictionary of Irish Biography*
EHR	*English Historical Review*
ESTC	English Short Title Catalogue
Grosart (ed.), *Lismore Papers*	A.B. Grosart (ed.), *The Lismore Papers* (10 vols in 2 series, 1886–88)
Hamilton Manuscripts	T.K. Lowry (ed.), *The Hamilton Manuscripts* (Belfast, 1867)
HJ	*Historical Journal*
Hist. Res.	*Historical Research*
HMC	Historical Manuscripts Commission
IHS	*Irish Historical Studies*
Lenihan, *Confederate Catholics at War*	Padraig Lenihan, *Confederate Catholics at War, 1642–1649* (Cork, 2001)
LJ	*Journals of the House of Lords*
LJI	*Journals of the House of Lords of Ireland* (8 vols. Dublin 1779–1800)
Montgomery Manuscripts	George Hill (ed.), *The Montgomery Manuscripts* (Belfast, 1869)
NHI	T. Moody, F. Martin and F. Byrne (eds), *A New History of Ireland* (vol. iii), *Early Modern Ireland 1534–1691* (Oxford, 1976)
NLI	National Library of Ireland, Dublin
ODNB	*Oxford Dictionary of National Biography*
Ó hAnnracháin, *Rinuccini*	Tadhg Ó hAnnracháin, *Catholic Reformation in Ireland: The Mission of Rinuccini, 1645–1649* (Cambridge, 2002)
Ó Siochrú, *Confederate Ireland*	Micheál Ó Siochrú, *Confederate Ireland, 1642–1649: a constitutional and political analysis* (Dublin, 1999)
Ohlmeyer, *Making Ireland English*	Jane Ohlmeyer, *Making Ireland English: the Irish aristocracy in the seventeenth century* (New Haven, 2012)

PRONI	Public Record Office of Northern Ireland, Belfast
RIA	Royal Irish Academy, Dublin
TCD	Trinity College, Dublin
Temple, *Irish Rebellion*	Sir John Temple, *The Irish Rebellion* (1646)
TNA	The National Archives, Kew

Introduction:
the confederate wars revisited

PATRICK LITTLE

The wars of the 1640s have always been one of the most controversial episodes in Irish history. Beginning with the Ulster rebellion of October 1641, with the massacre and eviction of thousands of Protestant settlers, the decade of periodic warfare, intermittent negotiation and constant threat of violence came to an end only with the Cromwellian invasion of 1649 and the brutal conquest of the whole island, completed in 1653. Irish historians have treated this pivotal period with a mixture of fascination and hesitation. It is curious that arguably the most influential historian of early modern Ireland, Aidan Clarke, wrote books that covered the period before and after the 1640s, but made only tentative forays, in article form, into the decade itself.[1] Donal Cregan's exemplary work on the Catholic Confederation of Kilkenny was fragmentary, and his *magnum opus* remains an unpublished thesis.[2] Similarly, Patrick Corish published only one major article on the 1640s, but his survey of the period in the third volume of the *New History of Ireland*, published in 1975, set the agenda for much of the debate that followed.[3] Their work was reinforced by that of other historians, notably John Lowe, whose essays on the royalist/confederate negotiations have stood the test of time,[4] and John Murphy, who produced a series of articles focusing on Munster.[5]

From the parliamentarian point of view, Karl Bottigheimer's book on the adventurers for Irish land proved the most influential, but when it came to Ireland itself his focus was very much on Munster.[6] Only a smattering of studies of individuals appeared during this period. J.C. Beckett's brief study of Ormond was a useful introduction but short on detail, Jerrold Casway's biography of Owen Roe O'Neill was a model of its kind, while Jane Ohlmeyer's portrait of the earl of Antrim was the first attempt to put a key player in Irish history into a 'three kingdoms' context.[7] Indeed, the 'wars of the three kingdoms' provided much of the impetus for renewed interest in the period during the early 1990s, as the so-called 'New British History' movement, associated with Conrad Russell and others in the pre-civil war period, was extended to cover the 1640s.[8]

Arguably, the golden age of study of the confederate wars was the decade from 1995 to 2005. Jane Ohlmeyer's edited volume, *Ireland from Independence to Occupation*, published in 1995, included essays by such well respected authorities as Nicholas Canny, Raymond Gillespie, Toby Barnard and James Scott Wheeler, covering topics including the 1641 rebellion, warfare, the economy and the Protestant interest. The fashion for putting Ireland into its wider British and European contexts was represented by John Adamson's exploration of Viscount Lisle's lieutenancy in 1646–47 and Ohlmeyer's own chapter on confederate foreign policy.[9] The volume was the harbinger of a series of four important monographs, derived from doctoral theses, which provided in-depth studies of particular aspects of the period. Micheál Ó Siochrú's ground-breaking political and constitutional analysis of confederate government appeared in 1999.[10] Ó Siochrú's largely secular focus was balanced by Tadhg Ó hAnnracháin's scholarly account of Archbishop Rinuccini's mission to Ireland, which came out in 2002.[11] A year earlier, Pádraig Lenihan published a comprehensive study of the confederate war machine.[12] The final book of the quartet, published in 2005, was Robert Armstrong's masterly study of the Irish wars from the Protestant point of view.[13]

The Big Four were complemented by a series of articles covering different aspects of the period, notably Ó hAnnracháin's two essays looking at the Catholic clergy, and his thought-provoking piece on the conflicted loyalties of the confederates more generally.[14] On the Protestant side of the equation, Ormond came into the spotlight thanks to Armstrong's study of his peace talks with the Catholics in the mid-1640s and my own article on his parallel negotiations with the English Parliament.[15] Other important individuals, including the earl of Clanricarde, Colonel John Barry and Lord Broghill also received much-needed attention.[16] Some of the best work was brought together in Ó Siochrú's 2001 volume of essays, entitled (with a nod to the 'New British History'), *Kingdoms in Crisis*.[17] A further collection of essays, appropriately dedicated to Aidan Clarke, appeared in 2005, and included pieces by Ó Siochrú on the constitutional relationship of Ireland and England, and Armstrong on the Protestant clergy during the 1640s.[18]

After 2005, the confederate period went off the boil. The focus of Irish historical attention shifted instead both earlier and later: to the outbreak of rebellion in 1641 (thanks to the Trinity College Dublin 'depositions' project, which generated a plethora of attendant publications) and to the Cromwellian conquest after 1649.[19] An important factor in this cooling of interest was the abandonment of the 'New British History' by its leading proponents, as new bandwagons hoved into view.[20] Yet in Ireland there were still younger scholars coming through who were focusing on the period, asking different questions of the sources, and finding new areas to study. With notable exceptions, earlier research on the decade had tended to concentrate on leading figures and central governments, but this was now offset by a renewed interest in the war as experienced in the regions. The benefit of this approach had already been demonstrated by Mary O'Dowd on co. Sligo, Raymond Gillespie on co. Cavan, and David Edwards's work on the collapse of the Ormond lordship in Kilkenny, and it was now extended by Aoife Duignan's article on the Protestant community in northern Connacht, drawn from her PhD thesis, which was published in 2006.[21] In 2007–8 Kevin Forkan added an important new facet to our understanding of Ormond's position with an article on his 'secret contacts' with various Protestant groups in Ulster, as well as studies of the Scottish community and its reaction to the Engagement in 1647–48.[22] Western Ulster was the subject of a thesis on co. Fermanagh by Charlene McCoy and a study of the Protestants of the 'Laggan' army by Kevin McKenny.[23] Individuals also received more detailed attention, especially Clanricarde, who was the subject of a 2006 PhD by Harriet Sexton and a 2009 article by Demetri Debe.[24] Robert Armstrong contributed an article focused on Viscount Montgomery of the Ards, also in 2009, and Andrew Robinson's thesis on Sir John Clotworthy appeared in 2013.[25] Military affairs saw considerable interest. On the back of the 1641 depositions project there was new research into massacres and violence in the early years of the war, and a continuing fascination with Cromwell's nefarious activities at Drogheda and Wexford in 1649, while the definitive account of naval warfare by Elaine Murphy was published in 2012.[26] Another development – influenced by a recent trend in English history – is an upsurge of interest in royalism, as manifested in Barry Robertson's important study of *Royalists at War*, published in 2014.[27]

Much of the recent work on the 1640s has been of high quality, but has had less of an impact than that of the previous decade, for two reasons: historical fashions have moved away from traditional political and religious history, and the recent economic crisis in Ireland and elsewhere has drastically restricted the opportunities for good doctoral students to develop their ideas and to publish material from their theses. A glance at the list of contributors to this book will show how many are now in untenured or non-academic jobs.

The primary aim of the present volume is to revive interest in the confederate wars by presenting the latest findings by younger as well as more experienced scholars and to point to new ways of approaching the period in the future. The quality and variety of these chapters suggest that the time for a revival is long overdue. The essays follow a broadly chronological sequence, beginning with detailed studies of individuals facing rebellion and warfare in their immediate localities, as with David Edwards's investigations of the first earl of Cork's private army, and the difficulty he had in defending his estates in the Blackwater Valley during the early years of the Irish wars (not least because the lord president of Munster, Sir William St Leger, had other priorities). Aoife Duignan's chapter considers Clanricarde's 'increasingly lonely struggle' as (it seemed) the only Catholic royalist in the province. As a man of honour, Clanricarde found the ambiguities of his situation difficult to face: although he remained faithful to the king he was constantly passed over or rebuffed by his royal master; and although he could not join his confederate friends and relatives in rebellion, he could (just) stomach cooperating with them against a bigger enemy, such as the Protestant army of Sir Charles Coote.

The interactions between Ireland and England are the focus of of Chapters 2 and 4. David Brown's painstaking reconstruction of the Sea Adventure as it pillaged the south and west coasts in 1642 reveals the importance of existing mercantile networks, especially in Munster, and the way in which 'piratical' colonial practices could easily be transferred to the Irish coast, with destabilising consequences. Andrew Robinson's account of the efforts of Sir John Clotworthy to increase the supplies sent from England to the armies in Ulster takes the story into the mid-1640s. Clotworthy's success in wresting the initiative away from the adventurers, aided by 'the gentlemen of Ireland' – a kaleidoscopic array of Irish Protestants from all four provinces engaged in lobbying the parliamentarian authorities – reminds us of the importance of personal connections during this period. In particular, the way in which the Carrickfergus merchant, John Davies, stole a march on his London rivals to monopolise the supply lines shows how war presented opportunities to those who were both enterprising and unscrupulous.

Chapters 5 and 6 address the neglected topic of the Irish Parliament in the 1640s. Many historians assume that, having played a pivotal role in the fall of the earl of Strafford, Parliament came to an end in 1641, before the outbreak of rebellion. Coleman Dennehy reminds us that Parliament continued to meet, however infrequently, until 1648 and technically it was only dissolved on the execution of Charles I in January 1649. His chapter investigates attendance in the houses and the business conducted there, including passing legislation and hearing petitions. He also considers why an apparently defunct institution was kept on life support by Ormond and the Dublin administration, concluding that part of the reason was to ratify a peace treaty with the confederates that never took effect. Dennehy's chapter is complemented by that of Bríd McGrath, who considers the MPs 'recruited' to the Irish Parliament between 1642 and 1647. Her analysis of the eighty-seven identified MPs added to the Commons during that period reveals that they mostly represented Leinster seats (especially those under the control of the government in Dublin), two-thirds were Protestant New English, and most were soldiers or government officials. The problems of conducting wartime elections meant that many MPs were 'elected' by the use of blank returns or effectively chosen by the local sheriffs, and the numbers varied considerably through the decade, with peaks in 1642 (to replace ejected Catholics), 1644 and 1647. Despite this, there was a considerable variety of political views, reflecting the increasingly divided Protestant community, and this contributed to the ineffectiveness of the Irish Parliament as an institution, even as its symbolic power as guarantor of any peace treaty increased.

Other chapters approach familiar subjects from unfamiliar angles: Ormond is the focus of two chapters looking at very different aspects of his role as lord lieutenant. My own eschews the normal political route to focus on Ormond's involvement with Archbishop Ussher and the running of the Church of Ireland, specifically the appointment of bishops. This shows not only Ormond's determination to keep the church hierarchy filled with suitably able men – which was especially important during the negotiations with the confederates, in which the future of church property was paramount – but also his sympathies with Calvinist divines such as Dr Henry Jones of Clogher, who could provide robust opposition to the covenanters as well as the Catholics. The chapter thus provides yet another layer to the complicated negotiations conducted by Ormond in the mid-1640s, reinforcing the impression that the lord lieutenant was a politician of considerable ingenuity; it also suggests that the role of the Church of Ireland as a support for the royalist government needs further consideration. Ormond's position as political ringmaster did not last. His ignominious surrender of Dublin to the English Parliament in 1647 and his return to Ireland with instructions to settle with the confederates at any price in 1648 made his position untenable. The leaching away of support for his lieutenancy in Ulster in 1649 is chronicled by Kevin Forkan in Chapter 8. Viscount Montgomery of the Ards seemed a good choice to lead the royalist 'non-sectarian coalition' in the north, but he could not convince the Presbyterian ministers, who turned against him, and his position was further weakened by the activities of Sir George Monro as a rival commander in the west of the province.

The final brace of chapters focuses more directly on the Catholic side of the equation. Eamon Darcy makes a foray into the notoriously difficult topic of early modern popular politics within a confederate context. He considers the importance of communication in the period, and especially the role of bilingual 'brokers' in spreading propaganda and of the role of oath-taking as a means of securing allegiance, and also looks at print culture and popular politics. The conclusion for the Confederate Association is not at all positive, as its leaders remained wary of the ordinary people, blaming them for lawlessness and violence during the rebellion, and dismissing their beliefs; instead it was left to the Catholic Church to seize the initiative, with the rejection of the first Ormond Peace, 'the ultimate popular act' of the decade, showing the power of the religious elite over their secular counterpart. The Catholic Church also plays an important part in John Morrill's concluding chapter, which looks at Cromwell's polemical dispute with the Catholic hierarchy in the winter of 1649–50. Morrill argues that Cromwell's rhetoric was not primarily anti-Catholic; rather his targets were those guilty of the massacres of 1641, the clergy he saw as behind the violence throughout the decade, and the recalcitrant royalists. Controversially, he concludes that the bigotry of the conquest of Ireland in the years that followed was the fault of others.

As will already be clear, these essays provide a multitude of different perspectives, many of which tie in with important ongoing research topics such as regionalism and royalism and 'British' history which provide insights into the political and religious experiences of all communities in Ireland during the 1640s. The chapters not only shed more light on the experiences of a wide range of individuals (from major political players such as Ormond and Clanricarde to lesser figures, notably the Carrickfergus merchant, John Davies) but also address the hitherto neglected topic of institutional history (specifically the Irish Parliament and the Church of Ireland). Each of these important themes might be explored further, challenging the existing literature; but for the remainder of this introduction I concentrate on another major issue that provides a thread running through almost all the chapters in this volume: the crisis of authority.

During the 1640s, prolonged rebellion and civil war led to a deterioration of already fraught political relationships within early modern Ireland. In times of peace the ultimate source of civil authority was the king, although there were concerns at outside interference, especially by the Catholic Church, while the role of the English government, and specifically the Westminster Parliament, was something of a grey area.[28] In a period of rebellion and civil war there was a fracturing of the normal order, with every side claiming some sort of justification, and seeking a measure of legitimacy for their actions. This complicated the picture enormously, and caused contemporaries to question their own assumptions. As Aidan Clarke, one of a handful of historians to have considered the problem, puts it: 'it was not until the breakdown of authority in the multiple Stuart kingdoms in the early 1640s that the underlying assumptions of Irish politics were found to be in need of definition and justification'.[29] The emphasis here is not on abstract political thought or abstruse constitutional theory but on the very real problems caused by the breakdown of a system that had been widely accepted, and was functional if not exactly smooth-running, in the four decades before the outbreak of rebellion in 1641.

As all political authority was derived from the king, the royalists – and especially Ormond as lord lieutenant – should have been more secure in their position than their rivals. The king demanded loyalty as of right, and so did his viceroy and other officers of state. This was taken as read by most of the Irish people, whether Protestant or Catholic. To take but two examples, Clanricarde's almost instinctive royalism led him to resist the blandishments of his confederate friends in Connacht, as Aoife Duignan demonstrates; likewise in April 1645 Sir Richard Osborne refused to surrender Knockmoan Castle in co. Waterford to the confederate forces under the earl of Castlehaven precisely because of the duty of allegiance he owed to the king and his lord lieutenant.[30] During the middle years of the decade Ormond had the additional advantages that went with his possession of the capital city, as he held not only the traditional seat of government at Dublin Castle, but also controlled the Parliament and law courts, as well as the university and two of the most important cathedrals. All enhanced his claim to be the representative of the king and to exercise lawful government of church and state, even if, geographically, most of Ireland was outside his control. Ormond was extremely jealous of his position as the king's viceroy. His dignified response, in June 1646, to the Scottish officers in Ulster, who had addressed a letter to him personally, as marquess, rather than to the lord lieutenant and council – 'in which capacity only, and not otherwise, we have power to treat with you' – was not just pulling rank.[31]

By including the council in his reprimand to the Scots, Ormond was merely stating a fact: as John Lowe has noted, the lieutenant 'insisted punctiliously on consulting at every stage in negotiations' with the confederates, and the moral support of senior councillors was vitally important.[32] The continuation of the Irish Parliament also served to bolster Ormond's authority during his negotiations. As Coleman Dennehy points out, that may provide one reason why the houses were not dissolved early in the decade, and the continuing importance of Parliament is also suggested by the continued efforts to 'recruit' its membership, as explored by Bríd McGrath. Likewise, Ormond's concern to maintain the Church of Ireland with a full complement of bishops can be linked with the need to bolster royal authority more generally. This chimes with Robert Armstrong's observation 'that churchmen and laymen could, as in England, stand by the church by law established because it was established'.[33] Such symbols of authority were vital when dealing with the confederate rebels. On the publication of the first Ormond Peace in 1646, Ormond sent Dr William Roberts, Ulster king of arms, to proclaim the treaty in Limerick and other confederate strongholds 'with the king's coat of arms upon him', as a powerful statement that central authority was being restored.[34] Parliament, the church and the officers of state were thus seen as pillars supporting Ormond's authority, even if his effective military power was restricted to the enclave around Dublin. Indeed, it might be argued that the weaker his position became, the more he came to rely on such props to his dignity. Any challenge to Ormond's own authority had to be taken very seriously – hence the frosty response to the Scots in June 1646, and the appalled reaction to the physical assault on Dr Roberts by the 'tumultuous rabble' at Limerick in August of the same year.[35] A few months earlier the earl of Glamorgan's secret dealings with the confederates had angered Ormond not only because he was prepared to make unacceptable religious concessions, but also because he was acting independently of the Dublin government, with a royal commission of dubious legitimacy.[36] It is also interesting that Glamorgan's arrest was ordered formally by the lord lieutenant and council, as if to highlight the informality of his own activities.[37]

The Glamorgan mission also highlights the extent to which Ormond's position was undermined by the king's interference in Irish affairs, and in this he was not alone. Aoife Duignan emphasises that the refusal of Charles I to make Clanricarde lord president of Connacht hampered the earl's ability to unite the local inhabitants behind the crown. There are strong parallels with the situation faced by Lord Inchiquin as vice-president of Munster after the death of Sir William St Leger left the presidency itself up for grabs in 1642. The lord president and his council were crucial to the southern province, as 'its very existence helped to give an administrative area a real existence' and it thus represented 'the collective will of the English interest' there.[38] This was particularly important in time of war, when the president was expected to unite and command the local forces. In Munster, as David Edwards demonstrates, tensions between the earl of Cork and St Leger as president had already hampered the war effort in the immediate aftermath of rebellion. Worse was to follow. The appointment of the earl of Portland, a courtier with no experience of Ireland, as St Leger's replacement, was one of the factors which lay behind Inchiquin's defection to Parliament in 1644. According to Arthur Trevor, Inchiquin was 'as full of anger as his buttons will endure' at the appointment of Portland in February 1644, and in the following May Inchiquin was feeling the after-effects in Cork City, where 'the mayor does already question my authority for the issuing of some warrants that do not please him'.[39]

The similarities with Clanricarde's precarious position in Connacht are very close, and the appointment of another courtier, Henry Wilmot, as joint president of that province alongside Viscount Dillon, suggests that the king's main priority was to please his courtiers at Oxford rather than fight an effective war in Ireland – a policy that led to a disjuncture between authority and power that severely hampered the royalist war effort in the regions. Ironically, the presidency in both provinces only stabilised when the English Parliament took upon itself the appointment of its own lords president in the new year of 1645. Inchiquin in Munster soon took charge of the military situation, even if his position was challenged in the longer term; and Sir Charles Coote in Connacht managed to unite the Protestant interest and create an effective fighting force in the later 1640s.[40] The value placed on the office of president can also be seen after Inchiquin's defection to the king in April 1648, as pains were taken to supply him with a new commission from the prince of Wales, his parliamentary authority having lapsed.⁴¹

Ormond was the primary focus for royalist legitimacy in the middle years of the decade, but with his surrender of Dublin to the Westminster Parliament in June 1647 his position was severely damaged. Indeed, Ormond not only surrendered the royalist garrisons but also his sword of office and 'other ensigns of royalty' – a point insisted upon by parliamentarians, who hoped thereby to undermine his influence in Ireland.⁴² In this they were successful. Although he remained titular lord lieutenant, on his return to Ireland in September 1648 Ormond found his authority questioned at every turn. When negotiations with the confederate General Assembly restarted in October, that body even demanded proof that Ormond had the right to conclude a treaty; and instead of treating the General Assembly with disdain, he now needed it as guarantor of the settlement. His position was further weakened by the order of Charles I, made at the insistence of the Parliament in November, that all talks with the confederates be broken off.⁴³ The 'lavish ceremony'⁴⁴ which inaugurated the second Ormond Peace in January 1649 did little to disguise the shakiness of the authority that underlay it. Unlike the first treaty in 1646, there was no role for the Ulster king of arms, resplendent in the royal livery; and the lord lieutenant's discomfiture could only have worsened by having to listen to Richard Blake's speech, praising the 'bond of unity' that had been brokered by the General Assembly as 'the representative body of the Roman Catholics of this kingdom'. After the second Ormond Peace was signed the foundations of Ormond's authority began to subside even more alarmingly. Part of the problem was that the lieutenancy had at that stage lost much of its institutional underpinning: instead of presiding over his government in Dublin Castle, Ormond was forced to operate out of his own home at Kilkenny; the Irish Parliament had been brought to an end; the Church of Ireland had all but collapsed; and the Irish council was no more. Instead, the treaty left Ormond with twelve Catholic commissioners, drawn from the four provinces of Ireland, and with the official backing of the Catholic Church.⁴⁵ Once it was clear that the centre could not hold, things fell apart in the regions. Ormond's proclamation in July 1649 that all Ulster must obey him as lord lieutenant was a sign of his desperation. It was hardly surprising, as Kevin Forkan notes, that Montgomery of the Ards kept his royal commission secret at first, and when he was forced to produce it to overawe the garrison at Belfast, he found it created more problems than it solved; and it was perhaps ironic that Montgomery's position was made impossible by the activities of another man with a royal commission, Sir George Monro.⁴⁶ There are obvious similarities with Munster, where Inchiquin spent 1649 trying to prevent his troops from mutinying as royal authority gradually declined. He headed off trouble caused by arresting disloyal officers, threatening the clergy and making concessions to Catholics under the terms of the second Ormond Peace, but could not prevent his troops from deserting in droves during the summer, nor could a new round of arrests prevent the final collapse in November, when the Protestant garrisons threw in their lot with Cromwell.[47]

Ormond's authority may have eroded rapidly towards the end of the decade, but when it came to legitimacy the confederates were on the back foot from the start. Historians in the past have mentioned confederate difficulties in this regard, but in most cases without dwelling on them,[48] and Ó Siochrú in particular was at pains to portray their government as 'a unitary state' with 'a highly sophisticated system of representative government'; indeed, 'the fact that the confederates never claimed sovereignty, and were ultimately prepared to accept Charles as head of state, does not negate the radical nature of their actions'.[49] Yet the surviving evidence suggests that the confederate leadership was far from radical, and the concern for true authority was no mere 'cloak of legitimacy'.[50] From the onset, the Irish rebellion was framed in terms of defending the king, and 'the point was driven home by the publication of a forged commission in which Charles was represented as commanding them to take arms in his defence'.[51] The confederate oath of association famously defended God, king and country, and the reluctance of the lords of the Pale to join in the rebellion speaks volumes for their instinctive loyalty to the crown.[52] Something of the confederates' awareness of the delicacy of their position can be seen in the institutional structures at Kilkenny: the unicameral General Assembly was specifically designed not to be a rival Parliament; the Supreme Council studiously avoided becoming a privy council in waiting; and the continuing respect accorded to the Irish Parliament, and its central importance as a guarantor of successive peace treaties, is striking.[53] When a genuinely radical alternative was proposed by the exiled Jesuit, Conor O'Mahony, in his *Disputatio Apologetica* of 1645, it was condemned by the vast majority of confederate leaders, alarmed by claims that the Irish could reject their king because his authority came not from God but from the people of Ireland. As Ó hAnnracháin comments, the violence of such opinions 'carried the risk of becoming a dangerous hostage to fortune, legitimising Protestant distrust and persecution of Catholics'.[54]

Confederate hostility towards O'Mahony's book may have been heightened by his argument that authority rested in the people rather than the king. As Eamon Darcy points out in Chapter 9, the government in Kilkenny harboured an ill-concealed distrust of the common people. This can be traced back to the early days of the rebellion, when local leaders such as Sir Phelim O'Neill in Ulster struggled to assert their authority over the rebel forces.[55] After the chaos of rebellion it was hardly surprising that the confederate leadership was reluctant to appeal to 'the many-headed beast, the multitude',[56] or to use more than the minimum amount of propaganda. For the confederate elites, popular lawlessness undermined their strenuous efforts to assert the legitimacy of their government and their fundamental loyalty to the crown. But the government could not close down debate, not least because it relied on the plain people of Ireland for troops and taxes, and the principal tool for ensuring loyalty was the parish clergy who were beyond their jurisdiction. The confederate leadership – drawn disproportionately from the Old English landowners of the Pale and Dublin-based lawyers – also lacked sensitivity when it came to regional power structures. For example, moves against the traditional lords of Sligo, the O'Connors, in early 1643 left a power vacuum, while in neighbouring Mayo the obvious candidate to lead the confederate forces, Viscount Mayo, was passed over in favour of John Burke, creating a rivalry that provoked Mayo's rejection of confederate authority in 1644, and made the area vulnerable to an increasingly aggressive Protestant interest led by Sir Charles Coote.[57] Mary O'Dowd is surely justified in her damning verdict on north Connacht, where 'the Kilkenny Assembly was insensitive to [traditional] loyalties' and 'the weak local government structure of the confederates undermined the solidarity of their support'.[58] The failure by the confederates to confer authority where power already lay has striking similarities to royalist policy in the provinces: both seem to have been the result of political short-sightedness that put factional concerns above military necessities.

As Cromwell recognised, the Catholic Church provided an immensely important alternative source of authority in Ireland. This had been the case since the very beginning of the rebellion, when the oath of association (by which 'the confederates tackled the awkward problem of legitimising the structure which they had created') was given further weight by the fact it was administered by the parish priests after confession and Mass. As a result, 'the authority of the church and its sacraments was thus thrown behind the oath, which emphasised the enormity of the sin which perjury would entail'.[59] In the early years of the war the clergy were careful to include professions of loyalty to the king in their public statements, but in the later 1640s the confederates had become more dependent on the support of the Catholic hierarchy in all its panoply.[60] The presence of papal representatives, Scarampi and Rinuccini, lent the regime considerable prestige and, domestically, the revival of bishops across Ireland in the previous decades – 'as a shadow church and not as a mission', as Ó hAnnracháin puts it – meant that 'when the 1641 rebellion engulfed Ireland, an extremely experienced Catholic hierarchy was already in existence in the island'.[61] The authority exercised by the church was crucial to the legitimacy of the confederate government, and at times it was not entirely clear who was in charge. Nowhere is that more apparent than in August 1646, when the first Ormond Peace was rejected by Rinuccini and the Irish bishops. Indeed, in the aftermath, the nuncio hijacked the confederacy, establishing himself as president of the Supreme Council, and reinforced his dominance by cementing alliances with the two most powerful confederate generals, Owen Roe O'Neill and Thomas Preston.[62] Interestingly, even before his coup Rinuccini was not exactly a fan of the confederate government, questioning its loyalty to the Pope, distrusting its desire to make peace with a Protestant king, and making sure the subsidies he brought from Rome remained under his control. He also despised the confederate administration, criticising what he saw as its ham-fisted diplomacy, disorderly finances and lack of forward planning. In return, the confederates treated Rinuccini with suspicion, keeping details of their peace negotiations, and even of the terms of the treaty, secret from the nuncio during the early months of 1646.[63]

Perhaps the most important tool of the Catholic hierarchy was the ecclesiastical synod, described by Ó hAnnracháin as 'a powerful forum from which to present a unified position', and these were a regular feature of the 1640s: the national synod at Kilkenny in May 1642 'explicitly legitimised participation in the rebellion on the grounds of protection of the Catholic religion'; the first Ormond Peace of 1646 was overturned by another synod at Waterford; and Rinuccini's position during the excommunication crisis in May 1648 was weakened because the Supreme Council sent troops to prevent a synod from being held at Galway.[64] The power of the synod was that it represented the whole institution of the church, with authority derived immediately from God. As Ó hAnnracháin argues, these meetings 'reflected the active guidance of the Holy Spirit and were thus close to infallible'.[65] This ties in closely with a point made in his chapter by John Morrill: that the archbishops, bishops and clergy that met at Clonmacnoise in 1649 to denounce Cromwell were making a powerful statement *ex cathedra*. The ancient monastery at the heart of Ireland was replete with symbolism – and the intention was to unite the Irish as Catholics, relying on the authority of the church rather than that of the crown. Cromwell's reaction was understandably violent.

There is also a wider point here, as Morrill indicates, for the language Cromwell used to denounce the Catholic theocracy in Ireland was almost identical to that he deployed against its Presbyterian counterpart in Scotland. Both churches demanded allegiance independent of the state, and enforced it by oath. Just like the Catholics with the oath of association, so the ministers in Ulster 'set themselves up as guardians and interpreters of the Covenant' which was subscribed as a 'public, communal and religious activity', often taken in conjunction 'with that other communal rite of Presbyterianism, large-scale communions'. For Presbyterians the Covenant contained a 'spiritual imperative' that demanded allegiance, and the claims of loyalty made by the king were only accepted because they were incorporated into the Covenant.[66] The popular appeal of such personal commitments can be seen in both west Ulster and Munster, where pressure to subscribe came from below, with regimental commanders like Sir William Cole at Enniskillen struggling to contain the enthusiasm of their troops.[67] The Covenant continued to cast a spell even after the regicide. During the crisis in Ulster in the summer of 1649, the Presbytery's declaration against Viscount Montgomery helped turn the tables against the royalists in the province. Ormond had been wary of dealing with covenanters earlier in the decade, and his antipathy towards them was one of the few things he had in common with Cromwell.

A key concern of the confederates was to deny the status of the English Parliament as a rival source of authority to the crown. Parliament's claim to authority over Ireland was also derived from the king, who had (it was argued) delegated the running of the war to them through the Adventurers' Act of April 1642 and the appointment of commissioners for Irish affairs drawn from both houses of Parliament. As David Brown emphasises (in Chapter 2), contemporaries were not necessarily taken in by this: the Sea Adventure was authorised by a separate ordinance, with a commission that was eminently 'deniable'; and Lord Forbes's false claim at Galway that he held the king's commission was technically treason. Nevertheless, the argument that 'the managing of that war is wholly committed' to Parliament was deployed repeatedly during the decade that followed. To take but one example, in their declaration rejecting the cessation and siding with Parliament, the Munster Protestants cited the king's assent to the Adventurers' Act, which had 'communicated to the Parliament that power which before was solely in himself'.[68] Whether this included the right to appoint their own lords president in 1645, and even to appoint Viscount Lisle as a rival lord lieutenant in 1646, was at best a moot point. In making such appointments, Parliament was consciously usurping royal authority, as a way of bolstering its own rather dodgy claim to interfere in Ireland. Significantly, the instructions issued to Inchiquin were modelled on those for pre-war presidents, giving him legal as well as military authority as governor of the province.[69] Likewise, the exact nature of the office of chief governor was also given careful consideration, with a sub-committee being appointed by the Star Chamber Committee of Irish Affairs in December 1645 to consider what powers were exercised by previous incumbents.[70] When it was finally issued, Lisle's credentials were based on 'precedents of former instructions and commissions to lord lieutenants of Ireland', written in Latin and authenticated by the great seal (itself a symbol purloined from the king).[71] He was also provided with a sword of office, as 'an ensign of honour and authority' and a privy council – 'the first body to bear that title without the prior approval of the king'.[72]

The rules governing Lisle's relations with other officials also followed traditional lines. On his arrival in Cork in February 1647, Lisle 'had his commission read … by the master of the rolls' and made a formal speech in which he emphasised 'how really he would follow the public good, without bias or partiality'.[73] Despite this, and his earlier assurances to Inchiquin that 'it is far from my intentions either to stretch my authority or diminish yours', Lisle's arrival in Munster naturally led to the lord president's authority being compromised, and he set about interfering with the day-to-day running of the province, not least by imposing his own officers to senior positions. When he relinquished his position in April 1647 it was even argued by some that presidency also 'determined upon the passing of the lord lieutenant's commission'.[74] With Lisle's term expired and Ormond gone, there was a vacuum at the top of Irish politics from the summer of 1647, and the Protestant community felt it keenly. There were persistent rumours that Ormond would return as lord lieutenant as late as September 1647,[75] and even Michael Jones was uncomfortable that his authority as governor of Dublin was based on such shaky foundations, representing to Parliament in February 1648 'the necessity of a commander in chief' who might have 'countenance and abilities above mine'.[76]

Lisle's commission would provide the model for the lieutenancy granted to Cromwell in 1649, even though the latter was issued by a commonwealth government that had just abolished the monarchy.[77] This attachment to the office of lord lieutenant was doubly odd, as Cromwell did not even try to behave as one. Unlike Lisle, he did not surround himself with councillors and the trappings of power or have himself read-in on arrival. His instinctive solution to the problem of lack of legitimacy was to fall back on military force, backed by claims of 'necessity'. But even Cromwell accepted that this was not enough, and it is interesting that in his exchange with the Catholic clergy he directly addressed the people of Ireland, in an attempt to convince them not to throw away their lives in defence of clerical tyranny. It was more typical of Cromwell to appeal to the highest authority when seeking justification for his actions. In September 1649, immediately after the storming of Drogheda, he told Speaker Lenthall, 'it was set upon some of your hearts that a great thing should be done not by power or might but by the Spirit of God… and therefore it is good that God alone have all the glory'.[78]

Ireland in the 1640s experienced a number of interlocking crises, political, military, religious, social and economic; but it has been argued here that central to all of them was a crisis of authority that affected every part of Ireland, and all kinds of civil government, from the lord lieutenant to the lords president, the confederate Supreme Council to the Association's representatives in the provinces. This challenges traditional histories that concentrate on treaty negotiations conducted like games of chess, or on military campaigns represented by arrows on maps: the reality was a lot more chaotic and contingent than that. Ormond can no longer be seen as some kind of malicious puppet master; instead the weakness of his position should be recognised. It is also misleading to portray the confederates as having set up an effective parallel state, or to claim that they achieved even a modicum of 'independence' during the upheavals of the decade. Indeed, from the mid-1640s the position of confederate Ireland became increasingly fragile, at the same time that Ormond's own authority started to implode; it was small wonder that the first Ormond Peace of 1646 failed almost before the ink had dried, and a similar fate awaited the second peace signed in the new year of 1649. By then, the most credible sources of authority in this failed state were not secular but religious. The Catholic Church and the Covenant already provided alternative sources of authority to rival civil governments fatally weakened by years of conflict, but the laurels would belong to another set of religious fundamentalists, led by Oliver Cromwell. As soldiers answerable only to God, the Cromwellians were not hampered by questions of legitimacy or concerns about authority, and the sword of state was soon replaced by one of cold steel.

NOTES

1 A. Clarke, *The Old English in Ireland* (London, 1966); A. Clarke, *Prelude to Restoration in Ireland: the end of the Commonwealth, 1659–1660* (Cambridge, 1999); A. Clarke, 'Colonial constitutional attitudes in Ireland, 1640–60', *Royal Irish Academy Proceedings* 90, C (1990), pp. 357–75; A. Clarke, 'Patrick Darcy and the constitutional relationship between Ireland and Britain', in J.H. Ohlmeyer (ed.), *Political Thought in Seventeenth Century Ireland* (Dublin, 2001), pp. 35–55; A. Clarke, 'The Commission for the Despoiled Subject, 1641–47', in B. Mac Cuarta (ed.), *Reshaping Ireland 1550–1700: colonization and its consequences* (Dublin, 2011), pp. 241–60.
2 D. Cregan, 'The Confederation of Kilkenny: its organisation, personnel and history (PhD thesis, University College Dublin, 1947); D. Cregan, 'Daniel O'Neill, a royalist agent in Ireland, 1644–50', *IHS* 2 (1940–41), pp. 398–414; D. Cregan, 'The Confederate Catholics of Ireland: the personnel of the Confederacy 1642–9', *IHS* 29 (1995), pp. 490–512.
3 P.J. Corish, 'Bishop Nicholas French and the second Ormond Peace, 1648–9', *IHS* 6 (1948), pp. 83–100; see also *NHI*, 289–335.
4 J. Lowe, 'The Glamorgan mission to Ireland, 1645–6', *Studia Hibernica* 4 (1964), pp. 155–96.
5 J.A. Murphy, 'The politics of the Munster Protestants, 1641–49', *Journal of the Cork Historical and Archaeological Society* 76 (1971), pp. 1–20.
6 K.S. Bottigheimer, *English Money and Irish Land* (Oxford, 1971).
7 J.C. Beckett, *The Cavalier Duke: a life of James Butler first Duke of Ormond, 1610–1688* (Belfast, 1990); J. Casway *Owen Roe O'Neill and the struggle for Catholic Ireland* (Philadelphia, 1984); J.H. Ohlmeyer, *Civil War and Restoration in the Three Stuart Kingdoms: the career of Randal MacDonnell, marquis of Antrim, 1609–1683* (Cambridge, 1993).
8 One of the first to embrace this approach was Michael Perceval-Maxwell, whose *Outbreak of the Irish Rebellion of 1641* (Montreal, 1994) provided a 'three kingdoms' account of 1641–42; the best 'integrated' account of the whole decade is D. Scott, *Politics and War in the Three Stuart Kingdoms, 1637–49* (Basingstoke, 2004).

9 J. Ohlmeyer, *Ireland from Independence to Occupation* (Cambridge, 1995), chapters 2, 3, 5, 7 and 8.
10 Ó Siochrú, *Confederate Ireland*.
11 Ó hAnnracháin, *Rinuccini*.
12 Lenihan, *Confederate Catholics at War*.
13 Armstrong, *Protestant War*.
14 T. Ó hAnnracháin, 'Rebels and Confederates: the stance of the Irish clergy in the 1640s', in J.R. Young (ed.), *Celtic Dimensions of the British Civil Wars* (Edinburgh, 1997), pp. 96–115; T. Ó hAnnracháin, 'Lost in Rinuccini's shadow: the Irish clergy, 1645-9', in M. Ó Siochrú (ed.), *Kingdoms in Crisis: Ireland in the 1640s* (Dublin, 2001), pp. 176–91; T. Ó hAnnracháin, 'Conflicting loyalties, conflicted Rebels: political and religious allegiance among the confederate Catholics of Ireland', *EHR* 119 (2004), pp. 851–72.
15 R. Armstrong, 'Ormond, the Confederate peace talks, and Protestant Royalism', in Ó Siochrú (ed.), *Kingdoms in Crisis*, pp. 122–40; P. Little, 'The Marquess of Ormond and the English Parliament', in T. Barnard and J. Fenlon (eds), *The Dukes of Ormonde, 1610–45* (Woodbridge, Suffolk, 2000), pp. 83–100.
16 P. Little, '"Blood and Friendship": the earl of Essex's efforts to protect the earl of Clanricarde's interests, 1641-6', *EHR* 112 (1997), 927–41; B. Kelly, 'John Barry: an Irish Catholic royalist in the 1640s', in Ó Siochrú (ed.), *Kingdoms in Crisis*, pp. 141–57; P. Little, *Lord Broghill and the Cromwellian Union with Ireland and Scotland* (Woodbridge, Suffolk, 2004).
17 Ó Siochrú (ed.), *Kingdoms in Crisis*.
18 M. Ó Siochrú, 'Catholic Confederates and the constitutional relationship between Ireland and England, 1641-1649' and R. Armstrong, 'Protestant churchmen and the Confederate Wars', both in C. Brady and J. Ohlmeyer (eds), *British Interventions in Early Modern Ireland* (Cambridge, 2005), pp. 207–29 and 230–51.
19 J. Ohlmeyer and M. Ó Siochrú (eds), *Ireland 1641: contexts and reactions* (Manchester, 2013); E. Darcy, *The Irish Rebellion and the Wars of the Three Kingdoms* (Woodbridge, Suffolk, 2013); M. Ó Siochrú, *God's Executioner: Oliver Cromwell and the conquest of Ireland* (London, 2008); J. Cunningham, *Conquest and the Land in Ireland: the transplantation to Connacht, 1649–1680* (Woodbridge, Suffolk, 2011); J. Wells, 'English law, Irish trials and Cromwellian state building in the 1650s', *Past and Present* 227 (2015), pp. 77–119.
20 It is interesting that the author of a recent groundbreaking book on Scotland in the 1640s deliberately avoided making comparisons with Ireland: see L.A.M. Stewart, *Rethinking the Scottish Revolution: covenanted Scotland, 1637–1651* (Oxford, 2016), pp. 4, 305.
21 M. O'Dowd, *Power, Politics and Land: early modern Sligo, 1568–1688* (Belfast, 1991); R. Gillespie (ed.), *Cavan: essays on the history of an Irish county* (Dublin, 1995); D. Edwards, 'The poisoned chalice: the Ormond inheritance, sectarian division and the emergence of James Butler, 1614–1642', in Barnard and Fenlon (eds), *Duke of Ormonde*, pp. 55–82; A. Duignan, '"All in a confused opposition to each other": politics and war in Connacht, 1641-9' (PhD thesis, University College Dublin, 2005).

22 K. Forkan, 'The Ulster Scots and the Engagement, 1647-8', *IHS* 35 (2007), pp. 455-76; K. Forkan, 'Ormond's alternative: the lord-lieutenant's secret contacts with Protestant Ulster, 1645-6', *Hist Res.* 81 (2008), pp. 610-35; K. Forkan, '"The fatal ingredient of the Covenant": the place of the Ulster Scottish colonial community during the 1640s', in B. Mac Cuarta (ed.), *Reshaping Ireland, 1550-1700: colonization and its consequences* (Dublin, 2011), 261-80; see also K. Forkan, 'Scottish Protestant Ulster and the crisis of the Three Kingdoms' (PhD thesis, NUI Galway, 2003).

23 C. McCoy, 'War and Revolution: County Fermanagh and its borders, c.1640-c.1660 (PhD thesis, Trinity College Dublin, 2007); K. McKenny, *The Laggan Army in Ireland, 1640-85: the landed interests, political ideologies and military campaigns of the north-west Ulster settlers* (Dublin, 2005).

24 H.M. Sexton, 'Clanricarde and the Confederate Wars: a study of Ulick Burke's career in Ireland, 1641-52' (Unpublished PhD Thesis, National University of Ireland, Cork, 2006); D. Debe, 'The fifth earl of Clanricarde and the founding of the Confederate Catholic government, 1641-3', *IHS* 36 (2009), pp. 315-33.

25 R. Armstrong, 'Viscount Ards and the Presbytery: politics and religion among the Scots of Ulster in the 1640s', in W.P. Kelly and J.R. Young (eds), *Scotland and the Ulster Plantations: explorations in the British settlements of Stuart Ireland* (Dublin, 2009), pp. 18-40; A. Robinson, '"Not otherwise worthy to be named, but as a firebrand brought from Ireland to inflame this kingdom": the political and cultural milieu of Sir John Clotworthy during the Stuart Civil Wars' (PhD thesis, Ulster University, 2013).

26 See the essays in D. Edwards, P. Lenihan and C. Tait (eds), *Age of Atrocity: violence and political conflict in early modern Ireland* (Dublin, 2007); E. Murphy, *Ireland and the War at Sea, 1641-1653* (Woodbridge Suffolk, 2012).

27 B. Robertson, *Royalists at War in Scotland and Ireland, 1638-1650* (Farnham, Surrey, 2014).

28 See Ohlmeyer (ed.) *Political Thought*, pp. 18-19.

29 Clarke, 'Patrick Darcy', p. 35.

30 Bodl. MS Carte 14, fo. 409: Sir Richard Osborne to Ormond, 19 Apr. 1645.

31 Bodl. MS Carte 63, fo. 441: Ormond and council to Scottish officers, 22 June 1646; for a parallel example see ibid., MS Carte 16, fo. 573: Ormond to Ulster commissioners, 2 Mar. 1646.

32 Lowe, 'Glamorgan Mission', p. 158.

33 Armstrong, 'Ormond [and] Confederate peace talks', p. 136.

34 *Clanricarde Letter-Book*, pp. 349-50.

35 Ibid.

36 Lowe, 'Glamorgan Mission', pp. 171, 180, 185.

37 *HMC Egmont MSS*, i. 267.

38 Murphy, 'Munster Protestants', p. 4; see also L. Irwin, 'The suppression of the Irish presidency system', *IHS* 22 (1980), pp. 21-32.

39 Bodl. MS Carte 9, fo. 243: Arthur Trevor to Ormond, 19 Feb. 1644; Bodl. MS Carte 10, fo. 654v: Inchiquin to Ormond, 20 May 1644.

40 Little, *Broghill*, chapter 2; McKenny, *Laggan Army*, p. 81.

41 Bodl. MS Carte 67, fo. 315: note of commission to Inchiquin, 2 July 1648.
42 Bodl. MS Carte 176, fo. 213: Dublin Articles, 18 June 1647.
43 Ó Siochrú, *Confederate Ireland*, pp. 188–91, 195n.
44 see Ó Siochrú, *Confederate Ireland*, p. 201; Ó Siochrú, *God's Executioner*, p. 52; and Ó Siochrú, 'Catholic Confederates', p. 207.
45 Ó Siochrú, *God's Executioner*, pp. 56–7.
46 Robertson, *Royalists at War*, p. 170.
47 Murphy, 'Munster Protestants', pp. 18–19.
48 An exception is Ó hAnnracháin, 'Conflicting loyalties'.
49 Ó Siochrú, *Confederate Ireland*, pp. 11, 243.
50 Ibid., p. 54.
51 Clarke, 'Patrick Darcy', p. 46.
52 Robertson, *Royalists at War*, pp. 88–91.
53 Ó Siochrú, *Confederate Ireland*, pp. 44–5, 49–50, 58.
54 T. Ó hAnnracháin, '"Though Hereticks and Politicians should misinterpret their good zeal": political ideology and Catholicism in early modern Ireland', in Ohlmeyer (ed.), *Political Thought*, pp. 155–75, at pp. 162–3.
55 Lenihan, *Confederates at War*, pp. 31–2.
56 Gilbert, *Irish Confederation*, ii. 90–1.
57 O'Dowd, *Sligo*, pp. 127–9.
58 Ibid., p. 130.
59 Ó hAnnracháin, 'Rebels and Confederates', p. 99; for the oath(s) see J. Morrill, 'An Irish protestation? Oaths and the Confederation of Kilkenny', in M.J. Braddick and P. Withington (eds), *Popular Culture and Political Agency in Early Modern England and Ireland* (Woodbridge, Suffolk, 2017), pp. 243–66.
60 Ó hAnnracháin, 'Conflicting loyalties', pp. 855–6.
61 Ó hAnnracháin, 'Rinuccini's shadow', p. 178; Ó hAnnracháin, 'Rebels and Confederates', p. 97.
62 Ó hAnnracháin, *Rinuccini*, pp. 125, 153–8.
63 Ibid., pp. 127, 132–7, 154.
64 Ó hAnnracháin, 'Rebels and Confederates', pp. 96–8, 100–1, 108; Ó hAnnracháin, 'Rinuccini's shadow', pp. 184, 188.
65 Ó hAnnracháin, 'Rinuccini's Shadow', p. 186.
66 Armstrong, 'Viscount Ards and the Presbytery', pp. 21–2, 40.
67 McCoy, 'Fermanagh', pp. 237–8; Murphy, 'Munster Protestants', p. 11.
68 BL, Add. MS 25287, fo. 6: unanimous declaration of the Munster Protestants, [July] 1644.
69 Bodl. MS Carte 67, fos 104–5: instructions to Inchiquin as lord president, 14 Jan. 1645.
70 Bodl. MS Nalson 21, fo. 49: Star Chamber committee's proceedings, 15 Dec. 1645.
71 Little, 'English Parliament and Irish Constitution', pp. 116–7.
72 TNA, SP 21/26 (Derby House Committee, foul book of orders, 1646–48), p. 2; J. Adamson, 'Strafford's ghost: the British context of Viscount Lisle's lieutenancy of Ireland', in Ohlmeyer, *Ireland from Independence to Occupation*, pp. 128–59, at p. 136.

73 *HMC Egmont MSS*, i. 365.
74 Ibid., i. 312; Bodl. MS Nalson 6, fo. 80: Sir Adam Loftus and Sir John Temple to Speaker Lenthall, 23 Apr. 1647.
75 *HMC Egmont MSS*, i. 468–9.
76 Bodl. MS Nalson 6, fo. 182: Michael Jones to Speaker Lenthall, 26 Feb. 1648.
77 Little, 'English Parliament and Irish Constitution', pp. 119–20; P. Little, 'Cromwell and Ireland before 1649', in P. Little (ed.), *Oliver Cromwell: new perspectives* (Basingstoke, 2008), pp. 116–41, at p. 134.
78 W.C. Abbott (ed.), *The Writings and Speeches of Oliver Cromwell* (4 vols, Cambridge, Mass., 1937–47), ii. 127.

1

Holding on: the earl of Cork's Blackwater army and the defence of Protestant Munster, 1641–43

DAVID EDWARDS

In *Making Ireland British*, published in 2001, Nicholas Canny observed a major gap in the military and political history of the 1640s to that point – the dearth of detailed local studies of the spiralling ethnic and religious conflict that spread throughout the country after October 1641, affecting almost every area.[1] There has been but a modest improvement in the interim. With the notable exceptions of Kevin McKenny's exemplary analysis of the Laggan Valley and Aoife Duignan's as yet unpublished thesis tracing the 1640s story in Connacht, few local or regional studies of the conflict have been attempted.[2] There remains a pressing need for detailed investigation of the fractures experienced by local communities in the traditional 'four loyal shires' of the Pale, for instance, and the continued absence of any serious consideration of the midlands as a distinct military and political theatre is likewise frustrating.

Arguably the biggest gap in regional coverage of the early 1640s, however, is the southern province of Munster. Although simultaneously the chief destination of English and Protestant colonists arriving in early Stuart Ireland, and the region most open to continental and Catholic influence along its Atlantic seaboard, the conflict that erupted in the province has received almost no close scrutiny. Prior to Canny's overview, the prevailing outline of events in the south could be traced backed directly to Richard Cox's highly partisan history, published in England in 1689.[3] The account of the 1640s given by Charles Smith, the eighteenth-century antiquarian of counties Cork, Waterford and Kerry, was heavily reliant on Cox; in turn, Smith's version, several times republished, informed later outlines that appeared in the Victorian period.[4] More recently Pádraig Lenihan, Robert Armstrong and David Dickson each brought a welcome academic rigour to discussions of the province during 1641–49; yet, engaged as they were in more general studies, they tended to sweep quickly over the pattern of events in Munster, especially when commenting on the pivotal early phase of the conflict, between autumn 1641 and autumn 1643.[5] This chapter is a contribution towards plugging that gap.

Focusing on the wealthiest and most powerful figure in the province, Richard Boyle, first earl of Cork, the chapter attempts to reconstruct the pattern of events as the conflict between planter and native, Protestant and Catholic unfolded in the two-year period prior to the earl's death at Youghal in September 1643. It has long been recognised that Cork and his family played a significant role in the Munster war, particularly in the Blackwater Valley that runs through the borderlands of counties Waterford and Cork.[6] Indeed, it has become the accepted view to state that the army of tenants that Earl Richard put in the field was a key factor in ensuring the failure of the insurgents to secure the strategically vital strip of coastline from Youghal to Kinsale. By helping to keep the supply lines from England open, the old earl's final achievement before his death was to preserve the English Protestant presence in the province. In broad terms this interpretation is correct. However, it is also misleading, failing to grasp the complexity of the situation on the ground. In the Blackwater Valley by September 1643 the Protestant and government interest had to rely on the confederate Catholic leadership in Kilkenny, and the terms of a ceasefire it had negotiated with King Charles's government, to survive.[7] The civil war in England, and the confederates' desire to help the king saved the Munster Protestants. The defensive line that had been sustained by the earl of Cork was actually on the brink of collapse. His achievement had been to prevent it collapsing earlier.

Drawing upon Cork's extensive archive of private letters and estate papers, this chapter shows how, from the onset of hostilities in the province in late 1641, the task assigned to the earl and his followers of guarding Youghal and the Blackwater was difficult and uncertain. While historians have noted the earl's political rivalry with the English lord president, Sir William St Leger, the extent to which their differences destabilised the Protestant war effort has not been fully appreciated. Of particular importance, St Leger's harsh policies towards the native population cut across the old earl's regional influence, and reduced his military capacity by alienating many of his Irish soldiers – a key component of the earl's 'colonial' army. Then there was the scale of the threat presented to Cork by the Catholic insurgents; this was both more sustained and more penetrative than hitherto acknowledged. The battle of Liscarroll made little difference. Long thought to have broken the Catholics' military strength, in the Blackwater region it proved otherwise. In the last months of his life the earl faced a relentless enemy moving ever closer to overrunning all of his positions.

The chapter gives marked attention to individuals and groups usually overlooked in histories of the period – those living beneath the earl and his family: from neighbouring knights and fellow landowners to his servants and tenants.

The composition and organisation of the earl's tenant army are described for the first time, partly because his papers record such information in considerable detail,[8] but also because it allows us to better appreciate the fact that the Blackwater Valley was a community as well as a possession. As shown, the strains placed on such people by the 1641–43 war led to the utter transformation of the region, from a place where English and Irish, Protestant and Catholic had muddled along side by side for years, sometimes uneasily, but without significant confrontation, to a region increasingly characterised by religious and ethnic hatred, suspicion and polarisation. This would prove a more lasting legacy than the survival of the Blackwater forts or the guarding of Youghal.

When the earl of Cork returned to Ireland from the English court in October 1641,[9] he was confident that his main holdings in Munster were ready, if necessary, to withstand an insurgent assault. His confidence seemed well founded. For nearly four decades, following his purchase from Sir Walter Raleigh of the great Blackwater seigniory of Inchiquin (December 1602), he had paid scrupulous attention to the question of plantation security. From the outset he had invested in native informers to keep close watch on the movements of former rebels, requiring his agents to give specific heed to their contacts with the exiled Irish military community in Spain and the Low Countries. He had actively recruited former captains and junior officers decommissioned by the crown after the Nine Years War to take up tenancies on his estates and to help him keep the natives of the region in check. He had acquired large quantities of weapons and other military equipment, which he later had stored in his armoury at Lismore Castle. Most significantly, he had seized the opportunity to earn royal approval by creating a large tenant militia – a private army – on his plantation lands, initially establishing a force in the Blackwater Valley which mustered annually at Tallow, before later authorising a second force in the Bandon Valley which mustered at Bandonbridge.[10]

Although it was a part-time force, from very early on the earl's tenant army had become the single largest component in the military defence of Munster. Every year it greatly outnumbered the permanent forces directly commanded by the lord president of the province. For instance, during the period 1611–36 the president had had between 25 and 50 horsemen and 100 and 150 foot soldiers under his charge,[11] whereas the earl's Tallow and Bandon militias had risen to a total of more than 1,500 men in arms, comprising 260 horse and 1,270 foot.[12] Moreover, the earl's army had a professional leadership. Formal responsibility for the training of the men was handled by the earl's tenant-in-chief – and after 1612 his kinsman by marriage – Sir Robert Tynte, as muster-master.[13] Other officers included Captain Richard Joliffe, Lieutenant Edward Russell, Ensign Hugh Croker and Sergeant Christmas Harford on his lands in counties Waterford and Cork, and Captain John Strongman in co. Tipperary.

Importantly, all of these were still living as tenants and followers of the earl in 1641.¹⁴ Indeed, in the intervening years they had introduced their sons and other kin into the tenant army's command structure: hence the appearance in records of the early 1640s of Robert Tynte Junior of Ballycrenane, John Smith of Ballinascarty (Christmas Harford's stepson), and of Walter, Christopher and John Croker.¹⁵ For these men, their families and wider associates, a role in the defence of the English plantation had become a proud part of their identity. It was something they took seriously.

While English settlers comprised the bulk of the Boyle army, it had a native element as well. The Boyle estates were not culturally or ethnically exclusive, but were mixed, with Irish tenants living and farming on every manor or parcel inside and outside the various plantation areas.¹⁶ Reflecting this, the militias that assembled each year at Tallow and Bandon contained Irish members at each level, from the gentlemen commanders of cavalry or 'horse', to the rank-and-file 'pike' and 'shot'. Consider the military contributions required of the tenants inhabiting the portion of Earl Richard's holdings that was assigned to his eldest son and heir Richard, Viscount Dungarvan in counties Waterford and Cork. The schedule book of leases that was prepared for the viscount recorded how his lessees were to provide him with 27 horse and 80 foot for his part of the Tallow militia. Reading through the terms of each lease in the book it emerges that five of the viscount's horsemen (nearly a fifth) were furnished by native tenants, as were eighteen of the foot (nearly a quarter). The providers of horsemen included Morris Condon, who leased land near Fermoy, and Morris Oge O'Hagherin, a long-standing tenant in the barony of Kinatalloon. The suppliers of foot included Gaelic and 'Old English' tenants living at Lismore, Ardmore, Lisfinny, Tallow, Youghal, Fermoy and Inchiquin – the very heartland of the English plantation.¹⁷ In the portion set aside by the earl for his second son, Lewis, Viscount Kinalmeaky, in west co. Cork, the contribution to defence required of native tenants was slightly higher. Gaelic and Old English tenants furnished the young lord with more than a fifth of his foot and nearly half of his horsemen.¹⁸ Regrettably, no schedule books survive for the earl's third and fourth sons Roger, Lord Broghill, or Francis Boyle, making a precise comparison with the arrangements on Dungarvan and Kinalmeaky's estates impossible. However, from the schedule book of his youngest son Robert Boyle, as for that of the earl himself, it is clear that at least a quarter of the tenants contributing to the two militias were of native origin.¹⁹

Plainly this has important implications for how we should try to comprehend the earl's Munster colony as it entered the early 1640s. Earl Richard was a pragmatist. In his view, to have rigidly adhered to the 'Articles of Plantation' imposed by the government since 1586 would have risked creating a chain of small-sized English Protestant islands in a sea of Irish Catholics.²⁰ As a younger man he had witnessed at first-hand the ineffectiveness of Elizabethan plantation defences, when in 1598 he had had to flee the province to escape being killed by MacCarthy rebels who easily picked off isolated English settlers in west Cork and Kerry.[21] Following his return to the province and his acquisition of Raleigh's seigniory, he calculated that the surest – and cheapest – way to protect his investments was to offer a place on his lands and a role in his schemes to natives willing to cooperate. He had already developed a native affinity in counties Limerick, Kerry and Tipperary through his first marriage, in the 1590s.[22] On moving to the Blackwater Valley after 1602 he had seized the opportunity to keep his new lands occupied and his rental full through the marriage of his sister into the local Old English lineage, the Powers of Carrigphilip; thereafter the Powers and their kin helped find him tenants.[23] His later pursuit of much grander marriage alliances with the powerful Fitzgerald and Barry dynasties helped consolidate his position, and further ensured that Irish tenants retained a marked presence on his estates.[24] Analysis of his rentals shows that throughout the 1630s just over 40 per cent of his tenants were of Gaelic or Old English extraction.[25]

Their yearly contribution to the earl's army was important in a number of respects. By consenting to provide him with a horseman and a horse 'fully furnished', or a foot soldier armed with a pike or musket, the Irish tenants demonstrated their willingness to help defend his colony and to contribute to it in the same way as his New English tenants and followers. In a very real sense they were accepting the earl as their overlord and leader, as their forebears had once accepted the rule and military demands of Irish lords and chieftains. In return, they expected to receive the earl's protection and support, and so secure the future of their families under the new colonial order that he dominated in the south. The extent to which by 1641 some of his Irish tenants and clients had attained positions of military responsibility at Lismore Castle, his principal seat, is noteworthy. 'The watch' was presided over by Teige O'Rowerty, a local Gael who was also bailiff of the barony of Coshanmore and Coshbride;[26] the porter at the castle was another native, the Old Englishman John Gough.[27] Most revealing of all, perhaps, the twice-yearly task of cleaning and repairing all the weapons and armour stored in the armoury at Lismore was performed by Thomas O'Flynn.[28] In December 1641, on realising that the outbreak of the Irish rebellion in Ulster had spread to Munster, Earl Richard turned to the native builder Thomas Kelly to inspect the outer walls and other defences of his main strongholds, initially at Lismore and then at other castles in the Blackwater. He saw no contradiction in further requiring the Irishman to reinforce them.[29] The earl expected 'his' Irishmen to help out in the unfolding emergency; they always had.

Cork's relationship with the lord president of Munster, Sir William St Leger, was destined to significantly affect the war in the Blackwater region. As is well known the two men were political adversaries. During the mid–late

1630s, when the earl's wealth and power was suddenly challenged by the viceroy, Viscount Wentworth (later earl of Strafford), the difficulties confronting him and his family had been compounded by St Leger, who supported Strafford at every turn and expected to have his presidential authority boosted as a result.[30] Following Strafford's impeachment and execution in England in early 1641, St Leger, like other Straffordites in Ireland, was left anxiously awaiting Cork's return from the royal court, where he had played a part in Strafford's downfall.[31] However, events overtook the pair of them. In response to the spreading insurrection Sir William and Earl Richard were expected to bury their differences and to work together for the defence of the kingdom.

From the very start cooperation proved difficult. It was not until 7 November (two weeks after the Ulster outbreak) that St Leger wrote to Cork suggesting they set aside 'all private resentments'. They should combine their efforts to secure the province, he said, lest the panicked demands of the Dublin government left the south bereft of adequate forces.[32] The earl was slow to respond. In addition to his 'private resentments', he had been troubled by St Leger's conduct of military policing ever since his return. In co. Tipperary, where Cork had native kin from his first marriage, the president had led a punitive expedition through the centre of the county, towards Cashel, believing a show of force and the liberal deployment of martial law to be the surest means to dissuade local Catholics from rebellion. In the village of Golden, eleven men, women and children were summarily killed, none of them, apparently, in rebellion. Moving on to Clonoulty, the provost marshal, Captain William Peisley (another Straffordite),[33] shot dead its main Gaelic occupant, a man named Philip Ryan (alias O'Mulryan), who had come out of his house to talk with him.[34] As one of the Ryans of Sologhed, Philip was actually related to Earl Richard, who had maintained links to the Ryan family since the 1590s and in a diary entry of 1632 even referred to the head of the line, William Ryan, as 'my cousin'.[35]

Viewed from St Leger's perspective, recourse to such pre-emptive severity seemed justified. Since early 1641 the president had been alarmed by the growing signs of defiance to the government in the province. By the spring he had already used martial law against elements of the general population, and no further disturbances appear to have occurred there during the summer (further convincing him of the efficacy of a hard-line approach).[36] He reckoned that another dose of the same medicine should have a similar effect now.

Cork felt otherwise. Despite some of his later statements to political contacts in England, stressing his own and his family's eagerness for military action,[37] his initial response to the reports of unrest had been to covertly despatch informers among the native Catholic landowners of the Blackwater Valley. Writing to St Leger from Lismore on 17 November he stated that his spies had identified the main danger as stemming from Catholic clergy, who had held a series of meetings and 'conventicles' across the region. If they could be effectively suppressed, it was his view that more general trouble could probably be avoided, for the majority of local people desired 'quietness' more than anything else.[38] It was something he had been urging for years – the rooting out of 'Papist' clergy, without whose malign influence he thought the kingdom at large could settle down to 'good order' and lasting economic prosperity.

Yet already the situation was spiralling out of control. Bringing Captain Peisley with him to Clonmel, St Leger had threatened to hang all the Catholic gentry and their followers who had assembled there to meet him, calling them traitors. Departing in a rush towards Waterford, later partisan accounts record that his men killed 'many harmless poor people' along the way.[39] By his own testimony, though, it is clear that he expected to reap obedience from terror. Seizing fifty prisoners in co. Waterford early in December he reported to the Dublin government that he had hanged them all by martial law, certain that the local lords and gentry would get the message. They would 'melt like snow before the [heat of his] sun'.[40] A full-scale uprising soon spread across the region.

St Leger's behaviour made Cork uneasy in other ways also. Although Sir William conceded that the earl's tenant army would need to carry the main burden of defending the province until such time as reinforcements arrived from England,[41] during the winter of 1641–42 his officers were slow to issue additional arms and ammunition to the earl's men from the government stores in Cork City.[42] The earl grew suspicious when commissions of martial law promised to his sons Dungarvan, Kinalmeaky and Broghill, and to trusty followers such as Sir Richard Osborne and Hugh Croker, were delayed for several weeks; moreover, on finally being issued, the powers they contained turned out to be less comprehensive than expected.[43]

From mid-November 1641 to mid-January 1642 Cork and St Leger put on an outward show of collaboration. In reality, though, they did little to help each other. Because it affected his reputation, the earl agreed to subsidise the cost of the crown forces in Munster, there then being no money in the government's coffers to meet their charges, but he was careful to specify that it was a loan 'for his majesty's service', not for St Leger's personal use.[44] Otherwise, the earl openly defied the president. He refused point blank to pay him the Irish parliamentary subsidy that had fallen due.[45] He backed out of an agreement worth £1,000 to underwrite the refitting of the king's ship *The Swallow* that lay at Kinsale, not trusting St Leger's terms and conditions for repayment.[46] He supported the mayor of Youghal in refusing to deliver to St Leger's officers guns or gunpowder taken from ships anchored in the harbour, to be carried away to Sir William's use; indeed, the earl admitted to having himself disobeyed the president's instructions, by sending a forfeited barrel of powder to his brother-in-law, Sir William Fenton, at Mitchelstown.[47] Most serious of all, Earl Richard utterly ignored St Leger's repeated requests to join with the government forces on campaign, and to draw towards Fermoy. Given the bloodshed recently committed by St Leger's companies in Tipperary and Waterford, and the outbreak of a general rebellion across the region, it seems the earl expected to better protect his lands and interests (and perhaps eventually to help calm the situation down) by holding back from the president.[48]

The fate of Cork's tenant army became another source of ill feeling. The incendiary impact of St Leger's campaigning was largely due to the indiscriminate nature of the attacks and punishments meted out by his forces, which affected all the Irish, loyalist or dissident, who lay in their path. One result of this, long unnoticed by scholars, was the disappearance of the majority of the native 'horse' and 'foot' that were enrolled in the Blackwater contingent of the earl's tenant militia. In December 1641, following St Leger's expedition through co. Waterford, many of them had slipped away – most likely to hide from him, but perhaps also to go to the aid of family and kin harmed by his forces. By 6 January 1642 St Leger had received a report from the earl about this.[49] Replying a few days later, he stated that the only way to remedy the problem of desertion was by execution. Accordingly, he ordered the earl to issue warrants for the apprehension of the missing men, and, proceeding under the terms of the martial law commission he had granted to Viscount Dungarvan, to then hang them all. But, he added, this procedure should apply only to those who failed to return voluntarily to the earl. If possible, the earl should endeavour to woo most of the runaways back to his service, by offering to continue paying them 'weekly by the pole', as before. Then he should execute the voluntary returnees also.[50] There is no evidence that Cork followed St Leger's instructions. Sir William apparently did not want any Irish or 'Papists' serving in the government forces.[51] The earl differed. Without Irish troops his tenant army would be seriously under strength. Besides, he had known many of them and their families for years. He was still their overlord: they would surely return, wouldn't they? A document among his private papers shows that he disregarded the president's orders and persuaded many of the runaways to return. But it also suggests that a sizeable proportion never returned.

The item in question is a set of accounts for two new companies raised from the ranks of the Boyle tenants to defend the Blackwater Valley. Commanded by Captains Richard Joliffe and James Finch, it had been agreed that they were to have their wages covered by the English Parliament.[52] Hence the account, which details the weekly charges of both companies, and lists their periods of service soldier by soldier. Regarding the ethnic composition of the force, it shows that of 216 officers and foot retained by the earl between 1 March and 1 July 1642, 30 of them were native men.[53] Ideally, of course, at least a quarter of those who mustered for Earl Richard in the Blackwater should have been natives. Moreover, while Joliffe's company had Irish as well as English junior officers, Finch's company was led entirely by Englishmen.[54] It was not an ideal start.

Across much of counties Waterford and Cork the onslaught from rebel forces began in earnest in January 1642, following the emergence of an organised Catholic army in Tipperary and Kilkenny led by Viscount Mountgarret and Richard Butler of Kilcash.[55] In the Blackwater Valley hostilities commenced with an attack on Dungarvan Castle, in the conduct of which the insurgents appear to have sent a detachment towards Lismore in order to pre-occupy the 'ward', or garrison, that Cork had placed there under Lord Broghill.[56] A second wave of attacks commenced about the feast of Candlemas (2 February) following what was described as a 'great meeting' of Munster Catholic leaders at Cashel.[57] This new campaign continued for several weeks and was far more extensive – and destructive – so that in co. Cork St Leger was persuaded to abandon his initial aim of holding on to the plantation lands north of the Blackwater in order to retain a Protestant land-corridor towards Limerick. By 26 February he had retreated to Cork City. Thenceforth he began to cooperate more closely with Earl Richard to secure the ports of Youghal, Cork and Kinsale and the chief castles and river-crossings that lay inland in between.[58] Belatedly, he issued an enhanced commission to the earl's officer Hugh Croker empowering him to raise a company of 100 foot from the earl's tenants to defend Cappoquin.[59]

While the ensuing military operations are sometimes seen as a straightforward assertion of Earl Richard's power, in reality confusion abounded and the earl's capacity to finance the government's war effort was soon under strain. Purely in monetary terms, as Raymond Gillespie has observed, Cork's officers collected less than £20 from his tenants in the first quarter of 1642; in normal times, before the rising, rents of almost £2,000 would have been realised during those months.[60] The earl was only able to subsidise his and the president's forces by drawing upon the residue of the previous year's revenues. On moving to Youghal in January he had emptied the treasury at Lismore Castle, boxing up £2,100 to bring with him.[61] It was quickly spent, augmented only by the proceeds of the sale of iron, and the delivery of money kept for him in England by his agent, Isaac Thornbury.[62] At Lismore, meanwhile, Lord Broghill and the receiver John Walley were left to manage on an ever-diminishing cash reserve that fell from £366 in January to just £30 by mid-April.[63]

A collapse in rents was just one facet of a much larger problem: the territorial implosion of the earl's colony. Because his estates were spread across all of the counties of Munster, Cork's tenants and farmers experienced attacks wherever the insurgents appeared. His holdings were generally highly developed and prosperous; they promised their attackers rich pickings. While it was no great surprise that his other estates in counties Limerick, Clare and Kerry were virtually cut off by early January,[64] the plight of his possessions in Waterford and Cork was soon serious as well. Besides the panic of his Irish tenants and neighbours trapped between St Leger's fury and the rebels' threats, many of his English tenants fled their holdings, some seeking sanctuary in the main castles of the region, others heading straight for the coast hoping for evacuation to England through Youghal and Kinsale. The landscape emptied. Large tracts of countryside situated more than two or three miles from the protection of towns, castles and strong-houses became vacant ground within just a few weeks. This would have serious implications for food supplies the longer the conflict lasted.

Then there was the problem of woodland. One of the paradoxes besetting the earl in 1642 was how all the forests and woods he had preserved and managed down the years, to supply his iron-smelting furnaces and his timber-provision and export businesses, were now transformed into areas of danger. Historians have tended to overlook this aspect of his 'model' colony, continuing incorrectly to view the earl as an archetypal New English forest-clearer and asset-stripper.[65] Archaeologists and historical geographers on the other hand have done much to identify the prevalence of woodlands on his main estates, revealing how they covered miles of the earl's Blackwater holdings, from Kilbree and Ballyraghter Woods close by Lismore, through Conna Woods between Tallow and Castlelyons, to the great forest of Kilworth north of Fermoy.[66] When the rebellion arrived the earl's woodlands facilitated a wave of surprise attacks by providing cover to bands of insurgent forces. As the earl expressed it in a letter to England, 'no place' was safe.[67]

Assembling his tenant army took longer than it should. This was partly due to ongoing difficulties with the president: whether intentionally or not, St Leger diminished the ability of Sir Robert Tynte, the muster-master of the Blackwater militia, to carry out his duties effectively for the earl by attempting to pursue him for an unpaid fine soon after the rebellion began. Tynte stayed away and out of reach, at Inchiquin. St Leger continued pursuing him for money throughout the hostilities.[68] Otherwise, though, the sheer confusion of the situation defied prompt action. Coinciding with the first attempt on Dungarvan, rebel attacks occurred all along the great southern river (as far, indeed, as Newmarket in north co. Cork).[69] With the disappearance of many Irish soldiers and the surge of rural refugees, the gathering of men was necessarily ad hoc. On 22 January John Walley reported that the garrison at Lismore amounted to only thirty-seven volunteers. Although the absence of the Irish soldiers angered him, he was reassured by the presence of Lord Broghill's captain – probably Robert Downing of Ballysaggart – who busied himself making the men practice their gunmanship. Walley was more worried by the situation at Tallow, the operational centre of the Blackwater army.

Table 1 Cork's command: castles and garrisons in the southern Blackwater Valley, 1642

Stronghold	Owner/tenant occupier	Garrison officers	Strength
Youghal	Youghal Corporation Richard, earl of Cork	Richard, earl of Cork Sergeant-Major Appleyard Captain James Finch	200 foot
Lismore Castle	Richard, earl of Cork	Roger, Lord Broghill Captain Broadrip Cornet Robert Downing	95 foot
Ballyduff stronghouse	Richard, earl of Cork Erasmus Burrows, tenant	Unclear	$c.$10 foot
Dungarvan Castle		Captain Robert Smith Lieutenant Henry Rossington	28 foot
Pilltown Castle	Richard, earl of Cork Sir Phil. Percival, tenant	Lieutenant Morgan	Unclear
Ardmore Castle		Richard, Lord Dungarvan	6 foot
Cappoquin Castle	Hugh Croker	Hugh Croker Captain John O'Farnane Lieutenant Rossington (from March)	100 foot
Lisfinny Castle	Richard, earl of Cork Edward Russell, tenant	Charles Pyne (from March)	Unclear
Tallow town	Tallow Corporation	Captain Richard Joliffe John O'Norrowne	100 foot
Camphire Castle	Francis Ffoulk	Unclear	10 foot
Tourin Castle		Unclear	9 foot
Knockmoan Castle	Sir Richard Osborne	Sir Richard Osborne Lieutenant Henry Rossington Sergeant Bateman	$c.$30 foot
Dromana Castle	Garret Fitzgerald	Mulmory Magrath	$c.$20 foot
Mocollop Castle	Henry Tyrrell et al.	Thomas Carter Jnr Owner	$c.$10 foot
Ballygarran Castle	Roger Power	Owner	$c.$3 foot
Castle Richard, alias Inchegeragh		Unclear	5 foot
Ballinetray Castle	Sir Percy Smith	Owner	10 foot
Shrancally Castle	James Ryves's assigns	Unclear	10 foot
Inchiquin Castle	Sir Robert Tynte	Owner	5 foot

Table 1 (*cont.*)

Stronghold	Owner/tenant occupier	Garrison officers	Strength
Curnaveigh Castle	William Llewellyn	Owner	4 foot
Castlelyons	Earl of Barrymore	Owner Captain Charles Vavasour	c.20 foot
Cahirmona Castle	Sir Richard Tynte	William Tynte	6 foot

Sources: NLI, MSS 6241, 6900; CHA, Cork MSS, CM/22–3; Grosart (ed.), *Lismore Papers*, 1st series, v. 203–18; ibid., 2nd series, iv, nos 500–4, 506–9, 512, 514–15; ibid., v, nos 518–22, 523, 526–31, 533, 536–8, 540–4, 546, 548–9, 561–4; TCD, MS 820, fos 68, 113, 180–1.

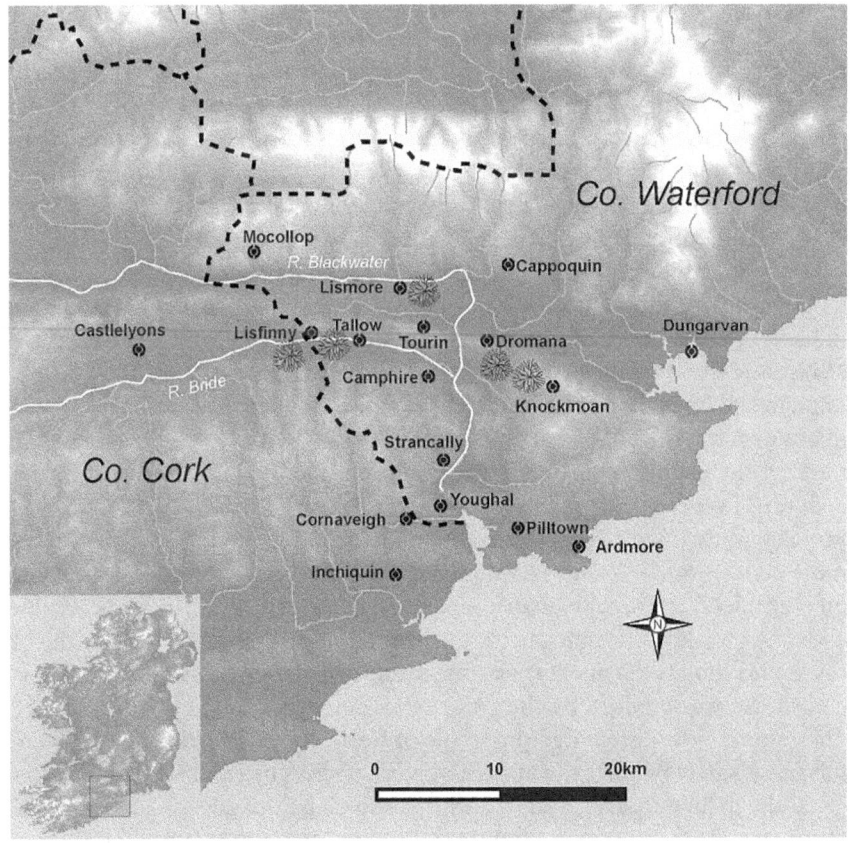

Figure 1 Map of the Blackwater Valley, 1641–43

With Captain Joliffe apparently not yet in place, the defence of the town was dependent on a band of thirty Irishmen commanded by John O'Norrowne, Gaelic tenant of an outlying parcel of Lismore manor.[70] Despite Walley's concerns, O'Norrowne's men held the town until Joliffe arrived to take charge.

From late January the earl's defensive line took shape as volunteers filed in, significant numbers of Irish returned, and arms and ammunition were distributed. As shown in Table 1 and the accompanying map, the Boyle garrison system was primarily a riverine one. In addition to five castles or strongholds situated along the Blackwater, from Mocollop south-east through Ballyduff, Lismore, Cappoquin and Dromana, and so to Youghal, it also contained an 'inner line' of another fifteen or so defensive points guarding the River Bride through Tallow as far as Castlelyons, as well as the spider's web of tributaries that brought the River Dissour to Inchiquin Castle and the sea. Likewise, the castles of Mogeely and Castlemartyr marked its western extremity, guarding the Kiltha River. Stretching a total of 36 miles (57 km) from Castleyons to Dungarvan the line was porous. In the east especially, the tracts of vacated territory that separated Dromana from Dungarvan attracted the rebels in large numbers, with Knockmoan and Pilltown standing as outposts in between. Under the brutally effective leadership of Edmund Fennell, who knew the region well, the rebels were able to strike almost at will, and disappear.[71] In addition, the combined rebel strength was vastly superior to the earl's force of some 700 men-in-arms – able, by his reckoning, to summon up to twenty times that number.[72]

With youthful exuberance, Roger, Lord Broghill never doubted the Boyle tenant army would prevail. In a letter to his father he boasted of his readiness to blow the roof in at Ballyeen Castle, with a 'long gun' placed on the terrace of Lismore, should Ballyeen's owner Roger Carew show any sign of wavering. Though the insurgents were returning again to the vicinity the baron urged that the main bridges be kept open the better to confront and chase them. He thought the enemy lacked supplies to sustain a long fight; they might soon be forced to leave.[73] But at this stage the rebels' appearance near Lismore was probably only a feint. They generally made inroads where their forces were most concentrated. Utilising woodland as cover they succeeded in cutting off land access to Dungarvan, before availing themselves of inside knowledge about the weakness of the garrison to launch a surprise attack and seize the castle and the little seaport it was meant to defend.[74] At a stroke, the insurgent cause was boosted by the prospect of imported supplies from Spain.[75] Their forces now dominated the whole of west co. Waterford to the banks of the Blackwater. Hoping to isolate Youghal, a series of raids ensued that targeted the main outposts loyal to Earl Richard along the river, at Knockmoan, Dromana, Cappoquin and Lismore.[76] Though attempts to cross the river at Youghal ferry and at Affane were repulsed, the rebels kept probing.

Ultimately, the earl's tenant force succeeded in holding on. Indeed, with the arrival in Youghal of reinforcements from England at the beginning of March the Protestant colony was finally able to counter-attack. Within days Lismore Castle, Cappoquin, Knockmoan and Castlelyons were relieved and reinforced, and on 3 March Dungarvan was retaken after a particularly bloody battle that reportedly left over two hundred insurgents and townspeople dead in the streets.[77] Furthermore, the recovery of the town and its castle was notable for witnessing close cooperation between the companies of the lord president and the earl. Cork's sons Viscount Dungarvan, and Lord Broghill participated in the engagement, as did a detachment from Knockmoan commanded by Sir Richard Osborne.[78]

Yet it is important to pay close attention to the chronology of military action so as not to over-estimate the strength of the Protestant fight-back. Consider Dungarvan: the insurgents managed to regain control of the town within just eight days (11 March), and to recapture the castle within twelve days (15 March).[79] As Osborne recounted, the enemy infiltrated Dungarvan's outskirts from the surrounding countryside, seized the mill, and brought in eighty musketeers from Waterford City to snipe at the new garrison of less than thirty men. During 10–11 March Knockmoan Castle was attacked again, the insurgents moving in from concealed positions when Osborne's soldiers left on a cattle prey and his second-in-command was preoccupied at Pilltown. Seven of Sir Richard's men were killed in the assault, others were badly wounded, leaving his ward 'much weakened', 'not able', he feared, 'to withstand a long siege'.[80] Lismore Castle was assaulted for the second time on or shortly before 14 March;[81] the following day Cappoquin Castle was preparing to face a 3,000-strong Catholic army;[82] Dromana was attacked 'about St Patrick's tide' (17 March);[83] Castlelyons was reported surrounded on 18 March;[84] and on 21 March the warders at Mocollop could see an advance party of their enemies gathering before them.[85]

Achieving more than they had managed in January, the Catholic insurgents stretched the earl's defensive line along its entire length, subjecting it to consecutive attacks in an evidently coordinated strategy. Their raid on Lisfinny Castle (25 March) deserves special notice, signifying that they had succeeded in crossing the Blackwater to reach the River Bride, approaching the castle through Conna Woods to the west. They were able to inflict considerable damage on the earl's lands and followers in this, the centre of his colony.[86] A letter by the earl's kinsman Robert Naylor, dean of Lismore, described the damage starkly. The entire parish of Lismore lay waste; Lisfinny village was stripped of anything of value; and the tenants of Kilmacow were in a desperate state. When he looked down from the top of a nearby hill towards the south-east the dean realised the full territorial extent of the onslaught of recent days. There were, he reckoned, 'at least 500 fires [burning] between the Blackwater and Dungarvan'.[87]

It was, then, only with the long-awaited landing of a second batch of English reinforcements and a large supply of weapons and munitions on 19 March that the insurgents were prevented from overrunning the earl's Blackwater defences and drawing close to Youghal. The alacrity with which Cork responded to the reinforcements' arrival hints at the strain he was under. Defying St Leger's explicit orders to transport *all* the delivered guns and powder to Cork City, where another large Catholic army was gathering to commence a siege,[88] the earl 'made stay' of the ship carrying the munitions, and requisitioned enough for his own companies at Youghal, and for Broghill at Lismore and Barrymore at Castlelyons.[89] The earl shared his officers' concerns about the Catholics' apparent access to weapons, knowing that at least one foreign consignment had recently reached Dungarvan following the insurgents' recapture of the town, and that Waterford was also being supplied.[90] The fact that the president was under siege in Cork did not apparently concern him. As the old nobleman saw it, if cooperating with St Leger meant constantly being deprived of available resources, his forces would not be able to maintain a defensive line for very long. Youghal, the colonists' best hope of salvation, would be at the insurgents' mercy.

And so it would continue until the final days of Earl Richard's life, with Catholic forces in the ascendant, inching towards a breakthrough, and the Protestant defensive efforts hampered by high-level discord. As Patrick Little has shown, even when Sir William St Leger died in June 1642 the relationship between the earl and the Munster presidency remained poor. St Leger was succeeded as the government's principal military commander by his protégé Murrough O'Brien, sixth baron of Inchiquin, who like him favoured an aggressive policy towards the insurgents, all the more so following the successful establishment of a confederate Catholic government at Kilkenny (also in June). The earl continued to desire a more cautious approach. Following his promotion Inchiquin immediately attempted to break the earl's influence, seeking what amounted to a monopoly of power in the province, and it was only through English mediation that a sharing of authority was reached.[91]

The major Protestant victory at the battle of Liscarroll in early September brought even that arrangement to an end. Not only was the earl's second son Viscount Kinalmeaky killed in the confrontation, but his son-in-law Barrymore was also fatally wounded – the very person with whom Inchiquin had been reluctantly persuaded to share power.[92] One of the more striking aspects of the earl of Cork's letters and papers post-Liscarroll is how little contact he had with Inchiquin. For nearly three months the baron could communicate with him only through Viscount Dungarvan, as the earl refused to answer his messages.[93] When direct correspondence eventually resumed (on Dungarvan's departure for England) it was chiefly to bicker over money and supplies, and expressed their mutual unwillingness to heed the requirements of the other.[94]

Contact between their forces was likewise minimal. The defence of Protestant Munster remained geographically as well as politically divided. Though histories of the period continue to speak of a strong defensive triangle joining Cork, Youghal and Kinsale, this does not fully match the facts. By land the three points remained for the most part separate; it was English naval shipping that linked them, and even that was barely adequate much of the time.[95]

Although Liscarroll was undoubtedly a major setback for the Catholic cause in the province,[96] its aftershock in south Munster was more limited than generally realised. Certainly, the extent of the territory controlled by Earl Richard's Blackwater forces steadily eroded. Dromana Castle was lost just weeks after the battle, thus nullifying any thoughts that the Confederate forces were really beaten. Predictably, its passage into Catholic hands brought no response from Inchiquin, so that within the valley the road south to Youghal soon became too dangerous to travel.[97] A fresh insurgent attack on Cappoquin at about the same time intensified the sense of siege.[98]

The earl's account books for February and March 1643 record his servants making entrenchments around Tallow, while his volunteer companies were reassembled and mustered at the town in readiness for an anticipated resumption of hostilities.[99] The attacks when they materialised came in the summer, in five discernible waves. The first occurred in late May, when a number of tenants bore the brunt of hit-and-run raiding. More seriously, early in June the earl's forces suffered a defeat on an expedition to relieve Castlelyons, losing seven officers and '300 common soldiers' – a huge loss given the size of their forces. Later that month a large-scale assault on Cappoquin was at length repulsed. In mid-July the confederates mounted a series of raids all along the line, but it was in early August, just in time for the harvest, that their troops impacted most forcefully. Lismore Castle was besieged for nine days, its reinforced walls withstanding the impact of '303 great shot' fired by the attackers (reflecting the quality of the defensive works carried out by Cork's Irish builder Thomas Kelly). The earl's main house was breached in several places.[100]

John Walley later wrote that the enemy destroyed what could not be dug up or removed. However, it is the locations he listed as affected that gives the clearest impression of what had occurred. In addition to the castles of Lismore and Cappoquin, the insurgents' usual targets, their troops advanced into Camphire, Ballyneety, Ballyeen, Affane and Tourin, all places that hitherto had seemed mostly safe, tucked in behind the earl's main strongholds.[101] Just a month before the earl died the Blackwater line was no longer fully functional. On the very day he died in Youghal a one-year ceasefire was announced between the Confederate leadership in Kilkenny and the king's government in Dublin. The local Catholic commanders were required to end their assault just as they were preparing for the final push. It would be interesting to discover if this fact contributed to the internal opposition to the cessation within the Confederate Assembly.

A final word about another internal world – that of the Blackwater Valley and the people that inhabited it, and those of the Bride Valley too. As 1642 turned into 1643 the community of the region was undergoing a redefinition along ethnic and religious lines that was no less painful than the waves of insurgent attacks. It will be recalled that a proportion of the earl's tenant army at the beginning of the conflict was comprised of local Irishmen, and that although significant numbers of these had left his service following St Leger's punitive treatment of native groups in Tipperary and Waterford, a sizeable proportion had stayed with the earl. This remained the case for most of the ensuing period of conflict. Available sources show that Irish troops had participated in repelling the main insurgent attacks. Indeed, the names of a few of them are to be found in the lists of casualties suffered by the earl's forces at the enemy's hands.[102] Even in May 1643, when Lismore was raided, Earl Richard was able to rely on a degree of Irish military support, including that of the sergeant of the garrison, John O'Dowan (tenant of some nearby mountain land), and three of the warders, one of whom, Maurice Roche, was killed in the attack.[103] Yet this proved insufficient to dispel the mounting anxiety felt by many Protestant settlers towards the Irish who remained among them. Successful confederate incursions were generally attributed to native duplicity: it was feared that the earl's Irishmen were traitors in disguise.

It was understandable, of course. The antics of local Irish Catholic commanders such as Edmund Fennell and John Sherlock may have been motivated by vengeance, but the viciousness of what they and their troops did in the Blackwater area by way of retaliation, allied with clear evidence they were aided by natives living in the valley, ensured that most of its English inhabitants came to view the Irish in general as inherently unreliable, and dangerous.[104] Reprisals were taken, every bit as indiscriminate as St Leger had committed before. The commander of the Mocollop garrison, Thomas Carter, was one of the first to act, ordering his men to burn the land of a neighbouring Irish gentleman who had protected his father's goods and property. Soon after there was trouble at Lismore, in the manorial village, the English troops (some of them new arrivals) pouring out of the castle after the rebels had gone to rough up the villagers.[105] Likewise Lisfinny: according to Dean Robert Naylor, English soldiers and what he described as 'a mob' of tenants could be seen robbing and stripping 'the poor harmless Irish'. The rest of the Irish, wanting to protect themselves, gathered up their movable possessions and were observed 'driving away' across the Blackwater.[106] Ethnic clearances had begun.

It had long been part of the earl of Cork's vanity to convince himself that his colonial holdings in Munster were the most settled and harmonious anywhere in Ireland. For the royal government in Dublin and Whitehall he had for years performed the role of 'model planter', emphasising his deep commitment to growing English settlement levels and the expansion of English government and of England's Protestant religion. But on his Munster estates his pursuit of a stronger English presence had always been moderated by his concern to accommodate the local Irish to the project, to recruit them and have them contribute to its success. Reading through his wartime papers 1641–43 it is clear that any satisfaction he felt at holding the line for English Protestantism on the Blackwater was countered by a deep disappointment at all that he and his family had lost. His son Kinalmeaky was dead, buried at Lismore; so too his son-in-law Barrymore, buried at Youghal. His vast fortune was gone, his lands either ruined or going waste – unless they were occupied by resurgent Catholic forces ready and waiting to finally push him and all of his associates out of the country.

One example will suffice to encapsulate the darkening atmosphere that surrounded the earl in these his last days. In April 1643, while he was in his chamber in Youghal, a new prisoner was brought in chains to the jail at Lismore, John O'Leighy. Located and arrested after a prolonged search for him, O'Leighy was in trouble with his English captors not for anything he had done, but for what he was reported to have said. He had been overheard making 'rebellious speeches', in which he allegedly called the Irish still living in the area 'fools' and 'apes' for trusting in the English, who were heretics after all, and as such could never be saved. His captors sought the earl's permission to execute him.[107] The earl would have been struck by the man's identity. John O'Leighy was the eldest son of Cork's long-time native servant, the builder Daniel O'Leighy. Years earlier his father had sought the earl's permission for John to grow up at Lismore as a companion for the Boyle children. Through the earl's influence he had also had his second son, John's brother Teige, sent to England to enter the household of the Protestant archbishop of Canterbury.[108] It was all so long ago.

NOTES

Research for this chapter was undertaken as part of a project at University College Cork funded by the Irish Research Council, 'Colonial Landscapes of Richard Boyle, 1st Earl of Cork, c.1602–43'.

1 N. Canny, *Making Ireland British, 1580–1650* (Oxford, 2001), p. 534.
2 K. McKenny, *The Laggan Army in Ireland, 1640–1685: the landed interests, political ideologies and military campaigns of the north-west Ulster settlers* (Dublin, 2005); A. Duignan, '"All in a confused opposition to each other": politics and war in Connacht, 1641–9' (PhD thesis, University College Dublin, 2006); otherwise, see D. Edwards, *The Ormond Lordship in County Kilkenny, 1515–1642: the rise and fall of Butler feudal power* (Dublin, 2003), pp. 309–32; J. McHugh, 'For our owne defence': Catholic insurrection in Wexford, 1641–2', in B. Mac Cuarta

(ed.), *Reshaping Ireland, 1550–1700: colonization and its consequences* (Dublin, 2011), pp. 214–40; and A. Duignan, 'The Scottish response to the 1641 Rebellion in Connacht: the case of Sir Frederick Hamilton', in D. Edwards and S. Egan (eds), *The Scots in Early Stuart Ireland: union and separation in two kingdoms* (Manchester, 2016), pp. 230–50.

3   R. Cox, *Hibernia Anglicana, or the history of Ireland from the conquest thereof by the English to this present time* (1689).

4   C. Smith, *The Antient and Present State of the County and City of Waterford* (Dublin, 1746); C. Smith, *The Antient and Present State of the County and City of Cork* (2 vols, Dublin, 1750); C. Smith, *The Antient and Present State of the County of Kerry* (Dublin, 1756).

5   P. Lenihan, *Confederate Catholics at War*; R. Armstrong, *Protestant War*; D. Dickson, *Old World Colony: Cork and South Munster, 1630–1830* (Cork, 2005); also notable, and still very useful, is J.A. Murphy, 'The politics of the Munster Protestants, 1641–9', *Journal of the Cork Historical and Archaeological Society* [*JCHAS*] 76 (1971), pp. 1–20.

6   The earl's role in the defence of the Bandon Valley is currently being explored by David Heffernan, and will be subject of an essay he is writing for the *JCHAS*.

7   Armstrong, *Protestant War*, chapter 3; Ó Siochrú, *Confederate Ireland*, pp. 62–8.

8   The arrangements made for colonial defence have only recently been attracting serious study: in addition to McKenny (note 2 above) see R.J. Hunter (ed.), *'Men and Arms': the Ulster settlers, c.1630* (Belfast, 2012), and K. Forkan, 'Army list of the Ulster British Forces, 1642–6', *Archivium Hibernicum* 59 (2005), pp. 51–65.

9   He landed at Youghal on 18 October 1641: Chatsworth House Archives [CHA], Cork MSS, CM/22/138: Cork to Perkins, 27 Jan. 1642.

10 D. Edwards, 'Boyle's private army: the creation of a colonial security force in early Stuart Munster', in D. Edwards and C. Rynne (eds), *The Colonial World of Richard Boyle, first Earl of Cork* (Dublin, 2018), pp. 223–44.

11 *Cal. Carew MSS, 1603–24*, pp. 217–8; Sheffield City Library, Wentworth Woodhouse Muniments, Strafford Papers [Str. P.] 24-25/236: list of the army in Ireland, n.d. c.1627; ibid., Str. P.24-25/267: list of entertainments for horse and foot, 1636.

12 R. Dunlop (ed.), 'An unpublished survey of the Plantation of Munster, 1622', *Journal of the Royal Society of Antiquaries of Ireland*, 6th series, 14 (1924), pp. 141–2; Grosart (ed.), *Lismore Papers*, 1st series, ii. 54.

13 *Cal. Carew MSS, 1603–24*, no. 64; C. Tait, 'Good ladies and ill wives: women on Boyle's estates', in Edwards and Rynne (eds), *The Colonial World*, pp. 205–222, at pp. 221–2.

14 NLI, MS 6248, pp. 15, 35, 55, 57, 67.

15 For more on their ties to the earl see NLI, MS 6142, pp. 27, 30, 158, 163; see also will of Sir Robert Tynte, 1643 (PCC, Wills and Administrations, 18 Fines).

16 Canny, *Making Ireland British*, pp. 322–8 is an important statement, but see D. Heffernan, 'Theory and practice in the Munster Plantation: the estates of Richard Boyle, first earl of Cork', in Edwards and Rynne (eds), *The Colonial World*, pp. 48–53.

17 NLI, MS 6140, pp. 5, 6, 14, 54, 69, 71–2, 111, 116, 127, 151, 158, 172, 180, 181–3, 229, 253.
18 Twenty-eight out of 130 foot, and four out of nine horse: NLI, MS 6129, pp. iii, 14, 16, 19, 21, 23, 24, 25–6, 28, 45, 51, 68, 73–4, 91, 95 and 111.
19 NLI, MSS 6142, 6244.
20 Heffernan, 'Theory and practice', pp. 43–63.
21 D. Edwards, 'From Land Thief to Planter: Kerry transactions and the rise of Richard Boyle, 1st earl of Cork', in M. Bríc (ed.), *Kerry: history and society* (Dublin, forthcoming).
22 D. Edwards, 'The land-grabber's accomplices: Richard Boyle's Munster affinity, 1588–1603', in Edwards and Rynne (eds), *The Colonial World*, pp. 170–82.
23 D. Edwards, 'Boyle's private army', pp. 232–3.
24 P. Little, 'The Geraldine ambitions of the first Earl of Cork', *IHS* 33 (2002), pp. 151–68.
25 NLI, MSS 6242 (Easter 1629 rental) and 6248 (Michaelmas 1642 rental), passim.
26 NLI, MS 43267/3: commissioners' warrant, 8 Aug. 1639.
27 NLI, MS 6240, entry for 1–7 Sept. 1639.
28 E.g., NLI, MS 6899, entries for 24–28 Sept. 1637, 22–26 April 1638.
29 NLI, MS 6900, entries for 19–25 Dec. 1641, 26 Dec. 1641–1 Jan. 1642.
30 N. Canny, *The Upstart Earl: a study of the social and mental world of Richard Boyle, first earl of Cork, 1566–1643* (Cambridge, 1982), p. 134; M. Perceval-Maxwell, *The Outbreak of the Irish Rebellion of 1641* (Montreal, 1994), p. 69; E. Murphy, 'Sir William St Leger', *DIB*.
31 P. Little, 'The Earl of Cork and the fall of the Earl of Strafford, 1638–41', *HJ* 39 (1996), pp. 619–35.
32 Chatsworth House Archives, Cork MSS, CM/22/84: St Leger to Cork, 7 Nov. 1641.
33 National Archives of Ireland, Catalogue and Index of Fiants, Charles I, no. 3136; M. Empey (ed.), *Early Stuart Irish Warrants, 1623–1639* (Dublin, 2015), no. 269.
34 R.S., *A Collection of some of the Massacres and Murthers committed on the Irish in Ireland since the 23rd of October 1641* (1662); suppressed at the time of publication, this Catholic account was later reprinted as an appendix to Edward, earl of Clarendon, *The History of the Rebellion and the Civil Wars in Ireland* (1720); see p. 358; its importance is discussed in K. Nicholls, 'The Other Massacre: English killings of Irish, 1641–3', in D. Edwards, P. Lenihan and C. Tait (eds), *Age of Atrocity: violence and political conflict in early modern Ireland* (Dublin, 2007), pp. 176–91, at pp. 176–7, 181–2; and P. Lenihan, *Consolidating Conquest: Ireland 1603–1727* (Harlow, 2008), p. 101.
35 Grosart (ed.), *Lismore Papers*, 1st series, iii. 162.
36 D. Edwards, 'Out of the Blue? Provincial unrest in Ireland before 1641', in M. Ó Siochrú and J. Ohlmeyer (eds), *Ireland 1641: contexts and reactions* (Manchester, 2013), pp. 95–114, at p. 109.
37 Grosart (ed.), *Lismore Papers*, 2nd series, v, no. 559.
38 Ibid., iv. 221–6.
39 M. Hickson, *Ireland in the Seventeenth Century, or the Irish Massacres of 1642* (2 vols, 1884), ii, pp. 242–3.

40 Bodl. Carte MS 63, fos 116r–117v: St Leger to lord justices and council, 4 Dec. 1641; Perceval-Maxwell, *Outbreak*, p. 257.
41 CHA, Cork MSS CM/22/84 and 96: St Leger to Cork, 6 and 7 Nov. 1641.
42 Grosart (ed.), *Lismore Papers*, 2nd series, iv. 218–21.
43 Ibid., pp. 224–5; CHA, Cork MSS, CM/22/91 and 122; St Leger to Cork, 20 Nov. 1641 and 5 Jan. 1642.
44 Grosart (ed.), *Lismore Papers*, 1st series, v. 202; the two argued over the terms of the loan.
45 Grosart (ed.), *Lismore Papers*, 2nd series, iv. 230; it was not unexpected: the earl had been accusing St Leger of abusing the subsidy collection for months: see CHA, Cork MSS, CM/21/96: grievances of inhabitants of co. Cork, 24 Mar. 1641.
46 Grosart (ed.), *Lismore Papers*, 1st series, v. 205; ibid., 2nd series, iv. 229–30; *The Swallow* remained at Kinsale thereafter: J.Hogan (ed.), *Letters and Papers Relating to the Irish Rebellion, 1642-6* (Dublin 1936), pp. 38–9, 65–7, 87–8.
47 Grosart (ed.), *Lismore Papers*, 2nd series, iv. 225.
48 St Leger requested the attendance of Cork's forces on campaigns in his letters of 6, 7, 10, 12, 20 and 28 Nov., 19, 20 and 25 Dec. 1641, and 16 Jan. 1642.
49 The letter, unfortunately, is not extant; I have ascertained its content from St Leger's reply.
50 NLI, MS 43266/19: St Leger to Cork, 10 Jan. 1642.
51 Gilbert, *Irish Confederation*, i. 231.
52 CHA, Cork MSS, CM/22/89: Perkins to Cork, 16 Nov. 1641; Grosart (ed.), *Lismore Papers*, 1st series, v. 214.
53 NLI, MS 6241, pp. 9–14; these were, of the foot, Edward O'Scanlon, William Fitzgerald, Teige O'Connell, Arthur O'Kelly, George Wadding, Daniel O'Driscoll, Morris Cragh, Teige O'Connellan, Cornelius O'Sullivan, John Devaney, Edward Tobin, Thomas Merry (alias O'Houlighane), Richard Mellifont, Richard English, Edmund O'Flynn, David Clancy, William Coveney, Nicholas Fitzgerald, John Downey, Richard Power, Lawrence O'Lyne, Donal O'Keeffe, Robert Stout, William Heale (alias O'Healy), William Donnyn or Dineen, and Garret Flanagan; Thomas White may have been another.
54 At least three of Joliffe's six junior officers were natives (ibid., p. 12).
55 Edwards, *Ormond Lordship*, pp. 309–22; Canny, *Making Ireland British*, pp. 525–8.
56 Grosart (ed.), *Lismore Papers*, 2nd series, iv. 246; Bodl. Carte MS 2, fo. 284: Broghill to Cork, 11 Jan. 1642; TCD, MS 820, fos 44, 57, 68, 70, 113, 183: depositions of Mary Boulter, Anice Lee, Barnaby Gosse, Tobias Brewer, George Monnocky and Daniel Spicer.
57 BL, Egerton MS 80, pp. 85–6: Fenton to Cork, 1 Feb. 1642.
58 Grosart (ed.), *Lismore Papers*, 2nd series, v. 5–6.
59 Ibid., iv. 249–50.
60 R. Gillespie, 'The Irish economy at war, 1641–52', in J. Ohlmeyer (ed.), *Ireland from Independence to Occupation, 1641-60* (Cambridge, 1995), pp. 160–80, at p. 165.
61 NLI, MS 6900, weekly accounts, 26 Dec. 1641 to 1 Jan. 1642.

62 Grosart (ed.), *Lismore Papers*, 1st series, v. 204, 206-7.
63 NLI, MS 6900, weekly accounts, 2-8 Jan., 17-23 April 1642.
64 CHA, Cork MSS, CM/22/123: sovereign and townsmen of Dingle to Cork, 9 Jan. 1642; Grosart (ed.), *Lismore Papers*, 2nd series, iv. 241-3.
65 Canny, *Making Ireland British*, pp. 310-15.
66 Rynne, 'Colonial entrepreneur and urban developer', pp. 106-7; C. Ketch, 'Landownership in County Waterford c.1640: the evidence from the Civil Survey', in W. Nolan and T. Power (eds), *Waterford: history and society* (Dublin, 1992), pp. 199-226, at pp. 210-11. See also NLI, MS 6140, pp. 6, 8, 122, 141, 169, 172, 230, 253, 255, 307.
67 CHA, Cork MSS, CM/22/138: Cork to Perkins, 27 Jan. 1642.
68 Grosart (ed.), *Lismore Papers*, 1st series, v. 205, 209-10; ibid., 2nd series, v. 33-5; in fairness, St Leger needed the money, and Tynte's dodging of payment set a precedent that could hardly be tolerated.
69 Ibid., 2nd series, iv. 247-8; TCD, MS 822, fo. 22: deposition of Ralph Steeres.
70 NLI, MS 13237/27: Walley to Cork, 22 Jan. 1642; ibid., MS 6248, p. 33.
71 For Fennell see TCD, MS 820, fos 44, 54-5, 68, 92-3, 138-9, 167, 174: depositions of Mary Boulter, Hugh Croker, Barnaby Goss, Edward Crockford, Nicholas Osborne, George Horson and Walter Power.
72 CHA, CM/22/138: Cork to Perkins, 27 Jan. 1642.
73 Grosart (ed.), *Lismore Papers*, 2nd series, iv. 254-6.
74 Ibid., pp. 246-7.
75 CHA, CM/22/140, 142: St Leger to Cork and Bradshaw to same, both 30 Jan. 1642.
76 Grosart (ed.), *Lismore Papers*, 2nd series, iv. 252-3.
77 Grosart, *Lismore Papers*, 1st series, v. 207-8.
78 Ibid.; NLI, MS 43266/19: Osborne to Cork, 12 Mar. 1642.
79 TCD, MS 820, fo. 149: deposition of Robert Sanders.
80 Ibid., fo. 221: deposition of Sir Richard Osborne; NLI, MS 43266/19: Osborne to Cork, 12 Mar. 1642.
81 NLI, MS 13237/27: Walley to Cork, 14 Mar. 1642.
82 CHA, CM/22/172: Croker to Cork, 15 Mar. 1642.
83 TCD, MS 820, fo. 105: deposition of Katherine Fowher.
84 Grosart, *Lismore Papers*, 2nd series, v. 24-5.
85 CHA, CM/22/175: Carter to Cork, 21 Mar. 1642.
86 Ibid., CM/23/1: Pyne to Cork, 25 Mar. 1642.
87 Ibid., CM/22/163: Naylor to Cork, Mar. 1642.
88 Hogan (ed.), *Letters and Papers*, pp. 14-16.
89 Grosart, *Lismore Papers*, 1st series, v. 209.
90 NLI, MS 43266/19: Osborne to Cork, 24 Mar. 1642.
91 Little, *Lord Broghill*, pp. 26-7.
92 James Buckley, 'The Battle of Liscarroll, 1642', *JCHAS* 4 (1898), pp. 83-100.
93 CHA, CM/23/127-8, 130-1, 139-40, 143: Inchiquin to Dungarvan, 20, 21, 28 Sept., 14 and 18 Oct. 1642.
94 ibid., CM/23/163, 166, 170, 179, 191: Inchiquin to Cork, 30 Nov., 7, 14 Dec. 1642, 10, 31 Jan. 1643; ibid., CM/23/20; Cork to Dungarvan, 16 Mar. 1643.

95 E. Murphy, *Ireland and the War at Sea, 1641–1653* (Woodbridge, Suffolk, 2012), pp. 17–34, 151–3.
96 Lenihan, *Confederate Catholics*, pp. 63–4.
97 Grosart, *Lismore Papers*, 1st series, v. 214; TCD, MS 820, fos 136r, 180r: depositions of Ursula Winyard and Richard Rely.
98 Ibid., fo. 110r: deposition of James Tomson.
99 NLI, MS 6900, weekly accounts, 12–18 Feb., 26 Feb.–4 Mar., 12–18 and 19–24 Mar. 1643.
100 Ibid., weekly accounts, 28 May–3 June, 9–15 July, 30 July–5 Aug., 6–12 Aug. and 27 Aug.–2 Sept. 1643; the earl of Cork's diary, one of the main sources for the war, is defective for these crucial weeks, the manuscript (CHA, CM/27) being badly torn in places: Grosart (ed.), *Lismore Papers*, 1st series, v. 228–31.
101 NLI, MS 13237/28: Walley to Cork, 22 July, 7 Aug. and 1 Sept. 1643.
102 TCD, MS 820, fos 66, 221: depositions of John Rowse and Sir Richard Osborne.
103 Grosart (ed.), *Lismore Papers*, 1st series, v. 227; NLI, MS 6248, pp. 27, 31.
104 Some of Fennell's alleged atrocities are described in depositions of Katherine Croker, George Horson, John Dartnell (TCD, MS 820, fos 161–2, 167r, 168r).
105 CHA, CM/23/17: Walley to Cork, 22 April 1642.
106 Grosart (ed.), *Lismore Papers*, 2nd series, v. 16–18.
107 CHA, CM/24/8: information against O'Leighy, 12 April 1643.
108 NLI, MS 13237/6: Nichollet to Cork, 4 Dec. 1623.

2

The Sea Adventure to Munster and Connacht, July and August 1642

DAVID BROWN

The additional Sea Adventure to Ireland of 1642, dismissed by Karl Bottigheimer as a 'floating mockery of the conquering expedition the adventurers had desired', was the direct response of militant puritan merchants in London to Charles I's declaration, on 14 April 1642, that he would travel to Ireland and take command of his forces.[1] Almost all of the historiography for the Sea Adventure is based on a single source, the hagiographical account of the voyage written in 1642 by Hugh Peter, the puritan divine who was its pastor.[2] Relying on this report, Robert Brenner identified the close correlation between the investors in the Sea Adventure and the contractors to the earl of Warwick's Providence Island Company, a pirate's nest masquerading as a hopelessly unviable plantation colony off the coast of modern-day Guatemala.[3] The Providence Island Company was owned by the 'junta' of opposition peers and a small number of equally influential MPs, including John Pym.[4] John Adamson has presented the events preceding the English revolution as a revolt led primarily by this section of the peerage, specifically Robert Rich, earl of Warwick, Robert Greville, Lord Brooke and William Fiennes, Viscount Saye and Sele. This thesis was developed further by Karen Ordahl Kupperman who, using the records of the Providence Island Company, demonstrated that a close relationship had existed for some time between Warwick and the leading sea adventurers, especially Maurice Thompson, who became the main contractor of naval services for the company.[5]

The Adventure for Irish land was initially the brainchild of Richard Boyle, 1st earl of Cork, communicated by letter to the earl of Warwick in January 1642. Boyle proposed the complete removal of Irish Catholics from Ireland, recommended a complete conquest and subsequent plantation with English settlers. In Boyle's words, 'if it would please his majesty, with assent of Parliament, to cause an act to be passed there, to attaint them all of high treason, and to confiscate their lands and estates to the crown, it would utterly dishearten them, and encourage the English to serve courageously against them in hope to be settled in the lands of them they shall kill or otherwise destroy'.[6] On 19 March 1642, this proposal had morphed into the Adventure for Irish land, a shared-ownership speculation in the conquest of Ireland.[7] The intention of the speculators was that money contributed towards a private army, under the command of the investors, would crush the Irish rebellion of October 1641, and be repaid quickly in land.[8] The Act assumed that the rebellion in Ireland was a general one and that all Catholic-owned land in Ireland would be subject to forfeiture.[9] The Adventure raised approximately £300,000 between March and July 1642.

The Sea Adventure was an off-shoot of the Adventure for Irish land, conceived as a naval expedition to complement the land expedition envisioned by the original scheme, with a quickly raised budget of £46,000.[10] Tensions between king and Parliament had prevented the adventurers' army from taking the field, although it was assembled and exercised near London in the summer of 1642. The adventurers had established their own committee, the Committee of Adventurers for Ireland that included neither peers nor MPs and met at Grocers' Hall in London, away from parliamentary scrutiny.[11] In an attempt to seize control of the private army, Charles I announced on 6 April that he would lead the expeditionary force to Ireland, an idea swiftly rebuffed by Parliament. This may have been his intention since 19 March when he signed the Adventurers' Act.

Taking the king's announcement as a threat to take over their army, the adventurers responded with a petition to Parliament on 14 April, offering to 'relieve their brethren who are in distress' and to 'further supply by sea for coming thither and to spoil and waste those rebels by land, do propose to this honourable assembly to set out at their own charge five, six or seven ships and pinnaces with 500 soldiers as an additional supply to their former subscription'. The petition stipulated that the subscribers would have 'freedom to choose all officers employed in this service'.[12] A clearly piratical venture, all spoil and prizes were to be divided among the crew and the Sea Adventure's financial backers who, furthermore, were to receive Irish land at the same rate as the original Adventure. There were no restrictions on who could be attacked and the vessels were exempted from being forced under the command of the English navy. *An Additional Declaration of the Lords and Commons*, of April 1642, emphasised the adventurers' position, stating that 'the king's going to Ireland ... will cause men to believe that it is out of design to discourage the undertakers and hinder the other propositions for raising money for the defence of Ireland'.[13] Having engineered an opportunity to acquire Irish estates on very attractive terms, what the adventurers feared most in April 1642 was peace.

The Sea Adventure tapped into existing mercantile and colonial networks. Perhaps the key figure was the London merchant and Virginia planter, Maurice Thompson. Thompson and his family were involved in a merchant network centred on the Boyles in Munster, initially through Thompson's brother-in-law, Captain William Tucker, the Virginia colony's captain-general.[14] In another role, William Tucker was the factor in Virginia for Daniel Gookin, the business manager for the 1st earl of Cork, who had migrated to Virginia in 1621 but returned frequently to Ireland and England.[15] Daniel Gookin was an active transporter of servants, cattle and other supplies to Virginia and owned several hundred acres there. While in England, Gookin made use of Boyle's contacts in Bristol to build ships of his own to service his colonial trade.[16] Gookin sent out at least one ship each year, delivering Irish and English servants and cattle on alternate years.[17] Boyle's purported niece, Hannah, also lived in Virginia, a tenant of the Tuckers and neighbour of the Thompsons in Elizabeth City.[18] Quite distinct from the men who made their money predominantly from trade, a separate class of investors, undertakers who invested in the development of new landed estates, entered the Virginia and Irish land markets in large numbers in the 1620s and it was common for English undertakers to have investments in both.[19]

By the 1630s the Thompson/Tucker partnership dominated the Virginia tobacco business and spread their interests to the Caribbean. St Kitts already had a large population of Catholic Irish indentured labourers who had been forcibly transplanted from Wexford by Sir Arthur Chichester to make way for incoming English settlers.[20] In 1629, Thompson secured a patent on the island for 1,000 acres in return for a loan provided to the financially troubled James Hay, earl of Carlisle. Hay had, also in 1629, acquired a patent for all of the western islands in the Caribbean for ten years, followed by a monopoly for the import of tobacco into Ireland in 1630.[21] The St Kitts venture brought Maurice Thompson once again into the world of Richard Boyle, and his business connections. Phane Beecher, for example, was originally granted land in co. Cork by Elizabeth I in 1586, which was inherited by his eldest son, Henry.[22] Henry Beecher built the town of Bandon and sold it on to Richard Boyle in 1618.[23] A second son, also Phane Beecher, left Ireland for St Kitts in 1627 to establish a plantation financed by New English settlers in Ireland, led by Captain Thomas Vallett of Aghmarten, one of Boyle's tenants.[24] In 1642, Phane led an unsuccessful rebellion on St Kitts against Carlisle's proprietorship and was forced to return to Ireland by Carlisle's governor, Sir Thomas Warner.[25] Warner, in turn, was financed by three London merchants, two of whom – Maurice Thompson and William Pennoyer – would take the lead in supplying Munster with munitions and other supplies in 1642, and a third, Thomas Povey, whose brother Edward was yet another tenant of Boyle in Carrigaline.[26] Carlisle's tobacco was imported through the city of Cork, where

Francis Boyle, the son of Richard (and future first Viscount Shannon) was the collector for customs.[27]

Nevis, an island close to St Kitts in the Caribbean Antilles, also had a large population of indentured Irish labourers in the 1620s. The Nevis colony was planted by a London-based cousin of the Thompson brothers, Edward Thompson.[28] The island was attacked by the Spanish in 1628 and the Irish population was moved to the nearby island of Montserrat, which received further imports of servants from Galway.[29] Montserrat continued to have an almost entirely Irish, and therefore Catholic, population throughout the mid-seventeenth century. The colony was governed by Captain Anthony Briskett – formerly a Wexford planter who had moved on in the hope of richer rewards in the Caribbean – financed from Virginia by a consortium led by George Thompson.[30] Commencing in 1631, entire cargoes of Montserrat tobacco were sent by George Thompson to Virginia and these consignments were shipped on by George and his brother Maurice to Cork.[31] All of these arrangements, although quite fluid, demonstrate the very close partnerships between Richard Boyle's circle on one side, and Maurice Thompson's on the other.

Although it is convenient to describe the Sea Adventure as yet another episode in England's great seventeenth-century western enterprise, most of the backing came from entrepreneurs involved in the Barbary Company, chartered in 1638 to perform punitive raids on the coast of North Africa.[32] Two naval crusades were planned by the earls of Essex and Warwick to commence in the spring of 1642.[33] The first was to the Caribbean, with the goal of retaking Providence Island from the Spanish, who had tired of constant attacks on their traffic to and from Mexico and overran the outpost. This project was delegated to John Pym, and the expected profits were to be divided between the Electoral Palatinate, the crucible of the Thirty Years War, and the Providence Island Company. The second mission, contracted to the powerful maritime Rainsborough family, was intended to attack pirates at their base in Algiers. This mission had most recently been discussed by Parliament on 9 February 1642 and three ships in the process of being fitted out for Algiers were made available for the time being to Parliament, for service in Irish waters.[34]

The legal basis for issuing parliamentary letters of marque for a privateering mission, without troubling the king or the privy council as was the norm, was provided by a vote in Parliament of 14 March 1642 declaring that where the king was unavailable 'due to ill counsel', and royal assent unobtainable, Parliament could provide such assent.[35] Parliament had thus enabled itself to launch privateering missions of its own. The distinction between privateering and piracy was a blurred one, but letters of marque issued by the state permitted an attack on a named party, in this case the Irish, to obtain redress for an earlier infraction. Although the Sea Adventure was promoted and organised by Maurice Thompson, Warwick's most reliable privateering contractor, it was in essence a piratical venture, enabled by a coalition of the two groups planning quite separate missions. In addition to the naval aspect of the venture, the Sea Adventure carried with it a sizeable land force. The introduction of a mercenary army to the shores of Munster and Connacht in the summer of 1642 brought with it the most brutal aspects of the Thirty Years War: the conduct of war for annihilation and plunder. As David Parrott put it: 'The officers' aim was to increase their profits from paying little or nothing to their – disposable – soldiers, while making still larger gains from systematic plunder and looting.'[36] Total destruction was a by-product of this type of warfare and practised by Gustavus Adolphus of Sweden during his northern European campaigns, where Alexander Lord Forbes, a Scottish professional soldier, served as an under-officer.[37] At a time when the Irish rebellion might have blown itself out due to lack of resources, Parliament's similar posture of unconditional surrender, exemplified by the mercenary army envisioned by the Adventurers' Act and demonstrated with the Sea Adventure, made this impossible.

Unlike the Adventure for Irish land, however, Charles I refused to sanction the Sea Adventure with a royal commission.[38] The Sea Adventure thus marked a significant escalation in Parliament's assumption of military authority by authorising a navy to attack one of the king's dominions. Furthermore, without a royal commission, a privateering mission of this type normally required letters of marque from the lord high admiral, but this was not obtained before the Sea Adventure sailed on 29 June, conveniently under the command of neither king nor Parliament, but with an ordinance of Parliament in defiance of the king's expressed wish.[39] For Parliament and the earl of Warwick, who was appointed lord admiral by Parliament on 2 July, this arrangement provided an opportunity for 'deniability', should the mission go badly.

In terms of English naval strength in June 1642, the Sea Adventure was a substantial undertaking. The Committee for Irish Affairs reviewed the strength of the navy on 13 June and found it comprised 21 ships, four in the Irish Sea chartered from Maurice Thompson at the start of the year, an additional seventeen to guard the English coast and a further two vessels, only chartered on 3 June, that had yet to be assigned any specific duties.[40] The eleven ships assembled for the Sea Adventure were, by comparison, a sizeable force. The Sea Adventure raised £42,906 in cash or in kind for its mission from 180 subscribers. Of these, thirty-three were associates of Maurice Thompson with a colonial trading background, and put up 30 per cent of the money.[41]

The entire Sea Adventure fund was paid directly to Maurice Thompson who managed the campaign.[42] Hugh Peter, who became associated with the Providence Island grandees in the Netherlands during the 1620s, was appointed the sea adventurers' chaplain.[43] Hugh Peter's brother, Benjamin, was appointed admiral of the sea force.[44] Alexander Forbes, veteran of the continental 'total war', was in overall command of the 1,000-strong mercenary land force. Forbes also held a patent by inheritance to Castle Forbes in co. Longford and was the only officer or committee member of the Sea Adventure to have any personal investment in Ireland.[45] Together with Thompson, who had deep links with the Calvinist St Augustine's Church in London, the leadership of the Sea Adventure was distinctively puritan and more continental than Atlantic in outlook, despite their colonial experiences. They were embarking on a religious war of conquest, not a colonial enterprise for profit.

Maurice Thompson convened a committee to manage the mission that included his brothers George and William, recently returned from Virginia where they had lived since childhood. The other members comprised Sir Nicholas Crisp and Abraham Chamberlain of the Guinea Company, who both opted to support Charles in the aftermath of the mission. The Crisp family were the principal backers of the Barbary Company and subscribed £2,550 to the Sea Adventure. John Wood and Humphrey Slany were also Barbary Company men, although Slany partnered with Thompson in financing an illegal colony at Maryland in the 1630s and was, with Crisp, Boyle's main customer for Munster bar iron, the source of much of his cash for land aggregation.[46] Thomas Rainsborough was the son of William Rainsborough, a Levant Company grandee and veteran of the Sallee raid in 1637.[47] Gregory Clement was a veteran of the East India Company until he was dismissed in 1630 for illegal trading practices. Clement was a long-time partner of Maurice Thompson, both in the tobacco trade and in privateering.[48] William Pennoyer partnered with Clement and Maurice Thompson in capturing a Spanish ship in the West Indies and bringing it in to Plymouth as a prize on 23 October 1641.[49] William Willoughby, an experienced captain trading with New England, was part owner of the *Elizabeth of London* with Maurice Thompson, attacked by Barbary pirates in the bay of Penzance, Cornwall, in the spring of 1640.[50] The combined committee comprised a 'dream team' of seventeenth-century English piracy.

Of this committee, Maurice Thompson and William Pennoyer, the leading conveyors of Caribbean tobacco to Munster, had taken the lead in provisioning Protestant forces in Ireland immediately following the outbreak of the 1641 rebellion. Pennoyer, who concentrated on Munster, undertook to ship gunpowder and shot from Holland to Ireland in ships owned by Samuel Vassall, a prominent puritan MP, founder of the Massachusetts Bay Company, and active in the sale of Moorish slaves in Livorno, Italy.[51] Maurice Thompson chartered four armed merchantmen to Algernon Percy, earl of Northumberland and lord high admiral, on 20 November 1641, to supply English and Scottish forces intended for Ireland and to guard the Irish Sea.[52] The *Charity* was commissioned to carry munitions to Carrickfergus Castle, along with £20,000 in silver bullion to pay soldiers.[53] Another, the enormous

Ruth, later used for Thompson's Indian ventures, was hired to deliver £6,000 to Boyle to pay the army in Munster.[54] This money was despatched directly, despite the entreaties of the lord lieutenant, the earl of Leicester, for funds to enable him to mount a campaign under the king's colours.[55] A petition sent directly to the king for arrears of pay and further provision was similarly ignored in the closing weeks of 1641.[56] Despite the fact that the Irish rebellion had spread throughout the country, Parliament and its merchant contractors were highly selective in choosing who to support. If the Protestant forces had no London connections, or were not connected to Boyle, whose closeness to Warwick ensured some support, nothing short of a direct family connection with the London contractors could ensure supply. Benjamin Whetcombe, for example, a New England trader whose family had invested in the Massachusetts Bay Company with Hugh Peter and Samuel Vassall, and whose brother was mayor of Dungarvan, undertook to provide biscuits, peas and cheese to the Munster forces to the value of £150.[57] These suppliers bore heavy costs, however, and Maurice Thompson lost one ship, *Blessing of London*, in July 1642, taken near Wexford while on a voyage to Derry.

The event in Ireland that directly triggered the Sea Adventure involved another merchant vessel. On 9 March 1642, a group of Galway merchants seized a merchant ship commanded by Captain Robert Clarke and took away a consignment of arms intended for St Augustine's fort outside the town.[58] A stand-off ensued between the town and the garrison of the fort, under the command of Captain Anthony Willoughby. As the town prepared to besiege the fort, Captain Willoughby set fire to its outer suburbs and fired shots over its walls. As far as the authorities in Dublin were concerned, and based on intelligence communicated to them by the earl of Clanricarde, the town was in open rebellion and had 'joined in an oath of confederacy'.[59] On 23 April a second supply ship, the *Employment* (owned by the ubiquitous Maurice Thompson and under the command of Captain Ashley), was diverted from Dublin with supplies and munitions for the fort.[60] Ashley successfully petitioned Clanricarde to stabilise the situation. In their submission to Clanricarde on 6 May, the townsmen declared their allegiance to Charles I, prompted by the king's announcement that he was to come over to Ireland. Their fear was that the arming of the fort by parliamentarians represented a threat to the Catholic inhabitants of the town and they requested that the town be put under royal protection.[61] Through Clanricarde's efforts, peace was restored between the fort and the town on 11 May, although tensions remained high.[62] Ashley continued to be a problem, however, remaining in Galway Bay, refusing to respond to Clanricarde's orders and encouraging Willoughby to maintain a posture of defiance. Although Clanricarde made enquiries with Sir Henry Stradling, the vice-admiral of the Irish coasts, no commander seemed able to instruct Ashley to leave Galway despite Stradling issuing a direct order.[63]

Details of Clanricarde's arrangements reached Parliament's Committee for Irish Affairs on 21 June. This meeting, held in Grocers' Hall rather than at Westminster, was attended by earls of Warwick, Essex, Pembroke and Holland, Lords Saye and Brooke, John Pym and the committee's secretary, William Hawkins, who was another of Maurice Thompson's brothers-in-law.[64] The committee decided that the town of Galway should be included in the forfeited lands to be made available to the adventurers for Irish land, a decision that would require its surrender to the adventurers' forces and that John Pym be despatched to the House of Commons to secure an ordinance in that regard. In his presentation to Parliament the following day, Pym produced a letter written by the earl of Clanricarde at Portumna, dated 18 May, that detailed the terms for the pacification of Galway, making it clear that Clanricarde had taken the town under his majesty's protection with Willoughby's collusion.[65] Pym was particularly incensed that under the terms of the agreement, the practice of Catholicism would continue to be allowed in the town, and he moved that the agreement with Clanricarde should not be allowed:

> That this form of protection, as it is granted to that city [Galway] is against the act of Parliament lately made, against the declaration of Parliament touching the advancement of Protestant religion in that kingdom, against the peace and settlement intended to be had there, and the satisfaction which the inhabitants of that city ought to make to those of his majesty's subjects that have received losses and injuries by them.[66]

Oliver Cromwell moved that the matter be referred back to the Committee for Irish Affairs, of which he was also a member, leaving the committee to make any arrangements it thought fit.

The Committee for Irish Affairs in turn passed the Galway question to the Committee for Adventurers, who also met in Grocers' Hall. On 22 June, James Harvey, an ensign under Willoughby's command, arrived in London and invited the adventurers to mount an expedition against the town of Galway.[67] Maurice Thompson's armed vessel remained in Galway Bay throughout, heavily armed and with munitions for 1,000 men, originally intended for Dublin, and the *Ruth* lurked in the Shannon Estuary.[68] Despite Galway being under royal protection, a private army intended to seize it under a vague commission to help suppress the Irish rebellion, and this army was the Sea Adventure. In preparation for their arrival, Ashley blockaded the town, preventing Clanricarde from leaving for Dublin to make his protests.[69] It would have been a wasted journey in any case, for on 18 June, Clanricarde received a letter from the lords justices in Dublin, disowning his agreement with the Galway townsmen.

This set the stage for the fleet that departed the Thames on 29 June 1642 and made it to Plymouth on 6 July. There, the opportunism that was to plague the mission became clear. The largest investor by far in the Sea Adventure, with an investment of £5,200, was John Dyke, one of the earl of Warwick's longest-standing partners in piracy and the first deputy governor of the Providence Island Company.[70] Thomas Cunningham, a Scottish merchant with a large business in the Netherlands invested a further £1,800, and the pair contributed two ships between them.[71] Cunningham, like Thompson, was an early supplier of the Scottish forces in Ulster. Cunningham and Dyke's ships never saw service in Ireland but remained off Plymouth, blockading the port in search of royalist supply ships which could be taken as prizes.[72] Continuing on for Ireland, Wexford was the most obvious target for a force of such size, as the town had become a critical hub for supplies to Catholic Ireland from France and the Spanish Netherlands as well as developing as the principal Irish base for privateers.[73] Surprisingly, however, the Sea Adventure headed instead for Kinsale, arriving there on 10 July.[74]

The prize in Kinsale was the tobacco store built up by Lord Deputy Wentworth (later earl of Strafford) during the 1630s. Wentworth had in 1639 created and acquired the hugely profitable tobacco monopoly for Ireland with his close friend and deputy, Sir Christopher Wandesford,.[75] The licence for this monopoly was originally purchased for £7,000 per annum by Wentworth in 1633 in partnership with Sir Arthur Ingram and Francis Annesley, Lord Mountnorris, but in later years Wentworth appears to have bought or forced them out of the consortium. The death of Wandesford in 1640, and Wentworth in 1641, created an opportunity for the colonial merchants to take over the Irish tobacco market, with the monopoly unenforceable and the likely support of the earls of Cork and Warwick, a return to the Thompson-led monopoly that had existed before Wentworth's intervention. Wentworth had built up a store of tobacco worth £46,000 using money secretly borrowed from the Irish exchequer.[76] At the time of his execution he owed £107,000 to various creditors, including his suppliers of tobacco.[77] The tobacco store would put the adventurers into profit from the outset.

There were, however, also valid strategic reasons for the Kinsale stop. William Pennoyer had organised a small network of sutlers who operated along the coast and for a short distance inland.[78] The principal distributors were the Gookins, Sir Vincent and his son, who distributed supplies in a corridor from Kinsale to Bandon. A second sutler, Thomas Payne, who handled merchandise in Castletown, was another of Maurice Thompson's Virginia connections. Phane Beecher, the sutler in Abbeymahon parish, had recently returned from St Kitts. A third, Sir William Hull of Clonakilty, was the son of a noted pirate also closely associated with Boyle.[79] Hull managed military supplies for Drimoleague and Clonakilty while his son, also called William, was a captain in the sea adventurers' land force.[80] The distribution of military supplies was, therefore, conducted through a network of trusted agents, both of the Boyles and the colonial merchants.

Two ships of the king's fleet were already at Kinsale, under the command of Captain Thomas Kettleby. Kettleby was familiar in English Caribbean privateering circles and formerly governor of Nevis, the small Leeward Islands plantation that was primarily a Munster Irish colony.[81] Forbes conferred with the earl of Cork's son, Lewis Boyle, Lord Kinalmeaky, and it was agreed that the land forces would march eight miles inland to Bandon, commanded by Sir William Hull, recently supplied with gunpowder by Pennoyer.[82] The march began on 15 July, one force despatched to Bandon and a second to Clonakilty, slaughtering eighty Irishmen as they progressed and stealing all of the livestock. After conferring with Hull and agreeing to engage a company of Irish soldiers under MacCarthy Reagh in the area, the entire force converged on Clonakilty, driving the Irish into the sea and watching 600 men drown. Forbes lost 100 of his own men during this engagement and occupied the town, taking up lodging in Sir William Hull's home. On 17 July, Forbes's army returned to Bandon with 1,000 sheep and hundreds of cattle and horses, sold for a good price to starving Protestant refugees who had congregated in the town.[83] The Thirty Years War had arrived in Munster.

The next phase of the campaign was to relieve Drimoleague, Hull's second supply station, but on the way the campaign diverted to attack Timoleague, the home of Sir Roger O'Shaughnessy, a liegeman of the earl of Clanricarde currently serving near Galway. O'Shaughnessy was, therefore, party to Clanricarde's hated peace deal with Galway town. On a pretext of requiring lodging, Forbes's men arrived on 21 July and demanded that Lady O'Shaughnessy, who was in residence, yield the castle to them. Lady O'Shaughnessy refused in the absence of a command from Kinalmeaky, whereupon the adventurers burnt the town and carried away all of the livestock.[84] It must be stressed that the O'Shaughnessys were not in rebellion and that the attack was certainly revenge for the events in Galway. The mission to take the fight to the rebels, therefore, only lasted for the week that the adventurers assisted Hull's forces around Bandon. After Clonakilty, Forbes and his men made no distinction between rebels and Catholic royalists and, in fact, preferred royalist targets.

The naval squadron and some of the men left Kinsale on 24 July, and the next stop was Castlehaven where they destroyed O'Donovan's Castle, the town and all the ships in the harbour. Although Castlehaven had a large garrison, it held back from engaging the Sea Adventure, taunting them from a distance as Parliament or puritan-dogs.[85] Castlehaven's men simply did not know what to do. Although not in rebellion, Castlehaven had gone to Dublin to offer his support to the lords justices but was imprisoned, essentially for being a Catholic. His men in Castlehaven harbour were marooned without instructions when Forbes and his men turned up and they had no orders to engage a Protestant force. Without organised opposition, the fleet moved on to Baltimore, arriving on 27 July, and, while waiting to regroup, staged a revenge attack, burning O'Driscoll's castle in the town and many of the houses. The O'Driscolls were widely blamed for facilitating an attack on the town by Barbary pirates in June 1631, which resulted in the capture and enslavement of Baltimore's English inhabitants.[86] It was simple vendetta destruction. Hugh Peter's recollection of the campaign in Ireland, printed and sent to 'a leading London merchant', claimed that: 'If we had men and money here, I verily believe this summer would be an end of this rebellion.'[87] In Baltimore, the Sea Adventure was faced with a choice between suppressing the rebellion or prosecuting their own agenda. Two letters were received, one from the earl of Cork requesting that the fleet turn around and assist Duncannon, a fort outside Waterford that was under sustained rebel attack. The second was from Captain Ashley at Galway Bay, inviting the fleet to attack Galway. In the event, Galway was the preferred target.

The Sea Adventure sailed into Galway Bay on 9 August and Forbes announced himself as 'lieutenant-general of the additional forces by sea and land, sent by his majesty, our dread sovereign lord Charles, by the grace of God, king of Great Britain, France and Ireland, and the Parliament of England, for reducing of Ireland'.[88] Forbes had, of course, no commission of any sort, as the king had refused to sanction the mission. In fact, by claiming a royal commission, Forbes was committing treason, from which there could be no turning back. Forbes demanded the surrender of the town and threatened that there would be no pardon or mercy for its inhabitants. The terms of surrender – that the town was to place itself under Forbes's protection until such a time as the king persuaded Parliament to order him to withdraw – were impossible. In effect, the adventurers wanted to take possession of the town and have Clanricarde's authority taken away. Clanricarde's strategy was to contact Willoughby and demand that the fort not be made available to the adventurers. He also wrote to Sir Charles Coote senior, lord president of Connacht, imploring him to present a united front against the invaders.[89]

As no immediate response from Galway was forthcoming, Forbes adopted the scare tactic of landing men on the co. Clare side of the bay and burning a village within sight of Galway town.[90] The following day he landed men on the west side of the town, occupying St Mary's church under fire from the local residents, and destroyed the surrounding countryside. Now well within range of the town walls, siege artillery was brought ashore from the ships and began a bombardment.[91] In a report sent to the lords justices in Dublin, Clanricarde made it explicit that Galway was the adventurers' target. Dublin was quick to disown the mission, having received additional reports of the adventurers' indiscriminate attacks on supposed rebels and random targets in Munster. To demonstrate his anti-rebellion credentials, Forbes sent a party of 500 men to west Galway to burn what they could, but it was a duplicitous move. The following day, 11 August, the townspeople awoke to find the abbey destroyed and its timbers used as a platform for thirty-six of the adventurers' cannons.[92] In response, the townsmen raised batteries along the walls of the town, trained them on the adventurers, and sent out a raiding party to seize the land forces' horses.[93] Artillery fire was then exchanged between the two sides.[94]

This was standard siege warfare, fought between a town flying the king's colours and an armada holding a commission of sorts from the Parliament of England. This was no skirmish: it was a full-scale siege, conducted by an amphibious army of 1,200 men. Galway then, on 11 August 1642, was the place and day on which the civil war between king and Parliament began, some eleven days before the king raised his standard at Nottingham. Forbes had hoped that Sir Charles Coote would provide him with reinforcements, but was disappointed. Coote saw no reason to escalate the conflict or besiege the town, pointing out that the inhabitants had little choice but to defend themselves, as the alternative was total annihilation.[95] In addition, Coote had deep reservations about Forbes's plan to reinforce his expected prize with some of the Scottish forces then pouring into Ulster, opining that 'the cure is worse than the disease'.[96] Rumours had spread throughout the town that Forbes intended to remove the inhabitants and garrison it with 800 of his men, and such fears were reinforced by the presence in the town of 700 families from the surrounding countryside, chased into town by Forbes's men. The besieging soldiers were, however, beginning to become restless. Warfare by private enterprise was unsuited to protracted sieges, dependent as it was on continual spoils to keep the soldiers happy. The adventurers' cannon had proved ineffective against the town's fortifications, with the houses within the town 'being like castles, and the walls strong and hard to mine'.[97] Soldiers began to succumb to the 'country disease', possibly smallpox, the scourge of soldiers confined for long periods aboard ship. The mood was lifted when one of the ships broke away from the squadron and captured an incoming Barbados tobacco ship with a cargo worth £5,000, but with it intelligence that a French fleet had been despatched to Ireland with reinforcements, leading to a resolve by the adventurers to burn both Galway and Limerick.[98] Newly impatient, Forbes switched his attention to the fort, claiming it was in danger and that his force would die in Galway before abandoning it. Forbes let it be known that his forces would assault the town on 15 August.[99]

Clanricarde's arrival near Galway put a stop to this assault, and the ensuing lengthy negotiations left Forbes in no doubt that his presence would cause a full and united rebellion, directed against Parliament, with Catholic rebels and Catholic loyalists united against him.[100] Throughout this episode, Forbes had been spurred on by Hugh Peter but, faced with the courteous and diplomatic earl of Clanricarde, he decided to finally confer with his captains instead, who had already decided to leave and issued instructions to their men to steal whatever cattle they could and made ready to re-embark. Word had also reached the naval captains that Captain Kettleby had left Kinsale with the king's fleet and was possibly on his way to Galway under orders from Dublin. This, together with Coote's arrival on 22 August and obvious displeasure as to how events had unfolded, was the end of the affair. After gratefully accepting £400 in gold from Clanricarde to speed them on their journey, in return for a share in the tobacco ship, the adventurers made ready to depart.[101] Forbes, now accepting Clanricarde's authority, agreed to leave one pinnace behind under the command of Thomas Rainsborough, to convey letters to England. In parting, he plundered the western part of co. Clare for cattle, and presented his haul to the Galway townsmen as compensation for their own losses suffered a few weeks earlier.[102]

At this point, the Sea Adventure more or less fizzled out. Their services were offered to Barnaby O'Brien, earl of Thomond, who warily and politely declined. As soldiers continued to succumb to disease, the vessels converted from troop carriers to refugee ships and evacuated hundreds of displaced Protestant settlers from the Shannon estuary, for a reasonable fee.[103] The pillage continued in that area, but most goods of value were now secure within the walls of Limerick City. In mid-September, the fleet dispersed, some to remain in service as Parliament's Irish guard, some to perform other duties, while Hugh Peter returned to London to write his now well-known account.

In military terms, the Sea Adventure failed to make much of an impact, although, paradoxically, it enabled the leading Catholic and Protestant figures of authority in Connacht, the earl of Clanricarde and Sir Charles Coote, to make common cause. In a wider sphere, however, the confrontation between king and Parliament in England was projected very rapidly to the west of Ireland. Had Charles I come to Ireland in the summer of 1642 and made peace, he would have had loyal forces in Ireland at his disposal to support him against his adversaries in Westminster. A strongly fortified parliamentarian outpost in the west of Ireland would have made this much more difficult, forcing Clanricarde, in particular, to maintain considerable forces in the province. If there was a grand strategy, however, it was well disguised and the looting of Galway would probably have sufficed for Forbes and his men. Their activities in Munster had no obvious strategic purpose and were mainly directed at supporting business acquaintances of the Boyles or the Thompsons.

Although Maurice Thompson was the principal contractor, the chain of command began with the arm's-length agreement of the earls of Cork and Warwick and the vague authority under which the mission sailed. Civil war in England had yet to start, although it was looming, and Ireland – the 'laboratory of empire' – presented a useful, yet deniable, opportunity for a show of force. Moreover, Catholic Ireland was an irresistible target for the puritan merchants, sailors and preacher who organised and commanded the expedition, and the Scottish army that comprised its land army. The ships were an amalgamation of resources for two 'crusades', one against Muslim Algiers, the second against the Catholic Spanish Caribbean. Galway, following Pym's denunciation in Parliament of Clanricarde's toleration of Catholic worship in the town against the background of the Irish revolt, made it the perfect target for such a contingent. In this way, the Thirty Years War, which engulfed Europe in religious conflict from 1618 to 1648, reached its most westerly theatre.

A consequence of the Irish rebellion of 1641 was to bring Ireland, through the Adventurers' Act, within the acquisitive reach of the Thompsons and their wide circle of partners. The Sea Adventure was their first attempt to seize an Irish prize, but it would not be their last. The committee and its principal financial backers went on to form the backbone of Parliament's naval committees until the mid-1650s, a direct line of administrative genealogy that commenced in April 1642. In this context, the expedition was the precursor of the parliamentary navy and preceded Warwick's appointment as lord admiral by only a couple of days. It was not, as Karl Bottigheimer would have it, a poor substitute for the Adventure for Irish land, diverted in other ways, but a separate naval enterprise that used the emergency in Ireland to seize control of a substantial fleet and engineer the earliest major military confrontation between king and Parliament. Overall, therefore, this obscure and short-lived enterprise had a far wider significance than has previously been realised.

NOTES

1. K.S. Bottigheimer, *English Money and Irish Land* (Oxford, 1971), p. 81.
2. H. Peter, *A True Relation of the Passages of Gods Providence in a Voyage for Ireland* (1642).
3. R. Brenner, *Merchants and Revolution: commercial change, political conflict, and London's overseas traders, 1550–1653* (Princeton, 1993), pp. 400–9.
4. J. Adamson, *The Noble Revolt: the overthrow of Charles I* (London, 2007).
5. K.O. Kupperman, *Providence Island, 1630–1641: the other Puritan colony* (Cambridge, 1993); TNA, CO/125/1–2: records of the Providence Island Company.
6. C.F. Smith, *Mary Rich, Countess of Warwick (1625–1678), her family and friends* (1901), p. 100.
7. *Statutes of the Realm*, vol. 5: 1628–9 (1819), pp. 168–72.
8. Bottigheimer, *English Money and Irish Land*, p. 37.
9. J.P. Prendergast, *The Cromwellian Conquest of Ireland* (New York, 1868), pp. 72–9; for the legislation see *CSP Ire. Adventurers, 1642–59*; in addition to Bottigheimer, there are valuable studies by J.R. MacCormack, 'The Irish Adventurers and the English Civil War', *IHS* 10 (1956–57), pp. 45–67, and K. Lindley, 'Irish Adventurers and Godly Militants in the 1640s', *IHS* 29 (1994), pp. 1–12.
10. *A & O*, i. 9–12.
11. *CJ*, ii. 510; BL, Add. MS 4771 (Committee for Irish Affairs, day book), fo. 3v.

12 Library of Kings Inns, Dublin, Prendergast Papers 6, pp. 33–5.
13 *HMC Portland MSS*, i. 35.
14 S.M. Kingsbury (ed.), *Records of the Virginia Company*, IV (Washington, 1935), pp. 441–2.
15 H.R. McIlwaine (ed.), *Minutes of the Colonial and General Court of Colonial Virginia 1622–1632, 1670–1676* (Richmond, 1974), p. 30.
16 For Gookin's activities see J.C. Appleby (ed.), *Calendar of Material relating to Ireland from the High Court of Admiralty Examinations 1536–1641* (Dublin, 1992), p. 152.
17 A. Gwynn, 'Documents relating to the Irish in the West Indies', *Analecta Hibernia* 4 (1932), pp. 162–6.
18 W. Foster (ed.), *The Voyage of Thomas Best to the East Indies, 1612–1614* (London, 1930), p. 262.
19 Irish planters Humphrey Allen, Thomas Flowerdew, Sir Henry Pierce and Lt Charles Pointz invested in Virginia as did the families of William Barker, Robert Cartwright, Sir Robert Heiborne, Walter Hodges, Sir John Kingsmill, Sir George Mainwaring, Gabriel Throgmorton and Oliver St John. English landed interest in both Ireland and Virginia developed simultaneously in the 1620s; for these comparisons see V. Treadwell (ed.), *The Irish Commission of 1622: an investigation of the Irish administration 1615–22 and its consequences 1623–24* (Dublin, 2006) and Kingsbury, *Records of the Virginia Company*, both *passim*.
20 Gwynn, 'Irish in the West Indies', p. 159.
21 H.T. Barlow (ed.), *Colonising Expeditions to the West Indies and Guiana 1623–67* (London, 1925), p. 31; J. Morin (ed.), *Calendar of the Patent and Close Rolls of Ireland, Chancery, Charles I, I to VIII* (1863), p. 553.
22 M. MacCarthy-Morrogh, *The Munster Plantation: English migration to southern Ireland, 1583–1641* (Oxford, 1986), p. 253.
23 A. Hadfield, 'Gookin, Sir Vincent', *ODNB*; Gookin, an uncle of Daniel, was originally a tenant of Beecher before the transfer to Boyle.
24 Barlow, *Colonising Expeditions*, pp. 4–5; Grosart (ed.), *Lismore Papers*, 2nd series, iii. 226.
25 J.H. Bennett, 'The English Caribbees in the period of the Civil War, 1642–1646', *William and Mary Quarterly* 24 (1967), pp. 359–77.
26 Grosart (ed.), *Lismore Papers*, 2nd series, iii. 226.
27 J. Morin (ed.), *Calendar of the Patent and Close Rolls of Ireland*, p. 541.
28 Brenner, *Merchants and Revolution*, p. 185.
29 N.A. Zacek, *Settler Society in the English Leeward Islands 1630–1676* (Cambridge, 2010), p. 1634.
30 Brenner, *Merchants and Revolution*, p. 129.
31 Appleby (ed.), *High Court of Admiralty Examinations*, p. 152.
32 K. Andrews, *Ships, Money and Politics: seafaring and naval enterprise in the reign of Charles I* (Cambridge, 1991), pp. 183–4.
33 J. Adamson (ed.), *The English Civil War: conflict and contexts, 1640–49* (Basingstoke, 2009), p. 363.
34 *The Diurnal Occurences or The Heads of the proceedings in Parliament from the*

Seventh of February to the Fourteenth (1642), p. 3; for the shrunken Caribbean mission that left in July 1642 see V. Harlow, *The Voyage of Captain William Jackson* (Camden Misc. xiii (II), 1923).

35 J. Bruce (ed.), *Notes of Proceedings in Long Parliament, temp Charles I printed from original pencil memoranda taken in the House by Sir Ralph Verney, Knight ...* (London, 1884), p. 162.

36 D. Parrott, *The Business of War: military enterprise and military revolution in Early Modern Europe* (Cambridge, 2012), p. 150.

37 P.H. Wilson, 'Was the Thirty Years War a "Total War"?', in Erica Charters, Eve Rosenhaft and Hannah Smith (eds), *Civilians and War in Europe, 1618–1815* (Liverpool, 2012), pp. 21–35, at p. 27; C.B. Gibson, *The History of the County and City of Cork, vol. 2* (London, 1861), p. 507.

38 *His Majesties Message to the House of Commons concerning an Order made by them for the borrowing of one hundred thousand pounds of the Adventurers Money for Ireland, together with the Answer of the House of Commons in Ireland Thereunto* (1642), p. 4.

39 Peter, *True Relation*, p. 2.

40 NLI, MS 14305, p. 81: list of the victualling of the king's ships, 1642.

41 Brenner, *Merchants and Revolution*, pp. 405–7.

42 *CSP Ire: Adventurers*, p. 558.

43 F.J. Bremer and T. Webster (eds), *Puritans and Puritanism in Europe and America*, 1 (Santa Barbara, 2006), p. 387.

44 BL, Add MS 4771, fo. 164: list of shipping for service in Irish waters; of the sea commanders, Benjamin Peter was captain of the *Speedwell*, Thomas Rainsborough was vice-admiral and captain of the *Zant Merchant*, one of two committee men to sail with the fleet, the other William Thompson, captain of the *Goodhope* and Maurice Thompson's brother; the owners of the remaining eight ships, the *George Bonaventure, Mary Bonaventure, Achilles, Hopewell, Pennington, Dolphin, Lily* and *Laghorne* were drawn from a very small circle. See E. Murphy, *Ireland and the War at Sea* (Woodbridge, Suffolk, 2012), *passim*.

45 Treadwell (ed.), *Irish Commission of 1622*, p. 657.

46 P.W. Coldham, *English Adventurers and Emigrants 1609–1660* (Baltimore, 1984), pp. 100, 300; H. Kearney, 'Richard Boyle, ironmaster – a footnote to Irish economic history', *The Journal of the Royal Society of Antiquaries of Ireland* 83 (1953), pp. 157–61.

47 Andrews, *Ships, Money and Politics*, p. 160.

48 TNA, SP 16/343, fo.120: Sir Henry Marten to lords of admiralty, 7 June 1637; SP 16/130, fo. 34: letters of reprisal to Thompson and Clement, Mar. 1637.

49 *LJ*, iv. 403.

50 A. Tinniswood, *The Rainborowes* (London, 2013), p. 102.

51 W.H. Courtney, A. Steele and V. Snow (eds), *The Private Journals of the Long Parliament, 3 January to 5 March 1642* (New Haven, 1982), p. 423; Andrews, *Ships, Money and Politics*, p. 60; Vassall owned the *Mayflower* and his captain, Peter Andrews, commanded one of the Sea Adventurers' vessels.

52 Parliamentary Archives, HL/PO/JO/10/1/73: draft order of the Lords and

Commons for the lord high admiral to prepare four ships for the service of Ireland, 20 Nov. 1641.
53 *LJ*, iv. 422.
54 Ibid., iv. 425.
55 TNA, PRO 31/1/2 (Carte transcripts), p. 141: humble desires of the earl of Leicester, 1641.
56 Ibid., p. 149.
57 TNA, SP 28/1B, unfol.: payment warrant to Whetcombe 27 Apr. 1642.
58 For an earlier account of this incident see J. Hardiman, *History of the Town and County of the Town of Galway* ... (Galway, 1975), pp. 109–18.
59 TNA, PRO 31/1/3, p. 48: lords justices and council to Leicester, 23 Apr. 1642.
60 Murphy, *War at Sea*, p. 25.
61 Bodl. MS Carte 3, pp. 68–71: submission of the town of Galway, 6 May 1642.
62 *Clanricarde Memoirs*, p. 135.
63 Ibid., p. 158.
64 NLI, MS 14035, p. 89: committee for Irish affairs attendance list, 21 June 1642.
65 V.F. Snow and A.S. Young (eds), *The Private Journals of the Long Parliament 2 June to 17 September 1642* (London, 1992), pp. 119–20; for the details of these negotiations see *Clanricarde Memoirs*, pp. 119–35.
66 NLI, MS 14035, p. 90, lords justices touching the protection of Galway, 21 June 1642.
67 Ibid., p. 94; *Canricarde Memoirs*, p. 239.
68 Bodl. MS Carte 3, p. 116: Parsons to Ormond 24 May 1642; D. Edwards and T. Powell, 'The Ship's Journal of Captain Thomas Powell, 1642', *Analecta Hibernica* 37 (1998), pp. 251–84 (especially p. 274).
69 *Clanricarde Memoirs*, p. 164.
70 A.P. Newton, *The Colonising Activities of the English Puritans* (New Haven, 1914), p. 60.
71 For Cunningham's career see *The Journal of Thomas Cunningham of Campvere, 1640–1654: With his Thrissels-banner and Explication Thereof* (Edinburgh, 1928).
72 TNA, SP 63/322, fo. 181v: case of *Joseph Ruthorne v. William Barker, 1667*; the suit was brought to decide if the assignee of Cunningham and Dyke, Maurice Thompson, was entitled to Irish land as these ships never went to Ireland.
73 See Jane Ohlmeyer, 'The "Dunkirk of Ireland": Wexford privateers during the 1640s', *Journal of the Wexford Historical Society* 12 (1988–89), pp. 23–4.
74 TCD, MS 840, fos 47–48v: account of the rising in Munster by James Cleland.
75 J.P. Cooper, 'The fortune of Thomas Wentworth', *The Economic History Review* new series 11 (1958), p. 231.
76 Ibid., p. 245.
77 *HMC 4th Report* (1874), p. 79.
78 BL, Add MS 46926, fo. 6: memorandum relating to pilchard fishing off the coast of Munster.
79 George Thompson, a member of the committee of Sea Adventurers, organised the shipping of tobacco from St Kitts to Cork during Beecher's tenure there.
80 BL, Add MS 46926, fo. 64; Peter, *True Relation*, p. 4.

81 V.L. Oliver (ed.), *Caribbeana: being miscellaneous papers relating to the history, genealogy, topography, and antiquities of the British West Indies, vol. 2* (1912), p. 6.
82 Peter, *True Relation*, p. 4, TCD, MS 840, fos 47–48v.
83 Peter, *True Relation*, p. 9; TCD, MS 840, fo. 48.
84 TCD, MS 840, fo. 48v; Peter, *True Relation*, p. 9.
85 Peter, *True Relation*, 10.
86 T. Murray, 'From Baltimore to Barbary, the 1631 Sack of Baltimore', *History Ireland* 14 (2006).
87 Peter, *True Relation*, p. 6.
88 *Clanricarde Memoirs*, p. 205.
89 Ibid., pp. 206–7.
90 Peter, *True Relation*, p. 12.
91 *Clanricarde Memoirs*, p. 207.
92 Peter, *True Relation*, p. 13.
93 *Clanricarde Memoirs*, p. 213.
94 Peter, *True Relation*, p. 13.
95 *Clanricarde Memoirs*, p. 216.
96 Ibid., p. 224.
97 Peter, *True Relation*, p. 15.
98 Edwards, 'Journal of Captain Thomas Powell', p. 272.
99 *Clanricarde Memoirs*, p. 222.
100 Bodl. MS Carte 3, p. 237: Clanricarde's motives for not entertaining Lord Forbes, 9 Aug. 1642.
101 *Clanricarde Memoirs*, pp. 256, 274.
102 Ibid., p. 243.
103 Peter, *True Relation*, p. 19.

3

'To hold a good opinion of my loyalty and zealous affections': the earl of Clanricarde and the royalist cause in Connacht, 1643–46

AOIFE DUIGNAN

Writing to Lord Cottington in early May 1644, Ulick Burke, fifth earl of Clanricarde, expressed uncertainty about whether he should travel to England and offer his support to King Charles in person, or remain in Connacht and defend the royal position on the ground. Although he inclined towards the latter course, he feared that his distance from the king had already allowed others to undermine his position and standing.[1] The sentiments expressed in his letter did not mark a momentary crisis in confidence; rather his correspondence throughout the 1640s includes frequent ruminations on how best to serve his royal master. This chapter focuses on Clanricarde's experience in Connacht following the confederate-royalist truce in September 1643, from the perspective of his over-arching concern at how his political behaviour would be interpreted by others. It considers how this preoccupation manifested in attempts to secure official recognition of his position in the province, and informed his relationship with representatives of the Confederate Association, at local and national level.

Clanricarde's career has been the subject of recent historical attention, with Harriet Sexton's doctoral thesis providing a detailed narrative of his experiences from the outbreak of the 1641 rebellion to the Cromwellian conquest.[2] His role in the establishment of the Confederate Association has been debated, notably in the work of Micheál Ó Siochrú and Demetri Debe, while Patrick Little's analysis of his enduring relationship with the earl of Essex as civil war deepened in England reflects the ongoing three-kingdoms dimension of Clanricarde's experience.[3] In considering the uneasy balance that Clanricarde trod between pursuit of a war effort in the peripheral western province and adherence to his political principles, preoccupied by how others perceived his actions, this chapter offers an insight into the pressures of war at local level. Taken in conjunction with emerging analyses of 1640s Ireland from a regional perspective, including work by David Dickson, Kevin Forkan, Maighréad Ní Mhurchadha and Charlene McCoy, it facilitates a more nuanced understanding of the shared and diverging experiences of conflict across the country.[4] The response to the crisis in Ireland from those with whom Clanricarde may be most closely associated in social and political terms has been examined in recent work by Jane Ohlmeyer and Barry Robertson respectively.[5] This chapter builds on that work, interrogating the factors that shaped Clanricarde's particular outlook and actions, while also considering the relevance of broader themes such as the enduring significance of established hierarchies and social rank in a time of crisis.

Having served the king in England for many years, and fought for him in the first bishops' war, Clanricarde returned to Ireland in September 1641, taking up residence at the mansion built by his father at Portumna, eastern co. Galway. He thus witnessed at first hand the outbreak of the 1641 rising. As violence spread from Ulster into Connacht, Clanricarde was active in defence of the king's cause but grew increasingly frustrated at his isolation and what he perceived as neglect by the Dublin government. Following the outbreak of war, Clanricarde assembled prominent Galway gentlemen to coordinate the raising of an army, which he would command. He was proactive in defending his jurisdiction, travelling the breadth of the county to ensure that fortifications and garrisons were up to standard.[6] However, a shortage of resources inhibited his efforts. At the end of 1641 and throughout the first half of 1642 Clanricarde made repeated complaints to the administration about the lack of men and supplies in Connacht and also targeted his influential English connections – but relief was not forthcoming.[7] Clanricarde viewed this neglect as a personal affront and attributed it to official suspicions of his Catholicism.[8] His situation was not helped by his location far from the centre of political power in Dublin while his relatively recent arrival in the province, and indeed in Ireland, must have contributed to his sense of isolation.[9] His material interests also suffered, as the collection of rents and levies from his lands were interrupted by 'rude and disorderly persons', while he supported various companies out of his personal finances.[10]

Clanricarde's isolation was exacerbated as support for the English Parliament grew within Connacht Protestant society, resulting in a considerable erosion of the king's traditional support base within the province. Matters came to a head in September 1643, when the marquess of Ormond brokered an agreement with the confederates suspending hostilities, known as the 'cessation of arms'. This was supported by a substantial section of the Irish governmental elite, who had come to believe that their war effort was unsustainable and primarily due to a lack of support from England, while in Connacht confederate military progress was most apparent in their success at Galway fort.[11] The truce was beset by difficulties from the outset, as the application of its terms proved contentious for Connacht Protestants, and late autumn saw the garrisons in north Connacht contravene its terms.[12] Unrest intensified in 1644, acquiring a sharper significance with constant rumours of an invasion by 'British' and Scottish forces garrisoned in Ulster.[13] While the mass invasion predicted did not occur, the prevailing climate of uncertainty and paranoia had a destabilising influence on the behaviour of the local Protestant population, and prominent figures soon defected to the parliamentary cause.[14]

A declaration by Irish royalists in July 1644 identifies that party's key adherents in Connacht at that juncture: most prominent among them were Clanricarde, Viscount Ranelagh, Viscount Dillon and Viscount Taaffe.[15] This impressive list belies the fact that support for the king in the province was rapidly diminishing. By early 1645 royalist Connacht was confined to a small area surrounding the presidential seat at Athlone, three baronies within Clanricarde's sphere of influence in co. Galway and a small number of his castles on the frontiers, and as the decade progressed, Ranelagh, Dillon and Taaffe would all shift allegiance.[16] From Clanricarde's perspective, maintaining an increasingly lonely struggle in defence of the king's cause in Connacht made recognition of his efforts crucial. Yet, despite his prominence, throughout this period he lacked an official position in the government of the province. He had been passed over on 27 April 1644, when the king had directed that the office of provincial president be granted jointly to Henry, Viscount Wilmot, and Thomas, Viscount Dillon.[17] Two individuals were chosen because of Wilmot's role in the royalist army in England, but Wilmot's subsequent dismissal saw Dillon function as the primary agent of royal governance in Connacht.[18] Following the appointment, ambiguities would arise over the respective spheres of influence of the new presidents and Clanricarde. Although the earl had a good opinion of Dillon, he articulated concerns about how the local population would receive the new president, suggesting that the appointment would be interpreted as a slight against Clanricarde himself. He described Dillon as 'very distasteful to the English, and not acceptable to many of the natives' and argued that he himself might have enjoyed greater acceptance, owing to a closer affinity with those of English descent in the province. He tempered his judgement with the aspiration that Dillon's actions on assuming the post would provide reassurance.[19] Ormond also articulated reservations about the appointment, intimating that Clanricarde might have been the more suitable choice.[20]

Clanricarde's expressions of anxiety were no doubt influenced by his own sense of grievance at not having been offered the appointment. Unlike Clanricarde, who had defended the king's cause on the ground in Connacht since the start of the war, Dillon had been absent from Ireland since November 1641.[21] While Clanricarde had dismissed reports that he desired the presidency in March 1644, stating that his current position caused him enough disturbance,[22] by mid-June he described it as the only job that could have enhanced his usefulness to the king. While he claimed to have accepted the appointment of Dillon, his tone was one of martyred resignation, declaring 'it is my duty to remain satisfied therewith, and to contain myself within those limits that are allowed to me'.[23]

In addition, Dillon's appointment raised questions about Clanricarde's official status in the province. George Lord Digby wrote in May 1644 of the king's desire that Clanricarde should receive an official position, but added that nothing could be decided until Wilmot and Dillon had been consulted.[24] He subsequently wrote that both men were happy for Clanricarde to be given the command in chief of the forces in Connacht, suggesting a general belief that Clanricarde would have more clout on the ground – further evidence of his centrality to Connacht royalism.[25] However, Clanricarde was anxious that no confusion of authority should arise between himself and the new president, expressing an unwillingness to encroach upon Dillon's sphere of governance.[26] Alluding to rumours that he might be offered martial command in the province, the earl made it explicitly clear that he was wary of such a command as it would burden him with the duties of leadership but deny him any of the accompanying power and prestige.[27] Thus, he was determined that he should not be encumbered with further military responsibilities without some public acknowledgement of his services to the royalist cause.

Clanricarde's difficulties with the presidential incumbents extended beyond their initial appointment. It appears that in 1645 he expressed dissatisfaction with a clause in the presidential patents stipulating that the command of Galway should pass to the president after Clanricarde's death – a scenario which he deemed 'a very great discouragement' to his family. Galway had lain outside the jurisdiction of the Connacht presidency since Clanricarde's father relinquished that office in favour of the governorship of Galway town and county.[28] Lord Digby responded to reassure him that the king had been unaware of the clause's significance and sought instruction on how this injury might be addressed.[29] Later, in 1646, in the context of enhanced military cooperation between confederate and royalist forces, Dillon would oppose the prospect of Clanricarde commanding military forces across the province because it would infringe on presidential authority, hammering home the ambiguity of Clanricarde's position in Connacht.[30]

Publicly, Clanricarde protested that he lacked interest in the presidency. When his close associate, Justice James Donnellan, wrote to Ormond urging that the earl be endowed with 'some public mark of his majesty's favour', Clanricarde denied this, claiming that knowledge of the king's good opinion was sufficient. He admitted that some form of recognition would be appreciated, but said this was not for his own private satisfaction, but because it would bolster his influence in war-torn Connacht. Indeed, a royal intervention could help remove any perception that he was estranged from the king, in turn encouraging his followers and attracting others to their cause. Ultimately, however, he would leave it to Ormond's judgement whether the time was right to make any such application.[31]

However, Clanricarde was more forthright in contemporary correspondence with Donnellan, commending the efforts made on his behalf. He makes specific reference to his desire to become lord treasurer of Ireland, and then a privy councillor – which he felt would be supported by Ormond. Such appointments would suffice in the immediate term, and would not obstruct his future advancement. While Donnellan favoured seeking a marquessate for Clanricarde, the earl perceived a number of impediments. He felt that Ormond might not be supportive, as he might expect that only he should hold this title as he was the king's lord lieutenant. Clanricarde feared such advancement would also be distasteful to the English peers as he already held the earldom of St Albans and owned an estate in England, and this would not be in the king's best interest.[32] Furthermore, he declared himself unable to support such an increase in honour because of his indebtedness and the spoiling of his estates in Ireland and England. Finally, he confessed that his pride was such that he did not wish to seek the honour unless he was certain of its being bestowed.[33]

Clanricarde's royalist masters were aware of the need to bolster his reputation and his efforts received official recognition when he was created a marquess on 21 February 1645.[34] In June he also received notification of his appointment to the Irish privy council.[35] However, controversy accompanied both those honours, highlighting the rivalries that existed within the upper echelons of Irish royalism. Earlier that year another prominent Connacht royalist, Theobald, Viscount Taaffe, had sought appointment to the privy council, but Digby responded that in the event of a Catholic appointment, only Clanricarde could be considered on account of his widespread popularity, which extended to the Protestant population. Taaffe was apparently unhappy with this response, objecting that he was held in equally high regard.[36]

Clanricarde's creation as a marquess was also marred by a dispute over the order of precedence with Randall McDonnell, newly elevated from earl to marquess of Antrim. When this was decided in Antrim's favour, Clanricarde's English allies, including his sister, the marchioness of Hertford, had initially sought to prevent Clanricarde's patent from going ahead. Clanricarde's subsequent correspondence suggests that he was somewhat divorced from the controversy, piecing the details together through letters that managed to reach him from England. However, his writings indicate approval of the strategy adopted by his allies, and that for them to have done nothing 'would in truth have been the greatest of misfortunes that could befall me'.[37] Ultimately, however, his supporters decided that it was in Clanricarde's best interest not to obstruct the patent but that it should progress without his knowledge, on the basis that while the position was ultimately to his advantage, the slight to his honour was such that it could not be sanctioned by him.[38]

Precedence disputes were a regular feature of Irish political life during the first half of the seventeenth century.[39] Clanricarde's father, the fourth earl, was involved in a protracted dispute over precedence with the neighbouring earl of Thomond in the mid-1620s.[40] Clanricarde himself was conscious of this controversy, referring to it in the context of Donnellan's earlier suggestion that he seek a marquessate. Clanricarde commented that because such an honour would probably only apply to his line and not to other branches of his family, it would not bring any further advantage over the house of Thomond.[41] Clanricarde's correspondence throughout the period reveals his preoccupation with his own sense of honour and that of his family, therefore it is not surprising that he should be perturbed by the advances of another which diminished his own reputation.

The fact that it was Antrim who was the other party to the controversy is significant, in light of the diverging politico-military strategies pursued by both men during the period. In late 1643 Antrim had secured royal support for an invasion of Scotland using confederate forces. The following March, Clanricarde expressed his concerns about this strategy, namely that Antrim's close public cooperation with the confederates might harm the king's cause in England.[42] Less than two months later, however, he was drawing negative comparisons between official responses to his own and Antrim's efforts. When writing to Lord Cottington, raising concerns that his absence from court had allowed advantage to others, he specifically referred to Antrim. Antrim had secured the promise of a marquessate in exchange for his efforts against Scotland, and although the title was not conferred until the beginning of 1645 the impending honour was well known, with some contemporaries referring to him as the marquess of Antrim from January 1644.[43] Clanricarde articulated his view that Antrim 'has not advantage over me either in power or affection to be employed in high and eminent commands'; but the influence that he had secured clearly caused Clanricarde much distress, and for a time 'put great blemishes upon my person and proceedings'.[44] Underlying this personal element was a practical one: Antrim's willingness to openly engage with the confederates was in marked contrast to Clanricarde's more cautious approach, based on his unwavering loyalty to the crown. This fundamental difference of opinion also affected Clanricarde's relationship with his fellow Connacht Catholics in arms.

Clanricarde's enduring influence over the Old English community in southern Connacht had tempered their reaction to the initial outbreak of unrest in 1641. His role in subsequent attempts to organise the Catholic war effort has been debated elsewhere,[45] and although the interaction between the magnate and his Catholic neighbours who had taken up arms continued beyond the establishment of the Confederate Association, relations were not unproblematic. Tensions became particularly apparent after the cessation of arms of September 1643. During the negotiations the confederates had agreed to pay £30,000 to the king, and their commissioners signed up to explicitly defined provisions for the payment of this sum.[46] However, the transfer of monies did not proceed smoothly. By 3 October Clanricarde had expressed disquiet over confederate failure to provide the required supply from Connacht.[47] Ormond also voiced concerns over the situation but retained confidence in the co. Roscommon confederate, Sir Lucas Dillon, as a force for moderation.[48] However, the supply issue remained unresolved at the end of the month and Clanricarde, who came under pressure from the lord lieutenant because of Connacht's failure to deliver the cattle due, was highly critical of Dillon in this context.[49]

Disputes over quartering arrangements, emerging in the wake of the cessation, also had direct implications for Clanricarde, as Galway's confederate county council issued warrants on his entire estate. The earl responded by declaring his intention to take decisive action, on the grounds that his interests did not fall under confederate remit. This issue would re-emerge as a source of contention for the remainder of 1643 and 1644, with Clanricarde sufficiently troubled to threaten intermittently the use of force to protect his interests in the province. It was not finally resolved until February 1645, when the confederates eventually acceded to his demands.[50] Clanricarde's challenging financial situation throughout the 1640s, burdened by heavy debts, meant confederate encroachments into his quarters had immediate practical implications.[51] But he was also perturbed by the slight to his honour, perceiving the confederate failure to agree on acceptable quartering terms as a personal affront, reflecting their disregard for his status and influence. However tempted Clanricarde might have been to avenge such slights, he was restrained by an appreciation that any use of force might be used as an excuse to reignite hostilities.[52]

Clanricarde was critical of Sir Lucas Dillon regarding quartering disputes, but the deterioration in relations did not extend to all Connacht confederates. In particular, his long-standing relationship with key Galway confederates, particularly Sir Richard Blake and Patrick Darcy, endured the pressures of war.[53] Overall, the earl expressed his belief in the essential moderation of some of the insurgents who endeavoured to modify the demands of their more extreme associates, including the aforementioned among those diligent labourers for restraint. He posited that the confederates had unleashed a force beyond their control and many now longed for a return to a more stable order.[54] That Clanricarde's relationship was stronger with neighbouring confederates with whom he and his family had traditionally allied is not surprising, illustrating how established professional and social connections could survive the progress of war.

Clanricarde's concern about confederate military discipline and levels of organisation also emerged as a source of tension. Relations became strained once more in summer 1646 in the context of an impending military campaign led by General Thomas Preston. Earlier that year Clanricarde had expressed anxiety about the military situation in the province, criticising in particular confederate efforts to secure the region. Writing to Patrick Darcy in April 1646 Clanricarde complained about the lack of forces in the field, apart from a few maintained by the earl himself at Athleague, and about the shortage of provisions and ammunition in confederate garrisons. As Preston prepared to advance through the province, the marquess was highly critical of the measures taken by local confederates to provide the finance necessary and he accused them of delays in preparing their men for the field, despite the imminent threat posed by the parliamentarian forces under Sir Charles Coote.[55]

Irrespective of his dissatisfaction with the behaviour of key Connacht confederates, the increasing threat from the parliamentarians forced the earl to respond to proposals for a military alliance.[56] In the spring of 1644, Clanricarde opposed confederate demands for military action against those Protestant garrisons which contravened the terms of cessation, informing Richard Martin that the threat posed by the Protestant soldiers or those in Ulster was not sufficient to warrant military engagement by the confederates.[57] He also objected to correspondence received from his cousin, the confederate Captain Richard Burke, and Captain Mleaghlin Donelaine (sic), which ordered the earl to gather together his supporters and fight under the Confederate commander, the earl of Castlehaven. Clanricarde viewed this as yet another personal affront and an encroachment upon his authority.[58]

The proper nature of his relationship with the confederates preoccupied the earl and to this end he submitted a number of propositions to Ormond to clarify his own role. In the event of a Scottish invasion during the cessation, he queried whether he might assist the confederates. If so, what form would this assistance take and would it apply only in Galway or throughout the province? Were he to assist them, what title should he assume? Were covenanter forces to be regarded in breach of the cessation and enemies of the king?[59] Ultimately, while some official sanction was given for Clanricarde's assistance of the confederates in the event of an invasion from Ulster, the proper nature of the relationship remained unclear.[60]

Clanricarde was adamant that he receive definite and specific instructions on what would be deemed legitimate interaction with local confederates and here we can see his absolute determination that his behaviour could not subsequently be depicted as rebellious. He had resisted confederate pressure to formally join their ranks but as deteriorating conditions in the province rendered a degree of informal cooperation between royalist and confederate forces militarily expedient, he was anxious that embarking on this course should not prompt accusations of rebellion. Central in this regard was the security of his English lands in Kent and Herefordshire. While Clanricarde's role in brokering the 1643 cessation had resulted in a parliamentary order to confiscate his lands in November 1643, a subsequent order directed that the benefit of his estates should be directed towards his half-brother, the earl of Essex. In this way, Essex was able to protect Clanricarde's interests as he had done from the outbreak of insurrection in Ireland. Despite Essex's marginalisation within the parliamentary camp from late 1643 on, Clanricarde's interests remained relatively secure until his half-brother's death in September 1646.[61] However, should Clanricarde be seen to act outside the law by entering into an unsanctioned military arrangement with the Connacht confederates, it is unlikely that Essex would have been able, or willing, to continue as his protector.

Despite Clanricarde's personal anxieties, the prospect of cooperation between the confederate and royalist forces in Connacht grew more palatable as the province became increasingly destabilised. In July 1644 Clanricarde, Taaffe, Ranelagh and Dillon emphasised the importance of appealing to moderate opinion, while simultaneously advocating a proactive stance against the Scots and their adherents, which could potentially involve some interaction with the confederates.[62] In Connacht, Clanricarde's correspondence indicated a greater personal willingness to work with confederate military forces. In December 1644 he responded positively to their commissioners' request that he lend them his castles at Athleague and Bellagare – the only winter passages from Galway to Roscommon, passages which Clanricarde himself had insufficient resources to secure.[63] In this context, Clanricarde's subsequent request that Patrick Darcy send more wardens to increase security at his castles in Galway may indicate that some level of military cooperation had been attained.[64] Those links would strengthen in 1645, as royalists and confederates presented an increasingly united front against an ever more assertive common enemy.

Developments at national level influenced Clanricarde's attitude towards an alliance with the confederates. In January 1645 he resisted Patrick Darcy's request for approval of confederate action against disobedient Roscommon garrisons, as he was concerned at recent developments in Kilkenny, where attitudes towards Ormond were suspect, and dangerous factions within the Confederate Association posed a threat to the future stability of the kingdom. Consequently, he would not cooperate until such issues had been addressed to his satisfaction.[65]

In the summer of 1645 Clanricarde observed at first hand those he termed 'the violent faction' when he attended the Confederate Assembly in Kilkenny as Ormond's intermediary.[66] Mícheal Ó Siochrú and Tadhg Ó hAnnracháin have interrogated his correspondence with the lord lieutenant as the confederates debated proposed peace terms, for insights gleaned into shifting political allegiances within the Association, and Clanricarde's own views on the relationship between religious allegiance and political loyalty. Both historians have discussed the confederate negotiators' appeal to the doctrine of St Ambrose on passive obedience as they argued against the inclusion of a specific article relating to the restitution of church lands.[67] Ó hAnnracháin argues that they were somewhat disingenuous in invoking this doctrine, using it to placate both the clerical wing and Ormond in mutually incompatible stances. Significantly, he also suggests that they were able to conceal this subterfuge from Clarnicarde.[68]

Despite his presence in Kilkenny and his long-standing relationship with key confederates, Clanricarde's letters to Ormond during this period reveal his difficulty in gauging the political mood. He declared himself reluctant to predict whether Ormond's terms would be accepted, and commented on those who expressed agreement in private but 'when they mix with their associates at their committee or grand assembly, they ever want courage or judgement to cope with the sages of law, who have a prevailing power to pervert the best ways and means of persuasion to a false and mischievous construction of their own'.[69] Notwithstanding the lack of clarity around confederate intentions, he clearly articulated his belief that the survival of the royalist cause depended on the king securing Catholic support, both in Ireland and in England.[70] The concerns expressed by Clanricarde are representative of the real and enduring reservations surrounding an alliance with the confederates. However, as the parliamentary threat grew, particularly after the fall of Sligo in the summer of 1645, it became imperative that relations be formalised.

In the spring of 1646, General Preston's impending advance into Connacht with 3,000 foot and six troops of horse raised the thorny issue of command once more, specifically Clanricarde's official position in the context of confederate and royalist forces campaigning alongside each other.[71] In certain quarters it was hoped that conditions in Connacht would encourage Clanricarde to embrace the Catholic cause, as evidenced by Rinuccini's belief that the marquess was edging closer towards the confederates.[72] Clanricarde himself referred to speculation that he would be chosen as commander in chief of Preston's men in Connacht and his tone suggests a willingness to assume that role, albeit as ever clouded by vocal protestations of his unsuitability for the task. Ultimately, however, any formal cooperation hinged on Clanricarde receiving explicit sanction from Ormond as the king's lord lieutenant.[73]

Explicit sanction was not forthcoming. Ormond directed Clanricarde to command those forces he could assemble to push back the parliamentarian advance, and asserted that he would 'want neither authority nor instruction (as far as possible to give either)' to command any force he could gather together in defence of the province and the king's rights. However, Ormond did not expressly order Clanricarde to command Preston's army. His qualification, 'as far as possible to give either' suggests he was unable or unwilling to give direct authorisation.[74] Clanricarde was equally cautious, insisting that Ormond formally declare him general of Connacht before he accepted confederate offers of command, so as not to risk 'that hazard and danger as to be a generall [sic] without commission'.[75] Anxious as ever not to be seen to be acting outside the law, he was wary about adopting a formal position in Connacht while the recently concluded first Ormond Peace remained unpublished.[76]

Uncertainty about how events would unfold on the national stage also influenced Ormond's response when the parliamentarians struck at the foundations of royalist influence in Connacht in 1646. Prior to Preston's campaign, Clanricarde's personal interests had been threatened as Sir Charles Coote and the parliamentary forces penetrated deep into Galway, ending in an unsuccessful siege of his house at Portumna. Ormond's suggestion that General Owen Roe O'Neill pursue the parliamentary forces in Connacht has been interpreted as a reflection of the lord lieutenant's determination that the province remain out of parliamentary hands, no doubt informed by contemporary fears of a full-scale joint Scottish-parliamentary campaign in the west.[77] But despite his resolve, Ormond proved reluctant to make an outright declaration of war against the parliamentarians. After the Portumna siege Clanricarde requested that Ormond explicitly declare Sir Charles Coote to be one of the king's enemies,[78] terming him 'an insolent viper that glories in the destruction of his preserver and brags of the justness of his cause'.[79] Ormond responded by trying to bypass the issue, saying that such a declaration was unnecessary since it was a man's act rather than any royal pronouncement that made him a traitor. Further, as agreement with the confederates was uncertain at that point, Ormond was loathe to declare against Coote and his party, as it could create an impression of royalist reliance upon the confederates, thus encouraging the latter to increase their demands.[80]

Robert Armstrong argues that, for Clanricarde, Ormond's refusal to condemn Coote was related to opposition within the Irish council, and Clanricarde wanted Ormond to work with him to break this opposition. However, Ormond did not take up this challenge, as if he lost the support of his council he would lose his influence in Protestant Ireland.[81] Additionally, as the clandestine peace with the confederates remained in an uncertain condition, Ormond's reluctance to make an explicit declaration against Coote may have reflected a desire to keep his options open.[82] It seems he could not afford to alienate those with whom he might need to negotiate in the future. This would fit with work on Irish royalism by Barry Robertson, which highlights the challenges posed by the inconsistent strategies pursued by Charles and the difficulties Ormond faced in obtaining clear instructions on how to approach negotiations with the confederates.[83] In an evolving politico-military situation it is not surprising that key protagonists were reluctant to make any outright declarations that could close off future possibilities. This is particularly true of one like Clanricarde, located far from the epicentre of royalist power.

Clanricarde's anxiety about how his behaviour would be interpreted, and his generally cautious approach, had already attracted criticism. In the midst of the order of precedence controversy, Clanricarde received reports that Lord Digby had criticised him for not taking up arms against the Ulster Scots. Clanricarde protested that he had not received clear instructions for such an expedition and to undertake it would have required him to join with the confederates without command or authority. Such a departure, Clanricarde conceived, would have contravened his honour and loyalty. Had he viewed such a course as the best way to serve the king, then he might have received the same priority as Antrim, instead 'now there can be nothing of merit in Clanricarde or power of recompense in his majesty that will take off his disgrace'.[84] Reaction to Clanricarde's efforts to bolster the faltering peace deal with the confederates in the latter half of 1646 suggests that his concern at not being seen to act outside the boundaries of acceptable behaviour was well founded. Clanricarde's activity from the initial outbreak of the insurrection reflects his anxiety that a peace deal be speedily concluded between the royalists and confederates. Unsurprisingly, he formally declared his support for the first Ormond Peace when it was published in August 1646, articulating its benefits for the country and for Connacht specifically. He decried its subsequent repudiation by the clerical wing of the confederates, and although his correspondence indicates that he had some difficulty justifying his stance among his co-religionists, he would play a pivotal role in efforts to revive the agreement in the closing months of 1646 through negotiations with General Preston. While his efforts resulted in Preston and his officers pledging acceptance to a peace with additional religious concessions, it was not enough to satisfy the nuncio and his adherents and the venture ultimately collapsed.[85]

Robert Armstrong has argued that this peace initiative originated with Clanricarde and Digby, but hints at some divergence in the strategies employed by both men to broker a peace. Clanricarde appeared to be negotiating with the confederates in their entirety, including Rinuccini, while Digby seems to have tried to isolate Preston and use him against the nuncio, his party and O Neill's followers, as this was as far as Ormond would go.[86] Ó Siochrú touched on this issue when, in the context of Clanricarde's propositions for a Catholic lieutenant general, he queried the sincerity of the marquess's involvement in the initiative, suggesting that his intention at this point may have been merely to split confederate ranks. However, the notion of Clanricarde as an honest broker is supported by his overtures to the nuncio. Further, a sense of distance from Ormond emanates from letters revealing some uncertainty over Clanricarde's mission, and a sense that his objectives may not have corresponded neatly with those of the lord lieutenant. On 24 November Clanricarde complained that while he had become involved in the endeavour for the king and Ormond's benefit, his efforts appear to have kept him at a remove from the lord lieutenant. While Clanricarde had initially believed there was a clear understanding between Ormond and Digby, and that Digby had royal authority to deliver on any undertakings made, he expressed fears that he may have been mistaken.[87]

Clanricarde also gently reprimanded Ormond for his attitude to Preston, suggesting that the lord lieutenant's failure to encourage the general threatened to jeopardise the chances for peace, and thus cautioned Ormond not to delay further.[88] He was also conscious of the parliamentary presence at Dublin, writing to Preston of his resolve to travel to Dublin because of recent events there and his fears that some 'ill affected persons' might have attempted to influence Ormond. While he expressed confidence in the lord lieutenant, his correspondence bore a mildly critical tinge, describing Ormond as 'accompanied with more in caution then the necessities of this time will permit'.[89]

With the prospect of any peace settlement at an impasse and deteriorating conditions in Connacht, Clanricarde resolved to leave Ireland in 1647. He wrote to his half-sister, the marchioness of Hertford, requesting that she obtain material assistance for his resettlement abroad. However, she was unable to procure aid in England because of the negative reports in circulation about him, noting that many 'take much offence at something in print that passed here as a great undertaking of yours without the minister of state's knowledge'.[90] This is a reference to Clanricarde's efforts to advance agreement with Preston. Subsequent correspondence reveals Clanricarde's acute concern that he could be viewed as having acted without authority or that his actions might be misconstrued. Thus he offered a lengthy justification for the agreement reached.[91] However, the reactions to his half-sister's efforts to solicit aid suggest that his justifications were in vain. Despite his frequently proclaimed intention to depart, Clanricarde would not leave Ireland in 1647. Rather he would assume an increasingly prominent role in the altered politico-military landscape following the negotiation of a royalist-confederate peace and subsequent onset of the Cromwellian wars.

Clanricarde's experiences in the period from the conclusion of the cessation of arms in 1643 to the collapse of his negotiations with General Preston in 1646 offer insights into not only his personal character but also the environment in which he operated. The desire for recognition from the king, shared by Clanricarde and his fellow Irish royalists, reveals the enduring significance of established hierarchies and social rank in spite of the engulfing political and military upheaval. As Jane Ohlmeyer has noted, 'in a society consumed by status, marks of royal favour were highly prized'.[92] Clanricarde provides a concrete example of how public recognition of his majesty's pleasure held even more currency in time of crisis, as he found himself financially stretched and politically isolated in the remote western province. Ever-loyal servant to his king, and always anxious that he be perceived in this way, Clanricarde was not vocal in seeking advancement. But it is clear that he was perturbed by ambiguities arising out of the appointment of others as lord president, on account of its impact on the royalist war effort in Connacht and what it implied about his own position in the region.

Clanricarde's resentment at the manner in which Antrim obtained precedence over him points to a dilemma at the heart of his political strategy. The marquess came under sustained pressure to ally with the Connacht confederates, both from their agents and from elements within the royalist camp, as the threat from the parliamentarians intensified. The practical tensions that emerged post-cessation reflect on the ground pressures of war, as Clanricarde perceived his material interests threatened. But his correspondence also reflects his sense of injury that provincial confederate actions and attitudes constituted an affront to his status and honour. Clanricarde was cautious in the face of formal requests for cooperation, anxious that his actions be in no way misconstrued. Undoubtedly, he was influenced by a desire to preserve his own interests, but his cautious approach also reflected the evolving political and military situation, and other contemporaries shared this tendency. Clanricarde's frequent presence in the remote western province during the decade, at a distance from the centre of royalist power and hindered by disrupted communications, would have made the wider situation even more difficult to read. External reaction to his negotiations with Preston intimate that some caution was justified. Clanricarde's inherent belief that Ireland must rally behind Charles I to survive, and his awareness that the only hope for preserving his own interests in Connacht and beyond was to avoid any hint of what might be termed rebellious activity, made him resistant to confederate overtures, with the possibility of cooperation only conceivable within explicitly defined parameters.

NOTES

1 *Clanricarde Letter-Book*, pp. 80–1.
2 H.M. Sexton, 'Clanricarde and the Confederate Wars: a study of Ulick Burke's career in Ireland, 1641–52' (PhD thesis, NUI Cork, 2006).
3 D. Debe, 'The fifth Earl of Clanricarde and the founding of the Confederate Catholic government, 1641–3', *IHS* 36 (2009), pp. 315–33; Ó Siochrú, *Confederate Ireland*, pp. 33–40; P. Little, '"Blood and Friendship": the earl of Essex's protection of the earl of Clanricarde's interests, 1641–6', *EHR* 112 (1997), pp. 927–41.
4 Studies of 1640s Ireland from a regional perspective include D. Dickson, *Old World Colony: Cork and South Munster, 1630–1830* (Cork, 2005), pp. 29–40; A. Duignan,

'"All in a confused opposition to each other": politics and war in Connacht, 1641-9' (PhD thesis, University College Dublin, 2005); K. Forkan, 'Scottish Protestant Ulster and the crisis of the Three Kingdoms' (PhD thesis, NUI Galway, 2003); M. Ní Mhurchadha, *Fingal 1603-60: contending neighbours in North Dublin* (Dublin, 2005), pp. 229-84; C. McCoy, 'War and Revolution: co. Fermanagh and its borders, c.1640-c.1660 (PhD thesis, Trinity College Dublin, 2007).

5 Ohlmeyer, *Making Ireland English*; Barry Robertson, *Royalists at War in Scotland and Ireland, 1638-1650*.
6 *Clanricarde Memoirs*, pp. 10, 13; Gilbert, *Irish Confederation*, i. 54.
7 *Clanricarde Memoirs*, pp. 26, 29, 32-3; Bodl. Carte MS 2, fo. 181: Clanricarde to Charles I, 20 Jan. 1642; Carte MS 68, fo. 394: lords justices and Irish council to Leicester, 2 Jan. 1642; Carte MS 68, fo. 51: lords justices and Irish council, 7 June 1642.
8 Gilbert, *Irish Confederation*, i, 54.
9 Bodl. Carte MS 3, fo. 114: Clanricarde to Ormond, 23 May 1642; BL, Add. MS 46188, fo. 158: Clanricarde to Essex, 13 Sept. 1641; Bodl. Carte MS 3, fo. 105: Clanricarde to Ormond, 19 May 1642.
10 *Clanricarde Letter-Book*, p. 29.
11 Bodl. Carte MS 6, fo. 512: declaration by Clanricarde, Roscommon, Dungarvan, Edward Brabazon and others, 15 Sept. 1643; *Clanricarde Letter-Book*, p. 1.
12 P. Lenihan, 'The Catholic Confederacy 1642-9: an Irish state at war' (PhD thesis, NUI Galway, 1995), p. 161; M. O'Dowd, *Power, Politics and Land: early modern Sligo, 1568-1668* (Belfast, 1991), p. 127; Bodl. Carte MS 7, fo. 625: Sir Robert Newcomen and Sir George St George, 29 Nov. 1643; Carte MS 9, fo. 1: Captain Francis King to Ormond, 19 Jan. 1644; Carte MS 10, fo. 195: Taaffe to Ormond, 13 Apr. 1644.
13 D. Stevenson, *Scottish Covenanters and Irish Confederates: Scottish-Irish relations in the mid seventeenth century* (Belfast, 1981), examines the experiences of Scots forces stationed in Ulster during the 1640s.
14 A. Duignan, 'Shifting allegiances: the Protestant community in Connacht, 1643-45', in R. Armstrong and T. Ó hAnnracháin (eds), *Community in Early Modern Ireland* (Dublin, 2006), pp. 120-32.
15 *Clanricarde Letter-Book*, pp. 93-5.
16 Ibid., pp. 144-5; Ó hAnnracháin, *Rinuccini*, p. 181; G. Aiazza, *The Embassy in Ireland of Monsignor G. B. Rinuccini, archbishop of Fermo in the years 1645-9* transl. by A. Hutton (Dublin, 1873), pp. 223, 385; Gilbert, *Irish Confederation*, vii, 88; Gilbert, *Contemporary History*, i, part i, 136; Bodl. Carte MS 20, fo. 56: Oliver Jones to Ormond, 6 Jan. 1647; Carte MS 20, fo. 62: Sir James Dillon to Ormond, 6 Jan. 1647; Ó Siochrú, *Confederate Ireland*, p. 253, n. 11.
17 Bodl. Carte MS 10, fo. 441: Digby to Ormond, 27 Apr. 1644.
18 *Dictionary of National Biography*, vol. XXI (London, 1909), p. 533.
19 *Clanricarde Letter-Book*, pp. 62, 81.
20 Bodl. Carte MS, fo. 543: Ormond to Digby, 22 July 1644.
21 E. Murphy, 'Dillon, Thomas 4th Viscount Dillon', *DIB*.
22 *Clanricarde Letter-Book*, pp. 58, 62.

23 Ibid., p. 88.
24 Ibid., p. 83.
25 Bodl. Carte MS 10, fo. 579: Digby to Ormond, 9 May 1644; Carte MS 11, fo. 60: commission by lord lieutenant and Irish council, 29 May 1644.
26 Bodl. Carte MS 11, fo. 62: Clanricarde to Ormond, 29 May 1644.
27 *Clanricarde Letter-Book*, pp. 88, 111.
28 B. Cunningham, 'From warlords to landlords: political and social change in Galway, 1540–1640', in G. Moran (ed.), *Galway: history and society* (Dublin, 1996), pp. 97–129, at p. 113.
29 *Clanricarde Letter-Book*, p. 152.
30 Ibid., p. 273.
31 Ibid., pp. 23–4.
32 The Irish peerage had undergone a dramatic inflation after 1620, which encompassed elevations within the peerage; this inflation alarmed many throughout the Stuart kingdoms; Clanricarde's concern should be viewed in this context: see Jane Ohlmeyer, 'The Irish peers, political power and parliament, 1640–41', in C. Brady and J. Ohlmeyer (eds), *British Interventions in Early Modern Ireland* (Cambridge, 2004), pp. 161–85, at p. 135; Ohlmeyer, *Making Ireland English,* pp. 37–41.
33 *Clanricarde Letter-Book*, p. 25.
34 Carte, *Life of Ormond,* vi. 77, 106, 114; *Clanricarde Letter-Book*, p. xviii.
35 *Clanricarde Letter-Book*, pp. 159–62.
36 Carte, *Life of Ormond,* vi. 163.
37 *Clanricarde Letter-Book*, p. 150.
38 Ibid., pp. 153–4.
39 B. Kane, *The Politics and Culture of Honour in Britain and Ireland, 1541–1641* (Cambridge, 2010), pp. 199–203; Ohlmeyer, *Making Ireland English,* p. 76.
40 The case was eventually decided in Clanricarde's favour, on the basis that while Thomond's creation was older it was not continuous, having passed from one line to another; despite this the matter did not die, but revived after the Restoration: see Kane, *Politics and Culture of Honour,* pp. 190–1; B. Cunningham (ed.), 'Clanricard letters', in *Journal of the Galway Archaeological and Historical Society* 48 (1996), pp. 162–208, at pp. 187–9, 200, 204.
41 *Clanricarde Letter-Book*, p. 25.
42 Carte, *Life of Ormond,* vi, p. 163; *Clanricarde Letter-Book*, pp. 63–4; J. Ohlmeyer, *Civil War and Restoration in the Three Stuart Kingdoms: the career of Randal MacDonnell, marquis of Antrim, 1609–83* (Dublin, 2001), p. 135.
43 Ohlmeyer, *Civil War and Restoration,* p. 131, n. 21.
44 *Clanricarde Letter-Book*, pp. 80–1.
45 Duignan, '"All in a confused opposition to each other"', pp. 130–41, 170–7; Ó Siochrú, *Confederate Ireland,* pp. 29–39; Debe, 'The fifth Earl of Clanricarde and the founding of the Confederate Catholic government', pp. 127–58.
46 Ó hAnnracháin, *Rinuccini,* p. 27; Gilbert, *Contemporary History,* ii, 379.
47 Bodl. Carte MS 7, fo. 9: Clanricarde to Ormond, 3 Oct. 1643; Carte MS 7, fo. 78: Clanricarde to Ormond, 8 Oct. 1643.
48 Bodl. Carte MS 7, fo. 190: Ormond to Sir Lucas Dillon, 19 Oct. 1643.

49 Bodl. Carte MS 7, fo. 240: Clanricarde to Sir Richard Blake, 24 Oct. 1643; *Clanricarde Letter-Book,* pp. 9, 12, 485.
50 See *Clanricarde Letter-Book*, pp. 7–8, for an outline of Clanricarde's demands concerning quarters; also ibid., pp. 6, 12–13, 17, 22, 42–3, 60, 118–19, 143–4; Bodl. Carte MS 7, fo. 240: Clanricarde to Sir Richard Blake, 24 Oct. 1643; Carte MS 7, fo. 331: Clanricarde to Ormond, 2 Nov. 1643; Carte MS 10, fo. 415: Sir George St George to Ormond, 26 Apr. 1644; Carte MS 10, fo. 721: Clanricarde to Ormond, 21 May 1644.
51 Sexton, 'Clanricarde and the Confederate Wars', p. 18; Ohlmeyer, *Making Ireland English*, p. 396.
52 Bodl. Carte MS 7, fo. 331: Clanricarde to Ormond, 2 Nov. 1643.
53 Bodl. Carte MS 7, fo. 295: Sir Richard Blake to Ormond, 30 Oct. 1643; *Clanricarde Letter-Book*, pp. 12, 17.
54 Bodl. Carte MS 8, fo. 49: Clanricarde to Ormond, 6 Dec. 1643.
55 Bodl. Carte MS 17, fo. 119: Clanricarde to Patrick Darcy, 12 Apr. 1646.
56 *Clanricarde Letter-Book*, pp. 32, 34.
57 *Clanricarde Letter-Book* p. 57; Bodl. Carte MS 10, fo. 24: Thomas Cashel, Malachy Tuam, Jo Clonfert, Rob Lynch, Lucas Dillon and others to Ormond, 26 Mar. 1644.
58 *Clanricarde Letter-Book*, p. 74.
59 Bodl. Carte MS 10, fo. 324: Clanricarde to Ormond, 22 Apr. 1644.
60 Bodl. Carte MS 11, fo. 62: Clanricarde to Ormond, 29 May 1644.
61 Little, 'Blood and Friendship', pp. 935–38.
62 Bodl. Carte MS 11, fo. 446: Thomond, Clanricarde, Taaffe, Ranelagh, Dillon, Fitzwilliam and Howth to Charles I, 15 July 1644.
63 *Clanricarde Letter-Book*, p. 121.
64 Ibid., p. 136.
65 Ibid., pp. 132–4.
66 Ibid., p. 167.
67 Both diverge somewhat in their analysis of emerging divisions within the Confederate Association during this Assembly; see Ó Siochrú, *Confederate Ireland*, pp. 90–2; T. Ó hAnnracháin, 'Conflicting loyalties, conflicted Rebels: political and religious allegiance among the Confederate Catholics of Ireland', *EHR* 119 (2004), pp. 851–72, at pp. 862–5.
68 Ó hAnnracháin, 'Conflicting loyalties, conflicted Rebels', p. 865.
69 *Clanricarde Letter-Book*, pp. 173–4.
70 Ibid., p. 176.
71 Ibid., pp. 219–20.
72 Aiazza, *The Embassy in Ireland*, p. 158.
73 *Clanricarde Letter-Book*, p. 220; Bodl. Carte MS 17, fo. 119: Clanricarde to Patrick Darcy, 12 Apr. 1646.
74 Robert Armstrong argues that the informal arrangement advocated here was merely a repeat of the unsuccessful confederate–royalist offensive in the province in summer 1645: R. Armstrong, 'Protestant Ireland and the English Parliament, 1641–7' (PhD thesis, Trinity College Dublin, 1995) p. 221.
75 *Clanricarde Letter-Book*, p. 236; Bodl. Carte MS 17, fo. 412: Clanricarde to Ormond, 26 May 1646.

76 Armstrong, 'Protestant Ireland and the English Parliament', p. 224.
77 *Clanricarde Letter-Book*, p. 241; Armstrong, 'Protestant Ireland and the English Parliament', p. 224; P. Lenihan, 'Confederate military strategy, 1643–7', in M. Ó Siochrú (ed.), *Kingdoms in Crisis: Ireland in the 1640s* (Dublin, 2001), pp. 158–75, at p. 166.
78 *Clanricarde Letter-Book*, p. 234.
79 Bodl. Carte MS 17, fo. 370: Clanricarde to Ormond, 11 May 1646.
80 *Clanricarde Letter-Book*, pp. 250–1.
81 Armstrong, 'Protestant Ireland and the English Parliament', p. 226.
82 Ó Siochrú, *Confederate Ireland*, p. 109, n. 110.
83 Robertson, *Royalists at War, pp. 194–5*.
84 *Clanricarde Letter-Book*, p. 151.
85 Bodl. Carte MS 18, fo. 394: Clanricarde's endorsement of the Confederate peace; Carte MS 17, fo. 412: Clanricarde to Ormond, 26 May 1646; *Clanricarde Letter-Book*, pp. 260, 284, 294–5, 300–1, 309–11, 312, 314, 316–17, 317–19; Bodl. Carte MS 18, fo. 531: Clanricarde to Ormond, 18 Sept. 1646; TNA, SP 63/262, fo. 10: Clanricarde to Preston, 20 Oct. 1646; Bodl. Carte MS 19, fo. 249: Taaffe to Ormond, 23 Oct. 1646; Carte MS 19, fo. 292: Digby to Ormond, 30 Oct. 1646; Carte MS 19, fo. 453: Digby to Ormond, 18 Nov. 1646; Gilbert, *Irish Confederation*, vi, 156–8; TNA, SP 63/262, fo. 22: Clanricarde's engagement, 19 Nov. 1646; Bodl. Carte MS 19, fos 482–5: Clanricarde to Rinuccini, 20 Nov. 1646; Aiazza, *The Mission in Ireland*, p. 216; Ó Siochrú, *Confederate Ireland*, pp. 91–2, 116 n. 143, 121 n. 16; T. Ó hAnnracháin, 'Conflicting loyalties, conflicted Rebels', p. 862.
86 Armstrong, 'Protestant Ireland and the English Parliament', p. 247; Ó Siochrú, *Confederate Ireland*, pp. 91–2, 122; Ó hAnnracháin, 'Conflicting loyalties, conflicted Rebels', p. 865.
87 Bodl. Carte MS 19, fo. 547: Clanricarde to Ormond, 24 Nov. 1646.
88 Ibid.
89 TNA, SP 63/262, fo. 444: Clanricarde to Preston, 25 Nov. 1646.
90 *Clanricarde Letter-Book*, pp. 427–8, 457.
91 Ibid., pp. 319–21, 321–2.
92 Ohlmeyer, *Making Ireland English*, p. 68.

4

'Clotworthy is a zealous man, yet hath his purse well lined': Sir John Clotworthy, John Davies and the politics of supply, 1644–45

ANDREW ROBINSON

In September 1643 Sir John Clotworthy would have been pardoned for feeling somewhat self-satisfied in his quest to safeguard decisive parliamentary military intervention in Ulster. He had successfully intervened to ensure Ireland was included in the Solemn League and Covenant, with the cessation of arms between the king and the Catholic confederates largely rejected by the Ulster British and the Scottish covenanter army. The field finally seemed set for a vigorous response to the situation in Ulster, while Clotworthy's position at Westminster, as the most influential voice in Irish affairs, had never seemed stronger.[1] Yet, by the summer of 1644 the political landscape had fundamentally altered. The Covenant in Ulster had not been embraced by the Ulster British and now, imposed at the point of the covenanting pike, it threatened to rip the Protestant community apart.[2] A coup by the British officers of Belfast, which facilitated its capture by Robert Monro from Colonel Arthur Chichester, and the potential repetition at Lisnagarvey (Lisburn), Newry and Dundalk provided a stark warning to the remaining British garrisons that they had little choice but to accept the Covenant and covenanting civil, religious and military subjugation. Clotworthy's plan to draw the British regiments to become a party for Parliament in the province, whether out of necessity or pragmatism, also failed. Monro's choleric confrontation with Lieutenant Colonel Edmund Matthews at Newry in early July 1644 suggested that Ulster teetered on the brink of civil war between the covenanters and any Protestant regiment that would not bend to the Scots' will.[3]

In the same period, Clotworthy encountered political problems of a very different kind at Westminster. His growing opposition to the covenanters in Ulster, together with his support for the earl of Essex (Parliament's lord general in England) in his feud with Sir William Waller,[4] led to former political allies becoming foes. In January 1644 Sir Walter Erle, who had collaborated with Clotworthy during the trial of the earl of Strafford three years earlier, accused him of having had a hand in the escape from the Tower of London of Colonel John Reade, a supposed conspirator in the 1641 rising, as part of an intrigue to bring the city of London and king Charles I into a rapprochement.[5] As a result, Clotworthy was excluded from the Committee of Both Kingdoms which was established on 16 February 1644. This new executive committee acquired near untrammelled powers to order and direct the managing of the war against the king in all three Stuart kingdoms and largely eclipsed the Committee of Irish Affairs which previously had given some limited direction to the Irish war through the allocation of supplies and provisions, working closely with the London adventurers based at Grocers' Hall.[6]

Clotworthy was not added to the Committee of Both Kingdoms until 6 May 1644, but even then the committee books suggest that he did not attend any of its meetings.[7] This was a bitter blow to Clotworthy's prestige at Westminster, hampering his attempts to help shape Parliament's response to the Irish war, and in particular, his persistent supplication for an enhanced role and material support for the Ulster British regiments. The effect of his absence was soon felt: in the Commons on 5 March Sir Henry Vane reported from the Committee of Both Kingdoms, confirming the Scottish supreme command of all the British forces in Ireland which Clotworthy had vociferously opposed in Parliament and in specially convened tripartite meetings between MP adventurers, Grocers' Hall and the Committee for Scottish Affairs at Goldsmiths' Hall.[8] The coalescing of supporters of pro-covenanting intervention in England and Ireland, whether principled or pragmatic, temporarily entrenched the influence of a small cabal of adventurers in the wartime financial machinery in both kingdoms. Individuals such as Maurice and George Thompson, William Pennoyer, Samuel Vassall, Thomas Andrewes, Sir David Watkins, John Towse, John Warner, William Tucker and William Hawkins sought reward in confiscated land for their speculation in the Irish war, with the covenanters rather than the Ulster British the key vehicle for its deliverance, backed with funding provided from confiscated royalist land in England. This knot of adventurers soon dominated almost every aspect of the financial and victualling apparatus of the Irish war in conjunction with the covenanters' political allies at Westminster. As a result, for much of 1644 Clotworthy was very much on the outside looking in, as strategic decisions about the war in Ireland were made without his advocacy or influence.

Rather than wading into the mire of factional politics in the House of Commons, Clotworthy pursued alternative means of ensuring parliamentary support for the Ulster British in prosecuting the war against the Irish confederates. His first move was to ally with a small number of fellow adventurer MPs not included in the Committee of Both Kingdoms, namely John Goodwyn and Robert Reynolds, and a wider 'convention' of citizen adventurers beyond the Grocers' Hall clique in promoting the virtues of the Ulster British and undermining the entrenched influence enjoyed by a small cabal of adventurers. Though sparsely attended by MPs and largely ignored by members of Grocers' Hall, this committee agreed on a number of innovative propositions to support those Ulster British who opposed the cessation of arms.[9] To ensure the financial sustainability of the Ulster British the committee proposed a partial adventure in Ulster alongside a six-month weekly assessment. Areas under British control – the vast majority of the province – would be confiscated, surveyed, and investors immediately charged with planting their proportions. Clotworthy's hand can be seen particularly in the third proposal, which enabled the Scots to gain lands in satisfaction of arrears in counties Cavan and Louth, but excluding them from Antrim and Down lest an influx of covenanted Scots challenge his existing patrimony and desire for an expansion of his sphere of influence at the expense of the earl of Antrim. While such propositions seemingly had the support of many despoiled Protestants in Ireland, particularly the emerging lobby group referred to as the 'gentlemen of Ireland', as well as the London adventurer Maurice Thompson, its construction came at a time when Clotworthy's credit had been diminished and the Committee of Both Kingdoms had, at least at this time, thrown their lot in with Grocers' Hall as its de facto Irish executive.[10]

The joint committee, made up of adventurer MPs and citizen adventurers, became a major irritant to the Grocers' Hall committee and the Committee of Both Kingdoms. One of the issues that confounded effective strategic leadership and direction in the Irish war was the layering of Irish committees, sometimes absorbing the powers of predecessors, meaning that their exact scope and decision-making authority was murky at best. Considerable confusion soon emerged with regard to the relative powers of the Grocers' Hall committee of adventurers and the newly constituted joint committee.[11] The joint committee acted upon its belief that it was a successor body to previous Irish committees, particularly the old parliamentary Adventurers' Committee which evolved into the Committee for the Affairs of Ireland, and the Committee for the Better Expediting the Affairs of Ireland, both of which held a range of powers relating to Dutch contributions to the Irish war and the shipping and disbursement of victuals, weapons and money to support Protestant regiments.[12] Aid procured from the United Provinces under the January 1643 loan and contribution scheme and the July 1643 ordinance appointing commissioners to receive subscriptions in Holland for Ireland became highly divisive as a significant resource to aid both the Ulster British and the covenanting army, and the joint committee and Grocers' Hall both believed they had the legitimacy to order the disbursement and auditing of the associated funds.[13] In a challenge to the Grocers' Hall committee, the joint committee expressed their concern that the treasurers for the scheme, namely

Sir Paul Pindar, Michael Casteel and the leading London adventurers John Kendrick, William Pennoyer, Maurice Thompson and Benjamin Goodwyn, had not dispersed any of the money collected. Sir John Clotworthy, John Browne, Thomas Erle, John Goodwyn, Robert Reynolds, William Jephson and, strangely, Maurice Thompson, who undoubtedly sought to protect the reputation of the adventurer treasurers, referred their enquiries to the earl of Manchester and discovered that a number of collectors and agents, particularly four named as William Hale, John Troughton, William Jennings and Thomas Fossan, had misappropriated the funds.[14]

The identification of Jennings is particularly noteworthy given his role as an agent for the Committee for Scottish Affairs at Goldsmiths' Hall, suggesting that the joint committee believed that he may have diverted money intended for the Ulster British to the covenanters in Ulster and northern England.[15] Though the treasurers of the loan and contribution scheme were not implicated by the joint committee's investigation, it was certainly a shot across their bows to stipulate that any money and victuals collected should be properly accounted for and allocated for the Irish war effort. The joint committee more overtly challenged Grocers' Hall when it stated that further contributions from the United Provinces should be transmitted to Britain or Ireland in cash rather than in goods owing to inflationary prices, with John Davies, the commissary at Carrickfergus, given the charge of purchasing goods at agreed prices and under conditions agreed with the joint committee. To avoid any accusations of impropriety the committee agreed that Davies's accounts be audited not only by William Collins, the auditor for the armies in Ireland, but Sir Thomas Trevor, baron of the exchequer.[16]

The joint committee also courted controversy in April 1644 by publicly challenging Grocers' Hall in a bitter dispute over control of all victuals, arms, ammunition or artillery collected for Ireland but still held in various stores. It emerged that one of the leading adventurers, Alderman James Bunce, had appropriated 128 snaphance muskets for the London militia which had originally been intended for Sir John Clotworthy. The joint committee asked that they be returned, replaced with arms of like quality or the cost reimbursed. Bunce's response to the joint committee did little but inflame tensions and was 'in no way satisfactory to them', leading to a missive to Grocers' Hall demanding a further explanation.[17] By 10 May the joint committee discovered that two commissaries, William Dobbins and Ralph Hardwick, had been ordered by Grocers' Hall not to dispose or deliver any goods to Ireland without their further order.[18] Affronted, the joint committee moved to call Sir David Watkins, the keeper of the adventurers' stores, to justify the order. Watkins refused to appear for questioning which members 'construe to be a contempt towards them'. They also attempted to require Jerome Alexander, the treasurer to the Grocers' Hall committee, to appear before them, but like Watkins he refused.[19]

Soon thereafter Watkins issued another order on behalf of the Grocers' Hall committee to require Hardwick to pass all his stored goods to two agents, the aforementioned William Jennings and Francis Smith, or find himself called to appear before the committee and answer for his reticence. The joint committee responded by calling for an audit of all those keeping supplies and money intended for Ireland and ordered Dobbins, Hardwick and other commissaries to move all goods intended for Ireland to one store and take a full account.[20] As the battle between the committees became increasingly unseemly, in mid-July the Committee of Both Kingdoms stepped in, placing a stay on the disputed firearms and referring the matter to the House of Commons. The Commons ordered that the arms be delivered into the keeping of William Pennoyer and Maurice Thompson – the latter a member of Grocers' Hall but a frequent attendee of the joint committee – until otherwise ordered by the house.[21]

The matter soon escalated when, a month later, the Commons divided on the motion of whether Jerome Alexander should be suspended from his role until his accounts had been audited. It caused two divisions in the house, the first tied with 46 votes to both yeas and noes. A second vote was won by the yeas by 49 votes to 44.[22] On 27 August, a day that otherwise proved to be a turning point in the Irish war effort, Clotworthy and Watkins had a spectacular falling out. The Antrim planter accused Watkins of being a 'beggarly, unworthy fellow' and reproached him for refusing to pay his full subscription to the adventurers fund. William Strode demonstrated that Watkins had disbursed £8,491 and other sums to the Scots, a £1,500 fine, and engaged £500 for John Pym, leading to the Commons publicly thanking him and proclaiming their satisfaction 'of his good affections to the service of England and Ireland'. As a result Dennis Bond moved that Clotworthy publicly ask Watkins's forgiveness.[23]

Despite this public set-back, by the end of August 1644 Clotworthy's determination to fight for the Ulster British eventually bore fruit. On 27 August the Commons ordered an ordinance be passed for a weekly assessment totalling £80,000 exclusively for the British regiments in Ireland, to be paid half in monies and half in supplies every three months. Despite recent spats, in the months that followed Clotworthy showed his ability to work with the London adventurers to ensure the successful passage of this ordinance. On 27 September he reported amendments and alterations with regard to how much each county was expected to raise. With the city of London struggling to raise money it was resolved they advance £300 per week after the common council protested they could not meet the initial figure of £550, 'provided that this rate shall be no precedent for the future, but is done for the ease of the city at this present'. Clotworthy drove through the safe passage of the assessment ordinance through successive debates and readings in the lower chamber, and personally carried it to the House of Lords on 10 October.[24]

Once minor changes and alterations had been finalised, the ordinance passed through the Lords on 18 October.[25] Thanks to Clotworthy's interventions, by the autumn of 1644 Parliament had belatedly placed the Ulster British on a footing through which they could actively demonstrate their desire to defeat the Irish confederates.

Yet his was only a partial and ephemeral victory for Clotworthy, as it was already clear that he and his political allies would have little direct influence on the strategic direction of the war in Ulster. On 27 August, the same day as the Commons agreed to the weekly ordinance to support the Ulster British, the lower chamber also granted the Committee of Both Kingdoms sole authority to carry out the levying of the Irish war, with the power to appoint sub-committees for the 'better acting and managing of that business' which, three days later, was amended to a power to appoint sub-committees out of the body of the adventurers for Ireland.[26] One month later the Committee of Both Kingdoms appointed a number of key 'citizen adventurers' to a sub-committee to assist them in the direction and control of the Irish war.[27]

Although the London adventurers seemed entrenched as the key facilitator for the Committee of Both Kingdom's plans, during the closing months of 1644 Parliament made a renewed and genuine effort to reach out and accommodate Protestant Ireland. There was a new urgency about building a party for Parliament in Ireland during this period, as it was hoped such a move would diminish the authority of marquess of Ormond as lord lieutenant and ensure that the king was not able to bring confederate and royalist forces from Ireland to fight in the civil war in England. A major fillip to Parliament's paper war with the king had previously emerged on 1 June 1644 when Captain William Parsons, the nephew of the former lord justice, Sir William Parsons, appeared before the Commons to give an account on behalf of a group of Protestant agents who had attended the king at Oxford to protest against royalist attempts to broker a peace deal with the confederates. Clotworthy was brought in from his relative wilderness and named to a committee alongside Robert Reynolds, William Jephson and Lord Lisle to hold a series of hearings with Parsons and his fellow agents Captain Michael Jones, Captain MacWilliam Ridgeway and Sir Francis Hamilton, and then publish their findings. The committee was also tasked with ensuring that the agents were adequately accommodated in a sequestered property in Parliament's care, with furniture and other necessities provided by the Committee for Sequestrations.[28]

The Venetian ambassador rather haughtily dismissed Captain Parsons's intervention and its propaganda value, stating that Parliament's 'pockets will be closed by their powerlessness, and he will take away nothing but declarations and words, and in the mean time the army promised by that kingdom to his majesty is making ready'.[29] The ambassador's prognostication, however, proved to be misplaced. The feting of Parsons was an early sign that

Parliament genuinely sought to win the support of Protestant Ireland. In October 1644 Westminster proved to be particularly active in renewing its interest in Irish affairs. For example, on 6 October the House of Commons resolved to obtain the freedom of some of the Irish councillors imprisoned by Ormond the previous year, seeking to trade the freedom of Sir John Mallett for Sir John Temple, and ordering the Committee for Prisoners to consider fit persons to be exchanged for Sir Adam Loftus, Sir William Parsons and Sir Robert Meredith.[30] On 23 October Sir John Clotworthy was named to a committee alongside Reynolds, Denzil Holles and Miles Corbet to prepare an ordinance of no quarter for Irish rebels in England.[31] Perhaps the most significant move occurred on 16 October in the Committee of the Both Kingdoms when members referred to the adventurers' sub-committee to consider the addition of agents from each Irish province to their ranks.[32] This proved to be a pivotal intervention, for the intercession and lobbying of the 'gentlemen of Ireland' eventually led to the eclipsing of the adventurers' power over the award of contracts of supply for Protestant forces in Ireland, with the Carrickfergus merchant John Davies the main beneficiary, becoming in effect the official parliamentary supplier for Ireland in short order.

The fact that Protestant Ireland began to coalesce as a prominent and influential regional power bloc proved to be hugely significant and, to a limited degree, mimicked similar patterns in England where local issues across a number of counties effectively trumped party and faction.[33] The welcoming of the 'gentlemen of Ireland' into the parliamentary fold meant that they could now directly influence the strategic direction of the Irish war, taking advantage of the renewed parliamentary fervour for defeating the confederates. It is difficult to be sure of the membership of this disparate group, though a later petition sent to the House of Lords in August 1645 concerning a proposal for Davies to ship cloth in lieu of cash to British forces in across the island listed Clotworthy, Lord Broghill, Sir Arthur Loftus, Arthur Hill, Sir John Temple, Sir Phillip Percivalle, John Parsons (although more likely to be James Parsons, Sir William's son), Thomas Bettesworth and Lieutenant Colonel John McAdam.[34] Bettesworth is a notable figure, given his previous role as a commissioner to settle disputes in Munster during the term of the cessation,[35] symbolising the extent to which Ormond's attempts to win peace in Ireland to expand the king's war in England increasingly alienated Charles's Protestant subjects, bringing them into a reluctant rapprochement with Parliament. Sir John Temple, Sir Adam Loftus, Sir William Parsons and Sir Robert Meredith were still imprisoned in Dublin in October 1644, but the fact that Parliament put great stock in winning their support suggests that they had already been considered as a distinct group within Irish politics.[36]

Sir William Stewart would certainly have been another member of the Protestant pressure group, having arrived in London from Oxford as one of the disgruntled Protestant agents on 12 July alongside Sir Phillip Percivalle.³⁷ William Jephson too was active in Parliament at this time alongside Clotworthy and would doubtless be a prominent voice for Protestant Munster. Sir Robert King and Arthur Annesley could also be potential members of the lobby group, with both named in April 1645 as parliamentary commissioners alongside the London adventurer, Colonel William Beale, to reside in Ulster to give direction to the Ulster British and covenanters in prosecuting the war. The ordinance for their appointment passed by the Commons was carried to the Lords by Clotworthy, alongside a commission for Sir Charles Coote to be lord president of Connacht.³⁸ Sir Charles Coote or his brother Chidley had previously had some interaction in early 1644 with the committee of Irish affairs, led by Clotworthy, Jephson and Reynolds, as it prepared a report on the state of Ireland.³⁹ Despite previous efforts to limit the number of Irish agents thronging to Westminster to press their cases for the award of supplies,⁴⁰ other figures, such as the 'commissioners of the British forces in Ulster', namely Sir William Cole, James Trail, Sir John Kyrle and Captain MacGill, pressed the division of supplies among the various regiments and may also have been a factor in influencing the Committee of Both Kingdoms.⁴¹ Likewise a certificate from the Committee for Examinations noted that on 24 April 1645 Sir Hardress Waller, a leading figure in Munster and agent to Inchiquin; Thomas Badnedge, former agent for the 1st earl of Cork; Sir Francis Hamilton, a key ally of Sir Charles Coote and another Protestant agent at Oxford; Sir Percy Smith, kinsman and ally of Broghill; and William Dobbins, formerly an agent of Sir William St Leger and an ally of Inchiquin had all taken the Covenant.⁴² The confluence of these somewhat unnatural allies suggests that, for a short time at least, Protestant Ireland had moved away from competing and ineffective 'proxy lobbies'⁴³ to a more united and influential interest group, representative of all four provinces.

Whatever the precise make-up of the 'gentlemen of Ireland' in October 1644, their influence was clearly being felt in the corridors of power. On 21 October the Committee of Both Kingdoms divided the £80,000 that the assessment planned to raise, with £42,000 assigned to Ulster, £10,000 to Munster, £5,500 to Connacht and £2,500 to Duncannon. This was the product of the lobbying of the 'gentlemen of Ireland' who forwarded propositions concerning the rates and prices of arms, ammunition, clothes and victuals, as well as the timetable for delivery to the Protestant forces. The adventurers were only asked 'if they know any that will furnish the said conditions (with all the circumstances expressed) upon better terms for the good of the service'.⁴⁴ For roughly two weeks from 31 October the adventurers and the 'gentlemen of Ireland' were locked into a process of negotiation, with the committee books for the Committee of Both Kingdoms noting that Grocers' Hall had submitted 'remonstrances' for consideration – suggesting that they were not fully behind the propositions. The propositions for Ulster in particular appear to be a sticking point but the committee records are frustratingly silent on the nature of Grocers' Hall's grievances and provides little additional context on a penalty which was imposed on Davies if he failed to live up to the terms of the contract.[45] However grudgingly, the terms of Davies's contract were eventually accepted by Grocers' Hall.[46] On 27 November the committee ordered representatives of the adventurers to check the quality of the arms, clothes and victuals and it appears that no issues emerged from their examinations. On 11 January 1645 the Committee of Both Kingdoms prepared to send supplies to Strangford, Belfast and Ballyshannon and they invited Grocers' Hall to again test the quality of the goods and name two commissioners to accompany the arms, clothes and victuals. With the suppliers meeting Grocers' Hall's expectations, on 16 January the warrant for delivery of wools and linen for officers in Ulster was accepted, along with warrants for supplies to Ballyshannon, Strangford and Belfast.[47]

The intervention of the 'gentlemen of Ireland', encouraged by the Committee of Both Kingdoms, meant that Irish Protestants were now key partners in the war, particularly with regard to how supplies would be subdivided in each province once the contract with Davies had been agreed.[48] The Committee of Both Kingdoms clearly sought to take much more interest in the Irish war, offering leadership and strategic direction which had been severely lacking for the past three years. The Ulster British, the black sheep of the Protestant cause a few short months before, were now viewed as crucial to the war effort and the committee sought to use the northern province as its powerbase for further military interventions. They suggested for example on 27 December 1644 that 2,000 Ulster British foot could be employed in Munster, 1,500 in Connacht, supported by 2,500 covenanters.[49] This shows how quickly the tables had turned: similar proposals, undoubtedly originating from Clotworthy in the 'convention' of citizen adventurers and adventurer MPs, had been introduced in the Commons on 17 January 1644 and were not even granted a reading.[50]

Two pertinent questions require further consideration: why did the 'gentlemen of Ireland' press for John Davies to be awarded the supply contract, and why did the adventurers at Grocers' Hall agree to it, however reluctantly? Davies's association with Sir John Clotworthy and later accusations of corruption made against them obscure the fact that he was not a simple devotee of Clotworthy, plucked from obscurity to defraud the state for the sake of self-enrichment: he was in fact already a prominent merchant in Carrickfergus before the outbreak of the 1641 rising, having been appointed as an alderman in 1630, sheriff in 1633, mayor in 1640 and 1641, as well as the town's MP to the Irish Parliament in March 1640.[51] He was also made a freeman in neighbouring Belfast in June 1640 and a burgess in February 1642.[52] Davies's role as mayor of Carrickfergus is particularly significant given that it was one of Ireland's staple towns. The Irish staple was essentially a means of regulating money lending, allowing individuals to borrow or lend money on a bond. As mayor of the town Davies also acted as mayor of the staple, assisted by two burgesses who fulfilled a role as constables of the staple. They had significant legal powers in recording and regulating the recovery of debt, ensuring that the debtor repaid the creditor a fixed sum by an agreed date together with a rate of interest which fluctuating considerably in the seventeenth century between 10 per cent and 40 per cent.[53] Furthermore, as commissary for supplies to support the covenanters in Carrickfergus in the early years of the war he was well versed in the use of bills of exchange and certificates for payment to merchants who delivered goods to Ulster.

The certificate system itself originated from Clotworthy's intervention. He had brought a motion to the Commons in January 1642 to form a committee to liaise with merchants to supply victuals for Ireland, the out-workings of which included ensuring payment to merchants who adventured victuals and supplies to Ireland in return for a certificate on delivery from the treasurer or vice-treasurer or commissaries at the ports of Dublin, Carrickfergus, Derry and Youghal.[54] Davies's knowledge of the merchant network, including operating on credit and the use of bills of exchange meant he possessed a level of administrative knowledge and capacity which suggested that his elevation after 1644 as the key supplier to Protestant Ireland was based on merit and not on factional alignment or a predilection for deception and embezzlement. Indeed, his personal accounts appeared to be beyond reproach before the award of the November 1644 contract. Following his appointment by the joint committee of adventurer MPs and citizen adventurers to buy goods for Ireland with funds coming in from the Dutch loan and contribution, they described Davies as 'well known both to them and most men of note of the English and Scottish nation in the north of Ireland to be of good sufficiency and experience in this way'.[55] The committee also ordered his associated accounts be audited by Sir Thomas Trevor, baron of the exchequer, with no evidence of impropriety discovered.[56]

Not only did Davies become the preferred supplier to Protestant forces across the island, he came to be highly regarded by many key Protestant settlers for his efforts in victualing beleaguered regiments or in providing his agency and political guidance, including to Sir Charles Coote,[57] Sir James Montgomery[58] and Richard Fitzgerald, Percivalle's brother-in-law.[59] Indeed, Davies's correspondence with Sir Phillip Percivalle reveals him to be a shrewd political observer on a range of issues including the dangers posed to Protestants in Ireland in being drawn into Westminster factional dissonance – particularly in the row between Broghill and Inchiquin – as well as the affairs of men like Sir William Parsons and Sir Adam Loftus.[60] Davies also eruditely remarked on the calibre of the New Model army soldiers destined for Ireland,[61] and on Parliament's negotiations with Ormond for the surrender of Dublin between October 1645–March 1646, and September–November 1646.[62] Indeed, Davies was sufficiently trusted by a number of leading Irish Protestants that he undertook covert correspondence with Ormond's agent in England, Sir Maurice Eustace, and held meetings with two other Irish royalists, Sir Gerard Lowther and Sir Paul Davies.[63] This would certainly belie any suggestion that he was a mere empty shirt controlled by the Machiavellian Clotworthy.

As for Grocers' Hall, it seems that the central knot of adventurers reluctantly agreed to the proposals from the 'gentlemen of Ireland' only after they insisted on putting extensive checks on the quality of clothes, arms and victuals, ensuring they would be inspected before shipping to Ireland.[64] Likewise 'fit persons' were to be sent to each province to oversee their distribution.[65] More importantly the ordinance named their own men – Samuel Avery, John Kendrick, Thomas Foot and James Bunce – as treasurers responsible for receiving the assessment collections, thus ensuring the adventurers' continued role in parliamentary financial apparatus.[66] Perhaps an overriding arrogance in the security of their influence, given Parliament's reliance on them in the preceding three years in financially administering their war against the king, lulled them into a false confidence that their authority was unimpeachable. It also appears that Davies continued to buy a limited amount of supplies from adventurers, with perhaps eight from a total of approximately thirty-two continuing to profit from the Irish war.[67] The adventurers may also have been content to allow someone else to take on the risk of supplying Protestant Ireland considering so many of their debts had not yet been paid. For example, by July 1646 a consortium comprising Richard Turner, Richard Gethin, Tempest Milner, Richard Wollaston and William Hawkins petitioned Parliament in relation to an eye-watering debt of £34,000 from supplies shipped in 1641 and 1642. The House of Commons sent their petition to the Committee of Accounts to enquire into their arrears and to determine if they could be paid from the confiscated property of royalists.[68] Payment in such circumstances was not quickly forthcoming.

In a move symbolic of Davies's growing dominance of the Irish supply routes, on 16 April 1645 the Committee of Both Kingdoms noted the continuing problems of having county collections for the Irish assessment sent directly to the Grocers' Hall committee in London, owing to the 'trouble and danger' of transporting it. Therefore they commanded the treasurers to order collectors to pay Davies directly or, in his absence, to his partners and assignees Thomas Rodbard, John Cheston and Denis Gauden. The committee also desired he be compensated for money improperly diverted for other uses – perhaps an implication that they believed Grocers' Hall misappropriated money assigned to Davies to pay other suppliers, motivated by their personal enmity towards the Ulsterman.⁶⁹ This robust message to Grocers' Hall committee suggests that the Committee of Both Kingdoms no longer saw them as a key partner in the Irish war. This is confirmed by the granting, also in April 1645, of another significant contract to Davies, authorising him to supply the covenanters in Ulster – a move that was a significant challenge to the Grocers' Hall and Goldsmiths' Hall nexus which had previously controlled it.⁷⁰ On 5 June the Committee of Both Kingdoms saw fit to order the committee for Scottish affairs at Goldsmiths' Hall to grant Davies a reward for the delivery of previous supplies to Carrickfergus.⁷¹ On 21 June they further ordered that £3,750 should be paid from the sale of goods at York House in order to facilitate the delivery of £4,000 worth of supplies for Munster.⁷² That the Committee of Both Kingdoms sought to bypass Grocers' Hall in identifying potential sources of income to support Protestant Ireland speaks volumes for their growing antipathy towards the Irish adventurers.

The creation of another Irish committee on 1 July 1645, based in the Star Chamber, proved to be a major fillip for Clotworthy in his quest to drive forward a vigorously prosecuted war in Ireland with parliamentary backing. Established to draw up propositions for parliamentary relief of Protestant forces in Munster, the committee had a 'Presbyterian' hue, with Clotworthy joined by Denzil Holles, Robert Goodwyn, Robert Reynolds, and Inchiquin's ally, William Jephson.⁷³ Until May 1646, when an influx of 'Independent' members gave that faction a majority, this committee largely superseded the Committee of Both Kingdoms in the direction of the Irish war, thus giving Clotworthy the sort of power that he had long craved. It is no surprise to see in late July 1645 John Davies become the main supplier to the new parliamentary military intervention in Munster,⁷⁴ and on 30 August he also proposed contracts to supply victuals worth £20,000 for Munster, £2,500 for Connaught and £7,000 for Ulster.⁷⁵

The continued rise of John Davies and the fall of the London adventurers is further illustrated by the passage of another ordinance in September 1645 which further secured the Carrickfergus merchant's arrears. In the summer of 1645 Davies found that his debts from the October 1644 ordinance to supply the Ulster British had not been met and there appeared no mechanism for the payment of his proposed supply of April 1645 to the covenanting army and other provincial forces. Pressed by the Star Chamber Committee, Parliament gave a first reading to an ordinance on 23 August 1645 for a further supply to the Ulster British regiments and Scots in Ulster, with a separate committee, which included Clotworthy, appointed to determine how to raise and appoint the money required to supply the covenanters according to the contract agreed with Davies in April 1645.⁷⁶ On 23 September the Commons sent their draft ordinance to the Lords for their agreement.⁷⁷ Six days later the upper house gave their assent, permitting Davies and his assignees to have receipt of any surplus over the £80,000 of the October 1644 assessment to pay debts incurred from his 23 April 1645 proposals to supply the covenanters in eastern Ulster.[78] His alliance with Clotworthy ensured he received a level of financial protection and security that few other merchants enjoyed and in effect he had privatised the Irish assessment machinery. That is not to say that Parliament did not address in some form the debts of other merchants. For example, two ordinances passed through the Lords on 23 October required Grocers' Hall to provide £1,670 from the adventurers' money to Maurice Thompson for debts going back to 1642 for the pay of soldiers raised in Bristol by Lieutenant Colonel St Leger as well as supplies of cloth, match, lead, shot and fish; and, the use of his ship the *Hopewell of London* to guard the Irish coast. A separate ordinance required Grocers' Hall to assign around £233 owed to John Davies to Thompson as part of his debts to the adventurer merchant for the previous provision of salt and other necessities to the Ulster armies. Both ordinances required the money to be paid 'out of such monies as are or shall come to their hands' by virtue of the Adventure or the Sea Adventure, which was no better than a paper promise as both schemes were long since bankrupt.[79] One is left to wonder whether Parliament's decision to assign the debt to be repaid through bankrupt funds was a deliberate snub. It certainly sent a potent message to these prominent merchants and adventurers that they were not as integral a part of the parliamentary apparatus as they once believed.

By November 1645 the Grocers' Hall committee had reached the end of their tether after the city of London has been asked to lend a further £15,000 for Irish service.[80] Alderman John Foulke delivered a remonstrance to the house on 10 November which outlined the grievances of Grocers' Hall to Davies's continued domination of the Irish supply routes and the financial protection he enjoyed through successive assessment ordinances in 1644 and 1645. The Commons formed a thirty-eight man committee, which included key allies of Clotworthy such as Robert Reynolds and John Goodwyn, as well as leading adventurers Sir Thomas Soames, Samuel Vassall and Maurice Thompson, to consider the findings of a Committee of Accounts investigation into the activities of Clotworthy and Davies, the execution of Davies's contracts of supply with the Committee of Both Kingdoms, and what encouragement could be given to adventurers to make additional subscriptions.[81]

The adventurers' sought a sympathetic ear and took to the pamphlet press to put their arguments into the public sphere. *The State of Irish Affairs*, published in December 1645, outlined their key concerns and gave ample demonstration of the extent to which the adventurers had been cast to the peripheries of the Irish war. They complained that their once key partners in the Committee of Both Kingdoms had 'cooled and withdrawn the zeal and affections of the adventurers and others', happily spending the money they had been at pains to bring in for the preservation of Protestants in Ireland, but refusing to give them any oversight as to how it would be spent. They complained that Davies, in league with his partners, gained nearly all the supply contracts to Ireland and overcharged the state to the tune of some £12,000–15,000 while he 'failed in all his undertakings, both for time, manner and matter', and shipped 'such base and unserviceable commodities, as they were little worth'. Davies and his partners 'hunted after these bargains, to raise themselves fortunes this way, and care not how they deceive the common wealth, so they may enrich themselves, and put the money into their own purses; which not only makes the people unwilling, but many of them wilful to refuse the payment of these monies'.[82] As for the Ulster British forces themselves, the adventurers complained that commanders filled the ranks of the local regiments with their own tenants, meaning that their primary focus was to look no further than the 'smoke of their own chimneys' and preserve their own estates rather than vigorously pursue the confederates.[83]

As for the 1645 ordinance, the adventurers stated that only £50,000 had been received from the October 1644 assessment monies 'at the first beginning, when men were better able and disposed to the work'.[84] They argued that Davies and his 'emissaries and creditors' had hounded them for payment at a time when 'men are more and more exhausted in their estates', owing to the added financial pressures in maintaining Fairfax's New Model army and Alexander Leslie's covenanters in northern England. Grocers' Hall also claimed that many more people were 'a little troubled, to see the citizens of London, men of worth and integrity, unemployed in the service; and such a poor fellow as Davies, and a mere stranger, vaulting himself herein against the whole city'.[85] In their infinite generosity, the adventurers offered to hold the assessment income for Davies in safe-keeping until the Committee of Accounts completed its investigation into the Carrickfergus merchant's alleged malfeasance.[86] The accusations levelled by Grocers' Hall went on to form the backbone of the investigations by the Committee of Accounts, dominated by allies of the 'Presbyterian' party which was reflected in the jaundiced nature of its investigations.[87] The allegations directed against Clotworthy and Davies regarding their activities in supplying forces in Ireland with much needed victuals, ammunition and clothing became a running sore, and many of them would resurface when Clotworthy was investigated by the Commons later in the decade.[88] Most of the accusations charged him with differing degrees of embezzlement of money and supplies,[89] defrauding individual merchants as well as the state,[90] but worse, his own regiment in Antrim.[91]

General accusations of embezzlement and corruption were one thing, but denouncing him for cruel practices towards the men of his own regiment had the potential to fatally undermine him in the eyes of his allies and opponents alike. Davies found himself accused of a range of malfeasance, with embezzlement of supplies and money, as well as poor quality supplies being the most common, with the uniforms particularly unserviceable, made of cloth 'so bad as that it doth not deserve to be called by the name of cloth', and stitching of such poor quality that one witness claimed he could 'thrust his finger betwixt the stitches'. Foodstuffs were no better, with the quality of the butter, described as the 'coarsest that could be gotten'.[92] This was a clear attack on Davies's honesty and integrity and questioned whether he was suitable proponent of parliamentary support for Protestant Ireland.[93]

Despite this range of allegations, the Committee of Accounts appeared to be stoically unimpressed by the Grocers' Hall denunciations of Clotworthy and Davies. The committee demanded an explanation from the adventurers as one of the bodies responsible for effective and efficient administration of the Irish supply routes as to why they did not call Clotworthy and Davies to account long before late 1645.[94] Davies's accounts were certified by the Committee of Accounts, with William Prynne and Oliver Clobery signing off the detailed records submitted by the Carrickfergus merchant and his business partners.[95]

In the end, it was not the adventurers but the increasing gulf between the Presbyterian and Independent factions that brought an end to the power of Sir John Clotworthy and his allies. In January 1646 Parliament appointed the Independent grandee, Viscount Lisle, as chief governor of Ireland, and by May the Star Chamber Committee had been taken over by his Independent factional allies. These men had little sympathy with Clotworthy's aim to secure vigorous parliamentary military intervention in Ulster, and influenced by Lord Broghill their focus soon shifted to the southern province of Munster, taking most of the funding with them. This move caused the 'gentlemen of Ireland' to splinter apart in a return to the provincial rivalries of the early years of the war, and Sir Charles Coote in Connacht was not the only one left to complain of 'that torrent which carrieth all to Munster'.[96]

It was also in this period that the so-called 'Irish Independents' emerged as a distinct and influential group, opening up old divisions from 1630s and before.[97] Clotworthy, who had successfully avoided Westminster factionalism for most of the 1640s, eventually threw in his lot with the rival Presbyterian interest in a move that eventually led to his impeachment in 1647 on charges that included regurgitated corruption allegations from earlier in the decade. As one commentator sneered, 'Clotworthy is a zealous man, yet hath his purse well lined.'[98]

As for John Davies, he, perhaps characteristically, continued to thrive. He had been entrusted by the Committee of Both Kingdoms and Parliament as a whole for the supply of parliamentary garrisons in Ireland throughout 1645 and 1646,[99] and when Lisle and his cronies planned a new offensive in

Munster in the winter of 1646–47, Davies became the main contractor for shipping victuals and supplies in the southern province.[100] He complained about the calibre of the new English soldiers for the Munster expedition as the 'most untoward people in the world, and whose officers have no command over them, which makes it a hard business for a place where they are', and indicated that he hoped to 'get off from meddling any more', and stated that he longed for a quiet retirement with his wife and children.[101] Nonetheless, he continued to evidence his eye for profit, proving that even in Ireland in the late 1640s, business was business.

NOTES

1 For Clotworthy's career see A. Robinson, '"Not otherwise worthy to be named, but as a firebrand brought from Ireland to inflame this kingdom": the political and cultural milieu of Sir John Clotworthy during the Stuart Civil Wars' (PhD thesis, Ulster University, 2013), pp. 181–238.

2 Robinson, 'Not otherwise worthy to be named', pp. 286–94; K. Forkan, '"That fatal ingredient of the Covenant": the place of the Ulster Scottish colonial community during the 1640s', in B. Mac Cuarta (ed.), *Reshaping Ireland, 1550–1700: colonisation and its consequences* (Dublin, 2011), pp. 261–80, at pp. 269–73; Armstrong, *Protestant War*, pp. 101–4, 111–16; R. Armstrong, 'Ireland's Puritan revolution? The emergence of Ulster Presbyterianism reconsidered', *EHR* 121 (2006), pp. 1048–74, at pp. 1063–64; E. Furgol, 'The military and ministers as agents of Presbyterian imperialism in England and Ireland, 1640–1648', in J. Dwyer, R.A. Mason and A. Murdoch (eds), *New Perspectives on the Politics and Culture of Early Modern Scotland* (Edinburgh, 1982), pp. 95–115.

3 Bodl. MS Carte 10, fo. 642: Edmund Matthews to Ormond, 15 May 1644; ibid., fos 655–6: Theophilus Jones to Ormond, 16 May 1644; ibid., fos 745–6: Robert Monro to Ormond, May 1644; ibid., fo. 751: Theophilus Jones to Ormond, 23 May 1644; MS Carte 11, fo. 336: Theophilus Jones to Edmund Matthews, 1 July 1644; ibid., fo. 431: Seafoule Gibson to Ormond, 12 July 1644; ibid., fo. 440: Edmund Matthews to Ormond, 14 July 1644; Stevenson, *Scottish Covenanters*, pp. 161–3, 195–6.

4 *Baillie Letters and Journals*, ii. 141; J. Adamson, 'The triumph of oligarchy: the management of war and the Committee of Both Kingdoms, 1644–1645', in C.R. Kyle and J. Peacey (eds), *Parliament at Work: parliamentary committees, political power and public access in early modern England* (Woodbridge, Suffolk, 2002), pp. 101–29, at pp. 110–11.

5 BL, Add. MS 18778 (Walter Yonge's diary), fo. 82; Add. MS 18779 (Walter Yonge's diary), fo. 46; V. Pearl, 'Oliver St. John and the "Middle Group" in the Long Parliament, Aug. 1643-May 1644', *EHR* 81 (1966), pp. 490–519, at pp. 512–13; discussion on the accusations took place on 12 and 13 January and seems to have been promptly dropped; *CJ*, iii. 364, 366.

6 *A&O*, i. 381–2; Adamson, 'The triumph of oligarchy', pp. 107–10, 113–17; *LJ*, iv. 405, 430; *CJ*, iii. 504.

7 *LJ*, iv. 542; TNA, SP 21/7 and 21/8.
8 Armstrong, *Protestant War*, pp. 105–6; *CJ*, iii. 337–9, 349–50, 418; *LJ*, vi. 455, 458, 464; BL, Harl. MS 165 (Sir Simonds D'Ewes's diary), fos 254–6; PRONI, T525/5: copy of NLS Wodrow Folio MS 66.
9 *CJ*, iii. 353; BL, Add. MS 4771 (Joint Adventurers' Committee, minute book), fos 28–9.
10 *CJ*, iii. 368, 370; BL, Add. MS 4771, fos 4–9.
11 At this time the Grocers' Hall committee appears to be regularly sitting at Turners' Hall. For clarity and consistency the chapter continues to refer to that adventurers' committee as the Grocers' Hall committee.
12 R. Armstrong, 'Ireland at Westminster: the Long Parliament's Irish committees, 1641–1647', in Kyle and Peacey (eds), *Parliament at Work*, pp. 79–100, at pp. 86–8; Robinson, 'Not otherwise worthy to be named', pp. 271–3, 291.
13 *A&O*, i. 70–3, 220–1; TNA, SP 21/7 (Committee of Both Kingdoms, day book Feb.–Nov. 1644), fo. 64.
14 BL, Add MS 4771, fos 19v, 20, 39v, 43–v.
15 TNA, SP 28/253B [box 2, part 2] (Committee of Accounts, depositions on case of Clotworthy and Davies), fo. 91; SP 16/539/3, fo. 115: certificate of William Jennings and Francis Smith, c.1645.
16 BL, Add. MS 4771, fos 29v, 30, 37, 38v, 44v.
17 Ibid., fos 28–9, 37, 41; TNA, SP 21/7, fo. 46; SP 28/253B [box 2, part 2], fos 1, 8–9, 20–1; SP 16/539/4, fo. 133: notes for proofs of articles against Clotworthy and Davies, n.d.
18 BL, Add. MS 4771, fo. 43v.
19 Ibid., fos 43v–44v.
20 Ibid., fos 44, 49, 50; TNA, SP 21/7, fos 64, 102.
21 TNA, SP 21/7, fo. 125; *CJ*, iii. 564.
22 *CJ*, iii. 599.
23 TNA, SP 16/539/2, fo.189: copy of Commons' order, Aug. 1644; *CJ*, iii. 609.
24 *CJ*, iii. 615–17, 624, 627, 631, 634, 640, 659, 666; *LJ*, vii. 19, 21, 26, 27.
25 *CJ*, iii. 640; *A&O*, i. 531–3.
26 *CJ*, iii. 609, 612; *LJ*, vi. 693.
27 TNA, SP 21/7, fo. 207.
28 *CJ*, iii. 513–14, 520, 525–6, 560; BL, Add. MS 31116 (Lawrence Whitaker's diary), fo. 141–v; Armstrong, *Protestant War*, pp. 120–1; Armstrong, 'Ireland at Westminster', p. 90.
29 *CSP Ven.* 1643–47, pp. 107–8.
30 *CJ*, iii. 666; W.P. Kelly, 'The early career of James Butler, twelfth Earl and first Duke of Ormond, 1610–43' (PhD thesis, Cambridge University, 1995), pp. 375–84.
31 *CJ*, iii. 673, 675–6; *A&O*, i. 554–5.
32 TNA, SP 21/7, fo. 235.
33 D.A. Scott, 'The "Northern Gentlemen", the parliamentary independents, and Anglo-Scottish relations in the Long Parliament', *HJ* 42 (1999), pp. 347–75; L. Glow, 'Pym and Parliament: the methods of moderation', *Journal of Modern History* 36 (1964), pp. 373–97.

34 *LJ*, vii. 528.
35 Armstrong, *Protestant War*, pp. 111–12.
36 P. Little, 'The Irish "Independents" and Viscount Lisle's lieutenancy of Ireland', *HJ* 44 (2001), pp. 941–61.
37 See *CJ*, iii. 513–14, 520, 525–6, 560; BL, Add. MS 31116, fo. 141r-v.
38 *A&O*, i. 677; *CJ*, iv. 109–10, 127, 133, 134; *CSP Dom.* 1644–5, pp. 201, 283–4, 357–8, 391, 475–6.
39 *CJ*, iii. 404; BL, Add. MS 4771, fo. 27r-v.
40 BL, Add. MS 4782 (Committee for Irish Affairs, copy book), fo. 190r-v.
41 *CSP Dom.* 1644–5, p. 201.
42 Other subscribers included Captain Francis Speene, Michael Beresford, Lieutenant Colonel Walter Loftus, and Richard Wingfield. Broghill, Sir Arthur Loftus, Sir Charles Coote, Sir William Cole and John Davies also took the Covenant at this time. Bodl. MS Carte 14, fo. 425: committee for examinations certificate, 24 Apr. 1645; my thanks to Patrick Little for bringing this document to my attention.
43 Armstrong, 'Ireland at Westminster', p. 86.
44 TNA, SP 21/7, fos 241–2; Davies's propositions are found at ibid., SP 16/539/2, fos 202 and 204.
45 TNA, SP 21/7, fos 251, 257–8, 268.
46 TNA, SP 17/H, fos 170, 172, 173, 175r-v, 177–8v: account of Davies and others, certified 27 Feb. 1646; TNA, SP 21/7, fo. 259; *CJ*, iv. 15.
47 TNA, SP 21/8 (Committee of Both Kingdoms, day book Nov. 1644-July 1645), fos 13, 68, 72, 75, 89, 99; *CJ*, iv. 15.
48 TNA, SP 21/8, fos 19, 21, 36.
49 Ibid., fos 45–6, 47.
50 *CJ*, iii. 368, 370; BL, Harl. 165, fo. 279v.
51 PRONI, T707/1 (records of Carrickfergus), pp. 124, 126, 130; PRONI, D162/1 (Carrickfergus corporation), fos 40–2; B. McGrath, 'A biographical dictionary of the membership of the Irish House of Commons 1640–1641' (PhD thesis, Trinity College Dublin, 1998), pp. 127–8.
52 R.M. Young, *The Town Book of the Corporation of Belfast, 1613–1816* (Belfast, 1892), pp. 24, 249.
53 For further details on the Irish staple see J. Ohlmeyer & É. Ó Ciardha (eds), *The Irish Staple Books, 1596–1687* (Dublin, 1998).
54 *CJ*, ii. 391–2, 395; *LJ*, iv. 546; W.H. Coates, A.S. Young and V.F. Snow (eds), *The Private Journals of the Long Parliament, 3 January to 5 March 1642* (New Haven, 1982), pp. 147, 163, 165, 169–70.
55 BL, Add. MS 4771, fo. 29v.
56 Ibid., fos 29v, 30, 37-v, 38v, 44v.
57 Coote praised Davies, stating that had he not 'most kindly supplied me beyond that which was due on him, we had disbanded before now' (*HMC Egmont MSS*, i. 379).
58 Montgomery informed Sir Phillip Percivalle that Davies was 'your true friend' who worked tirelessly to argue against the assertion that Percivalle hindered

supplies to Ulster as his estates lay in Munster and Leinster. Montgomery also informed Percivalle that John Clotworthy 'esteems you highly' (ibid., pp. 358–9).

59 Fitzgerald deemed Davies to 'more generous than my great masters in Ireland, who requited me unworthily for my extraordinary fidelity and diligence' (ibid., pp. 342–3).
60 Ibid., pp. 338–9, 352–3.
61 Ibid., pp. 366, 370–1.
62 Ibid., pp. 336, 338.
63 Ibid., pp. 336, 337.
64 TNA, SP 21/8, fo. 13.
65 Ibid., fo. 17.
66 *CJ*, iii. 640; *A&O*, i. 531–3.
67 This is an estimate based in some cases on the surnames alone of some of the individuals. Davies's suppliers may have included Thomas Freeman, George Thoroughgood, Daniel Waldoe, Roger or Robert Smith, Richard Lasingby, Alderman Thomas Andrewes, John Potts and Captain Laurence Bromfield; other individuals listed may have had previous business associations with the most prominent adventurers, though this is unclear from the existing records. TNA, SP 16/539/3, fo. 124: list of merchants selling provisions for Ireland to Davies and others, Nov. 1645.
68 TNA, SP 16/539/3, fo. 212: orders of Commons, 15 July 1646; ibid., fos 214–16: accounts and vouchers, 23 July 1646; *CJ*, iv. 617; *CJ*, iii. 289; TNA, SP 16/539/2, fo. 90: order in Parliament, 26 Oct. 1643.
69 TNA, SP 21/20, fos 125–6: Committee of Both Kingdoms to treasurers at Grocers' Hall, 16 Apr. 1645; SP 21/8, fo. 221.
70 *CJ*, iv. 120–1.
71 TNA, SP 21/8, fo. 311.
72 Ibid., fo. 350.
73 *CJ*, iv. 191; *LJ*, vii. 469.
74 *CSP Ire.* 1633–47, p. 407; TNA, SP 21/21 (Committee of Both Kingdoms, entry book June–Oct. 1645), fo. 106.
75 *CSP Ire.* 1633–47, p. 412.
76 *CJ*, iv. 276.
77 *CJ*, iv. 282; *LJ*, vii. 592, 604.
78 This new ordinance stated that he would be paid £3,000 within one month, £3,750 the month after, and then the remaining £18,000 after that; it also provided for the payments of some of his other debts, including £9,045 for his supply of the Protestant armies in Ulster in 1642, and for £3,150 he owed to Maximillian Beard and Thomas Brown of Cheapside which should have come from the adventurers' fund, but never materialised (*LJ*, vii. 610–13, 776–83; *A&O*, i. 776–83; *CSP Dom.* 1625–49, p. 648).
79 *CJ*, iv. 276; *LJ*, vii. 657–8.
80 *CJ*, iv. 337, 341, 368
81 Ibid., pp. 337, 368.

82 Committee of Adventurers in London, *The State of the Irish Affairs for the Honourable Members of the Houses of Parliament* (1645), pp. 2–4, 6–8.
83 Ibid., pp. 2–4.
84 See TNA, SP 63/261 (Star Chamber Committee, minute book), fos 48v–9v for the Star Chamber committee's accounts relating to the 1644 assessment.
85 *The State of the Irish Affairs*, pp. 6–8, 14–16.
86 Ibid., pp. 16–18.
87 J. Peacey, 'Politics, accounts and propaganda in the Long Parliament', in Kyle and Peacey (eds), *Parliament at Work*, pp. 59–78.
88 TNA, SP 16/539/4 fos 132–5v: notes for proof of articles against Clotworthy and Davies, n.d.; this document is dated to be from 1647, but an extant copy from the committee of accounts records as part of another investigation by the council of state dates it from 19 April 1653 (TNA, SP 28/253B [box 1, part 2] unpaginated papers).
89 TNA, SP 28/253B [box 2, part 2], fos 18–19, 20, 21. 42–3, 45–6; SP 16/539/3 fo.115: certificate by William Jennings and Francis Smith, n.d. (1645); SP 16/540/3, fo. 280: papers concerning Clotworthy's accounts, n.d. (1646).
90 TNA, SP 16/539/4, fos 132, 133: notes for proofs of articles, n.d.; SP 16/539/2, fos 13, 32, 26v; *LJ*, v. 597, 598–9, 694, 696; *CJ*, ii. 956; *CJ*, iii. 564; *Analecta Hibernica*, iv. 46–7, 54–5, 57; TNA, SP 28/253B [box 1, part 2], fos 17–18; SP 28/253B [box 2, part 2], fos 1, 8–9, 23–4, 31–2, 43–4, 68, 69; SP 63/344, fo. 55; SP 18/1, fo. 166v: statement of George Wood to Council of State, 16 May 1649.
91 For the accusations against Clotworthy see TNA, SP 28/253B [box 1, part 2], fos 15–17, 19–21, 22, 27–8, 23–35; SP 28/253B [box 2, part 2], fos 15, 15–16, 22, 25, 26–7, 28, 29–30, 34, 37–8, 42–3, 50, 65, 68; SP 28/253B [box 1, part 5] unpaginated folio volume, entry dated 27 August 1646; SP 28/1B, fo. 329: earl of Leicester to Nicholas Loftus, 26 Jan. 1642; *CJ*, ii. 473; Coates, *D'Ewes*, pp. 119, 122; Bodl. MS Rawlinson D.932, fo. 12.
92 TNA, SP 16/539/4, fo. 135–v: notes of proofs of article; SP 28/253B [box 2, part 2], fos 75, 78, 79, 82–3, 87–8, 89, 90, 92, 93.
93 See for example the statement from Derry merchant Alexander Gearing who claimed that 'he was reputed to be worse than nought and owing many thousand pounds as reported and known generally in Carrickfergus'; TNA, SP 28/253B [box 2, part 2], fo. 96.
94 TNA, SP 16/540/3, fo. 280: papers concerning Clotworthy's accounts, n.d. (1646); SP 16/539/3, fo. 116: certificate by Daniel Prigg and others, 18 Aug. 1645; ibid., fo. 117: examination of Daniel Sprigg (*sic*) and others; ibid., fo. 120: examination of inspectors of clothes; ibid., fo. 121: examination of tailors; SP 28/253B [box 2, part 2], fos 73, 74, 75, 78, 79, 81, 82–3, 95.
95 TNA, SP 17/H, fos 168–80.
96 *HMC Egmont MSS*, i. 379.
97 Little, 'Irish Independents', pp. 947–58.
98 Anon., *The Members Justification* (1647).
99 *LJ*, viii. 441–2; TNA, SP 63/261, fo. 150; *CSP Dom.* 1625–49, p. 476, 738; TNA, SP 63/266 (Committee for Irish Affairs entry books, 1647–48), fo. 19; *CSP Ire.*

1633–47, pp. 478, 483, 484, 487, 491, 501–2, 503–4; TNA, SP 63/262 (Star Chamber Committee, minute books), fo. 110; SP 63/261, fos 145v, 158; SP 63/261, fos 164–5.
100 *HMC Egmont MSS*, i. 365–6.
101 Ibid., pp. 366, 370–1, 378–9.

5

The Irish Parliament after the rebellion, 1642–48

COLEMAN A. DENNEHY

Towards the end of the Restoration Parliament in Dublin in 1666, after a series of difficult conferences between the representatives of the Lords and the Commons, relatively convivial relations finally came to the end, as the members of the upper house abruptly left a conference with those from the lower house. It emerged later that the reason behind the fall-out was the right of the peers to sit while the Commons were meant to stand – an issue which caused umbrage between the houses throughout the early modern period.[1] At the breaking off of the intended free conference, the earl of Drogheda said: 'Gentlemen, you would all be lords', and Mr Adam Mollineux, MP for co. Longford, replied, 'Another rebellion may make us so, as well as a former made your ancestors.'[2]

This short exchange and the cheeky riposte well illustrate what is surely known about the very real effect that war can have on societies, the various social strata, governments, their functions and on constitutions. For if Charles Tilly made a point about war making states and states making wars, the same can surely be said about parliaments.[3] Indeed, this is nothing new to historians of parliament across most eras, particularly medieval parliaments.[4] It is certainly the case that the need to finance war is one factor, if not *the* single primary factor, explaining the growth of parliaments in medieval and early modern Ireland – as it is for virtually all other states at the time.[5] This would suggest, therefore, that the Irish wars of the 1640s, surely the most encompassing and far-reaching wars for several centuries on the island, would thus see a growth in the activity and influence of the Irish Parliament commensurate with the damage and destruction. After all, the Irish Parliament had played a large role in the attack on the government of Lord Deputy Wentworth in 1640–41, one that was organised in tandem with English political agitation at Westminster and while perhaps not playing a central role in the breakdown of relations in England the way the English Parliament did, it was certainly a central part in the development of the Irish theatre of conflict.[6]

In 1641, Lord Lambart (later earl of Cavan) highlighted his belief that 'if Poynings' Law be so understood as that Parliament can do nothing but pass bills, that is scarce a parliament'.[7] Surely he would have been even less impressed with a parliament that rarely even read a bill, such as the Irish Parliament during the mid-century civil wars. Although Lambart attended after the outbreak of fighting, being military governor of Dublin and thus usually in the vicinity, most of the membership of both houses fell away to a considerable extent. The decline in membership mirrored the decline in the amount of business that it undertook, certainly if the role of Parliament is interpreted so as to involve itself in great affairs of state and to play its part in the processing of legislation.

Perhaps it should not be surprising that almost all the history books, the chapters in collaborative collections and many references on, and to, the Irish Parliament refer to the parliamentary political event of the mid-seventeenth century crisis as the 'Irish Parliament, 1640–41'.[8] This is worthy of note, as the official Journals of Parliament – the day-to-day records of the House of Commons and the House of Lords – indicate that the institution in both of its constituent houses continued to meet until well into the late 1640s. It seems quite certain that those authors are aware of the continued meetings, but have not thought them worthy of attention, and considering the sessions that went before and the events played out in them, this is hardly surprising. There is little new in this. Historians will generally take account of causation and change, and historically dramatic moments will attract interest in ways that the less eventful do not. Even for those who study Parliament as an ongoing institution and less as a political event, most are probably willing to acknowledge that there are times when such dramatic periods can sometimes drive institutional change and therefore draw attention. As such, it is not surprising that the study of political stagnation, if the post-October 1641 Parliament is considered stagnant, does not seem all that important. However, there are many historians of the institution and the processes, for whom the work of Parliament in the 1640s is just as valid an example of procedure and procedural development as at any other time, and thus just as useful a source.

This chapter examines the nature of the Irish Parliament, how and why it sat through to 1648, and also what, if anything, might be learned from it about the tumultuous decade. It considers the work Parliament undertook, why it was kept sitting at all and to what extent this may have affected the development of the Irish institution at a time when parliaments in England and Scotland were developing at great speed with increasing degrees of autonomy to the point of being revolutionary, seeing themselves and their role in the state in a thoroughly different manner.[9]

In addition to historians' discrimination in favour of dramatic, violent change, the distinct lack of interest in the Irish Parliament after the outbreak of violence in October 1641 may be due a deficiency of source material. This is a well-worn and oft-used complaint in Irish history generally, but particularly for the parliamentary and legal historians of the middle ages and early modern period.[10] This following episode makes the cause for complaint all the more valid. In 1774 Michael Ignatius Duggan, a bookseller, agent and dealer in manuscripts, petitioned the Irish House of Commons.[11] Duggan indicated that he had come into possession of a manuscript of the *House of Commons Journals*, via Mary Kelly, widow of William, clerk to Sir Stephen Rice, chief baron of the exchequer under James II, and 'the petitioner is informed, they will be of use to this house, and is desirous to present it to them; and humbly hoping such recompense, as to the house shall seem meet'.[12] Indeed, Duggan was no stranger to missing manuscripts of Irish parliamentary Journals, as he had supplied a copy of the Irish *Commons' Journals* to Archbishop Robinson's Library at Armagh.[13] While in this case his source would appear to have been the aged widow of a Jacobite clerk, who would clearly have had access to the state repository, Bermingham's Tower in Dublin Castle, Duggan also had a close connection with John Lodge, deputy keeper of records in Bermingham's Tower, deputy clerk and keeper of rolls, later master of the rolls, to whom he left a number of items in his will.[14]

Although nothing is provable, it is interesting to note that a friend of the keeper of records, who dealt in missing manuscripts, made these finds and subsequently sold them back to the House of Commons. These were published in 1765 as an appendix to the printed Journals and subsequently included in all later editions from the third series onwards.[15] They cover the period from 16 November 1641 to 29 March 1647, and so if researchers look to either the first or second printed series of the *Commons' Journals*, both published before 1765, they might assume that Parliament did not sit in that period.[16] Several shorter sessions for the House of Lords are also missing, along with the important longer sessions from the prorogation of 4 March 1641 until 1 August 1642, although exactly where these journals disappeared to is unknown. The short and intermittent gatherings, coupled with the fact that the kingdom was in a bitter contest for survival, will probably have produced a laxity in record keeping, a standard that was low even by the Irish administration's already low standards.[17]

Indeed, the same issue concerns the record of legislation in the period. Many historians consulting the *Statutes at Large* will conclude that no legislation was passed in the 1640s after the outbreak of violence in October 1641. The official record for legislation for the reign of Charles I ends in 1641, with 15 Chas. I, c. 14 (*An act that this session of parliament shall not determine by his majesties royal assent to this and some other bills*), and continues thereafter with the introduction to the acts of Charles II's Parliament (1661–66).[18] Their assumption is largely correct, but there is one *Act for remitting to his majesty's Protestant subjects, and their adherents, all arrears of rent, services, compositions, first fruits and twentieth parts, due to his majesty at Michaelmas 1641, ever since, and at Easter 1645*, which passed the lower house in March 1645 and the Lords some time between then and 6 May 1645, when it received the royal assent.[19] It has not, it would appear, ever been designated with a regnal year or a chapter number, but presumably it would be 20 Chas. I, c. 1. While it is by no means an act of great importance, the fact that it is not included in the 1786 *Statutes at Large* conspires again to convince the reader that nothing of interest happened in Parliament during the period. Thus, for many historians, when they go to the two usually reliable points of contact for an initial study of Parliament – Journals and statutes – they will find little material of interest to political historians.

The sittings of the Irish Parliament after the eruption of violence in October 1641 until its automatic dissolution upon the demise of the crown on 30 January 1649 are shown in Table 2. It is difficult to gauge how well the peers attended. As a general rule, they did not attend as frequently as the Commons across the century. For example, in the previous Parliament of 1634–35, the Lords sat for a total of 78 days, as opposed to the Commons at 104. In the Restoration Parliament, the Commons also sat more frequently, 424 days, as compared with the peers' 266.[20] This is for the same reasons that are to be found in parliaments in less exceptional circumstances. The lower house was petitioned more than the upper, and bills were more often than not presented initially to the lower house to be passed, before being sent up to the Lords. Both of these create more work for the Commons than the peers. In addition, the Commons had a considerably larger and more active membership, so even though they were able to commit complex issues for discussion and decision to committee, the time spent on business in the Commons always took longer.

We know that attendance post-October 1641 was particularly poor, and for good reasons. Both Houses of Parliament adjourned themselves on 7 August 1641, with the intention of reconvening in November.[21] This was very much standard practice. The usual format for Parliament was a substantial session in May once the planting, lambing and calving had been dealt with, along with the assizes. By May the weather had improved making travel more comfortable, although obviously as communications improved with the passage of time, this would be less of a concern. The ending of the summer session would then allow for assizes in October and also harvesting in the autumn, which came ten days later than in the modern calendar. Thus many members had departed from Dublin and not returned for quite some time. However, it should also be remembered that with a significant number of members being place-men for the government – that is, office holders in the army or

Table 2 The length of sessions of the House of Commons

Sessions	Days sitting
9 November 1641–17 November 1641	3 days
11 January 1642–14 December 1642	24 days
20 April 1643	1 day
13 November 1643–18 December 1643	2 days
17 February 1644	1 day
6 April 1644–18 April 1644	11 days
6 May 1644	1 day
4 June 1644	1 day
11 July 1644	1 day
8 August 1644	1 day
5 September 1644	1 day
3 October 1644–31 October 1644	2 days
30 November 1644	1 day
20 January 1645	1 day
3 February 1645	1 day
17 February 1645	1 day
3 March 1645	1 day
17 March 1645–19 March 1645	3 days
30 April 1645–6 May 1645	3 days
20 May 1645	1 day
3 June 1645	1 day
1 July 1645	1 day
29 July 1645	1 day
26 August 1645	1 day
23 September 1645	1 day
21 October 1645	1 day
18 November 1645	1 day
24 January 1646	1 day
24 February 1646	1 day
2 May 1646	1 day
2 July 1646	1 day
27 August 1646	1 day
22 October 1646	1 day
7 November 1646	1 day
21 November 1646	1 day
30 November 1646	1 day
26 January 1647–18 June 1647	37 days
15 June 1648	1 day
38 sessions in total	115 days sitting in total

Source: CJI.

in administration who were also MPs – means that some may not have left. Indeed, for the same reasons, they may not have been regular attenders either.

From this point onwards, attendance was always slack, to say the least, although it was rarely at full capacity at any stage in the seventeenth century. The opening of Parliament or other days of great theatre, such as the giving of the royal assent or the arrival of a new lord lieutenant, would ensure a higher than average attendance in both houses, but there was never a complete complement of MPs or peers in attendance. Even then, it is quite likely that there were individuals among the peerage of Ireland who had no estate in the kingdom or any other connection, and were unlikely to have ever visited Parliament, or perhaps even the kingdom.[22] Such peers' proxies were under pressure from the 1630s onwards, as the executive's control over the exercise of proxies created a strong government interest in the house. Although in the 1634–35 Parliament attempts were made to force non-resident peers to purchase an estate in Ireland, this came to nothing, and the issue was voted a grievance in 1641.[23] After agreement with the king, it was settled that no more than two proxies could be held by each peer present, with this extended to three in the 1690s.[24] This may well have caused the subsequent lords justices (Sir William Parsons and Sir John Borlase) or the new lord lieutenant, the marquess of Ormond, to avoid being seen to control the house using proxies of peers with no genuine connection with the kingdom. However, as various peers departed, died or no longer attended, the proxy they held died too, so the original absent peer would remain unrepresented unless he registered another proxy, and with little activity in the house there may have been little point.

The reasons for the drops in attendance should be obvious: the initial outbreak of violence and the following bouts of violence and reciprocated actions meant that Ireland became very violent, very quickly. By the end of 1641, the rebellion had extended across the kingdom. During this time, and in the months that followed, many MPs and peers left the island as refugees to avoid the violence.[25] In addition, many other members of both houses had military and governmental responsibilities. Placing military, governmental, judicial or other state servants had long been governmental practice for controlling Parliament, particularly from the relatively newly created boroughs. If this were not the case before October 1641, then certainly after the outbreak of violence, there were more pressing matters to attend than sitting in Parliament with little business before it.[26] In addition, some joined the fighting, and others returned to their districts to try to preserve peace or their estates – mostly in a futile action. Catholic leaders, particularly the lawyers made a deep impression in the Catholic confederacy, as did some Catholic peers.[27] Obviously, once one became a member of one assembly, it was as good as impossible to be a member of its rival.

In any case, the Irish House of Commons decided by June 1642 to impose an oath of supremacy on its members. Although the English had passed a number of acts that would restrict Catholics, as crystallised in the second Test Act of 1678, Ireland had no religious test for entry to Parliament up to this point and indeed a Catholic majority in the lower house was only overturned for the first time in 1613.[28] The legality of this was dubious. In England, the move was based upon statute law, but the Irish Commons did not make mention of an act, and it is questionable whether the English act of 1609 or any others applied. It did not mention Ireland specifically, but then other acts were applied when it suited those in power. Certainly Westminster went on to bar Catholics from sitting in either house of the Irish Parliament by an English Act of Parliament in 1691, although this specifically did provide for Ireland.[29] In the early seventeenth century the Irish Parliament was swiftly moving towards self-regulation in this matter, in that the Commons decided on any issues of membership and disputed elections and not the government.[30] Despite royal orders to dispense with the 1642 oath, it continued in use as an obligatory test until the end of this Parliament – the last recorded mention was when Oliver Wheeler, Richard Kennedy and Oliver Walsh took it in June 1647.[31] The issue of an oath for the MPs was raised again when Parliament met after the restoration of Charles II, but was politely ignored by the executive and the lower house did seek not to antagonise a more Catholic-friendly monarch.[32] There is in this period no call for a judicial opinion on the matter and so, to a point, the fact that the Commons insisted upon the oath in the 1640s meant that it was legal, the Commons having already achieved self-regulation in matters of membership.

The Lords' house was a different matter. Whereas the Commons effectively became a Protestant-only gathering from mid-summer 1642 until its dissolution, the Lords made no such ruling, as far as can be ascertained. Although most Catholic peers either attended the Confederate Assembly at Kilkenny or stayed away from both, some Catholic peers did attend Parliament into the mid-1640s, although, owing to the fractured and incomplete nature of the Lords' Journals, it is difficult to ascertain exactly to what extent they were active. For the small number who did attend, they appear to have sat on committees, which would suggest ongoing involvement within the community of peers. Thomas Fitzwilliam, first Viscount Merrion, attended regularly and was active until the end of the record of the upper house (summer 1646).[33] Richard Nugent, second earl of Westmeath entered the house in April 1644 (introduced by Roscommon and Merrion).[34] He was less active and listed in 1645 as being fined for non-attendance to the tune of £100 (usually not paid by peers), and for fees to servants of the house.[35] Clanricarde was mentioned in the Journals as being fined for non-attendance, which would indicate that he was expected to sit and had access to parliamentary privilege, but the rare mentions of him relate to his failure to attend.[36] Westmeath was 'a late convert to the confederate cause', and indeed both Clanricarde and Merrion had formal and informal communications and negotiations with the Confederate Assembly, and the former sat on the Privy Council.[37] Of course, it is worth remembering that, even after the outbreak of violence, there remained a Catholic population within the city of Dublin for most of the 1640s. Whilst the usual accusations of dubious or split loyalties were levelled at them with increasing severity and regularity, it was not unknown to have Catholics in the midst of the city.[38]

One way to quantify the relative industry of both houses is by considering attendance rates. Obviously, attendance is not always necessarily an absolutely accurate guide to work rate, but in the absence of a more detailed record it can be a useful and largely indicative guide of a member's commitment to the work of the house. The figures for the House of Commons are based on divisions at various stages, usually when there was a contentious issue that warranted a formal division rather than a simple oral vote. The division required one side to leave the room to be counted, the other to remain. Thus with no opportunity to abstain, the number is accurate. The numbers for the Commons, meeting on the following days are shown in Table 3.

The Lords generally did not divide in Ireland, always giving an oral vote individually, with the most junior voting first. Their attendance record is noted by the occasional recording of individual attendance at the beginning of the record for each day in the Journals, both those who sat in person and those who sat by proxy – essentially, giving to another peer the responsibility of voting on one's behalf. The numbers for Lords are shown in Table 4 (present in person and without proxies, but not including the speaker who during this period was either the lord chancellor, Sir Richard Bolton or second justice of the king's bench, Sir William Ryves,[39] who replaced him as speaker of the upper house during the lord chancellor's impeachment).[40]

The Commons figures for November 1641 are relatively high compared to others as many Catholics were still sitting; most had not yet departed the

Table 3 Attendance levels of members of the House of Commons

Date of divisions	Members in attendance
17 November 1641	70
6 August 1642	34
18 December 1643	49
8 April 1644	56
18 April 1644	42
24 February 1646	32

Source: CJI.

Table 4 Attendance levels of members of the House of Lords

Date	Members in attendance
11 August 1642	14 (of which 7 are spiritual lords)
18 November 1642	9 (2)
6 April 1644	6 (2)
20 January 1645	10 (4)
3 February 1645	10 (4)
3 March 1645	10 (5)
20 May 1645	13 (6)
3 June 1645	13 (6)
24 February 1646	12 (7)
2 May 1646	8 (6)

Source: *LJI*.

house for neutrality or the confederate headquarters, or indeed had not yet been secluded by order of the lower house. From this point on, the numbers dip considerably lower than the potential 252 members for all of the reasons listed. There appears to be little else to say about attendance rates thereafter. The rate is almost consistently below 20 per cent of its potential number and there appears to be little recognisable trend thereafter, the Commons sitting in no particular pattern and generally only for a day or two at a time.

So too with the upper house: the overall total for attendance was much lower than the lower house due to the fact that it has a much lower potential number. Before the outbreak of violence, the official number of peers and spiritual lords was more than 120, but there was never that many in the house at any point over the century.[41] Although an elderly man might be less likely to become an MP, both bishops and lay peers were entitled to their writ of summons until their death. Thus age and infirmity was more of a factor in non-attendance by the membership than it would be in the Commons.[42] Interestingly, whereas bishops never totalled more than 24 in the seventeenth century, and therefore usually between a quarter and a fifth of the membership, in the statistics quoted above they usually make up considerable fraction of the overall house, much greater than in peace-time, and frequently represent a majority.[43] Such a strong episcopal presence, frequently closely aligned to the government's political strategy, at least in the seventeenth century, would have made for a more pliable House of Lords had the government engaged Parliament in a meaningful sense. However, had they actually engaged politically with Parliament post-October 1641, it is more likely that there would have been a larger lay peerage present.

Nowhere is this unwillingness to put serious political business before the Irish Parliament, nor Parliament's ability to grasp it, more obvious than in the case of legislation. Since 1495, with minor adaptations thereafter, the law on producing legislation in Ireland was that Parliament could only pass or reject legislation laid before it by the Dublin government, which had already been approved by the government in London. In theory, this meant that the government had firm control over the initiation and content of legislation. In the climate of the 1640s after the beginnings of the civil wars, particularly one in which both the Scottish and the English Parliaments were in open rebellion, it was unlikely that the executive was going to allow the Irish Parliament room to manoeuvre in terms of legislation, or indeed in any other matter. This would account for the dispersed and short sessions. However, there was some legislative activity in Ireland, although most is unknown and has effectively been disregarded by historians, perhaps with good reason.

To begin with the sole successful bill that was passed as an act *for remittal of rents, services, compositions, first fruits, and twentieth parts.* The Lords' Journals would appear to be inconsistent in their record for this act (despite an order by the speaker for enrolment and printing at this time[44]), but it is clear that it passed the Commons over two days, 17 and 18 March 1645, without committal.[45] It was immediately dispatched to the Lords and received the royal assent on 6 May. The relative speed of the passing would suggest the bill was not contentious, and indeed it would be likely that few would baulk at taking a drop in taxation, but this is not uncommon in the progress of Irish legislation generally. The full text, as with the other bills in the 1642–48 period, is not available, but its content seems to be concerned with remitting certain payments to the state.

For those bills that did not pass as acts, while some appear to have been scuppered by failing to get through in time, rather than being necessarily odious to the MPs, the fact that several were rejected (rather than not progressed) in consecutive order would suggest that political dissatisfaction was responsible. They may be addressed in two categories. The first are the four bills addressing the legal status of the Parliament. There are bills to confirm that the Parliament would not end upon the giving of the royal assent in 1642 and in 1647, and in the same years there were also bills to confirm the validity of the Parliament.[46] It is questionable whether such former acts were necessary, but as they were passed in most early modern parliaments with more than one session, so they were passed in the 1640s. The validity bills, although precise texts are not extant, probably addressed the impact the wars had on more normal constitutional arrangements. None of these bills appear to have made any progress in the upper house in 1642, and the record is not extant for 1647.

Some bills would appear to have had more substance to them in affecting practical change in the kingdom, had they made it past the Commons. Two related to jury composition: a bill 'that lessees in years, being worth in leases for years, and moveable goods and substance, to the clear value of £50 sterling, shall pass in trials'; a bill 'that men in cities, boroughs, and towns, which be clearly worth £40 in goods, shall pass in trials of murder'.[47] Again, without the text, the exact nature of the bills is impossible to ascertain, but it is most likely an attempt to enlarge the pool of possible jurors available to the courts, as was occasioned in later centuries.[48] Again relating to criminal law, a bill 'for explaining a statute made in the tenth year of King Henry VII, whereby murder of malice pretensed is made treason' moved through the Commons in November 1642, making it as far as committee stage, but no further.[49] What the nature of this amendment was is difficult to say, but considering the reluctance of the authorities and juries to pass a guilty verdict, owing to the especially harsh punishments in Ireland (hanging, drawing and quartering for males; burning for females, thereby preserving their modesty by not exposing their lower-half nakedness on the scaffold), it was quite possibly designed to give flexibility to the sentencing judge.[50] Finally, the lower house also considered a bill touching the power of testators, in devising their goods and chattels, reading it once in November 1642, rejected it after committal.[51]

Perhaps the most interesting is the singular attempt by the Commons, after the outbreak of violence, to initiate a heads of bill, a process more generally understood to be a development of the later seventeenth century.[52] Between 1 and 6 August 1642, the lower house read three times and committed a bill 'which they conceive necessary to be passed, to suspend a part of the statute, called Poynings' Act, concerning acts to be passed to abolish popery, and to attaint the rebels', subsequently sending it up to the Lords, very much in the fashion as if it were a bill.[53] At a conference between the houses concerning the 'draught of the act for abolishing popery, and for attainting the rebels', the Lords opined that the bill 'would be prejudicial to this kingdom, by admitting of the Parliament of England to be of force, to oblige us here, without being here confirmed'.[54] The objection to the influence of the English Parliament, and the time of the session in question, would seem to indicate that the English parliamentary influence was based around the passing of the Adventurers' Act in March 1642, and three ancilliary acts some months later.[55] Without the full text for these bills, it is difficult to elucidate the exact nature of the prospective legislation.

If one judges Parliament by the barometer of its ability and willingness to create law, and there may be good reason to counsel against such a perspective, there would be little activity. There was just one act that made a successful journey through both houses to be met on the other side by an assenting lord lieutenant. A total of nine bills were read in the house, plus one heads of bill – that is one which was initiated by the Commons and did not have the advance approbation by the king or the Irish Privy Council in advance, which would admittedly take more work than a regular bill, due to the drafting process. By way of comparison, the House of Lords in the mid-1630s averaged more than one bill a day (78 bills processed in 73 days, including 57 committals), whereas the post-1641 Parliament struggled to exceed one a year.[56] It is important to acknowledge the power of Poynings' Law, and by it the power of the executive to restrict legislative activity, despite the clear moves towards heads of bills in a fashion more common from the 1690s onwards. Because the executive did not bring any money bills before Parliament, whatever power the assembly had was neutered; in fact not only did it not raise any money, but its sole act reduced the tax raised on the kingdom. Partly because of this paltry amount of legislative business, and partly owing to the very fractured nature of gatherings – generally just a day or two at a time, attendance was equally poor.

All these facts would suggest that the Irish Parliament did very little from the time the violence began, yet it did sit for at least 115 days. So what did Parliament do, after the Commons moved from Dublin Castle to the Tholsel and the Lords to either the same venue, or possibly the Four Courts at Christ Church or the Convocation House at St Patrick's, from January 1642 onwards? And why was it kept in situ by the government when there was so little work before it, especially when one considers just how volatile and uncontrollable other parliaments in the archipelago had become?

In keeping with the trends established earlier in the same Parliament, partly as a political weapon but also in part as a genuine source of justice and the airing of grievances, the Irish Parliament continued to accept petitions of grievance from the public and its members alike. This would appear to have taken up a considerable amount of its time and its rate of work in this area would suggest that it did not stand out as being less committed, certainly when compared with the statistical portrayal of its legislative or attendance rates. Petitions, the most accessible way in which one can measure Parliament's defence of its members' privileges or the subject's rights generally, show an average rate in the seventeenth century of 1.277 per day (Table 5).

Table 5 Petitions presented to Parliament in the seventeenth century

House	Year	Days	Petitions	Average number per day
Commons	1613–15	60	33	0.550
Commons	1634–35	104	25	0.240
Lords	1634–35	73	12	0.164
Commons	1640–48	260	591	2.273
Lords	1640–48	116	140	1.207
Commons	1661–66	424	388	0.915
Lords	1661–66	266	475	1.786
Total		1303	1664	1.277

Source: LJI; CJI.

Extrapolating from the available record (never entirely complete) for the period post-October 1641 to the conclusion of the Parliament in the later 1640s, it would appear that a total of 213 petitions were submitted in the Commons over the course of 115 days. This would equate to an average of 1.85 petitons per day. For the Lords, in the more limited Journal source material, there are a total of 90 petitions for the 59 days' worth of record. This is an average of 1.53 petitions per day.

Table 5 shows that the overall rate is 1.277 petitions per day for the seventeenth century, where records are available. The mid-1630s Parliament is doubtless the one most under control of the executive – one where advance preparation was relatively high, and one which was carefully managed by the then lord deputy, Wentworth. Perhaps surprisingly and also perhaps as a direct result of his tight management, his next parliament was quite the opposite. After his departure to England in 1640, the Irish Parliament quickly emerged as the least well-managed Parliament of the century, putting a number of government-connected figures on trial and dismantling a number of unpopular policies.[57] A large part of this opposition strategy was to carefully manage petitions and to use the grievances as a launchpad for opposition. Some of these clearly continued even after Wentworth's execution and the outbreak of violence and can be considered high politics. For example, Patrick Plunkett, Lord Dunsany, petitioned several times relating to his confinement,[58] as did John Bramhall, bishop of Derry, in a successful effort to have the remaining charges against him dropped.[59]

Most other petitions concerned less controversial cases, as when William Hetherington petitioned the Commons for parliamentary protection from the suit of Christopher Weldon and Walter Cusack.[60] 'The petitions of divers of the Protestant inhabitants within the city and suburbs of Dublin, in the behalf of themselves and others concerning abatements of rents' was also read, and may well have been the origins of the sole bill that passed the Irish Parliament in this period.[61] It would also appear that the Irish House of Lords in the 1640s was more than a little cognisant of its responsibility as the formal apex of the justice system within the kingdom. They certainly heard some writs of error from the court of king's bench, such as *Verschoyle* v. *Hunt* (1644).[62] Indeed, soon after this case which was thrown out for the want of progress and failure to assign errors, the lord chancellor acquainted the House of Lords of 'divers writs of errors, returnable into this house'.[63] Exact classification of the nature of such expressions of grievance or call for justice (formal or somewhat less so) is difficult in a chapter such as this, as is the quantification of the number, but it would appear to comprise a wide range and was certainly plentiful in comparison to other parliaments. All this would suggest that for as much as the Parliament could not control how much time it spent sitting, nor, to an extent, what legislation it could pass, in areas such as petitions for grace, justice or favour, where it did have control, the Irish Parliament had a consistent workload throughout the period.

Although much of this chapter concentrates on the business Parliament undertook, or did not undertake, there were also political concerns relating to the continued presence of Parliament in the capital. In the first instance, as Robert Armstrong has noted, there was a certain degree of reassurance for the Protestant population in keeping Parliament in situ, albeit meeting only for short bursts of limited activity.[64] There is also little doubt that Parliament gave the Dublin regime a certain degree of legitimacy, in the same way as royal government and the courts did. The fact that the confederates had effectively established an alternative state to match their alternative power meant that lords justices and later the marquess of Ormond saw some value in keeping Parliament for the time being.[65] This, of course, could lead to problems, for although Parliament did lend a degree of legitimacy and reassurance to the population and to the state, it could be unpopular. For example it is very interesting to see prosecutions for breach of privilege for speaking in derogatory fashion about Parliament, asking 'will it ever be at an end', reflecting the commonplace dissatisfaction with parliamentary privilege when parliaments sat for too long.[66] This same episode revolved around a dispute between an MP and the provost marshal of the city, putting into strong relief the position of martial law versus parliamentary privilege.[67] Laurence Lambert, provost marshal general of Dublin assaulted Mr Thomas Johnson, an MP, dragging him out of his home by the hair exclaiming loudly that he had hung better Welshmen than Johnson.

There was clearly more to preserving Parliament than mere cosmetic reasons. What seems to be at least equally as important is that Parliament was kept alive to provide for legislation that never came before it. Ormond had prepared legislation in 1645 for 'avoiding all doubts concerning the validity of the late cessation' to provide protection for the interests of royalist soldiers and administrators. There was also an 'act declaring his majesty's grace and goodness', which appears to have been about the ability to provide security, estates and titles to Catholics and Protestants of wavering loyalties, who might then be persuaded to throw in their lot with Charles I and his adherents in Ireland and promote a peace.[68]

Although Parliament had the right to adjourn, which it did on occasion, the fundamental power of gathering and prorogation was held by the executive – in theory directly from the king, but this was generally devolved to his Dublin administration. Its continued existence and haphazard convening is therefore really down to the political powers in Dublin in particular, and to a lesser extent perhaps, Oxford. For example, when Patrick Darcy and a number of other Catholic MPs tried to effect contact with the northern rebels in November 1641, Parliament was prorogued very quickly afterwards.

This was almost certainly due to the reticence of Parsons and Borlase to have Parliament involved, and indeed perhaps to have a peace manifested with anything less than a Catholic defeat.[69] Once the Commons was effectively purged of Catholics from 1642 onwards, Ormond was slow to have meetings in 1643 for fear of criticism of the cessation,[70] but he did use it again in 1644 as it could be trusted to come out against the Covenant, as indeed it did.[71]

It is also the case that Parliament was mothballed throughout the 1640s for reasons of political potential. The well-informed were aware that at some point in the 1640s a peace would need to be formalised. As in both 1646 and in early 1649, the Irish Parliament was considered necessary to guarantee the peace and to pass legislation adapting the operation of Poynings' Law or perhaps passing a declaratory act.[72] As neither peace came to a real fruition in the course of time, it is difficult to say how it might have happened. For the second Ormond Peace, the king had been executed less than a fortnight after the peace had been agreed and so Parliament was dissolved on the death of the king. Obviously, this would create issues around membership. The upper house would also have to wait for the king's bench to vacate the outlawries of Catholic peers before they could be readmitted, something not eventually done until several months into the Restoration Parliament, the courts' term suspended until several important moves had been made by the Protestant community in Parliament.[73] Ormond's appointment of several bishops in the mid-1640s, politically reliable if somewhat Calvinist in their theology, would encourage a compliant Lords, one where the bishops could hold a working majority.

The Commons represented considerably larger problems. As Bríd McGrath shows in Chapter 6, the Commons held a series of by-elections to replace the secluded members who had deserted for the confederate camp or indeed were expelled due to the failure to take the oath. Should legislation necessitated by either peace treaty been put forward it may have seen some opposition in the lower house. Had Parliament been dissolved with a considerable majority of the island in confederate hands in 1646, the elections would surely have returned a strong Catholic majority to the Commons, which would likely have passed the provisions for the peace without difficulty. However, it would have served to weaken Dublin Castle, pushed many more Irish Protestants into the English parliamentary camp, and have had considerable repercussions in England.[74] Obviously a new Parliament in 1649 would necessitate sittings in either Dublin or Drogheda, but as Dublin was in the hands of the English Parliament, this could have been problematic.[75]

In short, as far as the political outlook stood, the Irish Parliament was to be kept to support matters deemed applicable for government and to pass legislation if necessary, but at the same time to be kept on a very short leash for fear of political action or opinion independent of the executive – for example, all of its prospective anti-Catholic legislation was thwarted each time by the executive for political reasons. Overall, it was just too dangerous to have yet another representative assembly acting in anything other than the most controlled fashion at this time, considering how things had gone in other parts of the archipelago.

The contact and interaction between Parliament and war is fascinating. In such situations the relative power and influence of Parliament grows, as it did in both Scotland and in England, to fill the vacuum created by the weakness of royal government. The Dublin Parliament remained relatively inactive and, as a general rule, was not involved in the political developments of the kingdom at war. This is partly because Dublin Castle did not ask the Irish Parliament to raise revenue for the war, nor did it allow it to sit for concentrated periods where either house could have shown political initiative. Had peace treaties survived to be put before Parliament, requiring legislation that might well have changed the Irish constitution in a major fashion, obviously the political responsibilities of, and interest in, Parliament would have grown considerably. For their part, the members of Parliament did not show much interest in attending to their representative responsibilities. However, as is seen by Parliament's record of dealing with petitions and the administration of justice, which was generally politically harmless, it was accessed by the community of the kingdom on a continual basis and showed an appetite and ability to dispatch its responsibilities.

NOTES

1 F.G. James, *Lords of the Ascendancy: the Irish House of Lords and its members, 1600–1800* (Dublin, 1995); J.H. Ohlmeyer, *Making Ireland English: the Irish aristocracy in the seventeenth century* (New Haven, 2012).
2 *LJI*, 16 July 1666.
3 C. Tilly, *Coercion, Capital, and European States, AD 990–1990* (Cambridge, Mass., 1990); See also, L.B. Kaspersen and J. Strandsbjerg (eds), *Does War make States? Investigations of Charles Tilly's historical sociology* (Cambridge, 2017).
4 P.T. Hoffmann and K. Norberg (eds), *Fiscal Crises, Liberty and Representative Government, 1450–1789* (Standford, 1994); J.F. Lydon, 'William of Windsor and the Irish Parliament', *EHR* 80 (1965), pp. 252–67; A. Marongiu, *Medieval Parliaments: a comparative study* (London, 1968); D. Stasavage, *States of Credit: size, power, and the development of European polities* (Princeton, 2011).
5 J.R. Maddicott, *The Origins of the English Parliament, 924–1327* (Oxford, 2010); H.G. Richards and G.O. Sayles, *The Irish Parliament in the Middle Ages* (Philadelphia, 1952), chapters 4, 5, 8.
6 J. McCafferty, '"To follow the late precedents of England": The Irish Impeachment Proceedings of 1641', in D.S. Greer and N.M. Dawson (eds), *Mysteries and Solutions in Irish Legal History: Irish Legal History Society discourses and other papers, 1996–1999* (Dublin, 2001), pp. 51–73.

7   NLI, MS 9607 (MS journal of Irish House of Lords, 1640–41), pp. 121–2.
8   A selection, by way of example, might be A. Clarke, *The Old English in Ireland, 1625–42* (2nd edn, Dublin, 2000); A. Clarke, 'Historical revision XVIII: The history of Poynings' Law, 1615–41', *IHS* 18 (1972–73); J. Kelly, *Poynings' Law and the making of Law in Ireland, 1660–1800* (Dublin, 2007); B. McGrath, 'The Irish Elections of 1640–1641', in C. Brady and J.H. Ohlmeyer (eds), *British Interventions in Early Modern Ireland* (Cambridge, 2005), pp. 186–206; M. Perceval-Maxwell, *The Outbreak of the Irish Rebellion of 1641* (Montreal, 1994).
9   For example, see C. Russell, *The Crisis of Parliaments: English history, 1509–1660* (Oxford, 1971); D.L. Smith, *The Stuart Parliaments, 1603–89* (London, 1999); J.R. Young, *The Scottish Parliament, 1639–1661: a political and constitutional analysis* (Edinburgh, 1996).
10 C.A. Dennehy, 'Institutional History and the Early Modern Irish State', in V. Carey, S. Covington and V. McGowan-Doyle (eds). *Early Modern Ireland: new sources, methods and perspectives* (New York, 2018).
11 M. Pollard, *Dictionary of Members of the Dublin Book Trade, 1550–1800* (Dublin, 2000), p. 171.
12 *CJI*, 4, 10 May 1764.
13 Armagh Public Library, MS P001497118; C.A. Dennehy, 'Surviving Sources for Irish Parliamentary History in the Seventeenth Century', *Parliaments, Estates and Representation* 30 (2010), pp. 129–43.
14 J.L.J. Hughes, *Patentee Officers in Ireland, 1173–1826, including High-Sheriffs, 1661–1684 and 1761–1816* (Dublin, 1960); T. O' Riordan, 'Lodge, John', *DIB*.
15 *An Appendix containing the Journals of the House of Commons of the Kingdom of Ireland, from the ninth day of November 1641, in the seventeenth year of the reign of King Charles the First, to the twenty-sixth day of March, 1647, exclusive* (Dublin, 1765).
16 H.D. Gribbon, *Journals of the Irish House of Commons: a list of the printings/editions* (unpublished memorandum: Belfast, c.1984). The author consulted this typed memorandum in University College Dublin Special Collections Library.
17 H.H. Wood, 'The destruction of the Public Records: the loss to Irish history', *An Irish Quarterly Review* 11 (1922), pp. 363–5.
18 *The Statutes at Large, passed in the Parliaments held in Ireland from the third year of Edward the Second, AD 1310 to the twenty sixth year of George the Third, AD 1786 inclusive* (20 vols, Dublin, 1786–1800), ii. 222–3.
19 *LJI*, 6 May 1645.
20 C.A. Dennehy, 'An administrative and legal history of the Irish Parliament, 1613–89' (PhD thesis, University College Dublin, 2011), pp. 71–2.
21 *CJI*, 4, 7 Aug. 1641.
22 H. Kearney, *Strafford in Ireland, 1633–41: a study in absolutism* (2nd edn, Cambridge, 1989), chapter 6; Ohlmeyer, *Making Ireland English*, chapter 2.
23 *LJI*, 26 July 1634, 13 Feb. 1641; TNA, SP259/14: resolution of the Irish House of Lords, 18 May 1641; SP260/1: answer of the king in council to the Irish grievances, 16 July 1641.
24 *LJI*, 10, 14 May and 11 June 1661; NLI, MS 2091: standing order 30.

25 J. Cope, *England and the 1641 Rebellion* (Woodbridge, 2009); J.R. Young, '"Escaping Massacre": refugees in Scotland in the aftermath of the 1641 Ulster rebellion', in D. Edwards, P. Lenihan and C. Tait (eds), *Age of Atrocity: violence and political conflict in early modern Ireland* (Dublin, 2007), pp. 219–41.
26 Kearney, *Strafford in Ireland*, p. 45.
27 J.H. Ohlmeyer, 'The Baronial context of the Irish Civil Wars', in J. Adamson (ed.), *The Civil Wars: politics and rebellion in the kingdoms of Charles I* (New York, 2008), pp. 106–24; Ó Siochrú, *Confederate Ireland.*, passim.
28 5 Eliz., c. 1, § XVI-XVII [Eng.]; 3 Jas. I, c. 4, § IV [Eng.]; 7 Jas. I, c. 6, § VIII [Eng.]; 30 Chas. II, St. 2, c. 1 [Eng.]; R.W. Perceval and P.D.G. Hayter, 'The Oath of Allegiance', *The Table* 33 (1964).
29 3 Will. & Mar., c. 2 [Eng.].
30 Dennehy, 'An administrative and legal history', pp. 264–5; For English examples, see the details of the Norfolk election in 1586; G.R. Elton, *The Tudor Constitution - documents and commentary* (Cambridge, 1960), pp. 275–7; Elton, *The Parliament of England, 1559–1581* (Cambridge, 1986), pp. 338–41.
31 *CJI*, 12 June 1647; Armstrong, *Protestant War*, p. 126.
32 *CJI*, 15 May 1661.
33 *LJI*, 2 May 1646; F.E. Ball, *A History of the County of Dublin: the people, parishes and antiquities from the earliest times to the close of the eighteenth century* (6 vols, Dublin, 1903), ii. 13.
34 *LJI*, 15 April 1644.
35 *LJI*, 4 June 1644, 29 July 1645; the exact figure is not available, but for Lord Broghill in 10 April 1644, William Roberts, Ulster king of arms noted having 'received for parliamentary fees of the Lord of Broghill by the hands of Sir Arthur Loftus' (£6 18s), Petworth House, MS 13,192, unfol; NLI, GO MS 1, 2, 4, 8, 14, 17, 50, 56, 95–6, 150, 200, 552–3: various fees relating to the peerage.
36 *LJI*, 4 June 1644.
37 Ó Siochrú, *Confederate Ireland*, p. 234.
38 D. Dickson, *Dublin: the making of a capital city* (London, 2014), pp. 65–9.
39 C.A. Dennehy, 'Speakers in the seventeenth-century Irish Parliament', in P. Seaward (ed.), *Speakers and the Speakership: presiding officers and the management of business from the middle ages to the twenty-first century* (Oxford, 2010), pp. 62–74.
40 The citation for all of the individual dates is *LJI*.
41 Kearney, *Strafford in Ireland*, p. 49.
42 James, *Lords of the Ascendancy*, chapter 9.
43 *LJI*, 2 May 1646; lords present, in person: archbishop of Dublin, earl of Kildare, Viscount Fitzwilliam of Merrion, bishops of Kildare, Down, Limerick, Elphin and Clonfert.
44 *LJI*, 17 Mar. 1645.
45 *CJI*, 17, 18 Mar. 1645.
46 *CJI*, 17, 18, 19 Nov. 1642, 2 June 1647.
47 *CJI*, 18 Nov. 1642, 12 Dec. 1642.
48 N. Garnham, *The Courts, Crime and the Criminal Law in Ireland, 1692–1760*

(Dublin, 1996), p. 135; N. Howlin, *Juries in Ireland: laypersons and law in the long nineteenth century* (Dublin, 2017), pp. 41–9; John H. Langbein, 'The English Criminal Trial Jury on the eve of the French Revolution', in A.P. Schioppa, *The Trial Jury in England, France, Germany, 1700-1900* (Berlin, 1987), pp. 13–39, at p. 25.

49 *CJI*, 18, 19 Nov. 1642; 10 Hen. VII, c. 21.
50 R. Dunlop, *Ireland under the Commonwealth* (2 vols, Manchester, 1913), i. 271; my thanks are due to Liam Hogan for drawing my attention to this reference.
51 *CJI*, 18 Nov. 1642, 14 Dec. 1642.
52 J. Kelly, *Poynings' Law and the making of Law in Ireland, 1660-1800* (Dublin, 2007), pp. 12–18.
53 *CJI*, 1, 3, 4, 6 Aug. 1642; *LJ Ire.*, 6 Aug. 1642.
54 *LJI*, 12 Aug. 1642.
55 16 Chas. I, cc. 33, 34, 35, 37 [Eng].
56 Dennehy, 'An administrative and legal history', p. 132.
57 Perceval-Maxwell, *Outbreak of the Irish Rebellion*, chapters 2–3, 5–6.
58 *LJI*, 16 Aug. 1642, 17 Nov. 1642, 17 Feb. 1644.
59 *LJI*, 20 Jan. 1645.
60 *CJI*, 17 Mar. 1645.
61 *CJI*, 9 Apr. 1644, *post-meridiem*.
62 *LJI*, 6, 13, 15, 18 Apr. 1644.
63 *LJI*, 12 Apr. 1644.
64 Armstrong, *Protestant War*, p. 101.
65 Ibid., p. 42.
66 *CJI*, 9 Aug. 1642.
67 A. McArdle, 'Power and authority: a comparative study of Martial Law in early Stuart Ireland, 1603–41' (PhD thesis, Trinity College Dublin, 2014).
68 TNA, SP 260/133; Ormond to the king, 22 Apr. 1645.
69 *CJI*, 17 Nov. 1641.
70 Armstrong, *Protestant War*, pp. 100–1.
71 *CJI*, 12, 13, 15 Apr. 1644.
72 A. Clarke, 'Patrick Darcy and the constitutional relationship between Ireland and Britain', in J.H. Ohlmeyer (ed), *Political Thought in Seventeenth-Century Ireland* (Cambridge, 2000), pp. 35–55, at pp. 49–50; M. Ó Siochrú, 'Catholic Confederates and the constitutional relationship between Ireland and England, 1641–1649', in Brady and Ohlmeyer (eds), *British Interventions*, pp. 207–29, at pp. 216–17.
73 *CSP Ire.* 1660-2, pp. 145 (22 Dec. 1660), 184 (15 Jan. 1661), 291–2 (3 Apr. 1661), 324–6 (6 May 1661), 335 (18 May 1661), 345 (3 June 1661); *LJI*, 9 May, 20 May, 5 July 1661; Oireachtas Library Ms. 8. H. 12: outlawries for treason issued from the king's bench in Ireland from 1640 to 1698.
74 Ó Siochrú, 'Catholic Confederates and the constitutional relationship', p. 216.
75 18 Edward IV, Session IV, c. VIII.

6

The recruiter returns to the Irish Parliament, 1642–48

BRÍD MCGRATH

An immediate consequence of the outbreak of the 1641 rebellion was to raise the question of whether the next session of the Irish Parliament, which had been adjourned on 7 August 1641 until the following 9 November, should proceed or not and, if so, for how long. In an attempt to control the increasingly volatile situation, the lords justice had issued proclamations denouncing the rebellion, proroguing Parliament, postponing the new law term and banishing all non-residents from Dublin – actions paralleled in Edinburgh, where a similar proclamation was issued in response to the difficult political situation there.[1] After protests by Catholic MPs such as Patrick Darcy and Geoffrey Browne, horrified by the rebellion and anxious to demonstrate their loyalty and ensure that Parliament had a role in dealing with the crisis and that its legislative programme, including bills to guarantee land titles, would proceed, the administration agreed that Parliament should meet as intended in brief session.[2] When MPs gathered on 9 November, in an atmosphere of intense intimidation, 'in regard the house was but thin, they adjourned themselves' for one week and met on 16 and 17 November. Parliament was then prorogued until 11 January 1642, when it assembled in the Tholsel (Guildhall) in Dublin, rather than Dublin Castle.[3]

This absence of Parliament was later cited by Richard Bellings as one of the reasons for the spread of the rebellion, as it left the majority Roman Catholic population without a forum in which to express their grievances and contribute to a peaceful resolution of the situation. Equally importantly it dashed any hope of a legislative means of securing their land titles, as promised in the Graces.[4] As Ó Siochrú noted, 'the decision of the lords justices … to prorogue the Parliament that same day fatally undermined any efforts at reconciliation, leaving the Catholics of the Pale isolated and vulnerable. In the circumstances, they had little alternative but to seek some form of accommodation with the rebels.'[5]

Very little official business was carried out during the November sittings, although Sir Phelim O'Neill, Rory Maguire and Philip O'Reilly were expelled from Parliament for their role in the rebellion and the Commons ordered writs for their replacement. Again, no serious business was recorded as being carried out on 11 January 1642 when only five MPs, all Protestant, were listed as present, in addition to the Speaker, Sir Maurice Eustace, although this may not reflect the actual attendance; instead of dealing with legislation or public affairs, the Commons was largely concerned with St Anne's Guild and the private concerns of two of the five MPs, brothers John and Robert Bysse.[6]

Events in England and Ireland and the deep mutual suspicion between both sides in Ireland polarised the situation. Confusion reigned, and even contemporaries were unclear as to the sequence of events.[7] Despite attempts by the Catholic lords Mountgarrett, Gormanston and Costello to retrieve the situation, the rebellion spread throughout Ireland and the Catholics were establishing an alternative form of government, including a quasi-parliament, the General Assembly which met in Kilkenny between October 24 and 21 November 1642.[8] As Susan Lentz puts it, by 21 June 1642, when the Irish Parliament met again, it

> had already been transformed by distrust and fear. Rather than becoming an instrument to aid in the suppression of the rebellion, as many members had proposed in November 1641, it was viewed by the Irish government, the English Parliament and the crown as an undependable factor in Irish affairs, as a possible threat, or even a danger ... Irish Protestants were thus left with little hope of succor and the rebels were left with nothing to lose.[9]

On 21 June, MPs established a committee, to report the following day, to examine which members were in rebellion, and the privy councillor Sir George Wentworth, Strafford's brother, was reinstated as burgess for Kildare from which he had been removed on 5 March 1641. The committee, which came prepared and informed, punctually reported its findings and MPs expelled forty-one Catholic members who were 'either in open rebellion or stand indicted of high treason' and ordered writs for their replacement; as these included O'Neill, Maguire and O'Reilly, the November orders had clearly not been followed. MPs also declared that no MP could continue to sit without taking the oath of supremacy openly in the house, that all other absent MPs who had no role in the rebellion, and any returned in future, should also publicly take the oath, effectively excluding Catholics. Implicitly recognising they had no authority to make this order, they appointed a committee to draft a bill to that effect to be sent to England for certification under the great seal, and passed as a law in the Irish Parliament. Catholic peers continued to sit in the House of Lords. The house again considered St Anne's Guild's affairs and adjourned to 1 August.

While historians have noted the expulsions, most have not drawn the obvious inference that the Irish Parliament continued to sit, and its continued meeting has been largely ignored, partly because the Journals for 16 November 1641 to 25 March 1647 were missing when the first edition of the *Commons Journals* was published in 1753, although they were subsequently printed in the 1796 edition.[10] Lentz's thesis remains the only study of the institution during this period, although Aidan Clarke noted the presence of the 'rump' Irish Parliament and Robert Armstrong also discusses its work.[11]

The original writs of return were destroyed in the 1922 Public Record Office fire, but, despite the paucity of sources for the Irish Commons' membership and proceedings during this period, it is possible to piece together a picture of its composition, albeit one that is certainly incomplete.[12] While the *Commons Journals* repeatedly refer to the house's very thin attendance, they record the continued if intermittent and mainly infrequent attendance at some point of at least 86 MPs returned before November 1641. In addition, working from the original writs of return, where they existed, John Lodge recorded 68 returns between 1642 and 1647 although the names of only 58 of the new MPs for those constituencies are given. The Journals provide the names of a further 29 men from unidentified constituencies, giving a total of 87 identified recruiter MPs. This is probably an underestimate of their numbers, but the state of the returns is even more chaotic than for the 1634 Parliament or the original 1640 elections, and there is a small number of inaccuracies in names given in the Journals and Francis Moore and Raphael Hunt are listed as returned in both 1642 and 1644.[13] What is certain is that between January 1642 and 1648 at least 173 MPs, almost all Protestant, attended, members were replaced, generally by returns rather than elections, all for Leinster seats, and some business was conducted, albeit very little legislation.

Given the confusion in returns, the figures are based only on individual MPs' first recorded return. The majority of returns were made in 1642, when 41 new MPs are first noticed, followed by 5, 17, 4, 6 and 16 respectively in the following five years; these figures are presented with caution, as, where the date of a return is unknown, the date of the MP's first appearance in the house is given and Hunt and Francis Moore are included for both 1642 and 1644, in this table only.

The large number of returns for 1642 is understandable, given the 41 members expelled for being in rebellion on 22 June 1642, the further 6 deemed to have excluded themselves on 6 August 1642, those, numbering at least 37, who died from natural causes or in warfare, resigned, succeeded to peerages (Robert and James Dillon and Henry Moore) and those, especially part of Strafford's circle, who left Ireland.[14] On the other hand, two former MPs who had resigned or been expelled were ordered to continue membership (Wentworth and Sir Francis Butler for Derry City (2 August 1642)).

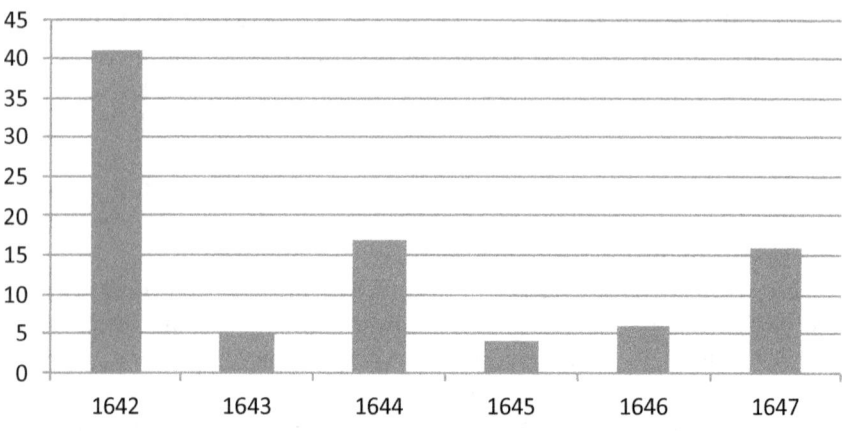

Figure 2 Known returns by year of first mention
Sources: R. Lascelles, *Liber Munerum Publicorum Hiberniae* (2 vols, 1824), ii, part 1, p. 1ff; *CJI*

All twenty-four MPs in the house on 22 June 1642 took the oath, only one of whom, the Dublin-based Dutch merchant Theodore Schout, was a new MP, although his constituency has not been identified; a private bill for his naturalisation passed in October 1640 made him eligible for membership of the Commons.[15] No other returns appear to have taken place by then, as Sir John Veele wrote to the MP William Cadogan on 22 June, making no mention of his membership of the Commons.[16] A series of returns was immediately made: Veele first appears on 1 August when he and Roger Moore (both from unidentified constituencies) were added to an expanded Committee of Privileges, and a further twenty-four MPs took the oath, nine of them newly returned (Sir John Temple and Thomas Ashe (Meath), Christopher Huetson and Charles Forster (Swords), Philip Lord Lisle (Louth), Sir Thomas Lucas (Drogheda), Henry Warren (Kildare), and Sylvester Kennedy and John Newman from unknown constituencies. In addition, Lodge records the returns of John Hatch (Dundalk), Alexander Burrows (Kildare town), William Flower and Thomas Leigh (Ballinakill), Walter Chambre (Old Leighlin), and William Ball (Kells), William Whyte and Walter Harding (Navan), George Graham (Grymes) (Queen's County), James White and George Peisley (Trim) and Ralph Wallis (Athboy). Lisle should not have taken the oath on 1 August, as his return, together with Lawrence Crawford's, was dated two days later, the day after Francis Moore's return for Dundalk, clear evidence of a return, rather than an election.[17] Three more returns are recorded for that month, Sir John Sherlock, the conforming son of the wealthy old English merchant, Christopher (MP for Naas, 1613–42)[18] replacing Peter Barnwall for Dublin County, Edmund Keating for NewcastleLyons (for Dongan or Talbot) and James Laughlin for Banagher for Jacob Lovell, who died at the siege of Drogheda in October 1641;

Captain Michael Jones, constituency unknown, took the oath on 3 August. Again, little business was undertaken, apart from discussing St Anne's Guild's affairs. The house adjourned until November, when Thomas Eustace, Mathew Ford, John Lewis, John Stoughton, Thomas Wakefield and John Whyte are first named in the Journals, although they may have been returned earlier; their constituencies are unknown.

On 13 December 1642, a committee was appointed to assess the membership and attendance of the Parliament and order writs for replacements; despite this, only five new MPs appear in 1643, Robert Kennedy, Thomas Coote, William Colley, Simon Lutterell and Terence McGrath for Kildare town, Trim, King's, Meath and Queen's counties respectively. John Hoyte (Dundalk), Thomas Trafford (Trim), Arthur Whyte (NewcastleLyons), Gerard and Francis Moore (Louth), Hunt (Ardee), Edward Trevor (Carlingford) and Henry Gilbert (Maryborough) and George Lane, John Harrison, Thomas Mapother, Charles Ryves, Daniel Foster, Thomas Whyte, Erasmus Burrows, Walter Plunkett, Charles Leigh, for unidentified constituencies, were all returned in 1644. In 1645 Robert Dixon (Bannagher), Patrick Tallant (Kells), Joshua Carpenter (Wicklow town) and Henry Jones were returned, followed in 1646 by Peter Wybrants (Old Leighlin), William Sacheverell (Wexford), Robert Cusack (Philipstown), William Peisley (King's County), Francis Edgeworth (Longford) and William Sandes (unidentified seat), despite the latter's position as deputy clerk of the Commons. Finally, Thomas Armstrong (co. Dublin), Oliver Wheeler and Richard Kennedy (Mullingar), Francis Barrington (Queen's), Robert Newcomen (Longford), Henry Kenny and Cosny Molloy (Newcastlelyons), Richard Lambert (Kilbeggan), Oliver Walsh (Fore), Thomas Clarke, Thomas Hea, ____ Bolt, ____ Glaughton, James Grace, John Newcomen and Gilbert Rawson were all returned in 1647.

In theory these elections were conducted in the normal way. Sheriffs were responsible for the returns from their counties and mayors, sovereigns and portreeves arranged elections in their towns; writs of return were completed by the returning officer and signed by a number of the electors and forwarded to the sheriff who delivered the counties' writs to the Chancery. In some cases, 'blank' returns were sent by the returning officer to an influential man, completed and endorsed by electors, but with space for that man to insert the name of his choice as MP. Given the upheaval of the times, the lack of sheriffs to undertake returns and the defections of so many towns, it is unsurprising that most counties did not hold elections or make returns and many expelled, deceased or lapsed members were not replaced. Where sheriffs were in control of at least part of their counties, they were able to manage returns, if not elections, but this was not the case in most of Ireland. In 1642 Westmeath's sheriff, Edward Tuite, and eleven Catholic freeholders remained loyal to the administration, but they may not have been prepared or able to make a return;

both knights were expelled on 22 June, but no return is recorded until 1647.[19] Erasmus Burrows, returned in 1644, was sheriff of Kildare in 1642, when he returned his brother Alexander for Kildare town, the local Henry Warren for the County and Dr Dudley Loftus for Naas. The following year Robert Kennedy was returned to replace Alexander.

Louth's sheriff is unidentified but the 1642 returns follow a clear pattern and were probably managed by Robert Bysse, recorder of Drogheda and MP for Roscommon town, and Sir Henry Tichbourne, privy councillor, governor of Drogheda, and, from April 1642, lord justice. Lodge records Hatch's return for Dundalk on 1 July, and Francis Moore's return just one month later, followed the next day by the soldiers Lisle and Crawford. When the other Drogheda MP, Worsley Brice, repeatedly avoided taking the oath of supremacy, he was replaced by the town clerk Richard Batten, who, with Hatch was described in 1645 as having 'a great interest with the discontented inhabitants of Drogheda'.[20] By 1644 Lisle and Crawford were based in England and expelled from the house, being replaced by Lord Drogheda's sons, Francis and Gerard Moore, even though Francis had already been returned in 1642; Raphael Hunt was recorded as returned from Ardee, despite having been listed as an MP for an unidentified constituency in 1642. Finally, Edward Trevor, son of the deceased privy councillor and brother of Marcus, MP for Downpatrick, was returned for Carlingford in 1644.

The Meath returns are easier to explain; a transcript survives of Ralph Wallis's return for Athboy on 28 July 1642, which is highly suggestive of the method of other returns.[21] Written, signed and sealed by Arthur Loftus, MP for Wexford and sheriff of Meath (a position he held illegally, as returning officers were barred from being MPs), it made no pretence of an election having been conducted by the proper returning officer, the portreeve, and was endorsed by only three men, two with local connections and the third linked only with Loftus's home place of Rathfarnham. On 23 July Loftus returned Temple, the Master of the Rolls, and Ashe for Meath; it would not have been possible to conduct an election locally, although the county returns might have been endorsed by Dublin-based freeholders of land in Meath. Five days later, Loftus returned Wallis, two MPs for Navan and one for Kells and three days later, for both Trim seats. Clearly, all were filled by Loftus without elections.

The 1642 returns demonstrated the difficulties in holding elections and the widespread use of making returns without elections. However, some locally conducted elections did occur, as the consternation displayed on the return of the suspected Catholics Terence McGrath and Simon Luttrell in 1643 demonstrates. Audley Mervyn anticipated filling vacant seats near Derry in 1645 and valued the credibility that genuine elections would provide.[22] When Tallant appeared in the house 19 May 1647, he was described as 'elected, and returned a burgess from Kells'. However, the vast majority of returns were at best legally dubious; some were illegal and contentious. On 9 April 1644, the Queen's County freeholders petitioned the Commons objecting to McGrath's election and in November 1644 Arthur Whyte's return for Newcastle was deemed invalid. On 21 October 1645 Robert Kennedy, MP and sheriff of Wicklow, objected to Joshua Carpenter's return for Wicklow town, arranged by Ormond in support of the Wentworths' interest, as 'no writ came into his hands'. Difficulties increased over time until on 18 May 1647 the Commons ordered that 'all those who are sheriffs, and are either absent, dead, or otherwise' be replaced and that sheriffs be appointed to fourteen named counties, all outside Leinster; this prompted the return of Wheeler, Walsh and Robert Kennedy, all for Westmeath constituencies and possibly John Newcomen and James Grace. The increasing reluctance to replace members suggests a clear policy, rather than carelessness or lassitude.

The Irish Commons moved quickly to recruit replacements; the English Commons was a great deal slower to take such action, even allowing for the rapid spread of the rebellion in Ireland. The question of electing new members to replace deceased MPs and 'disabled' royalists was raised in the English Commons several times in 1644 and the first writs to replace members were issued on 21 August 1645 and frequently thereafter.[23]

Expelling Catholics excluded them from any role in either managing the country or its settlement and the rush to exclude in 1642 took place at a time when Protestant MPs were anxious to control the house and cement their own positions. Despite the wholesale expulsions in 1642, care was taken to ensure that only those known to be in rebellion were excluded. Six Catholics were given repeated opportunities to attend Parliament and only expelled on their continued absence. Brice was only excluded after repeatedly failing to attend the house or swear the oath locally. Other Catholics known to be neutral, like John Fitzgerald and Nicholas Barnwall, were not expelled, and Alexander Hope, Edward Petitt and Patrick Barnwall were only replaced in 1647.[24] It is curious that many seats remained unfilled. It was, perhaps, more important to exclude Catholics than to replace them.

The quantity of 1642 returns makes it hard to discern a unified electoral strategy, but a number of features of the returns are noteworthy and demonstrate different influences. The return of privy councillors Temple and Lucas enhanced the administration's parliamentary liaison and control; Ormond's concern to protect the Wentworths' interests was demonstrated through George Wentworth and Butler's reinstatements, and the returns of Strafford's associates George, Francis and, later, William, Peisley and Carpenter; Lord Lieutenant Leicester's interests were served by the returns of his son Lisle, his very close family friend Temple and Falkland's former secretary and Temple's brother-in-law Veele. Temple's indissoluble friendship with Leicester's family went back to at least 1587, when his father William had been Sir Philip Sidney's secretary at Zutphen; Sidney had left William, later provost of Trinity College Dublin (which he represented in the 1613 Irish Parliament), an annuity of £30. John maintained the closest friendship with the Sidneys; his wife had died at Penshurst, where Lady Leicester had consoled him and Temple had been involved in negotiating Leicester's appointment as lord lieutenant of Ireland; after Temple left Ireland in 1644, Lisle arranged for his election for the English seat of Chichester.[25] The master of the Ordnance, Sir John Borlace, would also have been interested in the return of so many soldiers, including Lisle, Crawford, Lucas, Burrows, Flower, Chambre and Graham. No return suggests any Boyle or Thomond interests.

All the known returns are from Leinster; all Meath's MPs were replaced in 1642, and there were returns also from Louth, Dublin, Kildare, Carlow, Queen's and King's counties. While he sat for a Meath constituency, Temple's interests were in Carlow and he may have been the hand behind the returns of the unidentified MP for Carlow County and Chambre for Old Leighlin. Interestingly, only one return is recorded for Wexford (Sacheverell), despite nine expulsions. There are no recorded replacements for deceased MPs (e.g. Edmund Cossens for Coleraine), even when Mervyn considered it possible.[26] On 15 August 1642 the Commons questioned the clerk of the hanaper about returns and vacancies, implying a tardiness in the chancery.

Some Meath recruiters formed a tightly linked group: James White, eldest son of Walter White, MP in 1613 and 1634, was brother-in-law of Ashe, Harding and the existing MP Bryan Jones.[27] Equally interesting is the connection with St Anne's Guild in Dublin, whose associates included the recruiter MP Ball, his father Robert and father-in-law Robert Usher, Henry and Richard Ashe, Dixon and the MPs Richard Barry and the Bysses.[28] These and other returns of so many Dublin merchants highlight their determination to protect their own interests, including control of St Anne's Guild, which had long been a controversial issue. Strafford's over-enthusiastic campaign to ensure the guild's substantial rents should benefit Protestant clergy was cited as one of the four causes of his downfall.[29] In 1638 he preremptorily installed his own nominees to the guild but the old Dublin merchant families who controlled the city council and its trade were determined to hold on to their traditional rights, and they included the new MPs Charles Forster and his brother-in-law Huetson, Dixon, the Kennedies and Whites, Ashe, Ball (and his Usher in-laws), and current MPs Nicholas Loftus and the Bysses. This dispute between Protestant clergy and the guild, which fought tenaciously for its rights, occupied a great deal of the Commons' business during this period. At the time of his return, Ball was the guild's warden, responsible for pursuing the fight and managing the money raised for that purpose; he was re-elected warden for the following two years.[30]

The Bysses were not merely closely related to many of these merchants; they were recorders of Dublin and Drogheda and while studying at Lincoln's Inn had acted as manucaptors (guarantors) to many of their fellow students, including Ball, Sylvester Kennedy, Michael Jones, and Ford's son Nicholas. At least five other recruiter MPs (Temple, Walter Plunkett, Newman, Cusack and Richard Kennedy) had been fellow students at Lincoln's Inn, as had the Speaker, Sir Maurice Eustace, who had been manucaptor to John Bysse and Temple, and many sitting MPs and their relatives, including Roger Brereton, MP for Old Leighlin.[31] Speaker Eustace and Brereton were both paid by St Anne's Guild for legal advice on its case in Parliament in 1643 and 1644, despite the obvious conflict of interest.[32] Other mercantile interests were represented. Schout's return (and later that of his brother-in-law Wybrants), supports Sir John Clotworthy's assertion in the English Parliament that Dutch merchants would contribute to sorting Ireland; Dublin merchants were critical suppliers for Dublin Castle.[33]

It is difficult to establish recruiters' social status: titles are often not given in the records, men with multiple titles were always accorded the highest one (e.g. esquire and gentleman outranked alderman) and in time of war men who would usually have been listed as esquire or gentleman had military titles which were always used, unless they were knights, baronets or lords. There appeared to be a tendency to give Englishmen, even those without coats of arms, the title esquire. Titles, where they can be established, are given as at the time of returns; thus Erasmus Burrows who became a baronet in 1646 is listed as captain. Despite these difficulties, some analysis of social status is possible; the largest number of recruiters (35) were described as 'esquire'; 15 men's titles could not be established; 9 were soldiers, 8 knights and one a baronet at the time of their return, 4 were merchants, 3 aldermen and 7 were described as 'gent'; Loftus was a doctor. Four (Lisle, the Moores and Lambert) were peers' sons (see Figure 3).

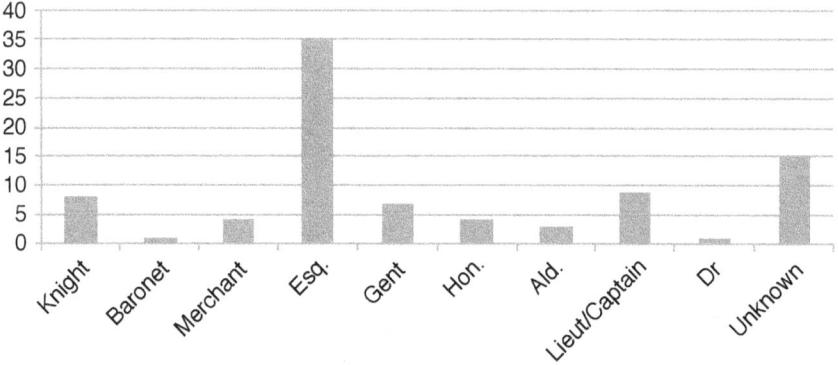

Figure 3 Social status of recruiter MPs
Source: B. McGrath, Data-set of recruiters returns, unpublished

There were notably fewer merchants and lawyers, and more soldiers and minor crown officials than usual in Irish Parliaments. Excluding Catholics disfranchised their staple constituencies of gentry, lawyers and merchants and opened space for more minor officials based in Dublin and available to sit in the Commons, especially since their workload was reduced by the war and the effective confederate government. The large number of Catholic lawyers, gentry and merchants involved in the Confederation left fewer men of that calibre and status available for Parliament.[34] As the civil war progressed, men moved to England, leaving the Parliament in the hands of lower-status men, with an inferior level of education, commercial knowledge and negotiating capacity.

Nevertheless, many came from the usual strata of society for Irish MPs; the Dublin merchants, Dudley Loftus, the privy councillors, the lawyer John Lewis, the gentry and peers' sons and Ormond's secretary Lane were certainly of the usual standard. Three recruiters were former MPs (Colley, Carpenter and William Peisley); at least six were sons of former MPs (Gilbert, Coote, Rawson, Ryves, Dudley Loftus and Trevor) and nine later sat in the 1659 Convention which was instrumental in restoring the monarchy in Ireland (Gilbert, Coote, Barrington, Rawson, Francis Peisley, Ryves, Plunkett, Dudley Loftus and Richard Kennedy).

The ethnic background of the new MPs is, perhaps, surprising: while 62 per cent were New English, less than one-fifth (17 per cent) were Old English; 8 per cent were of Gaelic origin (including the highly Anglicised Kennedys), 2 per cent were Dutch and 1 per cent each were Scottish and Welsh; the ethnic origins of nine (10 per cent) are unknown (Figure 4). These figures for the New English do not distinguish between those, such as Ashe, Chambre, Flower, Harding, Peisley, Loftus, Temple and the Burrows and Moores, whose families had been based in Ireland for some decades, and those recently arrived; the balance was overwhelmingly in favour of those settled for at least two generations, with only Armstrong, Batten, Carpenter, Hatch, Lane, Lisle, Lucas, Veele, Wakefield and Wallis, and possibly Bolt, Clarke, Hea, and Hunt being first generation New English; at least five of those had been in Ireland for at least ten years. All the convention members were at least second-generation new English, except for the natives, Plunkett and Kennedy.

Politically, the 1642 returns display diverse interests but no divisions. One year later the situation was very different. The developing civil war in England forced men there and in Ireland to choose to support the king or Parliament; more problematically, it was increasingly difficult for Irish Protestants to arrange for, or receive, help from England, and Ormond, lord lieutenant from 13 November 1643, was placed in the invidious position of being required to negotiate first a cessation of arms and then a peace treaty with the confeder-

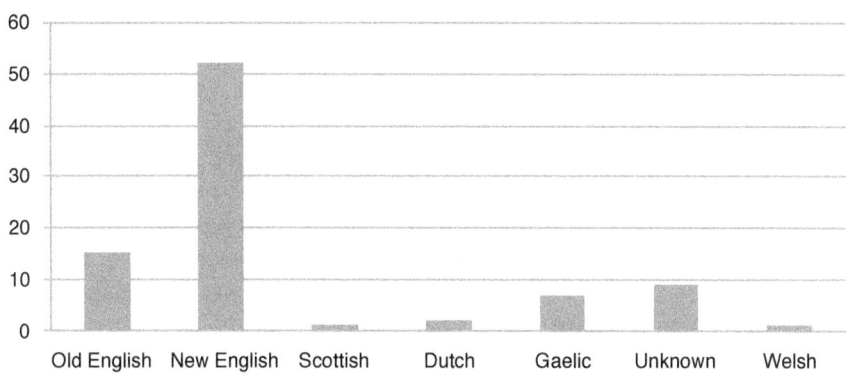

Figure 4 Ethnic origin of recruiter MPs
Source: B. McGrath, Data-set of recruiters returns, unpublished

ates, which it would be virtually impossible to persuade the Irish Parliament to endorse.

The cessation, agreed in September 1643 caused deep divisions in the administration and MPs were as divided as the rest of the population:

> the people of Ireland (who took a liberty at the uncertainty of affairs) were strangely divided, whether the cessation should be concluded or no. Some (who were sensibly touched with the injuries and cruelties of the rebels) could not brook it; others (hoping for their advantage by the change) daily expected it, whilst the city (in general) being burdened with taxes, quartering of soldiers etc, having no hopes of relief from abroad, willingly hearkened to their freedom: so as now the strong affections which had been commonly born against the rebels began to wither into an indifferency, and the course which had been then took to weather out the resolute, either for despair or terror humbled many, and as interest lay, several resolved what party to take in England, upon the conclusion of the cessation.

There were implications also for the Parliament:

> the consequences of dissolving the Parliament were not in the least in consideration at the council board, nor was there anything more desired by the rebels, who thereby hoped to be reseated in a new Parliament, which they questioned not to manage to their own ends and advantage.[35]

The administration splintered and the Protestant population became increasingly divided and open to extreme measures. The earl of Clanricarde ascribed Sir William Parsons, Temple, Sir Adam Loftus and Sir Robert Meredith's opposition to their having 'more regard to private spleen and particular interests than the general advantage gained to your majesty's service thereby'.[36] Nor were they alone. The November 1643 petition of Protestant subjects to the king opposing the cessation was signed by thirty-one current

MPs, and the Irish Parliament issued a remonstrance in similar terms; Ormond prorogued the Parliament in response. Six other signatories (Henry Jones, Wybrants, Erasmus Burrows, Wheeler, Forster and Kenny) subsequently became MPs.[37]

The cessation and the deepening divisions in England caused a number of Irish MPs to move to England to fight and to attempt to preserve their positions there, including Crawford, Richard FitzGerald (who remained there as agent), Lisle, Maule, Somers, Temple and Waller. Inevitably, the tensions appeared also in the Irish Commons. While the confederates were anxious that a new Parliament be called, which could approve a treaty, Ormond opposed this. As Parliaments could only be summoned by the king, and legislation only considered after it had been certified by the English Privy Council, while the Commons sat it had little business to conduct and factions within the house engaged in Fabian tactics, considering petitions, remonstrances and meetings, rather than any meaningful work. The house became increasingly fractious, and MPs focused on their own positions:

> It might well be wondered at wherewithal the time would be taken up, but it is (to speak freely) to hasten our own ruin, as if it came not on fast enough before. We are now doing that which the Irish would do in that which they call a free Parliament. It is by all means laboured that this kingdom may be declared independent, unto England: that the Act for the Adventurers having entrenched on the honour and independency of this kingdom may be protested against, than which what can be more pernicious and destructive to this poor state in our growing miseries. Easy as it is to fathom the bottom of this design. The well-affected among us have interposed, as far as it stood with their safety. It is strange to find, in so thin a house as ours must be, so many of the Irish faction, for ours, having no better way to hinder those proceedings than offering some matter for taking up time, propounded the taking of the remonstrance at Trim into consideration, wherein the honour of the house was so far reflected upon disparaging the members.[38]

Others expressed vitriol about their fellow MPs: 'Tell Mr. Loftus I hope to live to see him and his suffer as much as he makes me and mine ... I hope he and his friends will answer for it, either in this world or in the world to come ... Nich White is now going as fast as can be to God Almighty, I hope.'[39]

Ormond's focus was on holding as much of Ireland as possible for Charles and treating with the confederates and he was increasingly mindful of the need to control Parliament if any agreement with the Catholics was to be confirmed. While it would be a Protestant house, Ormond needed sufficient of his own supporters to ensure success. The absence of many MPs and limited efforts to replace others reduced attendance and increasing numbers of men associated with Ormond were returned to the house in 1644 and 1645, including his secretary, Lane, and other MPs were working for him in administrative capacities (Harrison, Stoughton, Harding) and soldiers under his command included MPs Wheeler, Mapother, Trafford, Lambert, Garrett and Francis Moore, Flower, Sherlock, Parsons, William Peisley, Sacheverell, Armstrong and possibly Thomas Eustace.[40] Grace and Walsh were probably also returned with Ormond's support and others were adhering to his side, including Wallis and Sir Robert Stewart, who had signed the November 1643 petition, but, by early 1645 was his supporter.[41]

Ormond's was not merely an impossible task, but also fraught with danger to his reputation. In this dilemma, Audley Mervyn, always an advocate for the institution, saw a role for the Irish Parliament:

> A peace with the Irish is generally a harsh sound to every ear, and the reason of this is diverse. Some in conscience hold no toleration of their religion; some judge the blood of their friends yet unrevenged; some their personal losses not to be repaired; others that it is beyond the reach of state to provide for our security in the future, and not a few because the country is pleasant and held too good for them … will be a very unthankful office of whosoever engageth himself in this work, and the malice he shall contract is better avoided than singly encountered. Therefore, if there be a necessity to transact such a matter,'tis wisdom to have many sharers, and those of such a nature as may both preserve your lordship and themselves … by a Parliament in this kingdom; this will take both aspersions from his majesty, which now is considerable when the people sit on the bench and stand not at the bar; it is a buckler betwixt your lordships and laws *a posteriori*; and if though many years after any inconvenience should ensue (which God forbid) the violence of our posterities would not deface your tomb as a cabinet actor of so public a concernment. Now there is no doubt of effecting whatsoever the justice of your lordship's thoughts would propound. I know the composure of your house the last time I sat. Many of the most violent spirits are away, there are many vacant places ought to be supplied by moderate persons. To this purpose if Sir Maurice Eustace cause the clerk of the House of Commons to give him a list of such vacant places, and writs immediately do issue for new elections, [it] will advance the work. Here are many members in the army that were not formerly present all of a sober temper … Here are ten places void which we can make good by legal elections, and I have wrote to Sir Maurice Eustace to cause writs to be sent down, and I shall see them returned, so that there is no dispute but that the moderate party shall sway all at pleasure. Pray, my lord, consider of this point.[42]

Ormond ignored this advice, certainly as relates to Ulster, with only four MPs returned in 1645. Usher, with others, remained wary of Ormond and his objectives: 'We are now taken up in our fatal work, the concluding of (shall I call it) a peace. [Ormond] hath too much power, all being left to him and yet if he observe it, he hath nothing at all, while he is limited to such a conclusion as shall be for the honour of his majesty and the security of his Protestant subjects.'[43]

Despite the recruiters, the number of members attending the House of Commons remained low and the house was repeatedly called (a mechanism for holding roll-calls used to encourage attendance), members were fined for non-attendance and the numbers were so low that the tellers were reduced to one on each side.[44] The poor attendance is understandable; the country was not merely at war, many MPs were soldiers, obliged to spend time in the field or defending their own homes,[45] or concerned to protect their own property or other interests outside Dublin, whether in Ireland or England and the business conducted by the house was limited and trivial. As early as 8 July 1642, the Irish council wrote to the commissioners in England asking them to oblige members of both Irish houses who were in England to return 'for that otherwise there will be but few to meet the next session in regards of those of both houses now in rebellion and in regards of the necessitated absence of others by reason of the rebellion kept from us, and in respect that sundry of the members of both houses may then be abroad with the army upon service'. Thomas Johnson reported disrespectful remarks about the length of time the house was sitting on 9 August 1642.[46] Few, if any, could have received wages and lack of payment, together with the relative unimportance of their business, presumably contributed to slacker attendance, apart from times of crisis and their own self-interest.

Some bills were transmitted and read in August and November 1642, but after that date the work of the house was almost entirely limited to dealing with petitions, motions, issues of privilege and almost no legislative work whatsoever was done.[47] Nonetheless, a hard core of roughly forty members sat regularly. The dominance of this small number, by no means representative of the population of Ireland, elected or paid by them and, for most of the time, unable to consult their constituencies, even had they wished to, raises the question of why this small rump of MPs continued to sit. Unlike the Confederation, the Irish Parliament had no military role, diplomatic agency or power to summon itself or initiate legislation and very little prestige or credibility. Its subservience to the English Privy Council left it especially marginalised when that body was experiencing dislocation and difficulty during the English civil war; Ireland was always low down the list of the English council's priorities; during a civil war, it was even less important and the decreasingly low social status of many of the MPs is testament to this. Contemporaries also ignored the Parliament's sitting; the representatives of the Irish Franciscans, keeping a close eye on developments in England and Ireland, mentioned the English Parliament and not the Irish. MPs Temple and Borlace, in their accounts of the Irish rebellion, ignored the existence of the Parliament of which they were members.[48] It was also progressively less representative of the Commons of Ireland as the defection of so many men to England, where they might have some influence over Ireland's fate, demonstrates.

One reason for Parliament's continued sitting was that any accommodation with the Catholics would have to have been approved by the Parliament, and while it was possible for by-elections to take place or, at least, for returns to be made, the lack of a functioning monarchy would have made it difficult, if not impossible, for a new Parliament to be summoned. Moreover, Ormond was determined not to call a new Parliament in which Catholics would be represented, although that was understandably one of their demands.

The Confederation of Kilkenny, unlike the House of Commons, was, by and large elected by the constituencies for which men sat, energetic in its meetings, and controlled, unlike the Irish Parliament, the entire structure of a state, including courts, an army and navy, coinage, printing presses, taxation assessors and collectors and diplomatic representatives abroad. This made it imperative that the Irish Parliament continue to sit to maintain the status of a national Parliament, no matter how skeletal a form it might have and how trivial its work.

The Commons also sat to ensure that its members' own, very narrow, interests were preserved, in the face of indifference in England. These included the threat to their own estates and personal positions from the Adventurers' Act in England in March 1642, which raised money to subdue Ireland on the security of Irish lands being given to Englishmen who subscribed money for that purpose. Motivation for seeking return included the obvious level of self-interest displayed by those associated with St Anne's Guild, who shamelessly used their positions to fight any encroachment of their control of the guild's assets, and the protection afforded by MPs' privilege from arrest and from cess and having soldiers billeted upon them.[49] The latter group may have included guild members, including Forster, Huetson and Dixon, as well as McGrath, Tallant, Grace, Molloy, Wentworth, George Carr and Carpenter, whom Ormond had already protected.[50] As a newly created Protestant elite in Ireland, their own social standing, economic interests and political welfare were all at risk, as much from the Confederate Catholics as from the English Parliament and its forces. As long as they continued to sit, and could prevent a new Parliament being called, which would include Catholics, they had a forum in which to protect their individual and collective interests. By and large, these were not men of any special power and influence outside the Parliament, even in Ireland; their influence, such as it was, was entirely bound up with their role as the official state Parliament of Ireland, and their adherence to that role is explained by what they had to lose by its dissolution.

Nevertheless, political exigencies required men to choose sides, and as John Morrill has argued, allegiances did not break down entirely on confessional grounds. Many different political positions were adopted by Protestants and Catholics in Ireland in the 1640s,[51] as demonstrated by Lawrence Crawford, who had to leave Ireland because he would not abjure the Covenant, and joined the army of the Eastern Association, fighting at Marston Moor. Mervyn, however, was obliged by political expediency to take the Covenant.

Some Catholics like John FitzGerald and Nicholas Barnwall remained neutral, others such as the expelled MP Henry Talbot fought for Charles in England, as did Fitzgerald's relatives. As the civil war in England progressed and Irish interests coalesced around the royalist Ormond in Ireland, Michael Jones and his colleagues in the parliamentary forces and the Independents Temple, Meredith, Borlase, Parsons, Adam Loftus and John Veele grouped around Lisle as rival lord lieutenant in 1646-47.[52]

The Irish Catholic position was neatly encapsulated in an anonymous poem:

> Most sacred majesty grant we may have
> Our ancient faith and lands, 'tis all we crave
> Your English and your Scotts not so content
> Claim all that's yours by act of Parliament
> Their tyranny we hate, confess your right
> 'Tis not against you, 'tis against them we fight
> Whilst you were king, we were your subjects
> Scorn to be their subjects, our fellow subjects borne
> Heavens bless your majesty, increase your powers
> You bring yourself again, we still are yours.[53]

A number of the recruiter MPs remained loyal to Charles, as shown in a 1649 list of Protestant delinquents (i.e. royalists) in Ireland with estates in Wexford, Carlow and Kildare includes Kenny, Dixon, Ford as well as Ormond.[54] In this, both the Protestant royalists and the neutral Catholic MPs were, like the confederates, worsted in the game.

NOTES

The author is grateful to Aidan Clarke, David Edwards, Micheál Ó Siochrú and Robert Armstrong for useful discussions on an earlier draft of this chapter.

1 A. Clarke, *The Old English in Ireland, 1625-42* (London, 1964), pp. 162-3; *His Majesties proclamation enent the unnecessary confluence of his Highnesse Lieges to Edinburgh, in the time of the Parliament, 1641* (Edinburgh, 1641).
2 Clarke, Old English, pp. 171-2; M. Perceval-Maxwell, *The Outbreak of the Irish Rebellion of 1641* (Montreal, 1994), pp. 287-8; E. Borlace, *The History of the Execrable Irish rebellion trac'd from many preceding acts, to the grand eruption the 23. of October 1641. And thence pursued to the Act of Settlement, MDCLXII* (1680), p. 32.
3 Perceval-Maxwell, *Outbreak*, p. 243; *CJI*, 9 Nov. 1641, 16-17 Nov., 11 Jan. 1641-42; all references to activities in the Commons are found in the Journals for the dates given.
4 Perceval Maxwell, *Outbreak*, pp. 287-8.
5 Ó Siochrú, *Confederate Ireland*, p. 25; for the process of communities deciding whether to join the rebellion, see B. McGrath, 'Mount Taragh's triumph: commitment and organisation in the early stages of the 1641 rebellion in Meath', in

E. Darcy, A. Margey and E. Murphy (eds), *The 1641 Depositions and the Irish Rebellion* (London, 2012), pp. 51–63; A. Margey, 'War and society in County Meath, 1641–1654', in F. Ludlow and A. Campsie (eds), *Meath: history and society* (Dublin, 2015), pp. 215–44.

6 Information on Irish MPs, returned before November 1641, and Theodore Schout, is drawn from B. McGrath, 'A biographical dictionary of the Irish House of Commons, 1640–1' (PhD thesis, Trinity College Dublin, 1998).

7 Pierpoint Morgan Library, MS Rulers of England, Box 7B/120: Dr Dudley Loftus to Ormond, n.d. (after 30 Mar. 1661).

8 Ó Siochrú, *Confederate Ireland*, pp. 37–8.

9 S.A. Lentz, 'The Irish Parliament during rebellion and Civil War, 1641–1648' (MA thesis, University of Wisconsin, 1974), pp. 108–9.

10 Certificate dated 22 May 1674 by John Keating, clerk of the Parliament of Dublin that 'a Parliament met at the Castle of Dublin on March 16, 1640 and by divers adjournments, etc. continued sitting until Oct. 23, 1641', after which he finds no Journals, but finds by orders and loose papers that it continued sitting until the year 1646 (*HMC Various Collections, Barrett Lennard Manuscripts. iii*. 244; *CJI*, i. 290.

11 Lentz, Irish Parliament; A. Clarke, *Prelude to Restoration in Ireland: the end of the Commonwealth, 1659–1660* (Cambridge, 1999), pp. 185, 194–5, 204, 206, 211, 258; Armstrong, *Protestant War*, pp. 7–10, 18–21, 23, 25–6, 41–2, 75–6, 84–5, 100–1, 112, 114, 120–1, 126, 137, 152, 196.

12 Lodge's compilation (Public Record Office of Ireland, MS. 1A/53/56), was printed in R. Lascelles, *Liber Munerum Publicorum Hiberniae* (2 vols, 1824), ii, part 1, pp. 1ff, and all references to returns, members and seats are drawn from this and the *Commons Journals*, unless otherwise stated; for the Parliament's orders, see J.L.C. Lindsay and R. Steele, *A Bibliography of Royal Proclamations of the Tudor and Stuart Sovereigns and of Others Published Under Authority, 1485–1714* (Oxford, 1910).

13 For the 1634 and 1640 returns respectively see B. McGrath, 'Sex, lies and rigged returns: the Kerry county parliamentary election of 11 June 1634 and its consequences', *Parliaments, Estates and Representation* 17 (2017), pp. 241–55, and B. McGrath, 'The Irish elections of 1640–1641', in C. Brady and J. Ohlmeyer (eds), *British Interventions in Early Modern Ireland* (Cambridge, 2005), pp. 186–206; for example, it is presumed that William Wallis is an error for Ralph, and Joseph Gifford an error for Sir John Gifford.

14 McGrath, 'Biographical Dictionary', pp. 88–94; for Wentworth's coterie see ibid., p. 33.

15 Ware noted that there were only 24 MPs on that date; see M. Empey (ed.), 'The Diary of Sir James Ware, 1623–66', *Analecta Hibernica* 45 (2014), pp. 53–146.

16 NLI, MS 2541, no. 3; Veele to Cadogan, 22 June 1642.

17 For blanks see B. McGrath, 'Irish Electoral law to 1648', in C. Dennehy (ed.), *Law and Revolution in Ireland: law and lawyers before, during and after the Cromwellian interregnum* (Dublin, 2019); for the podcast of the original conference paper see https://soundcloud.com/ucd-humanities/sets/law-and-revolution-in- ireland-law-and-lawyers-cromwellian-interregnum/

18　Expelled from the Commons, 10 Nov. 1642.
19　King's Inns, Carte transcription, Prendergast Papers, vol. III, part 1, p. 163.
20　T. Carte, *An History of the Life of James Duke of Ormond* (2 vols, 1736), i. 525.
21　B. McGrath, 'Athboy's election returns 1640 and 1642', *Riocht na Midhe* 21 (2010), pp. 65–72.
22　Audley Mervyn to Ormond, February 1645, in *HMC Ormonde*, old series, i. 90–5.
23　D. Brunton and D.H. Pennington, *Members of the Long Parliament* (Hamden, 1968), p. 21.
24　For FitzGerald see McGrath 'Sex, lies and rigged returns'; Barnwall was still described as a member of the House on 8 August 1644; for non-attendance 27 March 1647.
25　Morgan Library, MS. MA 1475.7 (17 Oct. 1609) and MA 1475.9 (17 Oct. 1621): receipts from William Temple, Stansted, Essex, to Robert Sidney, Lord Penshurst and Lisle, for payment of annuities of £30 left to Temple by Sir Philip Sidney; *DIB*; *HMC de Lisle and Dudley MSS*, vi. 359ff.
26　B. McGrath (ed.), *Acts of the Corporation of Coleraine, 1623–1669* (Dublin, 2017) makes no mention of replacing Cossens.
27　NLI, GO MS 72 (funeral entries, vol. 9, 1640–63), p. 49; for Walter White see B. McGrath, 'The Membership of the Irish House of Commons, 1613–15' (MLitt thesis, Trinity College Dublin, 1986), p. 106; for James White's lack of freehold in Meath see TCD, MS 813, fo. 282; ibid., MS 816, fo. 203: list of names belonging to extracts of petition of John Nettervill as escheator; the Hardings had been based in Queen's County since Elizabeth I's reign and Walter was the son of Thomas Harding of Maryborough; see NLI, GO MS. 71 (funeral entries, vol. 8, 1639–41).
28　Royal Irish Academy, MS 12.D.1 (account book of St Anne's Guild, 1584–1817), pp. 72, 80.
29　H.F. Berry, 'History of the religious guild of S. Anne, in St Audeon's Church Dublin, 1430–1740', *Proceedings of Royal Irish Academy* Section C, 25 (1904–5), pp. 21–106; C. Lennon, 'Charitable property the manuscripts of St Anne's Guild, Dublin', lecture given to the Royal Irish Academy (RIA), 1 March 2017, https://soundcloud.com/the-royal-irish-academy/charitable-property-the-manuscripts-of-st-annes-guild-dublin (accessed 17 February 2018).
30　For money collected for the case in Parliament, June 1642, see RIA, MS D.12.1, pp. 126ff; for sums disbursed for the suit in Parliament see ibid., pp. 152–3, 162–4.
31　B. McGrath, 'Ireland and the third University: attendance at the inns of court, 1603–1649', in D. Edwards (ed.), *Regions and Rulers in Ireland 1100–1650: essays for Kenneth Nicholls* (Dublin, 2004), pp. 217–36.
32　RIA, MS 12.D.1, pp. 162–4: payments to Eustace and Brereton.
33　Armstrong, *Protestant War*, p. 80; Temple, *Irish Rebellion*, p. 48.
34　B. McGrath, 'Parliament men and the Confederate Association', in M. Ó Siochrú (ed.), *Kingdoms in Crisis: Ireland in the 1640s* (Dublin, 2001), pp. 90–105.
35　Borlace, *History*, pp. 129, 131.
36　*Clanricarde Letter-Book*, p. 1.
37　*HMC Ormond MSS*, new series, ii. 341–2.
38　*HMC Egmont MSS*, i. 210–11.

39 Ibid., p. 235.
40 NLI, MS 2541, no. 103: list of Ormond's troops and those dealing with administration, n.d. (1647?); *HMC Ormonde MSS*, old series, i. 190ff.
41 Ibid., pp. 90–5.
42 Ibid.
43 *HMC Egmont MSS*, i. 237.
44 The House was 'called' on 8 Aug. 1642, 9 Apr. 1644, 17 Apr. 1644, 7 May 1647 and 27 May 1647.
45 Birr Castle, MS A/9 (diary of Capt. William Parsons) shows he was busy fighting at home in Parsonstown from October 1641 until the last date in the diary, 18 January 1643.
46 J. Hogan (ed.), *Letters and Papers relating to the Irish Rebellion between 1642–46*. (Dublin, 1936), pp. 68ff; unfortunately, the enclosed list of names has not survived.
47 For example, bills debated 1 August 1642.
48 *HMC Franciscan MSS*, pp. 114ff.
49 *CJI*, 13 Dec. 1642.
50 *CJI*, 6 Apr. 1644; ibid., 1 Aug. 1642, 20 Apr. 1643, 6 May 1644, 4 June 1644, 30 Nov. 1644; see *CJI*, 20 Apr. 1643 for Carpenter; T. Carte, *A Collection of original letters and papers concerning the affairs of England from the year 1641 to 1660 found among the Duke of Ormonde's Papers* (1739), p. 47.
51 J. Morrill, 'The English Revolution as a Civil War', *Hist. Res.* 90 (2017), pp. 726–41.
52 P. Little, 'The Irish "Independents" and Viscount Lisle's Lieutenancy of Ireland', *HJ* 44 (2001), pp. 941–61.
53 Folger Shakespeare Library, MS v.b.303, p. 320: anon, 'the Irish petition', included with a selection of other verses from 1641 to 1642.
54 NLI, MS 2541, unpaginated: a brief note of delinquents' estates set by us the undernamed by virtue of his excellencies the lord lieutenant's commission bearing the date 25th of May last, with the names of the delinquents propriate of such estates within the counties of Wexford, Carlow and Kildare in the present year 1649.

7

The politics of preferment: the marquess of Ormond, Archbishop Ussher and the appointment of Irish bishops, 1643–47

PATRICK LITTLE

In 2005, Robert Armstrong described the 1640s as 'the lost decade in the history of the Protestant church establishment in early modern Ireland'.[1] Compared with, for example, the Laudian intrusion during the 1630s, there has been very little research undertaken on the Church of Ireland during the confederate wars since the ground-breaking work of St John Drelincourt Seymour in the 1920s and 1930s.[2] Armstrong's article has helped to bring the story up to date, but in a short, general survey he was unable explore key issues in any great depth. When it comes to the appointment of bishops he ventures no further than a brief statement of fact: 'Of the twenty-five bishops of 1641, seven had died between the outbreak of the rising and the surrender of Dublin to Parliament in 1647. All were replaced, either by new consecrations or by promotions. The share-out of influence in new appointments between Ormond and the royal court at Oxford is unclear, though both were involved.'[3] This chapter offers a detailed exploration of these episcopal appointments – in particular those made during Ormond's active lieutenancy between the autumn of 1643 and the summer of 1647 – to identify the influences that lay behind them, and to put them within the wider religious and political contexts of this turbulent period of Irish history.

First, it is necessary to consider where the power of presentation actually lay during the early 1640s. It is easy to assume that with the Irish primate, Archbishop James Ussher, in England throughout this period there was a power vacuum at the top of the Church of Ireland. But this was clearly not the case. Before his journey to England in the spring of 1640, Ussher had already asserted his authority over the church in the traditional way, by presiding over the opening of convocation in Dublin. In the two years before the outbreak of civil war his position was strengthened by the shift in royal policy towards the Church of England, with the Laudians being replaced by men like

John Williams, archbishop of York, who were 'welcomed back into the king's counsels', while 'a series of new appointments to bishoprics in the years 1641–3 included a number of Calvinist divines'.[4] As Alan Ford has demonstrated, Ussher was at the heart of this wider movement, becoming 'a role model for the non-Laudian bishops'. In 1640 Ussher was 'entrusted by the king with the task of looking after the welfare of the episcopalian ministers who had fled from Scotland', and in 1641 he was 'clearly trusted by, and on intimate terms with the king and his advisers'.[5] This allowed the primate to unveil his scheme for 'reduced episcopacy' during the same year. Ussher continued to have the trust of the king after the outbreak of rebellion in Ireland. In February 1642 the king granted him the profits of the vacant see of Carlisle to make up for his lost revenues in Ulster, and after Ussher's decision to join the king at his Oxford headquarters in November 1642, the two remained close, with Charles making his public statement of loyalty to 'the established and true-reformed Protestant religion' during a service of Holy Communion led by Ussher in 1643.[6]

This new relationship with the king allowed Ussher to exercise considerable influence over the Irish church by remote control. In his absence, Ussher relied on his extensive network of friends and relatives in Ireland. In November 1642, when the puritan preacher, Stephen Jerome, took the opportunity of a Sunday sermon in Christ Church Cathedral to 'traduce both their majesties, his majesty's council, and his army', evidence against him was provided by a group a clergymen closely connected with Ussher, including his former pupil at Trinity College Dublin, William Golborne, his 'kinsman' James Nugent, and Joseph Travers (or Trevor), another Trinity man who was married to the archbishop's 'near kinswoman'.[7] Ussher was also behind a letter of 29 May 1643 in which the king complained to the lords justices about the continuing activities of 'factious and seditious preachers' in the Dublin churches, warning that such men were intent on turning the people against the crown and the 'established discipline' of the church, and ordering that they be punished.[8] The letter was written in the knowledge that the lords justices were themselves encouraging these troublesome preachers.[9] This was not a little local difficulty. The malign influence of the lords justices over the Dublin church was symptomatic of a wider crisis afflicting the Church of Ireland, which had seen much of its diocesan and parochial structure collapse, and the retreat of many of its bishops and clergy into the Protestant safe havens.

In response to such threats, Ussher did his best to fill episcopal vacancies as soon as they arose. Maintaining a full bench of bishops had always been an important symbol of the legitimacy and viability of the Church of Ireland: a point not lost on the Laudian reformer, Bishop Bramhall of Derry, in the 1630s or on the Roman Catholics who developed a church-in-waiting during the same period.[10] In the early years of the Irish wars, with much of the country now under Catholic control, and Ulster playing host to an aggressively Presbyterian Scottish army, there was an added sense of urgency when it came to appointing bishops. It was no surprise that at least two of the bishops consecrated in 1643–44 had existing connections with Ussher. Robert Sibthorpe, the former bishop of Kilfenora elevated to the see of Limerick by the king on 7 April 1643, had previously been recommended for the bishopric of Ossory by the primate.[11] Robert Maxwell, the new bishop of Kilmore consecrated at St Patrick's Cathedral on 24 March 1644, was one of the ejected Scottish ministers in Ussher's care.[12] Another candidate considered for Kilmore was Dr William Baillie, another Scot who had fled to Ireland in 1638 and now resided in Oxford, where he had been awarded a doctorate of divinity in February 1642.[13] Although Baillie was passed over this time, he was not forgotten, and on 22 December 1643 the king instructed Ormond, as the newly appointed lord lieutenant, to place him at Clonfert, 'waiving our former choice of him to the bishopric of Kilmore, which we have otherwise disposed'.[14] This order was fulfilled at Oxford on 2 May 1644, when Baillie was consecrated bishop of Clonfert by three Church of Ireland bishops: Ussher and two native Scots, John Maxwell of Killala and Henry Leslie of Down and Connor.[15] The involvement of the three prelates may seem unremarkable, as they were all in attendance at the royal court, but it is interesting that Ussher should have been flanked by two Irish bishops, rather than by English colleagues. The timing suggests that this demonstration of unity was in part a response to the favourable reception given to the confederate agents who a few weeks before had presented the king with their conditions for signing a peace treaty, including freedom of religion for Catholics.[16]

A letter from the very end of May 1644 confirms that the primate was playing an important role in episcopal appointments. On 29 May Ussher wrote to Ormond to tell him that the king had decided that William Golborne was to be the new bishop of Kildare.[17] (He presumably enclosed the official instruction from the king, dated 17 May, which detailed the livings to be held in commendam; Golborne was consecrated on 1 December.)[18] Golborne was the natural choice for Kildare, as he was the archdeacon of the diocese and had stayed in his post during the Irish rebellion, providing the government with details of its lands in March 1642.[19] This solidity in the face of Catholic pressure may have recommended Golborne as a suitable candidate on its own, but it was reinforced by his personal connection with Ussher and his opposition to Stephen Jerome in November 1642. Ussher also saw the potential of such an appointment in freeing junior posts to the advantage of his own family and friends. In the same letter he pointed out to Ormond that by this preferment 'the archdeaconry of that diocese falleth unto your lordship's disposition', and recommended his relative, Joseph Travers, who had helped to face down the seditious preachers. Ussher said he was prompted to make this request 'by the success which my former letters obtained in the recommendation of Baron [William] Hilton and Dean [Nicholas] Bernard, who both of them have amply recounted unto me the noble favour which thereupon you were pleased to vouchsafe unto them', and in the same letter he sent his respects to his nephew, the dean of Kilmore, Dr Henry Jones.[20] Ormond did as Ussher wanted, and Joseph Travers was duly appointed archdeacon of Kildare.[21] Nor, as we shall see, did he forget Henry Jones. In May 1644, at least, it looks like the usual process of the primate working with the lieutenant to influence the king was continuing to operate.

The promotions in May 1644 fit in with the general pattern that was emerging during the early years of the confederate wars. Through Ussher's influence, those chosen for preferment were a mixture of his relatives, long-standing members of the church hierarchy, or Scottish refugees under his care. Despite pressure from the confederates and the covenanters, Ussher was determined to assert at every opportunity the legitimacy and durability of the Irish church.

In the year after Golborne's appointment, the position of the Church of Ireland had weakened significantly. Ormond had received a formal commission from the king to treat with the Confederate Association on 24 June 1644; eight days later the king's army in England received a major defeat at Marston Moor. The inability of the Westminster Parliament to capitalise on their victory led to stalemate and renewed peace talks. The Uxbridge negotiations failed in February 1645, and immediately afterwards Charles instructed Ormond to conclude a deal with the confederates at any cost.[22] Perhaps in reaction to this, in the same month, Ussher left Oxford for the west country – ending up as a guest of his son-in-law, Sir Thomas Tyrrell, in Cardiff Castle.[23] In a later letter he voiced his enduring bitterness at the turn of events, as 'new furies affected me in England, which drove me out of Oxford into Wales'.[24] With Ussher absent from the royal court, control of the Church of Ireland appears to have fallen, by default, into the hands of the lord lieutenant, working with the king and his advisers in Oxford.

Ormond lost no time in nominating bishops for approval by the king. On 16 April 1645 he wrote two letters to Oxford concerning the church. The first, to the secretary of state, George Lord Digby, was accompanied by 'drafts of letters for the advancement in this church of the lord bishop of Killala and Dr Sibbald, both persons of great learning, piety and affections to the king's service'. Observing the correct protocol, Ormond added: 'I do humbly beseech your lordship to move his majesty in their behalfs.'[25] The second letter, to Sir George Radcliffe, concerned the arrival of the bishop of Killala from Oxford, just before three parliamentarian ships blockaded the harbour. Ormond added, almost as an aside, that Killala was the man 'who I desire may be archbishop of Tuam'.[26] It is significant that both of the men recommended by Ormond were Scottish episcopalians, and renowned enemies of the Covenant.

John Maxwell, the former bishop of Ross, who had fled to England after the covenanter rebellion and was consecrated as bishop of Killala in October 1641. He had a growing reputation as a polemicist, upholding monarchy and attacking the covenanters in such works as the *Epistle Congratulatorie of Lysimachus Nicanor* of 1640 and *Episcopacy not Abjured in his Majesties Realm of Scotland* of 1641, and after being forced from his residence, and physically assaulted in the early stages of the Irish rebellion, he made his way to Oxford and the royal court. Ormond's approval of Maxwell can be seen in his letter introducing the bishop to the king of 11 April 1643, in which he praised him as 'a venerable light of the Protestant church'.[27] The other divine recommended by Ormond was Dr James Sibbald, one of the 'Aberdeen doctors' who had opposed the covenanters in 1638, crossed to Ireland in 1640, and now lived in Dublin, as reader of St Werburgh's Church. He too was known as a fierce critic of the Covenant, and was thus a potentially useful ally, especially against the Scots in the north of Ireland, and had recently been recommended to Ormond by the king, as 'a person of great abilities, and worthy of all encouragement'.[28]

There were three interconnected reasons why Ormond supported these appointments. The first was a desire to maintain continuity with the Ussherian church: the preferment of Scots in particular looks like a continuation of the primate's practice earlier in the decade. The second was of more immediate concern: the need to assert the position of the Church of Ireland during a new round of peace talks with the confederates. Ormond has been blamed for jeopardising these talks by increasing his religious demands, in particular the requirement that the church property seized by the Catholic clergy should be returned to the established church, but others have argued that this only became a central bone of contention because the Catholic clergy were becoming more assertive in the spring of 1645. In any case, it was a good time to uphold the Church of Ireland through the appointment of new bishops, especially when the dioceses in question were mostly under confederate control.[29] The third reason was equally pressing. In April 1645 Ormond was not only busy restarting talks with the confederates but also entertaining an alternative plan in the north, described by Armstrong as his 'summer strategy for the creation of a cross-religious third force to which, ideally, disillusioned confederates and covenanters could attach themselves'.[30] This policy was principally aimed at Ulster but it applied equally to Connacht, increasingly targeted by pro-parliamentarian forces, led by Sir Charles Coote, who were busy undermining the loyalty of the Protestant community towards Ormond and the king. The archdiocese of Tuam and its subordinate diocese of Killala were in the firing line, and it was fortuitous that they now came into Ormond's hands at a crucial point. More importantly, in the war of words against the covenanters, polemical champions such as Maxwell and Sibbald were a tremendous asset. This had been recognised the previous year by Ormond, who told the king that Bishop Maxwell 'said more to vindicate your rights against the furious invaders upon them of this age than most men had the courage or were able to say'; and one of the British commanders in Ulster, Sir James Montgomery, had written to Ormond asking for a copy of one of Maxwell's books 'in the hope of deploying it against Presbyterian clergy there'.[31] In any case, Ormond only partly got his way. Maxwell was consecrated as archbishop of Tuam on 30 August 1645.[32] Sibbald, however, refused the promotion, remaining for the rest of the decade the reader of St Werburgh's.[33]

On 13 May 1645 Lord Digby wrote to Ormond to discuss further 'church preferments', saying that 'his majesty is engaged unto Dr Fuller, bishop of Kerry [i.e. Ardfert], to remove him to a better bishopric than what he now holds', and pointing out that the see of Clogher in the province of Armagh was now vacant. Digby made it clear this was a request, not an order: 'I do not send any letter for Dr Fuller's advancement to that because I think a less will content him, and I shall expect your excellency's further directions which you think fittest to be removed to which.'[34] Digby hinted that Ormond had a free hand when it came to appointments, although he also indicated the king had his own preferences, and would make the final decision. Perhaps Digby sensed that Thomas Fuller (or Fulwar) of Ardfert, an Englishman who had spent the civil war years in Oxford, would not be Ormond's first choice as the man to tackle a strategically important diocese like Clogher, which included a swathe of confederate-held territory in southern Ulster.[35] If so, Digby was not immediately successful in persuading the king to change his mind, as a supplementary letter of 21 May suggests: 'I thought it not necessary to renew those letters for the promotion of the clergymen, since the king's engagement to Dr Fuller, mentioned in my former letter, may perhaps beget an alteration in the whole.'[36]

It was not until August 1645 that Ormond made his own recommendations. On 14th of that month he wrote to Digby, sending for his approval a draft letter

> for preferring of Dr Henry Jones to the bishopric of Clogher, of whose advancement in this church, and especially to that see, I conceive very good use may be made, as there would be by advancing Dr Edward Parry to that of Killala (declined by Dr Sibbalds) if his majesty were not engaged to Dr Fuller.[37]

Ormond's choices were interesting. He made no mention of the English Fuller, despite the king's stated preference. Parry was an Ulsterman by birth, but his career had largely been in the south, as the 'reliably Laudian' chaplain to Archbishop Lancelot Bulkeley of Dublin in the 1630s, and then as dean of Waterford and Lismore, holding the latter alongside the archdeaconry of Glendalough.[38] Parry was also an intellectual, who had defended the church against Catholicism in 1641, and more recently advised Ormond on a theological response to the Covenant.³⁹ He would be a useful replacement for Maxwell at Killala. There were good reasons for appointing Parry, but the man Ormond really wanted to promote at this juncture was Henry Jones.

Dr Henry Jones had impeccable New English and Church of Ireland credentials, as the 40-year-old son of Lewis Jones, bishop of Killaloe and (importantly) nephew of Archbishop Ussher. But Jones was also a controversial figure.⁴⁰ As the author of the violently anti-Catholic *Remonstrance of Divers Remarkable Passages Concerning the Church and Kingdom of Ireland*, which contained a digest of the depositions of those who had suffered at the hands of the insurgents in 1641 and argued that the massacre had been the work of Antichrist, Jones was already famous for his extreme views. He was also loathed by the king. When the book appeared in March 1642 Charles I had objected to the 'great scandals raised upon himself' in Jones's book, 'wherein some examinations were set down (how improbable or impossible soever,) which might make an impression on the minds of many of his weak subjects'.⁴¹ Jones had gone on to oppose the cessation of arms of September 1643, again using the deposition evidence to demonstrate Catholic barbarism. Ormond's sponsorship of Jones might demonstrate his commitment to Ussher personally and the Church of Ireland more generally, even though it carried a clear risk of irritating the king. Yet it could be argued that Ormond had other, more urgent, concerns in the late summer of 1645.

The letter of 14 August recommending Jones was written at a particularly difficult time for Ormond. News of the catastrophic defeat of the king's army at Naseby had reached him on 29 June, only six weeks before.⁴² In the meantime, his negotiations with the confederates had further denuded his authority in Ulster and Connacht. In July, the bishop of Cloyne advised Ormond of the need to sound out the officers of the 'old British forces', inviting them to restart negotiations with Dublin and talking up the forthcoming treaty with the confederates as 'an honourable and safe peace, accompanied with all possible advantages that may be for the Protestant party'.⁴³ On 26 July Archdeacon Galbraith of Clogher wrote to Ormond from Magavelin near Derry concerning his efforts to persuade the 'British' of Ulster of the benefits of peace.⁴⁴ Neither adviser was confident of success. Ormond was also under pressure from his bishops. On 2 August eight of them wrote a paper objecting in the strongest terms to some of the concessions demanded by the Catholic Church, especially concerning the retention of church property in areas under their control, and this was used as the basis for an official reply to the confederates on 5 August.⁴⁵

At the same time, Ormond was at loggerheads with one of his own commanders, Viscount Taaffe, over the treatment of Henry Tilson, bishop of Elphin, whose position had become increasingly untenable during the previous weeks. In order to shore up his own position in Connacht – especially against parliamentary agents who were proving successful in undermining the loyalty of the Protestants on the province – Ormond had, at the end of June, issued Taaffe with a commission to enforce the terms of the cessation of arms, working in conjunction with the local confederates. The results of this policy were disastrously counter-productive, as Aoife Duignan has chronicled.⁴⁶ On 7 August Ormond told Taaffe to control his men, adding that the bishop's 'calling and affections I am sure place him at sufficient distance from those that adhere to the Parliament at Westminster'.⁴⁷ A week later, and on the same day that Ormond wrote his letter to Digby, the bishop sent a letter to the lord lieutenant asking whether the town and garrison of Elphin really were to be surrendered to the confederates under the terms of the cessation. If so, he begged permission to leave, 'for I am resolved not to live with them and be a tenant at will, but rather to lose that little which is left'.⁴⁸ Nevertheless, the articles for the surrender of Elphin were signed on 19 August, and a few days later the bishop, now in the relative safety of Roscommon Castle, asked Ormond the very pertinent question: 'whether it might not alienate the hearts of the Protestant subjects as well in this kingdom as that other of England' and encourage waverers to throw in their lot with the Scots instead.⁴⁹ The triumphant Catholics soon installed their own bishop, and a later letter from Elphin to his brother-in-law, James Margetson, dean of Christ Church in Dublin, made plain the wider lesson that was to be drawn: 'As this army beginneth with us, so (if they can prevail) in the end will they deal with all the Protestant clergy also.'⁵⁰

When put in the context of growing hostility towards a peace deal with the confederates, and the fear that the 'British' of Ulster would make common cause with the Scots rather than stomach any such agreement, Ormond's ecclesiastical re-shuffle takes on a rather different light. The key phrase in Ormond's letter of 14 August was that 'very good use may be made' of Jones's placement at Clogher. Clogher was strategically as well as religiously important, and the 'placing' of a Calvinist divine there, however notionally, would reassure many in Ulster – not least Jones's own brother, Sir Theophilus, who was commander of the vital, and threatened, stronghold of Lisnagarvey (Lisburn). It would also offer a robust response to the confederates, who were intent on taking over neighbouring Elphin and ejecting the bishop as a step towards reclaiming church property across the north and west. Behind these considerations was the obvious connection – of churchmanship as well as blood – between Jones and Ussher, which again suggests that the lord lieutenant had the primate's preferences in mind. Remarkably, despite his enduring suspicion of Henry Jones, the king was willing to accede to the appointment, and at the beginning of October 1645 Ormond received a royal order appointing Jones as bishop of Clogher with commendam livings, including the archdeaconry of Killaloe.⁵¹ Jones was consecrated by the archbishop of Dublin and the bishops of Kildare and Cloyne on 9 November.[52] There was no more talk of Parry or Fuller becoming bishop of Killala, and the see remained vacant.

The political situation was also pressing in January 1646, when Ormond made his next suggestion for an episcopal promotion. The previous month had seen the exposure of the activities of the earl of Glamorgan, who had been negotiating a separate agreement between the king and the confederates behind Ormond's back for much of the previous six months.[53] Glamorgan's draft treaty offered far-reaching religious concessions to the confederates, allowing freedom of worship and possession of churches already in their hands – terms that were clearly anathema to the Church of Ireland.[54] On 5 January Ormond and his council (including Anthony Martin, bishop of Meath) sent a strongly worded letter to Secretary Nicholas warning that the Glamorgan articles amounted to 'no less than an absolute giving up of the king's ecclesiastical supremacy within this kingdom, and in lieu of it introducing the fullness of papal power'.[55] In the same month, as Kevin Forkan has shown, Ormond was gearing up for negotiations with the Ulster Scots, sending 'remembrances' to his agent, Archdeacon Galbraith, based on the articles agreed between the English Parliament and the Scots on 6 August 1642.[56] These included a crucial compromise: that the Covenant, having been signed more than a year after August 1642, would not be 'pressed' by the Scots on the rest of the population, who were free to continue using 'the form of divine service appointed and established by law in the Church of Ireland'; on the other hand,

> the chief governor will not press the using of the said form upon any, but that the same remain suspended and as a thing indifferent till it shall please God to settle the Church of England by his majesty and his Parliament unto which or the like settlement the subjects here will in all likelihood submit, and the like forbearance to be on both sides touching church government.[57]

Rather than insisting on conformity to the established church, Ormond was now prepared to offer a measure of toleration to the Presbyterians. This violent reaction against Glamorgan and simultaneous softening of tone towards the Scots provides the immediate context for Ormond's next proposed appointment.

On 19 January 1646, Ormond drafted a letter to Secretary Nicholas, reacting to news that Ussher had died: 'We understand this kingdom hath lost her greatest ornament of learning and example of piety in the death of the late lord primate, a loss so great to this church that it ought to be lamented by all that are truly of it.' The Church of Ireland could not be left without a head, and Ormond made a bold recommendation: 'I presume to offer to his majesty's choice for his successor Dr Henry Jones, bishop of Clogher, a man of great learning and piety and nephew to the said late lord primate', a promotion he hoped would be 'an advantage to the king's service in other regards as well as in those of the church'.[58] Reports of Ussher's death proved to be greatly exaggerated, and Jones missed his chance of the top job;[59] but the fact that Ormond was prepared to recommend him to the king as the new primate is interesting. Of all the bishops who might be promoted, Jones was the most recently appointed, the most controversial, the least acceptable to the king. Jones was on good terms with the English Parliament, and was hated by the Irish confederates. To appoint him was to take a huge gamble.

Again, the political context provides the key. In January 1646 as in August 1645, the advancement of Jones to Armagh would reassure the 'British' of Ulster by publicly snubbing the confederates, while at the same time positioning Ormond for possible talks with the covenanters. Ormond seems to have hinted at this when he framed the appointment as 'an advantage to the king's service in other regards as well as in those of the church'. It is also significant that Ormond emphasised that Jones was 'nephew to the said lord primate', just as, at the beginning of the letter, he heaped lavish praise on Ussher as Ireland's 'greatest ornament of learning and example of piety'. In the space of a few sentences, Ormond thus endorsed not just Ussher and Jones as individuals but also the Ussherian model of the Church of Ireland.

The moment for such confidence was soon past. Only weeks later, Ormond had abandoned his negotiations with the Scots and the Ulster commissioners, and revived the flagging peace talks with the confederates. The first Ormond Peace, signed privately in March 1646, did not make the concessions to the Catholic Church that Glamorgan had suggested, instead leaving ecclesiastical affairs – including the thorny problem of the possession of church property – to be decided at a later date. During the summer the situation in Ireland took a sudden turn for the worse. The victory of Owen Roe O'Neill against the Ulster Scots at Benburb on 5 June came immediately after news arrived that the king had fled Oxford and surrendered to the Scottish army besieging Newark. When the first Ormond Peace was made public at the end of July, it was welcomed by the Church of Ireland clergy but condemned by the more extreme Protestants and by the clerical party among the confederates. Renewed warfare was now inevitable. By this time, Ussher had accepted that the royalist cause was finished, and travelled to London to make his peace with Parliament. He arrived on 11 June 1646. Thereafter he was engaged in what Alan Ford has described as 'a delicate process of negotiation with the authorities in London, as he sought to meet his basic financial needs so that he could get back to his beloved research'. It was a slow business. In December of that year his books were returned, and it was not until a year later that he was given an official position, and a stipend, as lecturer at Lincoln's Inn.[60] Ussher played no discernible role in the Irish church throughout this period.

Ormond was also running out of options. In September 1646, as the confederate armies prepared to besiege Dublin, he turned to the English Parliament for a possible solution. Even at this point he was reluctant to make firm religious – as opposed to political – commitments, and told his agents to demand similar terms as had been discussed with the Ulster Scots the previous winter: 'that we may not be pressed to the Covenant until it be warranted by act of Parliament; and secondly desire that nothing be at this time pressed which may give occasion of division amongst the Protestant party'. When it came to the formularies of the church,

> if the suppressing of the Book of Common Prayer be pressed you may offer the same considerations concerning that as formerly concerning the Covenant, yet with this addition that in case any shall desire the use of the Directory [for Public Worship] here, that the use thereof be permitted them.[61]

This was the same deal he had offered the Ulster Scots in October 1645, based on the 1642 treaty.[62] The official declaration justifying the opening of peace talks with the parliamentary commissioners in Dublin at the beginning of November 1646 was framed in very broad terms: a treaty was vital to 'the maintenance of the Protestant religion in the kingdom of Ireland [and] the strengthening thereof in all the reformed churches'.[63]

Throughout the subsequent negotiations, the 'Protestant religion' was invoked time and again, but with no mention of specific forms, and no guarantees of the liturgy and hierarchy of the established church. It was only as the talks broke down at the end of November, that the lord lieutenant raised concerns that some of the ordinances 'require the Covenant to be generally taken' while the use of the Prayer Book would be banned, 'which form of service and no other is by a law of force in this kingdom'. This elicited the surprising reply from the commissioners that 'we know of no ordinance of Parliament that requires the Covenant to be taken in the kingdom of Ireland' and 'we have no ways instructed to suppress the Book of Common Prayer or impose the Directory, though your lordship represented in your own instructions that the Directory might be used here'. Sulkily, Ormond pointed out that Ulster and Munster had already had the Covenant imposed.[64] He knew full well that the Church of Ireland was unlikely to survive a treaty with the English Parliament.

Soon after Ormond's negotiations with Parliament failed, the confederates closed in on Dublin. Ormond despaired of assistance from the king, who was still a prisoner of the Scots, and refused to countenance a new deal with the Catholics. In an anguished letter to Digby, written on Christmas Day, Ormond made clear where – in public at least – he drew the line: 'no man knows better than your lordship where in this particular I stick, yet I hold it not amiss to remember you that it is in what concerns any concession that may seem to perpetuate to the Roman Catholics either churches or church livings or that may essentially take from ours or give to their clergy ecclesiastical jurisdiction', although he was willing to allow 'the quiet exercise of their religion'.[65] Only four days later, on 29 December, Charles wrote to Ormond from Newcastle, noting the death of Lewis Jones, bishop of Killaloe (and father of Henry Jones) and recommending to the post Dr Edward Parry, who had missed out from preferment last time round. Parry was to hold the see alongside his existing jobs as treasurer of Christ Church Cathedral, archdeacon of Glendalough and vicar of the Dublin parish of St Nicholas Without.[66] The preferment of Parry may have been a royal initiative, in keeping with the 'Laudian revival' among the king's ecclesiastical advisers during the mid- to late 1640s,[67] but it evidently received enthusiastic support from Ormond, who had earmarked Parry for a bishopric two years earlier. On 9 March the lord lieutenant issued orders to the secretary of the Irish council to draw up a fiant for the grant to Parry; and a few days later he arranged for the deanery of Lismore, vacated by Edward Parry, to pass to his brother, Robert Parry.[68] The letters patent for this appointment were signed on 20 March 1647, and Parry was consecrated at Christ Church by the archbishop of Dublin and the bishops of Kildare and Cloyne on 28 March.[69]

The legal processes and ecclesiastical ceremonies had been observed, but all was not as it seemed. During the short period between Parry's nomination and his consecration, the political situation had changed yet again. At the end of December it seemed that Ormond had at last run out of alternatives; but in February he resolved to make new approaches to the Westminster Parliament. This move was not universally popular among the clergy, who feared for the very survival of their church. When John Maxwell, archbishop of Tuam, died in the same month, rumours soon circulated in Dublin: 'some say (and the bishop of Down at his funeral sermon said) it was grief (that the things go here as they do) killed him'.[70] Ormond's own discomfort can perhaps be seen in his decision to continue to avoid religious complications in his talks with Parliament. On 16 March, in his instructions to his negotiating team, the sixth point was that 'you are to desire that the form of religious service now used here may be continued'; but there was no mention of the protection of the clergy or their livings, or guarantees that the Covenant would not be imposed from above.[71] The next day Ormond justified his actions to the king, writing that a deal with Parliament would be 'better ... in all probability, for religion, your crown and faithful servants here'.[72] Again, the detail is lacking. Perhaps keeping things vague was the only way to secure a deal; there was also the pressure of time. As Robert Armstrong puts it, 'Ormond's actions in the latter half of March suggest he was tidying up loose ends ahead of his departure.'[73] Nevertheless, it is difficult to see how the consecration of a new bishop – and especially one of decidedly Laudian views – fits in with Ormond's closing-down sale. He may have felt obliged to continue with the consecration, not only through a sense of personal obligation towards Parry, but also in the hope that it would provide a crumb of comfort for those clergy who feared for the future of the church under parliamentarian rule.

If so, it was the smallest of crumbs. The Dublin Articles signed between Ormond and the parliamentary commissioners on 18 June made no mention of the rights of the church, merely referring to protection for 'Irish Protestants'. Despite a vigorous protest from the 'Protestant clergy of Dublin', on 24 June the parliamentary commissioners issued an order that the use of 'the Common Prayer Book and ceremonies in the churches of this kingdom' would be 'discontinued' and the Presbyterian Directory for Public Worship imposed instead.[74] A group of pro-Laudian clergy, associated with the city's cathedrals and headed by Bishop Parry, protested, but to no avail.[75] The mood in Dublin at the beginning of July, just days before Ormond's departure, was grim: 'all our divines are silenced for not accepting the Directory, and are upon departing the kingdom. Those that were never esteemed for any parts they had are preferred. This the Protestants here do much take to heart.'[76]

This chapter has sought to add something to our knowledge of the 'lost decade' of the Church of Ireland by looking at the episcopal appointments within their wider context. Despite his absence in England, Archbishop Ussher continued to play an important role in the appointment process in 1643–44, and this period saw the preferment of men of his own stamp, such as Baillie of Clonfert and Golborne of Kildare, who, it was hoped, would hold the line against both confederates and covenanters. After Ussher's departure from Oxford in early 1645, responsibility for appointments was assumed by Ormond as lord lieutenant, who continued to promote those associated with Ussher, including Henry Jones of Clogher. Gradually, during 1645, ecclesiastical appointments became more overtly political. This was especially so when vacancies occurred in the north and west – Tuam, Killala, Clogher, and possibly Armagh itself – and this fits neatly with what Kevin Forkan has uncovered of Ormond's plan of constructing a 'royalist alliance' in the north that ran alongside (and ultimately counter to) his negotiations with the confederate Irish and with the Scottish covenanters and their parliamentarian allies. By recommending the appointment of Ussher's nephew, the Calvinist and violently anti-Catholic Henry Jones, as the new archbishop of Armagh in January 1646, Ormond was playing a trump card in a bigger political game. But Ormond never had such a strong hand again. The narrowing of his political options as the year progressed forced him to approach the English Parliament with little room to manoeuvre over religious issues. His tactic of refusing to define terms, which had worked well for a time with the confederates and may have become the basis for an agreement with the Scots, now became a liability. Ormond left Dublin without any safeguards for the Church of Ireland, and the last-minute appointment of a new bishop of Killaloe did nothing to offset that.

Central to this narrative is the relationship between Ormond and Ussher. There seems to have been considerable sympathy between the two men. Ormond had been brought up in household of Archbishop George Abbot of Canterbury, who saw eye to eye with Ussher theologically; he retained elements of the 'older puritanism', not least in the strength of his belief in Providence and he based his religion on notions of 'honour and duty' towards the crown as much as the church and its hierarchy.[77] This last point is important: whether or not the two men shared a religious outlook (and the case of Edward Parry suggests they did not always concur), they were in total agreement when it came to loyalty to the crown.[78] Alan Ford's statement that Ussher's 'primary political loyalty remained to his king' could just as well be applied to Ormond.[79] Ormond seems to have supported Ussher through a sense of duty towards the church and its hierarchy, almost to the point of seeing his role as that of deputy to the archbishop as well as to the king. This may help to explain his eagerness to promote Ussher's candidates to the episcopacy, to protect his protégé, Nicholas Bernard, in Drogheda, and his efforts to secure the archbishop's release from prison in Wales and to raise funds for his family.[80] The suggestion of Henry Jones as primate in January 1646 was the high point of this collaboration, but it was also the end point.

With the king in Parliament's hands, and Ussher in London, Ormond's final appointment in March 1647 was of a very different kind. Instead of backing another Ussherian candidate, he instead went along with the appointment of the pro-Laudian Edward Parry, as the new bishop of Killaloe. It would be easy to accuse Ormond of hypocrisy, championing Calvinists when it suited his political strategy, favouring a Laudian when this seemed most appropriate, and dumping the whole church when he left Dublin in July 1647, but it would be a mistake to ignore the difficulty of his situation, as events throughout the British Isles ran far beyond his control.

NOTES

I would like to thank Alan Ford and Robert Armstrong for their comments on an earlier draft of this chapter.

1 R. Armstrong, 'Protestant churchmen and the Confederate Wars', in C. Brady and J. Ohlmeyer (eds), *British Interventions in Early Modern Ireland* (Cambridge, 2005), pp. 230–51, at p. 230.
2 A. Ford, *The Protestant Reformation in Ireland, 1590–1641* (2nd edn, Dublin 1996); J. McCafferty, *The Reconstruction of the Church of Ireland: Bishop Bramhall and the Laudian reforms, 1633–1641* (Cambridge, 2007); St J.D. Seymour, *The Puritans in Ireland, 1647–1661* (Oxford, 1921); St J.D. Seymour, 'The Church under persecution', in W.A. Phillips (ed.), *History of the Church of Ireland* (3 vols, Oxford, 1933),

iii. 59–116; some general studies extend into the period: see A. Ford, 'Dependent or Independent: the Church of Ireland and its colonial context, 1536–1647', *The Seventeenth Century* 10 (1995), pp. 163–87.

3   Armstrong, 'Protestant churchmen', p. 247.
4   A. Milton, 'Anglicanism and Royalism in the 1640s', in J. Adamson (ed.), *The English Civil War: conflict and contexts, 1640–49* (Basingstoke, 2009), pp. 61–81, at pp. 63–4.
5   A. Ford, *James Ussher: theology, history, and politics in early-modern Ireland and England* (Oxford, 2007), pp. 230, 234.
6   Ford, *Ussher*, pp. 255, 260; Milton, 'Anglicanism and Royalism', p. 64.
7   Bodl. MS Carte 4, fos 37, 40, 54, 56, 62: examinations of witnesses, 26 Nov. 1642; for Nugent see E. Boran (ed.), *The Correspondence of James Ussher, 1600–1656* (3 vols, Dublin, 2015). iii. 901, for Travers see Bodl. MS Carte 11, fo. 30: Ussher to Ormond, 20 May 1644.
8   *CSP Ire. 1633–47*, p. 383.
9   See Carte, *Life of Ormonde*, v. 520.
10 J. McCafferty, 'Protestant prelates or godly pastors? The dilemma of the early Stuart episcopate', in A. Ford and J. McCafferty (eds), *The Origins of Sectarianism in Early Modern Ireland* (Cambridge, 2005), pp. 54–72, at pp. 65, 68–9; T. Ó hAnnracháin, '"In Imitation of that Holy Patron of Prelates the Blessed St Charles": episcopal activity in Ireland and the formation of a confessional identity, 1618–1653', in Ford and McCafferty (eds), *Origins of Sectarianism*, pp. 73–94, at pp. 79–81, 90.
11 *CSP Ire. 1633–47*, p. 379 (the king ordered that he was to continue to hold the rectory of Tradry in Killaloe diocese in commendam); J.B. Leslie, *Clergy of Killaloe, Kilfenora, Clonfert and Kilmacduagh* (new edn, 2010), p. 687 (for Sibthorpe); *The Whole Works of Sir James Ware Concerning Ireland, Revised and Improved ... by Walter Harris, Esq* (2 vols, Dublin, 1764), i. 515, dates Sibthorp's translation as 7 Apr. 1642.
12 *Works of Sir James Ware*, i. 243.
13 *CSP Ire. 1633–47*, p. 380; Leslie, *Clergy of Killaloe*, p. 296; *Works of Sir James Ware*, i. 643.
14 Bodl. MS Carte 8, fo. 197: Charles I to Ormond, 22 Dec. 1643; *CSP Ire. 1633–47*, p. 389.
15 Armstrong, 'Protestant Churchmen', p. 243; *Works of Sir James Ware*, i. 643.
16 Ó Siochrú, *Confederate Ireland*, pp. 70–2.
17 Bodl. MS Carte 11, fo. 30: Ussher to Ormond, 20 May 1644.
18 *CSP Ire. 1633–47*, p. 394; the see was to be held with prebendary of Dunlavan (St Patrick's Cathedral) and Castropetre (Kildare Cathedral) and the vicarage of Bodenstown, Kildare diocese; *Works of Sir James Ware*, i. 393.
19 TCD, MS 813, fo. 264: deposition of William Golborne, 24 Mar. 1642.
20 Bodl. MS Carte 11, fo. 30: Ussher to Ormond, 20 May 1644.
21 Bodl. MS Carte 21, fo. 557: list of clergy, *c*.1647.
22 Ó Siochrú, *Confederate Ireland*, p. 82.
23 Ford, *Ussher*, p. 266.
24 Boran (ed.), *Corresp. of James Ussher*, iii. 905.

25 Carte, *Life of Ormonde*, vi. 277.
26 Bodl. MS Carte 63, fo. 329: Ormond to Radcliffe, 16 Apr. 1645; cf. *CSP Ire.* 1633–47, p. 400, which suggests there was alternative plan to translate Killala to Clogher.
27 Carte, *Life of Ormonde*, v. 436.
28 Bodl. MS Carte 14, fo. 235: Charles I to Ormond, 9 Mar. 1645.
29 Ó Siochrú, *Confederate Ireland*, pp. 80–2; T. Ó hAnnracháin, 'Rebels and Confederates: the stance of the Irish clergy in the 1640s', in J.R. Young (ed.), *Celtic Dimensions of the British Civil Wars* (Edinburgh, 1997), pp. 96–115, at pp. 104–7.
30 Armstrong, *Protestant War*, pp. 135, 138.
31 Armstrong, 'Protestant churchmen', p. 244; Carte, *Life of Ormonde*, v. 436.
32 *Works of Sir James Ware*, i. 617.
33 J.B. Leslie, *Clergy of Dublin and Glendalough* (new edn, 2001), p. 229; a planned reshuffle, with Griffith Williams of Ossory moving to Killala, and Sibbald becoming bishop of Ossory, does not seem to have been followed through: see Bodl. MS Carte 14, fo. 543: Charles I to Ormond, 13 May 1645.
34 Bodl. MS Carte 63, fo. 345: Digby to Ormond, 13 May 1645.
35 E. Venables (revised by J. McElligott), 'Fuller, Thomas', *ODNB*.
36 Carte, *Life of Ormonde*, vi. 287.
37 Bodl. MS Carte 63, fo. 345: Digby to Ormond, 13 May 1645; MS Carte 15, fo. 416: Ormond to Digby, 14 Aug. 1645.
38 Ford, *Ussher*, 162; C. Diamond,'Parry, Edward', *ODNB*; Leslie, *Clergy of Dublin*, p. 18.
39 Diamond, 'Edward Parry', *ODNB*; Armstrong, 'Protestant churchmen', p. 238n.
40 A. Clarke, 'Jones, Henry', *DIB*.
41 Clarendon, *History of the Rebellion*, ii. 38–9.
42 Bodl. MS Carte 15, fo. 111: Prince Rupert to Ormond, 22 June 1645 (marked as received on 29 June).
43 Bodl. MS Carte 15, fo. 162: bishop of Cloyne's notes, c.July 1645.
44 Bodl. MS Carte 15, fo. 297: Galbraith to Ormond, 26 July 1645.
45 Bodl. MS Carte 15, fo. 351: Irish bishops to Ormond, 2 Aug. 1645; ibid., fo. 357: Sir Gerard Lowther to Lord Muskerry, 5 Aug. 1645.
46 A. Duignan, 'Shifting allegiances: the Protestant community in Connacht, 1643–5', in R. Armstrong and T. Ó hAnnracháin (eds), *Community in Early Modern Ireland* (Dublin, 2006), pp. 120–32, at pp. 129–30.
47 Bodl. MS Carte 15, fo. 373v: Ormond to Taaffe, 7 Aug. 1645.
48 Bodl. MS Carte 15, fo. 420: Elphin to Ormond, 14 Aug. 1645.
49 Bodl. MS Carte 15, fo. 453: articles of surrender of Elphin, 19 Aug. 1645; ibid., fo. 510: Elphin to Ormond, 26 Aug. 1645.
50 Bodl. MS Carte 15, fo. 652v: Elphin to Margetson, 17 Sept. 1645.
51 Bodl. MS Carte 15, fo. 694: royal order, 29 Sept. 1645.
52 *Works of Sir James Ware*, i. 159; J.B. Leslie, *Clogher Clergy and Parishes* (Enniskillen, 1929), p. 11.
53 Ó Siochrú's argument that Ormond knew about the Glamorgan mission all along is not convincing: cf. K. Forkan, 'Ormond's alternative: the lord-lieutenant's secret contacts with Protestant Ulster, 1645–6', *Hist. Res.* 81 (2008), pp. 610–35.

54 Ó Siochrú, *Confederate Ireland*, pp. 93, 98.
55 Bodl. MS Carte 16, fo. 415: Eustace to Thomas Pigott, 11 Jan. 1646.
56 Forkan, 'Ormond's alternative', pp. 617-20.
57 Bodl. MS Carte 16, fo. 487r-v: Ormond's 'remembrances' for Galbraith, c.Jan. 1646.
58 Bodl. MS Carte 16, fo. 441: Ormond to Nicholas, 19 Jan. 1646.
59 Ford, *Ussher*, pp. 266-7.
60 Ibid., pp. 267-8.
61 Bodl. MS Carte 18, fos 590v-591: instructions of Ormond and Irish council, 26 Sept. 1646.
62 Forkan, 'Ormond's Alternative', pp. 618-9.
63 Bodl. MS Carte 19, fo. 324: justification of peace, 6 Nov. 1646.
64 Bodl. MS Carte 19, fos 463, 500-1: Ormond's answers to commissioners, Nov. 1646.
65 Bodl. MS Carte 19, fo. 702: Ormond to Digby, 25 Dec. 1646.
66 Bodl. MS Carte 19, fo. 763: Charles I to Ormond, 29 Dec. 1646.
67 Milton, 'Anglicanism and Royalism', pp. 65-8.
68 Bodl. MS Carte 164, pp. 392b-3: Ormond's order, 9 Mar. 1647; ibid., p. 408: Ormond to Sir Paul Davies, 24 Mar. 1647.
69 C. Diamond, 'Parry, Edward', *ODNB*.
70 *HMC Egmont MSS*, i. 363.
71 Bodl. MS Carte 20, fos 462v, 467: Ormond's instructions, 16 Mar. 1647.
72 Bodl. MS Carte 20, fo. 479: Ormond to Charles I, 17 Mar. 1647.
73 Armstrong, *Protestant War*, p. 198.
74 Bodl. MS Carte 21, fo. 241: order of commissioners, 24 June 1647; ibid., fos 241v-2: response by Dublin clergy, 22 June 1647.
75 Seymour, *Puritans in Ireland*, pp. 2-6; Armstrong, 'Protestant churchmen', p. 248.
76 *HMC Egmon MSS*, i. 425.
77 R. Gillespie, 'The religion of the first duke of Ormond', in Toby Barnard and Jane Fenlon (eds), *The Dukes of Ormonde, 1610-1745* (Woodbridge, Suffolk, 2000), pp. 101-14, at pp. 103, 105-6, 108-9.
78 Ussher seems to have had considerable respect for Ormond, reputedly describing him as 'truly noble' in the spring of 1647: see *HMC Ormonde MSS*, old series, i. 116.
79 Ford, *Ussher*, p. 230.
80 For an overview of the evidence see P. Little, 'Discord in Drogheda: a window on Irish church-state relations in the sixteen-forties', *Hist. Res.* 75 (2002), pp. 355-62, at p. 359.

8

The marquess of Ormond, Lord Montgomery of the Ards and the problem of authority in Ulster, 1649

KEVIN FORKAN

'The ministers before had preached so much against Ards' treachery, that few of his people had heart or hand to join him'.[1] This was Robert Baillie's cutting description of the reaction to efforts by Lord Montgomery of the Ards to shore up royalist support in Ulster during the second half of 1649. Montgomery, commander-in-chief of the Ulster royalist forces by commissions from both Charles II and the marquess of Ormond, lord lieutenant of Ireland, was at that time head of an army symbolic of the improbable alliances that marked the royalist cause during that year: Scottish redshanks, Catholic Connachtmen and Ulstermen, and Ulster Scottish Presbyterians ('blue bonnets') made up the ranks of the 3,000 foot and 300 horse under his command. This army was defeated and scattered at Lisnastrain in December, a battle that destroyed Protestant royalism in Ulster, a hammer-blow to the non-sectarian coalition that Ormond had built in Ireland during the year. Montgomery's failure to convince his kith and kin that the royalist cause was worth fighting for was symptomatic of Ormond's failure to impose his authority as the king's lord lieutenant on the northern province, despite that province being among the first and loudest condemners of the regicide and most enthusiastic proclaimers of Charles II as king.

This chapter analyses the attempts by the marquess of Ormond to impose his authority on Ulster following the execution of Charles I in January 1649, through to the defeat of Montgomery's army at the end of the year. Ormond's contacts and alliances with the Church of Ireland, Presbyterian and Catholic factions in Ulster are examined, in the context of his previous experience during the 1640s and of his newly formed alliance with the former confederate Catholics in the south of the kingdom. The sequence of events culminating in the proclamation of royal authority in the province by Montgomery are described, as well as the subsequent collapse of that authority under pressure from the competing power centres dominated by the Belfast Presbytery and the English parliamentarian interest. A conclusion offers reasons why royal authority as defined by Ormond and Charles II could not be imposed on Ulster during 1649, and how this failure contributed to the overall royalist defeat in Ireland.

The history of Ulster following the 1641 rising was traditionally dominated by two narratives: the Presbyterian/covenanting version of Patrick Adair, Robert Blair, Robert Ballie and J.S. Reid from the seventeenth century onwards,[2] and the royalist narrative of Thomas Carte in the eighteenth century, which was followed up by the editors of the Montgomery and Hamilton manuscripts in the nineteenth.[3] Mid-twentieth-century historiography mainly bypassed the 1640s, and certainly ignored the tortuous theological squabbling and shifting allegiances of the Ulster Protestants, preferring to study the negotiations between the royal government in England and Ireland and the confederate Catholics.[4] The *New History of Ireland* devoted scant attention to Ulster during the 1640s and the only major monograph to look at Ulster in depth was David Stevenson's 1981 study of the Scottish army in the province.[5] The historiographical revolution of the 1990s and early 2000s relating to 1640s Ireland did not, however, overlook Ulster, as the royalist and Presbyterian myths were teased apart and a comprehensive view of what actually happened in the province during the decade brought into focus.[6]

Nevertheless, gaps remain, especially when it comes to the later 1640s. This chapter is unashamed in seeking to recover the political and military situation *wie es eigentlich gewesen* (as it actually happened) during the period January–December 1649, a period when Ulster Protestants rapidly abandoned the alliance with the English Parliament that it had sustained earlier in the decade, a royalist commander took over almost the entire province in the name of Charles II, and the subsequent collapse of that takeover with extraordinary speed in the latter part of the year. The defeat of royalism in Ulster removed the major Protestant element from Ormond's coalition in Ireland and his dependence on Catholic arms increased, making his political position increasing untenable.[7] Understanding why events occurred as they did in Ulster during 1649 also helps us understand their effect on the larger political movements in the three kingdoms. In particular, discouraging news from Ireland made Charles II more likely to submit to the demands of the hardline covenanter government in Scotland. Without an understanding of these events, larger postulations on the significance or otherwise of Ulster and its interaction with the rest of Ireland and the three kingdoms as a whole is impossible.

When the marquess of Ormond returned to Ireland from France in September 1648, his mission was to secure that kingdom for the royalist cause. His previous eight years of service, first as lord general of the Irish army, and from November 1643 as lord lieutenant, afforded him insight into the myriad factions and powerful personalities that made up the political landscape of in each of the four provinces. Ulster, in particular, had been an awkward case. From trying to impose royal authority over the Ulster settler forces that were raised in the aftermath of the 1641 rising to dealing with the Scottish army under Robert Monro, which operated completely independently of the royal administration in Dublin, Ormond's Ulster experiences as lord general did not inspire confidence.[8] As lord lieutenant from the end of 1643, he lost all authority in Ulster following the cessation of arms with the confederates and the Solemn League and Covenant between the Scottish covenanters and the English Parliament, the latter being adopted with varying degrees of enthusiasm by the Protestant populace and elite of the province.[9] In 1645 and 1646 Ormond engaged in various plots to win back his authority in Ulster, but by mid-1647, with his overtures of alliance to both the Ulster Protestant forces and the Catholic confederates rejected, he concluded his position throughout Ireland was hopeless, and surrendered Dublin to the parliamentarians.[10] Returning to Ireland in late 1648, too late to aid the pro-royalist Scottish Engagers, Ormond's tortuous negotiations with the confederates were galvanised in December by news of the New Model army's intention to put Charles I on trial for his life. On 17 January 1649 a peace treaty was signed between Ormond and the confederates, creating a broad alliance of Catholic and Protestant royalist forces in Ireland, but this came too late to influence events in England. On 30 January, Charles I was executed.

News of the regicide probably arrived in Ulster days before Ormond received word. The Ulster Presbytery's reaction was swift and strident. Their *Necessary Representation* attacked the English sectarian party, primarily for the overthrow of the Covenant and for its perceived establishment of a 'universal tolerance of all religions ... so repugnant to the Word of God and the first two articles of the Covenant'.[11] Only after this came condemnation of the purge of the Westminster Parliament and the execution of Charles I – 'an act so horrible as no history, divine or human, ever had a precedent to the like'. Ormond saw the opportunity presented by the Presbytery's reaction, writing confidently that 'the Scots in the north are ready, upon any countenance of force, to act considerably against these hell-hounds'.[12] Yet his hopes of a new alliance between the Ulster Protestants and the Catholic and Protestant royalists under his command were compromised by the final paragraph of the tract, wherein the ministers warned Ulster Presbyterians against allying with 'known opposers of the Covenant ... papists and other malignants, especially such who have been chief promoters of the late Engagement against England'. An Ulster petition was also prepared for the new king, seeking security for Presbyterianism and the Covenant, entreating the king to take the Covenant himself, and urging him to disavow Ormond's recently signed peace treaty with the confederates.[13] The petition was probably sent via Scotland to Charles II, but on 12 February one of Ormond's south-east Ulster contacts, Robert Ward of Castleward, passed a copy to the royalist agent, Daniel O'Neill, for delivery to the lord lieutenant.[14]

Ward was part of a nexus of English royalists, many of whom had previously been under Ormond's command as part of his Leinster army, and based mainly in south co. Down and co. Louth, including Charles Townley and Sir Marcus Trevor. Ward was fully supportive of the confederate treaty, urging the lord lieutenant to reject the Ulster Scottish petition as a plot to make the province 'subordinate to Scotland … this I have often heard to be their design'. He advised the lord lieutenant to secure the English plantation areas in counties Londonderry, Antrim and Fermanagh, while as commander-in-chief he suggested reinstating Arthur, Viscount Chichester, who had been expelled from the province in 1644 for his resistance to the Covenant. All this seemed utterly incompatible with the Ulster Scottish demands. At the end of his communication Ward suggested that the most active and respected Ulster Scottish nobleman, Lord Montgomery of the Ards, be ordered to arrest the local allies of the parliamentarian commander in the north, Colonel George Monck, including Colonel Edward Conway and Major George Rawdon, by which means 'it will appear what obedience will be given to your commands'.[15] If royalist and Presbyterian priorities were still far apart, perhaps in the person of Montgomery a bridge could be found to span the gap, if only to facilitate the expulsion of the parliamentary forces.[16]

In west Ulster, more removed from the influence of the Belfast Presbytery and Scottish government, local royalists took the initiative themselves. In Enniskillen, junior officers seized the garrison, wrote to Charles II and Ormond expressing their loyalty, and contacted Archdeacon Humphrey Galbraith and other prominent royalists in co. Donegal.[17] Galbraith was by now seconded by his brothers (who held senior positions in the regiments of Sir Robert Stewart and Audley Mervyn), the Church of Ireland bishop of Raphoe, John Leslie, and other officers from the 'Laggan' regiments in an open avowal of the cause of Charles II.[18] In the meantime he urged Sir Charles Coote, commander of Derry City, to disown the regicides and 'unfeignedly contribute your endeavours to wipe away from these lands the guilt of so much innocent blood'.[19] Ormond, simultaneously receiving letters from Enniskillen and the Laggan, sent his own exhortation to Coote, and remodelled the west Ulster forces along royalist lines.[20] The covenanting variable in the north-west was represented by a group of Presbyterian ministers and by Sir Alexander Stewart, son and heir of the late Sir William Stewart, an influential landowner in counties Donegal and Tyrone from the 1630s who had been effective leader of the pro-Parliament and pro-Presbyterian faction in the area until his death in 1647.[21] The Belfast Presbytery, aware of the strong Church of Ireland influence as represented by Bishop Leslie and Archdeacon Galbraith, also took a keen interest in west Ulster, adding their voice to those imploring Coote to condemn the regicide.[22]

By early March, however, Coote had made up his mind to resist such pressure, informing the Presbytery of his belief that the New Model Army had 'been the instruments of redeeming England out of thralldom', and that his priority was to finish the war against the Irish rebels.[23] This latter point would resonate with the Presbytery, but not with Galbraith and his fellows, who prepared to go into action against the Derry garrison. At this point, Galbraith requested that Ormond send an auxiliary force to aid them, his only condition being that the soldiers would be 'not of our neighbouring Ulster Irish, whose ill usage towards us, in the beginning of the troubles of this kingdom, can not upon the sudden be so well digested'.[24] Galbraith's request – sensible from a military point of view and understandable in the heat of emotion following the regicide – set in course the events that would eventually shatter the uneasy alliance between royalists and covenanters that was developing in the province.

In east Ulster, Monck was backed into a corner. He had answered the Presbytery's call for a renewal of the Covenant with a request for them not to press matters until he had consulted with a council of war of the Ulster British forces, called for 21 March. In the meantime, the Covenant was resubscribed throughout Antrim and Down, the Presbytery sent a deputation to the Laggan to oversee a similar process, and Lord Montgomery was reported to have declared strongly against both sectaries and malignants.[25] At the council of war, held at Lisnagarvey (Lisburn), Monck attempted to deflect attention from the regicide by emphasising his opposition to the second Ormond Peace, but the local officers and country representatives insisted he take the Covenant and forswear the authority of the New Model Army.[26] Monck stalled for time, promising to defend all who supported the Covenant, while writing urgently to Colonel Michael Jones, the parliamentary commander in Dublin, and preparing to withdraw south to Dundalk.[27] The council of war then issued a declaration evocative of the *Necessary Representation*, heralding the creation of a covenanted people-in-arms, free from contamination by 'papists, sectaries and malignants', unconnected with Ormond's alliance with the Irish in the south of the kingdom.[28] In the meantime, Charles II was declared king with full pomp, and Montgomery acclaimed commander of the east Ulster British forces by the officers and Presbytery.[29] While being entrusted by the Presbytery with the civil and military governance of east Ulster, however, Montgomery sent a coded note to Ormond, assuring him 'how wholly I am your lordship's servant'.[30] Nineteen days later, Ormond signed a commission for Montgomery to be commander-in-chief of the royalist forces in Ulster.[31] On 29 May, Ormond assured Charles II's secretary that Montgomery was 'without condition or reserve resolved to serve the king', but would be unable to produce his commission openly until 'Scotland ... be persuaded to leave out of their declarations their usual destructive reservations'.[32]

The lord lieutenant was now marshalling his forces to take control of the whole kingdom. By his treaty with the confederates, their Association was dissolved, and the Catholic forces united with the Protestant Munster forces commanded by the Lord Inchiquin. In May Ormond advanced at the head of his army from Kilkenny, reaching Finglas, a few miles north of Dublin, by 28 June. He now answered Humphrey Galbraith's plea for assistance by authorising the first overtly royalist military intervention into Ulster affairs, a clear affront to the council of war's *Declaration* a few weeks earlier. His commander was a professional soldier, Sir George Monro, previously commander of the Scottish army's garrison at Coleraine, and much to the fore in royalist scheming during the 1647–48 period.[33] Ormond, somewhat optimistically, gave Monro the command of a force of about 1,600 men consisting of Catholic Old English dragoons, Catholic Scottish/Ulster Gaels under Colonel Alexander McDonnell, Connachtmen under Francis Taaffe and a regiment under Colonel Maguire, a defector from Owen Roe O'Neill's Catholic Ulster army.[34] Monro was also to be commander-in-chief of the Laggan army in western Ulster, an appointment not welcomed by Galbraith or the royalist officers there. These forces were intended to rendezvous at Roscommon on 20 May, capture Sligo, and proceed via Enniskillen to the Laggan, eventually reducing Derry and thus securing the overall royalist position in the province.[35] Monro was expected to liaise with, and respect the authority of, Lord Montgomery.[36]

In co. Down, Rawdon and Conway had by this time sworn the Covenant, leaving Monck to slip away to Dundalk, 'where he studies nothing else but fortification, [and] he talks of nothing more than Lieutenant General Cromwell'.[37] In west Ulster, the last week in March saw the beginning of what one of Coote's English officers described as 'a general revolt of the Scotch of all sides'.[38] Throughout April the Laggan forces closed in on Derry, entrenching themselves close to the walls, while on 26 May two of their commanders, Sir Robert Stewart and Audley Mervyn, returned to Ulster to conduct the siege.[39] However, despite requests from Ormond, the royalist navy under Prince Rupert remained to the south of Ireland and made no effort to prevent Coote from being supplied by sea, undermining the morale of the Laggan forces who lacked heavy cannon to breach the city's walls.[40] Meanwhile, Sir George Monro arrived in the area, capturing his former garrison town of Coleraine around the last week of June.[41] Around 26 June, Monro and his force left Coleraine and swept through co. Antrim, arriving outside the walls of Belfast. The next day Montgomery arrived, apparently to relieve the garrison, but upon gaining entry displaced the Presbyterian governor and publicly proclaimed his royal commission.[42] He then went on to secure Antrim town and Lisnagarvey, sending Monro on towards Carrickfergus, then the residence of the ministers of the Presbytery. Montgomery joined Monro outside Carrickfergus on 1 July and demanded its surrender. His promises to maintain the Covenant and Presbyterian church government rang hollow with the defenders and Presbytery as they observed Monro's Catholic Irish soldiers outside the walls, but their military weakness and divisions in the garrison made defence impossible.[43] The town surrendered on generous terms on 4 July, and Montgomery issued a declaration stating that his royal commission was necessary to maintain unity in the province, he would maintain Presbyterianism and would remove Monro and his unsavoury company as quickly as possible.[44] A further proclamation by Ormond ordered all in Ulster to obey him as lord lieutenant, and allowed for the imprisonment of any ministers who would 'presume to exercise the people in sedition or disobedience'.[45]

Yet in Montgomery's moment of triumph the seeds were sown for the collapse of the royalist position in Ulster. Even before the fall of Carrickfergus, he was attacked by the ministers of the Presbytery, who wrote to 'denounce judgement upon your person, family and all your party'.[46] Soon afterwards they issued yet another declaration to the Presbyterians of Ulster, condemning Montgomery's treachery in accepting a commission from an uncovenanted king and allying with Ormond and the Irish. This condemnation was in print in Scotland within three weeks, and from thence doubtless distributed throughout Ulster. It was read at the pulpits of the province, and the people exhorted to disassociate themselves from Montgomery and the malignants and to deny them 'the sinews of war, money and victuals'.[47] In their actions the ministers mirrored events in Scotland, where the Kirk party government was purging the military, civil and religious establishment of all tainted with malignancy, placing the defence of the Covenant far above restoration of the Stuarts.[48] Throughout the summer and autumn Montgomery's forces were slowly weakened as word of the condemnation took root. Late July, however, saw the apogee of royalist efforts throughout the kingdom. Monck, ensconced in Dundalk, had come to an agreement with the Catholic commander Owen Roe O'Neill that protected his position for the moment, but on 23 July Trevor and Inchiquin defeated a strong force from O'Neill's army just outside the town. Two days later the garrison changed sides, forcing Monck to flee to England, where his dealings with the Ulster general earned for him a censure in Parliament.[49] By then also, Ward and Trevor had ensured that the south-east Ulster garrisons of Newry, Carlingford, Rostrevor and Dundrum were in royalist hands. On 28 June Ormond reported the favourable situation to Charles II, noting the lack of opposition to Sir George Monro's progress in east Ulster. Three weeks later, however, the lord lieutenant admitted the Presbytery's condemnation of Montgomery's commissions, and that 'the fatal ingredient of the Covenant' could yet undermine royalist efforts in the province.[50]

Montgomery now travelled west to join the besiegers of Derry. Lack of supplies and the arrival of reinforcements for Coote from Connacht had forced the Lagganeers back from the walls on 20 July, but the viscount's arrival four days later with 800 horse and dragoons heartened them, and they offered battle to Coote and his men.[51] A tale of Montgomery's drinking bout with Coote (part of an attempt to win over the parliamentarian commander) may be apocryphal, used as it was to emphasise his profanity by the Presbyterian historian Patrick Adair, but it illustrated the divisions that were opening up among the Laggan forces.[52] Sir Alexander Stewart invited local Presbyterian ministers and those sent from the Belfast Presbytery to preach to the soldiers, but they were shocked at the strength of the royalist party. The ministers and Sir Alexander left the siege, taking with them many men.[53]

Threats by Sir Robert Stewart and Monro to imprison several ministers only widened the divisions.[54] On 29 July Montgomery reported the situation to Ormond.[55] All equipment necessary for a siege was lacking, the Laggan forces were reduced to 700 effective troops, and his own force wished to return to east Ulster. The countryside was devastated and provided scant relief; it was felt that the Derry garrison 'indeed did rather besiege us'. Coote played the national card, turning the English soldiers and populace of the city against the mainly Scottish Laggan forces. Since force was ineffective, Montgomery's only solution was for Ormond to send an eminent Englishman, or Inchiquin, to induce the defenders to join the royalists. In the first few days of August, Coote and his men sallied out and ravaged the Laggan army's quarters.[56] Soon after, in accordance with an agreement made in March, O'Neill's army arrived to relieve Derry, scattering the remaining Laggan soldiers.[57] Sir Robert Stewart now joined Montgomery in retreating to Antrim and Down, and Coote was given effective control of the north west.[58]

As Montgomery faced these reverses in Ulster, Ormond and the main royalist army closed in on Michael Jones in Dublin; but on 2 August the besieging forces were decisively defeated at Rathmines, Ormond's army was scattered and the initiative passed forcibly to the parliamentary commanders. Minimising the scale of his defeat to Charles II, the lord lieutenant determined not to re-engage until reinforcements had arrived from his provincial commanders, Inchiquin, Clanricarde and Montgomery.[59] Montgomery himself had retreated from the Laggan to his lands around Newtownards, where he found his forces weakened and divided. His neighbour the earl of Clanbrassil (formerly Lord Clandeboye) wished for an independent command while the earl of Ardglass, an English planter recently returned to his estates in co. Down, complained scathingly that had he received a commission from Ormond he would have marched south with 'better strength as a colonel than he [Montgomery] went up with now as a commander in chief'.[60] And all the while men streamed from their colours as the condemnation of the Presbytery continued its effect.[61] At a council of war Montgomery, Sir Robert Stewart and Sir George Monro discussed a response to Ormond's pleas for assistance, as Jones advanced towards Drogheda.[62] Montgomery mustered his forces at Dromore, co. Down, and led 600-odd cavalry south to reinforce the strategically important castle of Trim, co. Meath, while his 920 infantry were divided, some joining the cavalry while others were ordered to secure Antrim and Down.[63]

The Ulster forces arrived too late to hinder Oliver Cromwell's landing on 15 August, and upon news of the storm and slaughter at Drogheda on 11 September they fled northwards from Trim, allowing Cromwell to occupy the castle.[64] Before turning south to invade the confederate heartlands of south Leinster, Cromwell ordered Colonel Robert Venables to strike northwards. Dundalk, Carlingford and Newry quickly fell, as the east Ulster English forces under Trevor retreated to defend the approaches to Belfast and Carrickfergus.[65] On 27 September Trevor fell on Venables's quarters near Dromore, but treachery and the poor performance of his Irish cavalry led to his defeat, and the rapid capture of Lisnagarvey and Belfast by the parliamentarians.[66] Venables's next target was Carrickfergus, but as he advanced towards this, the last major stronghold in east Ulster, Sir George Monro and his force dashed southwards from Coleraine and burned Lisnagarvey, before retreating across the province to Enniskillen.[67] In the meantime, Coote advanced from Derry and took Coleraine, and he and Venables joined forces to summon the garrison of Carrickfergus on 2 November, where the commander agreed to surrender the town on 13 December if he had not been by then relieved.[68] In the meantime, Ormond and his allies were enduring a string of defeats in the south, as Wexford (11 October), New Ross (19 October) and Carrick-on-Suir (20 November) fell, and Inchiquin's Munster garrisons began to declare for Parliament.[69] By late November, however, Cromwell's assaults against Duncannon and Waterford had failed, his army held in check as reinforcements from Owen Roe O'Neill's army joined the royalists.[70] Suddenly, Ormond's prospects appeared brighter. He was aware by now that the king was in Jersey and still intended to sail to Ireland.[71] As yet, he did not know that having received the news of Drogheda, Charles was sending an emissary, Henry Seymour, to Ireland to report on the situation there before he himself travelled to the kingdom.[72] At the same time, the Scottish government, controlled by the Kirk party, resolved to reopen negotiations with Charles and invite him to Scotland, sending an emissary to search the courts of western Europe for their absentee king.[73] The terms offered did not differ substantially from those of the previous March, and so any favourable news from Ireland would almost certainly encourage Charles to go there instead.

Carrickfergus was the last major seaport held by the Ulster royalists, and its fall would signal the end of royalist hopes in the province and of any expectation Ormond had of significant aid from Montgomery and Monro. Its relief was therefore a priority. On Seymour's arrival in late November, Ormond prepared the desired report for Charles II, in which supplies of money and success in Ulster were defined as the preconditions for an eventual victory.[74] In order to achieve the latter, the lord lieutenant ordered Clanricarde to prepare a force from Connacht to aid his two Ulster commanders, feeling that such a conjunction should soon have 'annulled the bargain lending the surrender of Carrickfergus'.[75] These orders came much too late to influence events in Ulster during December, where Montgomery and Monro decided to bring matters to a head. Their forces, bolstered by the addition of a contingent of Ulster Irish soldiers from Charlemont, joined forces with Trevor and Clanbrassil at Armagh in early December. This heterogeneous body of Scottish Presbyterians, redshanks, and Catholic Connacht and Ulstermen remained at their strength of about 3,000 foot and 300 horse; the viscount tried to recruit on his own lands around Newtownards but was unsuccessful.[76] After an attempt to cross the River Lagan at Lisnagarvey was repulsed by the united forces of Coote and Venables, Montgomery made the decision to remain in the field rather than bypassing the parliamentarians with an overnight dash to Carrickfergus. The next day Coote and Venables caught up with the royalist rearguard at Lisnastrain, just west of Lisnagarvey, and broke it with a cavalry charge. Panic spread throughout the main body of the army and the soldiers scattered, with a few hundred chased down and killed by Coote's cavalry. Clanbrassil was taken prisoner, Montgomery and Monro fled ignominiously to Charlemont.[77] Montgomery wrote desperately to Ormond about his lack of means and desire to leave the service. Monro retired to Enniskillen to join with the forces Clanricarde had promised.[78]

Lisnastrain destroyed Protestant royalism in Ulster, and with it Ormond's non-sectarian coalition. Carrickfergus surrendered within a week. Montgomery's forces could not be reformed, his men returned to their homes as he straggled southward to join Clanricarde with a bare company.[79] Along with most of the remaining Protestant royalists, Montgomery surrendered to the Cromwellians at Clonmel in March 1650.[80] Sir George Monro, piqued at being overlooked for the command of Enniskillen and unimpressed with Clanricarde's forces, surrendered the town to Coote for £500 and licence to return to Scotland.[81] The process that began with the Presbytery's denunciation of Montgomery the previous July concluded in June 1650, when Venables declared that he would protect the Presbyterian ministers from the royalists.[82]

To the south, a similar process splitting the Catholic hierarchy from Ormond's coalition was underway, culminating in his repudiation by the bishops on 12 August. Irish royalism, as represented by Ormond, had been abandoned by the majority of both the Catholics and Protestants of the kingdom. Another blow fell shortly after. Seymour had returned to Jersey, on the heels of a Scottish emissary, in early January 1650. By now the defeats at

Drogheda and Wexford were well known, and it was increasingly unlikely that the king would risk travelling to Ireland. It was resolved that only through Scottish arms could Ireland be saved and England recovered, and that a treaty with the Kirk party must be concluded.[83] On 1 May the treaty of Breda was completed, and on his arrival in Scotland hard-line elements of the Kirk party demanded a public declaration against malignancy, the Irish treaty, and even the king's late father.[84] The publication of this declaration, made at Dunfermline on 16 August, and Charles's acknowledgement of 'the exceeding great sinfulness and unlawfulness, of that treaty and peace made with the bloody Irish rebels',[85] made Ormond's position in Ireland untenable, and on 11 December he left the kingdom, leaving the Catholic earl of Clanricarde to continue the hopeless struggle.

The *Necessary Representation*, the Ulster Petition to Charles II, and the acclamation of Lord Montgomery as leader of the anti-parliamentarian party in Ulster presented a major opportunity for the marquess of Ormond to achieve what he had been unable to do in the previous seven years: impose his authority and that of the king on Ulster. Initially, the plan was successful. By the early summer of 1649, Monck had fled from Ulster and Coote was besieged in Derry. A decision by Rupert to divert some ships north, or an alternative view by Coote on the matter of the regicide, would have secured the entire province and, perhaps, mobilised a strong and experienced fighting force to aid Ormond in his campaign against Dublin. This was a situation that needed to be handled delicately, and Ormond had ample experience from his previous dealings with Ulster that Presbyterian loyalty was conditional and subject to the Covenant. In 1645–47 he had been prepared to make significant concessions on the Covenant and the question of Presbyterian church government,[86] but in 1649 he was either unwilling to consider this, or did not communicate his willingness to take Ulster Presbyterian feelings into account. Perhaps Ormond felt that the shock of the regicide would override Ulster Scottish concerns and propel them into his new alliance. Ormond also had faith in Montgomery as a proxy royalist commander in the province. It was a shrewd choice. Montgomery was a proven commander against the Irish, who had suffered capture and imprisonment by Owen Roe O'Neill following the battle of Benburb, and was, as far as the Presbytery was concerned, untainted by 'malignancy'.[87] Montgomery was also a popular figure: his decision to make the market fountain in Newtownards run with wine at the proclamation of Charles II speaks to his deft touch concerning the man on the street.[88] Given time, Montgomery may well have cemented his Presbyterian-royalist alliance, secured the entire province, and released valuable reinforcements southwards for Ormond's army.

Ormond's single biggest mistake with regard to Ulster was the intervention of Sir George Monro's force into the province. For the political carnage that it caused, its military effectiveness was minimal: it did nothing to help in the siege of Derry, stayed in Coleraine most of the time, and its intervention before Carrickfergus and Belfast was unnecessary and disastrous for Montgomery. Before Monro's intervention, Montgomery had been acclaimed commander-in-chief of the Ulster Protestant forces and in all likelihood would have been welcomed into the towns. Following Monro's appearance at the walls, Montgomery had little choice but to acknowledge his alliance with him in order to prevent his own men and the defenders firing on them. Once he had acknowledged this alliance, he needed to justify it by displaying his royal commission, and announcing his alliance with Ormond. It was these three steps that broke his bond with the Presbytery, and set the scene for the collapse of his authority in the province. Ormond's subsequent blundering declarations in support of Montgomery and against the Presbyterian ministers compounded the initial mistake, but as support and soldiers leached away from Montgomery during the late summer and autumn the lord lieutenant prepared to repeat the mistake of sending a Catholic auxiliary force into Ulster before news of Lisnastrain made this plan redundant. The Ulster royalist revolt of 1649 presented a major opportunity to Ormond to restore the king's authority both in the province and throughout Ireland, but by viewing the province only through his own lens of post-regicide outrage he failed to learn from his own past experience, refused to take account of the nuances of Ulster politics, and ultimately destroyed Lord Montgomery, Charles II's hopes from Ireland, and his own position in the kingdom.

NOTES

1 *Baillie Letters and Journals*, ii. 346.
2 P. Adair, *A True Narrative of the Rise and Progress of the Presbyterian Church in Ireland*, ed. W.D. Killen (Belfast 1866); T. McCrie (ed.), *The Life of Mr Robert Blair* (Edinburgh, 1848); J.S. Reid, *History of the Presbyterian Church in Ireland* (3 vols, Belfast, 1867).
3 T. Carte, *An History of the Life of James Duke of Ormonde, from his birth in 1610, to his death in 1688*, 3 vols (1735); T.K. Lowry (ed.), *The Hamilton Manuscripts* (Belfast, 1867); G. Hill (ed.), *The Montgomery Manuscripts* (Belfast, 1869).
4 See for example J. Lowe, 'The Glamorgan mission to Ireland, 1645–6', *Studia Hibernica* 4 (1964), pp. 155–96; J. Lowe, 'Charles I and the Confederation of Kilkenny, 1643–9', *IHS* 14 (1964–65), pp. 1–19.
5 Only 29 lines out of 63 pages in the *NHI* are devoted to Ulster during the years 1641–53; D. Stevenson, *Scottish Covenanters and Irish Confederates. Scottish-Irish relations in the mid-seventeenth Century* (Belfast, 1981).
6 K. McKenny, *The Laggan Army in Ireland, 1640–85: the landed interests, political ideologies and military campaigns of the north-west Ulster settlers* (Dublin, 2005); K. Forkan, 'The South Ulster borderland as a political frontier in the 1640s, *Breifne*

10 (2004), pp. 270–89; K. Forkan, 'The Ulster Scots and the Engagement, 1647–8', *IHS* 35 (2007), pp. 455–76; K. Forkan, 'Ormond's alternative: the lord-lieutenant's secret contacts with Protestant Ulster, 1645–6', *Hist. Res.* 81 (2008), pp. 610–35; R. Armstrong, 'Viscount Ards and the Presbytery: politics and religion among the Scots of Ulster in the 1640s', in W.P. Kelly and J.R. Young (eds), *Scotland and the Ulster Plantations: explorations in the British settlements of Stuart Ireland* (Dublin, 2009), pp. 18–40; Forkan, '"The fatal ingredient of the Covenant": the place of the Ulster Scottish community during the 1640s', in B. Mac Cuarta (ed.), *Reshaping Ireland, 1550–1700: colonization and its consequences* (Dublin, 2011), pp. 261–80.
7 For the strength of the Ulster Protestant forces in late 1646 see *HMC Portland MSS*, i. 400.
8 K. Forkan, 'Scottish-Protestant Ulster and the Crisis of the Three Kingdoms, 1637–1652' (PhD thesis, NUI Galway, 1999), chapters 2–3; Armstrong, *Protestant War*, chapters 2–3.
9 M. Perceval-Maxwell, 'The adoption of the solemn league and covenant by the Scots in Ulster', *Scotia: American-Canadian journal of Scottish Studies* 2 (1978), pp. 3–18; Forkan, 'Scottish-Protestant Ulster', chapter 4.
10 See Forkan, 'Ormond's Alternative', passim.
11 *A Necessary Representation of the present evills, and eminent dangers to Religion, Lawes, and Liberties, arising from the late, and present practises of the Sectarian party in England: together with an Exhortation to duties relating to the Covenant, unto all within our Charge; and to all the well-affected within this Kingdome, by the Presbytery at Belfast, February 15th 1649* (Belfast, 1649).
12 Carte, *Ormonde*, iii. 608.
13 TNA, SP 63/275/2: Ulster petition to [Charles II], [1649]. This petition is addressed to 'the king' and survives as a copy dated to 1643 in the state papers, but internal evidence indicates that it was composed in early 1649.
14 Bodl. Carte MS 23, fo. 485: D. O'Neill to Ormond, 14 Feb. 1649.
15 Bodl. Carte MS 23, fos 230-1: [R. Ward] to [Ormond], [2 Feb. 1649]; another unsigned and undated letter, evidently from around this time and perhaps sent by one of the English officers at Lisnagarvey, advised Ormond to entrust Montgomery with the command of Ulster, and also to assure the Presbytery that their form of church government would be established throughout the kingdom should it be decided by a general assembly: see Bodl. Carte MS 26, fo. 448.
16 For an account of these events, focusing on Montgomery's relations with the Ulster Presbytery during the first half of 1649, see Armstrong, 'Viscount Ards and the Presbytery'.
17 *HMC Pepys MSS*, p. 277; Bodl. Carte MS 23, fo. 568: Enniskillen officers to Ormond, 26 Feb. 1649; Bodl. Carte MS 23, fos 570-1: Ormond to Enniskillen officers [16 Mar. 1649]; Carte MS 30, fo. 330: account of seizure of Enniskillen in Jan. 1649 [1651]; for Galbraith's activities during the mid-1640s see Forkan, 'Ormond's Alternative'.
18 Bodl. Carte MS 23, fo. 537: Galbraiths, Leslie and others to Ormond, 21 Feb. 1649.
19 Bodl. Carte MS 23, fo. 539: Galbraith to Coote, 20 Feb. 1649.
20 Bodl. Carte MS 23, fos 570-1: Ormond to Enniskillen officers, [16 Mar. 1649]; Bodl. Carte MS 24, fo. 59: Ormond to [Enniskillen or Laggan officers?], [16 Mar. 1649];

ibid., fo. 62: Ormond to Coote, 16 Mar. 1649; ibid., fo. 142: Ormond to Coote, 16 Mar. 1649; ibid., fo. 145: Ormond's notes re. Enniskillen, [Mar. 1649]; ibid., fo. 147: Ormond's notes re. the Laggan, [Mar. 1649]; ibid., fo. 169: Ormond to Galbraith, 19 Mar. 1649.
21 For Sir William Stewart see Forkan, 'Scottish Protestant Ulster', *passim*.
22 Edmund Borlase, *The History of the Execrable Irish Rebellion trac'd from many preceding acts to the grand eruption the 23 of October, 1641, and thence pursued to the Act of Settlement* (1680), p. 207.
23 Borlase, *Execrable Rebellion*, pp. 208-9; Coote appears to have dissembled in his replies to Galbraith, saying that should he receive direct orders from Charles II he would hold his garrisons for the royalists; see Bodl. Carte MS 24, fo. 171: H. Galbraith to Ormond, 19 Mar. 1649.
24 Bodl. Carte MS 24, fo. 324: H. Galbraith to Ormond, 30 Mar. 1649.
25 Adair, *True Narrative*, p. 156.
26 *HMC Hastings MSS*, ii. 355-60.
27 *HMC Hastings MSS*, ii. 359; *HMC Ormonde MSS*, old series, ii. 91.
28 *The Declaration of the Brittish in the North of Ireland* (1649), pp. 3-6; Armstrong, 'Viscount Ards and the Presbytery', pp. 29-30.
29 Hill, *Montgomery Manuscripts*, p. 178; Bodl. Carte MS 24, fo. 313: Ward to Ormond, 30 Mar. 1649.
30 Bodl. Carte MS 24, fo. 313: Ward to Ormond, 30 Mar. 1649; this note confirms that Montgomery had met with Ward at this point, and indicates that he was working for the royalist, rather than Presbyterian, cause throughout 1649.
31 Bodl. Carte MS 24, fo. 446: Ormond's commission to Montgomery, 18 Apr. 1649; ibid., fo. 706: Charles II's commission to Montgomery, 4/14 May, 1649; during May Charles II also prepared a commission for Montgomery to command in Ulster, probably having been assured of Montgomery's reliability by Sir George Monro and Sir Robert Stewart, who both passed through his court on their way back to Ulster in 1649; it is likely that Charles's commission was produced independently of Ormond's and this interpretation is supported by the instructions the king gave Sir Robert Stewart, who brought over the commission, to inform Ormond of its existence and receive his instructions in regard to it before delivering it to Montgomery: see Bodl. Carte MS 24, fos 709-10: Charles II's instructions to R. Stewart, 5/15 May 1649.
32 Bodl. Carte MS 24, fos 795-6: Ormond to Nicholas, 29 May 1649.
33 See Forkan, 'Ormond's alternative'; Forkan, 'The Ulster Scots and the Engagement'; Stevenson, *Scottish Covenanters*, pp. 254-60.
34 Gilbert, *Contemporary History*, i. 758-9.
35 Bodl. Carte MS 24, fo. 699: Ormond to Monro, 14 May 1649.
36 Bodl. Carte MS 24, fo. 699: Ormond to Monro, 14 May 1649; ibid., fo. 705: Ormond to Montgomery, 14 May 1649.
37 Bodl. Carte MS 24, fo. 456: T. Perkins to G. Lane, 29 Apr. 1649; ibid., fos 639-40: W. Constable to G. Lane, 7 May 1649.
38 Gilbert, *Contemporary History*, ii. 440-7 (H. Finch's relation of the siege of Derry, 19 June-14 August 1649, [hereafter 'Finch's relation']).

39 'Finch's relation', p. 441. Imprisoned in England following the Engagement, Stewart had escaped and fled to Holland, while Mervyn was released on promise of good behaviour.
40 Bodl. Carte MS 24, fos 401-2: Galbraith to Inchiquin, 10 Apr. 1649; ibid., fos 541-2: Ormond to Rupert, 29 Apr. 1649.
41 'Finch's relation', p. 443; Bodl. Carte MS 25, fo. 32: Clanricarde to Ormond, 9 July 1649; Monro had governed Coleraine as a garrison of the Scottish army in Ulster from 1642-8.
42 E. Hogan (ed.), *The History of the Warr of Ireland from 1641 to 1653. By a British officer, of the regiment of Sir John Clottworthy* (Dublin, 1873), pp. 77-8; Adair, *A True Narrative*, pp. 168-9; a letter, now apparently lost, written by Monro to Sir Robert Stewart and intercepted by the Presbytery, also appears to have implicated Montgomery in Monro's actions during the summer; this letter is referenced in *The Complaint of the Boutefeu, scorched in his owne kindlings. Or The backslider filled with his owne wayes:in two letters of the Presbytery at Carrick-Fergous to the Lord of Ardes* (1649), pp. 9-10.
43 National Records of Scotland [hereafter NRS], PA 7/23/2/64/2: Montgomery to Ellis, 28 June 1649; Bodl. Carte MS 25, fos 23-4: Montgomery to defenders of Carrickfergus, 2 July 1649; Hill, *Montgomery Manuscripts*, p. 187n; TCD, MS 838, fo. 269: deposition of A. Adair, 12 May 1653.
44 Bodl. Carte MS 25, fos 25-8: articles for the surrender of Carrickfergus, 4 July 1649; Hill (ed.), *Montgomery Manuscripts*, pp. 187-8n.
45 Borlase, *Execrable Rebellion*, pp. 215-7.
46 *Complaint of the Boutefeu*, p. 13.
47 *A declaration by the Presbytery at Bangor in Ireland* ([Edinburgh], 1649), p. 6; see also Armstong, 'Viscount Ards and the Presbytery', pp. 34-9.
48 D. Stevenson, *Revolution and Counter-revolution in Scotland, 1644-1651* (Edinburgh, 1977), pp. 152-4; A.I. Macinnes, 'The Scottish Constitution, 1638-1651. The rise and fall of oligarchic centralism', in J. Morrill (ed.), *The Scottish National Covenant in its British Context 1638-51* (Edinburgh, 1990), pp. 126-7.
49 HMC Ormonde MSS, old series, i. 91; Gilbert, *Contemporary History*, ii. 216-7; J. Casway, *Owen Roe O'Neill and the Struggle for Catholic Ireland* (Philadelphia, 1984), pp. 242-3.
50 Bodl. Carte MS 25, fos 19-22: Ormond to Charles II, 28 June 1649; ibid., fo. 58: Ormond to Nicholas, 19 July 1649; ibid., fo. 59: Ormond to Digby, 19 July 1649.
51 'Finch's relation', p. 444; Bodl. Carte MS 25, fo. 71: R. Stewart to Clanricarde, 24 July 1649; ibid., fo. 73: Montgomery to Clanricarde, 24 July 1649.
52 Adair, *A True Narrative*, pp. 163-5.
53 Adair, *A True Narrative*, pp. 163-5; Hill (ed.), *Montgomery Manuscripts*, pp. 189-90;
54 Bodl. Carte MS 25, fo. 105: G. Monro to Gemmill, Cunningham etc, 30 July 1649; ibid., fos 107-8: R. Stewart to Ormond, 30 July 1649.
55 Bodl. Carte MS 25, fo. 90: Montgomery to Ormond, 29 July 1649.
56 'Finch's relation', p. 445.
57 'Finch's relation', pp. 445-6; Bodl. Carte MS 25, fo. 41: Clanricard to J. Dillon, 16 [Aug.] 1649; *Warr of Ireland*, p. 80; Casway, *Owen Roe O'Neill*, p. 251.

58 The remaining Laggan officers agreed to surrender their garrisons to Coote by 31 August: see Bodl. Carte MS 25, fo. 248: Ormond to G. Monro, 24 Aug. 1649.
59 *The Marquesse of Ormond's letter to His Majestie concerning the late fight betwixt the forces under his command, and the garrison of Dublin* (1649), p. 3.
60 Bodl. Carte MS 25, fo. 81: articles between Clanbrassil and Montgomery, 27 July 1649; ibid., fos 150–1: R. Ward to G. Lane, 5 Aug. 1649.
61 *Baillie Letters and Journals*, ii. 345–6; NRS, GD 3/5/455: Montgomery to R. Stewart, 27 July 1649.
62 Bodl. Carte MS 25, fo. 237: Ormond to Montgomery; ibid., fo. 238: Ormond to Montgomery and Clanbrassil; NRS, GD 3/5/457: Lady Montgomery to countess of Eglinton, 24 Aug. 1649.
63 *HMC Ormonde MSS*, old series vol. i. 205–8; Bodl. Carte MS 25, fo. 274: J. Montgomery to Ormond, 16 Aug. 1649; ibid., fo. 296: Montgomery to Ormond, 17 Aug. 1649; ibid., fo. 298: M. Trevor to Ormond, 18 Aug. 1649; Montgomery and Stewart, along with Ormond, partook in a council of war in Drogheda on 23 August, eleven days before the town was invested by Cromwell: see Bodl. Carte MS 25, fo. 341: council of war at Drogheda, 23 Aug. 1649.
64 *Letters from Ireland, relating the several great successes it hath pleased God to give unto the Parliaments forces there in the taking of Drogheda, Trym, Dundalk, Carlingford, and the Nury* (1649), p. 9.
65 *Letters from Ireland*, pp. 15–16; Carte, *Ormonde*, ii. 98–9.
66 Bodl. Carte MS 25, fo. 623: M. Trevor to D. O'Neill, 28 Sept. 1649; *Warr of Ireland*, pp. 89–90; *HMC Leyborne-Popham*, pp. 44–5.
67 *Warr of Ireland*, pp. 92–6; Bodl. Carte MS 26, fo. 41: G. Monro to G. Moore, 27 Oct. 1649.
68 BL, Add. MS 4769B, fos 109–11: articles for the surrender of Carrickfergus, [2 Nov.] 1649; *HMC Leyborne-Popham MSS*, pp. 50–1.
69 James Scott Wheeler, *Cromwell in Ireland* (Dublin, 1999), pp. 98–104.
70 Wheeler, *Cromwell in Ireland*, pp. 108–17.
71 Bodl. Carte MS 25, fo. 518: Nicholas to Ormond, 11/21 Sept. 1649.
72 Bodl. Carte MS 25, fos 730–1: R. Long to Ormond, 12/22 Oct. 1649; ibid., fos 736–7: Nicholas to Ormond, 13/23 Oct. 1649.
73 Stevenson, *Counter-Revolution*, pp. 155–6.
74 Bodl. Carte MS 26, fos 286–9: report on the state of Ireland by Ormond, 30 Nov. 1649; ibid., fos 300–1: notes on Ireland by Ormond, [30 Nov.] 1649.
75 Bodl. Carte MS 26, fo. 365: Ormond to H. Galbraith, 12 Dec. 1649.
76 *Warr of Ireland*, pp. 97–9; *Baillie Letters and Journals*, ii. 345–6; Bodl. Carte MS 26, fo. 339: G. Monro to Ormond, 8 Dec. 1649.
77 *Warr of Ireland*, pp. 100–3; Bodl. Carte MS 26, fo. 339: G. Monro to Ormond, 8 Dec. 1649; ibid., fo. 341: Montgomery and G. Monro to Ormond, 8 Dec. 1649; Gilbert, *Contemporary History*, ii. 336–7; *Two Letters from Sir Charles Coote ... Relating the Rendition of the Town and Castle of Carrickfergus, to Sir Charles Coote, Together with the totall Defeate of the Scottish and Irish Forces in the North of Ireland, under the Command of the Lord Ards, Lord Claneboys, and Monro* (1650).
78 Bodl. Carte MS 26, fo. 353: Montgomery to Ormond, 10 Dec. 1649.

79 Bodl. Carte MS 26, fo. 564: Montgomery to Ormond, 28 Jan. 1650; ibid., fo. 634: Ormond to Montgomery, 7 Feb. 1650.
80 Gilbert, *Contemporary History*, ii. 393–6.
81 Bodl. Carte MS 26, fo. 712: Clanricarde to Ormond, 19 Feb. 1650; Stevenson, *Scottish Covenanters*, p. 278.
82 Adair, *A True Narrative*, pp. 175–6.
83 *The Nicholas Papers: the correspondence of Sir Edward Nicholas, secretary of state*, ed. G. F. Warner (4 vols, Camden, 1886–1920), i. 160–1; T. Carte, *A Collection of original letters and papers, concerning the affairs of England, from the year 1641 to 1660. Found among the Duke of Ormonde's papers* (2 vols, Dublin, 1759), i. 337–9; R. Hutton, *Charles the Second: King of England, Scotland, and Ireland* (Oxford, 1990), pp. 43–4.
84 Stevenson, *Counter-Revolution*, pp. 174–7.
85 *A Declaration by the Kings Majesty to his subjects of the Kingdomes of Scotland, England, and Ireland* (Edinburgh, 1650), pp. 6–7.
86 See Forkan, 'Ormond's Alternative', pp. 9–10.
87 Montgomery's support for the Engagement in 1648 seems to have escaped the attention of, or been ignored by, the Presbytery in the first half of 1649, see Forkan, 'Ulster Scots and the Engagement'.
88 Hill (ed.), *Montgomery Manuscripts*, p. 178.

9

The confederate Catholics of Ireland and popular politics

EAMON DARCY

On 12 July 1643 Richard Bourke, a former schoolmaster and rector living in Enniskillen, co. Fermanagh, appeared before two fellow Church of Ireland clergymen who sat on the 'commission for the despoiled subject'. His account of the wars of the 1640s reveals the challenges of using the 1641 depositions as historical evidence. Bourke recounted that he lost £900 as a result of the rebellion and that he had heard of 'the burning and killing of one hundred Protestants' in Tully Castle among other violent acts committed by Catholic 'rebels'. It is no surprise, therefore, that Bourke's account of what 'really happened' at Tully formed part of the narrative of cruelty in later histories that accentuated Catholic barbarity and Protestant victimhood, an enduring legacy of the 1641 rebellion.[1]

When one considers the immediate cultural and social contexts that shaped Bourke's deposition (setting aside the significant mediation of the commissioners), it is possible to understand the world in which he lived both before and during the rebellion. Of the 152 testimonies in the Fermanagh volume, 82 were recorded before 29 January 1642 and a further 40 by the end of the year.[2] Bourke was one of only seventeen Fermanagh residents who testified in 1643. His survival behind enemy lines for a considerable period after the initial eruption of rebellion contrasts sharply with public pronouncements from the deposition commissioners of the perils faced by Protestant settlers, particularly clergymen, at the hands of Catholic rebels.[3] Bourke knew his attackers and understood the organisation of the rebel army, suggesting a familiarity with Irish society and local clan groups – an aspect of native and newcomer social relations downplayed by the commissioners.[4] The rebels that attacked Bourke came from counties Cavan, Clare and Galway and their commanders were identified as either 'gent' or 'esquire'. Bourke also blamed Catholic clergy for encouraging people to participate. He accused Heber MacMahon, the

Catholic bishop of Clogher, of forcing Protestants in Limerick City to take an oath that they would neither oppose the practice of Catholicism nor deny the supremacy of the Pope. Meanwhile, priests on the continent, Bourke claimed, 'publicly preached applauded and commended ... [this] Catholic war in destroying of the puritans'. A range of media was deployed to promote the rebellion. Most notably, one rebel read a prophecy of St Patrick from 'an English book printed in the Low Countries' that called for the extirpation of the English 'and the settling of the whole kingdom in the Irish'. While others repeated the following prophecy:

> Do bhéarfar cath Dhún na Sciath, cuirfear Baile Átha Cliath ar gcúl, marbhfaidh Iarla Thrá Lí, Fear Ionaid an Rí in Áth Crú, which is thus Englished: at Donaskeagh a fight shall be and Dublin City shall be fane; the king his viceroy at Athcroe by the earl of Tralee shall be slain.[5]

Bourke's deposition describes the *continuation* of the rebellion as opposed to its *outbreak*. It provides vivid detail on how non-elites willingly participated in, or were cajoled into, confederate politics, suggesting that they played some role in their own governance – the very essence of early modern popular politics as outlined by Ethan Shagan.[6] Ordinary peoples' experiences of the wars of the 1640s, however, have been overlooked in narratives of high politics that have painstakingly captured the machinations of confederate, parliamentarian and royalist politics in Ireland.[7] Work by historians on English popular politics has transformed our understanding of the early modern period, particularly the turbulent events of the 1640s and 1650s. This research has demonstrated the multifaceted nature of English politics prior to the 1640s when, occasionally, elites engaged in political debates with subordinate groups and solicited their support.[8] Despite considerable work by Raymond Gillespie and Clodagh Tait about popular political thought and protest in early modern Ireland, there is still a historiographical need to investigate these issues in the 1640s.[9]

In this instance, when Bourke deposed those he deemed 'rebels' were allegedly describing their battle as a 'holy war of the confederate Catholics'. They had probably sworn the oath of association. The range of media used to encourage 'rebels' suggests that their participation and support were active considerations factored into the thoughts of elites. The processes of 'negotiation' (a term Brendan Kane takes umbrage with) between elites and non-elites hints that there was a limited exchange of views between the governors and the governed and that, occasionally, the commonalty could influence politics with varying degrees of success.[10] A study of the politics of early modern Irish non-elites, however, is fraught with difficulty, owing to conceptual issues and the elusive nature of the evidence. First, Tudor and Stuart State Papers from Ireland do not document the lower social orders in a consistent way. Second, political actions such as protests and riots were often viewed through a hostile lens. This forces historians to read against the grain of the evidence to infer the cultural and social significance of such actions, as the early modern state became the primary archivist of political activities.[11] Third, those of the lower social orders are 'truly subaltern' in an Irish context as very few surviving documents record their various doings or outlooks in their own words.[12] Fourth, the issue of language and oral communication emerges also: what language was used? English? Irish? What role did interpreters play? Can historians trust that state scribes faithfully represented the words of those they were investigating? Did the state always acknowledge the role of interpreters?[13] Fifth, to what extent can Irish language sources be integrated into a consideration of early modern Irish popular politics? Finally, there is a conceptual issue, often these actions are understood within the parameters of colonial resistance; this perspective overlooks, however, the complexities of Irish Catholic politics among both Irish and English speakers.

Any consideration of popular politics in an early modern Irish context, therefore, is predicated on educated guesswork and can only draw tentative conclusions, owing to the elusive nature of the evidence. Thus, this chapter is an initial and exploratory foray into the nebulous world of Irish popular politics in the 1640s. An analysis of how non-elites contributed to national debates about confederate politics is worthy of a book-length study. This chapter, however, aims to outline how the confederates cultivated and shaped the political participation of the lower social orders, which has largely been overlooked in earlier analyses that focus on high politics.

Since the Reformation in Britain and Ireland the welfare of non-elites was gradually integrated into political discussions and the plight of subordinate groups became a key factor in the political considerations of elites.[14] In Ireland, English commentators excoriated Irish lords for subjecting their inferiors to tyrannical rule as the responsibilities of the elites to protect the less fortunate and to foster the common good, or commonwealth, became a key part of contemporary rhetoric.[15] The question remains, however: to what extent did the confederate government promote a shared perception of the public good?

At a congregation in May 1642, leading Catholic clergymen resolved to preserve the commonwealth by encouraging unity between the socio-economic groups and punishing malefactors and enemies to the 'common' cause.[16] Such concerns were repeated in the first confederate General Assembly in October.[17] The confederates' first publications provide the clearest indicator of their thinking about governance. 'A discourse between two councillors of state' criticised the lords justices, Sir John Borlase and Sir William Parsons, for deliberately excluding the 'people' from political communication and for the use of excessive force by state troops against civilians.[18] Repeatedly, Catholic elites emphasised their status as loyal subjects to Charles I and highlighted the neglect of the colonial administration in protecting the lower social orders.

Clear distinctions were drawn between the 'commonalty' of respectable Catholic subjects and the 'multitude' that had perpetrated violent crimes after 23 October 1641. Furthermore, a 'humble apology' from Catholics of the Pale excused their recourse to arms as a defence of 'beneficial servants to the commonwealth, as being either husbandmen or tradesmen' persecuted by state forces.[19] Richard Bellings, secretary to the confederate Supreme Council, also distinguished between the commonalty of Ireland and the 'multitude' that engaged in criminality upon the outbreak of rebellion. Similarly, the Supreme Council denounced the actions of the 'many-headed beast, the multitude', noting that many had met their providential punishment, 'the fury of our enemies'.[20] The hostility of elites towards those they viewed as the criminal element of Irish society can be evidenced in the empowering of high sheriffs to hang laymen worth less than £5 found guilty of murder or theft.[21]

Clear attempts by Catholic elites to distance themselves from the alleged actions of malcontents from the lower social orders, however, should not be conflated with a lack of concern about the participation of non-elites in governance. Leading figures among the confederates recognised that they had an obligation to protect vulnerable members of society. This is not to suggest an emancipatory narrative, however, as their main concern was with those that could contribute to the confederate war effort, such as husbandmen and victuallers.[22] The integration of the lower social orders into broader political thought reflected the necessity of their participation in the administration of de facto, as opposed to de jure, authority[23] – an issue the confederate government was keenly aware of.[24] There is significant evidence, albeit only within the co. Wexford depositions, of the extent to which non-elites formed part of confederate governance by collecting revenues and taking the confederate oath.[25] This could be perceived as an act of political agency or the result of coercion.[26] Either way, it underlines how, despite the outbreak of war, pre-existing communities still had to function and had to be governed; in short, elites relied on the active support and collaboration of the lower social orders.[27]

Leading confederates also recognised the existence of divergent views on Irish Catholic politics and attempted to paper over these significant divisions. From the beginning attempts were made to integrate political factions into the confederate fold. The first pronouncements of the General Assembly capture contemporary fears over the deep divisions within Irish Catholicism that threatened confederate unity and stressed how these politics were shaped by ethnicity.[28] Order 14 called for the 'avoiding of national distinction' between Irish, Old English, Welsh, English and Scottish Catholics on the island. Such discord, they decreed, 'ought not to be endured in a well governed commonwealth'.[29] Crucially, 'all new converts' from any of the Stuart realms who joined the 'cause', were now considered 'Catholics and natives to all intents and purposes'.[30] Most interestingly, in an attempt to encourage settlers to participate in confederate politics (as Catholics), the confederates clearly identified their rival combatants and coined terms to demonise them. An order dated 29 October 1642 warned that 'every person or persons whatsoever talking or discoursing, in writing or otherwise, of the enemies, shall not call them by the name or names of English or Protestants, but shall call them by the names of puritanical or malignant party'.[31] This demonisation of the enemy as 'puritans' also occurred in the first days of the rebellion, whereas the term 'malignant' party seems to have been used after the establishment of the Confederation.[32] This attempt to manipulate the politics of non-elites reflected the politics of what would become the 'peace party' and also illustrates the broader British dimension to confederate politics. By demonising 'puritans', the actions of the lower social orders could be readily portrayed as a defence of Charles I in the face of growing parliamentary opposition.

The role of communication, that is, 'talking, or discoursing, in writing or otherwise', has transformed our understanding of the emergence of public debates about national politics. In England, the wars of the mid-seventeenth century are viewed as a pivotal period in the development of a public sphere to facilitate national political debates.[33] In Ireland, much like in Wales, however, historians face a number of challenges when considering political communication. Most notably, the barriers to communication played a key role in shaping popular participation. As Lloyd Bowen has demonstrated convincingly for Wales (where there was a similar linguistic landscape), bilingual cultural brokers profoundly influenced Welsh popular politics. Many of the Welsh gentry were bilingual and had a vested interest in promoting the Church of England and the Stuart monarchy. Thus, they disseminated and translated English-language news that reflected these political views among Welsh speakers. This, Bowen argues, explains the overwhelming support among Welsh people for royalism during the 1640s.[34] In Ireland, recent work has estimated that by the 1660s one third of the country's population was bilingual and that a 'hybrid linguistic group' emerged in socio-economic entrepôts, such as towns, cities and estates of multi-ethnic tenantries; yet there is little discussion around language use during the 1640s despite it being a pivotal consideration in terms of political communication.[35] The language barrier is critical to our understanding of Irish popular politics. Among elites the political discourse was conducted through English but as one moves through the social orders it is clear that bilingual people played a key role in facilitating political participation. Richard Bourke's memorisation and translation of a prophecy he allegedly overheard, mentioned in the introduction to this chapter, raises a key consideration of identity and language politics. Needless to say, the translation of an English language text by an Irish-speaking Church of Ireland cleric such as Bourke would differ from that of a bilingual Catholic priest and textual communities were aware of the role of translators in shaping reception.[36]

It is difficult to determine the extent of bilingualism in Ireland let alone define competencies among those who operated in multilingual worlds. One way of gauging language use is by investigating the role of interpreters, although the record that has survived on this matter is patchy at best.[37] Two groups of examinations that now form part of the 1641 depositions are the most pertinent to this discussion. The first is a collection of 80 testimonies of 'strangers' arrested in Dublin city on the night of 22 October 1641. These examinants came from all across the country but mostly from Ulster and the counties bordering Dublin.[38] Only nine needed an interpreter to make a statement in English. Although their occupation is not specified, it can be deduced from their evidence that they were for the most part of humble stock, such as farm labourers, servants and soldiers.[39] One examinant, Brian Odire from Thurles in co. Tipperary, travelled around the country selling cloth. His inability to speak English suggests that this was no barrier to his trade.[40] The second collection of examinations, taken in July 1642 by William Ryves, speaker of the Irish House of Commons, also implies a correlation between socio-economic status and language use. Ryves employed three men and one woman to interpret the examinations of fourteen people implicated in an attack on Clongowes Wood Castle. These boys and men were of humble origins, described variously as 'beggar boy', 'masterless boy', 'herdsman' and 'of no trade and had never a master'. They were not from gentry stock but it is tempting to assume that their status meant that they were less exposed to the English language – hence the need for an interpreter. One of the interpreters was Ambrose Bedell, presumably the son of William, bishop of Kilmore, who instituted a lecture in Irish at Trinity College Dublin and attempted to organise the translation of the Bible into Irish.[41] To further complicate matters, in his own deposition Ambrose claimed that he heard 'the mere Irish rebels' curse those of Old English stock: 'you churls with the great breeches, do you think that if we were rid of the English that we would spare you? No we would cut all your throats.'[42] Were these words uttered in English or in Irish? We do not know as he did not specify – an indication of how limited the depositions can be as evidence for language use. A handful of statements suggest how people could engage with English language news cultures. George Gonne translated his servant's examination from Irish into English as did Katherine Murry's husband.[43] John Winsmore, a man of gentry stock living near Mountmellick in Queen's County, witnessed an argument in Irish between two rebel commanders; an Irish neighbour subsequently translated their argument for his benefit, which he related to the deposition commission.[44]

At both gentry and elite levels there must have been greater bilingual competency. In a country where the majority of people spoke Irish but the political and print cultures were (for the most part) in English, the ability to read, speak and translate English into Irish was a critical feature of political communications. Donal Cregan argued that 'almost all of the confederate Catholics could speak Irish, with greater or lesser fluency'.[45] One possible exception was James Tuchet, the earl of Castlehaven and confederate commander. Castlehaven was reared in England and had limited exposure to Irish. In his memoirs, printed forty years after these events, Castlehaven claimed that few in the Supreme Council could read Irish, although he omitted this in the third edition of his memoirs.[46] Many who served in the Confederate Assembly had also been MPs or trained as lawyers suggesting that they could read English.[47] Beyond the Assembly there is tentative evidence of considerable competency in English among Irish speakers suggesting that some from the lower social orders were also bilingual. The 'Aphorismical Discovery of Treasonable Faction' mentions an exchange in English between Castlehaven and Gerald Fitzgerald before some of his Irish-speaking soldiers: 'Fitzgerald ... spoke to my lord in his Dutch like English, that he would lead them ... he that will not go where I appoint him, said he, give me leave to kill him.' The effect of this threat, however, was negated: 'All that heard him laughed heartily as well for his broken English as for his request.'[48] A similar exchange occurs in the early seventeenth century lampoon, 'Pairlement Chloinne Tomáis' where a churl speaking broken English with a strong and comical Irish accent is the butt of a joke.[49] This tentative investigation of bilingualism suggests that there was a growing sophistication to English language use in Ireland among some Irish speakers. More work is needed on the extent to which Irish speakers were exposed to the English language, as proximity to English speech communities – rather than socio-economic status – may be a more significant factor in determining the extent of bilingualism in Irish society.

Those who could read and translate English-language texts were central to the administration of, and political communication within, the confederate regime. For example, Dr William Roberts, the herald charged with disseminating the first Ormond Peace of 1646, had an Irish-speaking servant in his retinue who presumably translated the proclamation into Irish.[50] Limited evidence suggests also that bilingual brokers during the 1640s must have played a significant role in shaping the participation of the lower social orders. Before the outbreak of rebellion, key figures played upon fears of the 'puritan' Parliament in London.[51] Conor Maguire, baron of Enniskillen, heard the reading of a news packet in Dublin that detailed proclamations issued in England against Catholics. It is unsurprising, therefore, that Maguire's servants blamed 'the tyrannical government over them' for their actions.[52] Sir Phelim O'Neill, a co-conspirator, met Maguire in Dublin and this is presumably where he heard this news; subsequently O'Neill repeated this claim to his followers.[53] Deponents from Fermanagh, where Maguire was based, also alleged that rebels cited the actions of the 'puritans' as a justification for their actions.[54] Although more work is needed on the murky world of extempore translation as well as the extent of linguistic competency in Ireland, there is enough evidence here to suggest tentatively that bilingual interpreters were an integral part of everyday life. The actions of leading figures who organised the rebellion, furthermore, hints that bilingual brokers helped to shape political participation in the rebellion and confederate wars by disseminating news that stoked pre-existing fears.

The instructions concerning the taking of the confederate oath of association offer further clues about how elites attempted to manipulate the politics of the lower social orders. The first General Assembly requested that priests were to administer the oath 'and shall translate and expound the said oath … in Irish'; this suggests that they hoped to reach a broad audience; that bilingual speakers were readily available among the clergy; and that this reflected their role in disseminating news and facilitating political participation.[55] If oaths are viewed as acts of communication it is possible to see how various policies were promoted by elites to their subordinates and how non-elites could engage in contemporary politics. As noted by John Spurr, oaths became a key weapon in the arsenal of Stuart politicking and the refusal or acceptance of such oaths hints at their political agency.[56] Thus, the confederates were equally keen to ensure their movement was oath-bound. The problem was, however, that many of the earliest rebel forces swore a range of oaths that articulated different war aims, making them a useful indicator of popular political outlooks.

From the immediate outbreak of the rebellion, Owen Connolly, who revealed the plot to the lords justices, maintained that some rebels swore a 'national oath' not to have English governors. Later, several deponents repeated this claim, as did the deposition commissioners in their printed digests about the rebellion.[57] The 'Aphorismical Discovery' claimed that, at the first meeting between the Irish and the Old English at Crufty in co. Meath, those in attendance swore an oath 'maintaining the holy religion, defence of his majesty's prerogatives and vindication of the free liberty of the Irish nation'.[58] It was claimed that the propagation of this oath across the country encouraged others to partake in the rebellion as a war of religion as opposed to a defence of Charles I.[59] The variation in the prioritisation of war aims in these oaths reflects a wide spectrum of motivations and localised concerns among insurgents. An oath sworn by rebels in Wexford promised to uphold: first, monarchical rights, then the Catholic faith and, lastly, to defend Ireland from 'all oppressors'.[60] Another oath, sworn at Eglish in King's County, portrayed rebel actions as a defence of the king's prerogatives and the English queen, and constituted an attack on 'oppressors' of the commonwealth. Finally, they described themselves as a 'Catholic army against the puritans'.[61] The hierarchy of political desires, aims and outcomes reflects the spectrum of Catholic politics that gripped the island, meaning that these oaths can be understood as expressions of political views as well as instruments of manipulation.

An oath sworn by local civic and gentry leaders in Galway illustrates the careful crafting involved in composing, and the complexities in terms of interpreting the meaning of, an oath. The oath was designed to enlist the support of the wider locality *and* to entice the Old English Catholic earl of Clanricarde, Ulick Bourke, to join them. Its priorities were carefully expressed. They promised to first uphold Catholicism, then the common laws of Ireland, then the statutes of Magna Carta. Finally, they affirmed their supreme loyalty 'to our sovereign lord the king'.[62] Some of Clanricarde's kinsmen, most notably Viscount Clanmorris, ordered all gentry and civic officers of Galway to gather at the Tholsel for a speech 'conducing them to the association of Catholic union, who so far prevailed that he and the rest there swore the said oath'.[63] Clanricarde was deeply suspicious of the more radical element within Irish Catholicism and accused the clergy of being 'very violent and busy in persuading the people to join in a general commotion' and in tendering oaths. Clanricarde's views here were shaped by his ability in the 1630s to practise his faith and maintain a high profile politically in England despite prohibitions on Catholicism.[64]

We do not know from the evidence that has survived, however, what language was spoken during these public occasions. Presumably, bilingual brokers from the gentry and clergy translated the oath into Irish for those who knew no English. Therefore, despite the seemingly moderate expression of Catholic politics the performative context needs to be taken into consideration. This allowed some flexibility in terms of the oath's meaning. As the author of the 'Aphorismical Discovery' stated: 'An oath is to be interpreted not by him that takes it but by him that takes his assurance by it.'[65] This interpretation may have been influenced by the renunciation of the first Ormond Peace by the clerical party on the grounds that it constituted perjury as it contravened the oath of association.[66] Nonetheless, this highlights how the communal and performative element of oaths, as well as the role of interpreters in shaping wider perceptions and interpretation of the oaths, played a key role in shaping popular politics. Recently, John Morrill pondered whether an Irish language text of the oath ever existed or has survived. The crux of the issue is how the English text of the oath was translated into Irish by people of various political viewpoints in different contexts, responding to different audiences.[67] Despite the careful crafting of this oath as a statement of moderate Catholic politics, the power of interpretation (in this instance at least) lay in its translation, its communal performance and the public portrayal of its meaning. This contributed to the broader radicalisation of Galway Catholics, which drew Clanricarde's ire and affirmed his decision to stand aloof from the confederate wars.

As illustrated by Morrill, several versions of the confederate oath were circulating throughout the 1640s.[68] Their varying content is indicative of divergent political and regional motivations in fighting. Crucially, leading confederate literati viewed (or presented) their dispute as part of a broader post-Reformation European struggle. Therefore, they disseminated works in Latin, French and Spanish to solicit support from European leaders. Walter Enos, writing in 1646, captured the transnational outlook of the Confederation and claimed that its war aims were prioritised and articulated in the oath of association, the bicameral model of government and 'our remonstrance printed in France in 1642'.[69] In this French remonstrance, which was also published in Spanish and Latin, the rebellion was portrayed primarily as a war motivated by religion: 'Nous demandons, en premier lieu, la liberté de conscience et l'exercice public de notre religion' (We seek, in the first instance, freedom of conscience and the public exercise of our religion).[70] These publications contained a version of the confederate oath that differed significantly from the official oath disseminated in October 1642. This continental oath primarily aimed to defend Catholicism (until death) against heretics, atheists and other enemies of the church.[71] One could be tempted to assume that different factions promoted separate oaths as 'the' confederate oath, providing further evidence to the highly fractious nature of confederate politics at a popular level during this time. Perhaps there were other factors involved.

Over the course of the confederate wars the oath was evoked in a similar way to the modern parliamentary whip system, to cajole people to conform to prevailing political needs. In the crucial years of the mid-1640s, as confederate fortunes rose, the terms of a proposed settlement with Charles I proved a controversial subject that divided people. In July 1644, as part of a call for confederate unity the General Assembly warned their subordinates to adhere to the oath of association.[72] A year later another proclamation repeated this and warned that all conversations critical of the 'religious intentions' of the assembly were now considered 'high treason'.[73] The highly anticipated first Ormond Peace of 1646 proposed a speedy end to the war without public guarantees of Catholic toleration. It was roundly rejected by members of the wider populace. Vivid accounts by supporters and opponents of the peace argued that competing interpretations of the oath framed the responses of those who opposed the peace.[74] Afterward, having successfully thwarted the peace, Rinuccini, the papal nuncio and leader of the clerical faction, circulated a new oath to ensure the confederates would remember their religious obligations in any future settlements with the king.[75] From this it is evident that oaths were useful tools of political mobilisation and could promote political agendas and politicise non-elites.

The swearing of oaths, in some cases mediated by bilingual brokers, and the prioritisation of different war aims in local communities suggests that Catholic politics was hotly contested. In a sense, the confederate oath failed to bind these competing factions into a shared political vision. In the content of other political messages disseminated by various forms of contemporary media it is possible to witness the extent of these deep divisions within Irish Catholicism. Richard Bourke's testimony outlined in the introduction to this chapter reveals the political currency invested in prophecies during the seventeenth century. Since the middle ages successive English monarchs suppressed the telling of prophecies, recognising their ability to provoke unrest and political agitation. In both an Irish and English context, prophecies evoked revered or ancient authorities that provided convenient explanations and justifications for contemporary events, hence their valency as political propaganda.[76]

They were not without their contemporary critics, however. Bellings condescendingly commented that Dermot Kavanagh, whose death in battle had been prophesied and subsequently fulfilled, succumbed to 'powerful impressions his imaginations had received from some old prophecy, which by a fatal credulity it seems he would not falsify, though it cost him his life'.[77] In an interesting and telling contrast, the anonymous author of the 'Aphorismical Discovery', whose political and cultural background differed considerably from Bellings's, praised Kavanagh for partaking in battle and preparing a will beforehand, knowing it would be his final act.[78] Bellings was highly critical of those who harnessed the power of prophecies to stir others into action, particularly those 'easily induced to be the first to deceive themselves'.[79] His hostility is indicative of their political potency as witnessed by the frequent retelling of prophecies among the rebels.[80]

The prophecies mentioned by Richard Bourke in his deposition require further attention. Three in particular suggest the cultural contexts that contemporaries drew from, to rationalise and understand their experiences of warfare in the 1640s. The first, 'Do bhéarfar cath Dhún na Sciath', is a prophecy attributed to Maol Sheachlainn Óg Mac Amhlaoibh who was imprisoned for his involvement in the Nine Years War. Mac Amhlaoibh was the chief of Duhallow in co. Cork and this prophecy referred to Gearóid Iarla, the 3rd earl of Desmond (1338–98). It claimed that Gearóid Iarla would awake from his slumber in Lough Gur and lead the Irish against English invaders. Similar prophecies evoking Gearóid Iarla were popular in the sixteenth and seventeenth centuries.[81] The second prophecy, that 'the English' would be defeated at Singland in co. Limerick and expelled from Ireland is of an unclear provenance. It may be a prophecy of St Benigus of Armagh or another of Mac Amhlaoibh. Regardless this prophecy was occasionally mentioned in contemporary Irish literature and was still recited in nineteenth-century Ireland.[82] Finally, Bourke mentioned a prophecy of St Patrick, printed in an English book from the Low Countries. There are two possible candidates here. The first could be Patrick Mayerne's *The Pattern of all Pious Prayer*. This contained a 'divine ditty' that spoke of England's rejection of Catholicism and advocated the celebration of St Patrick's Day to honour the 'crimson cross'. An alternative suggested by Raymond Gillespie is *The Life of the Glorious Bishop Saint Patrick* (St Omer, 1625), which contained some prophecies attributed to Patrick.[83]

All of these prophecies were a celebration of Irish identity and the Irish language prophecies, in particular, demonised the English as an invading race. Thus, in some quarters the rebellion was promoted as an anti-English and anti-Protestant act. These messages appealed to a more hard-line element among the confederates, particularly those who supported the reversal of the plantations and the expulsion of English colonists as well as the restoration of the Catholic Church. Understandably, those members of the Supreme Council who favoured a conservative settlement with Charles I desperately sought to suppress such radical political views. This explains both the proclamations banning discussions of the terms of the first Ormond Peace and the order to burn Conor O'Mahony's controversial *Disputatio Hibernica* (Lisbon, 1645). The overwhelming conservatism (or pragmatism) among some Catholic elites on these issues may not have been as prevalent at a popular level, an issue that requires much deeper investigation.[84]

The reading, telling and retelling of manuscript and printed prophecies indicate the rich tapestry of oral and literate communication that shaped political participation in early modern Ireland as it did in England and Wales.[85] It also raises an important question about the role of print in shaping confederate governance and politics. The lack of Irish type, poor finances and low literacy levels were all obstacles that prevented the publication of Irish language materials.[86] The informal bilingual structures of communication outlined in this chapter provided an avenue through which unilingual Irish speakers could engage with confederate print. The production of materials in English as well as the original location of the press at Waterford, a port city, implies that confederate print was aimed at an English-speaking transnational audience. A crucial issue remains, however: to what extent did the confederates use print to encourage popular political participation in Ireland? It must first be noted that in comparison to other regional presses the confederates fared poorly, producing only sixty-two publications over the course of the 1640s.[87] The vast majority of confederate publications concerned administration: decrees of excommunication, orders, proclamations and publications concerning peace negotiations. A preface by Thomas Bourke, the confederate printer based at Waterford, outlined how his role was to disseminate works for 'the defence and propagation' of the Catholic faith against those roundheads who 'oppose themselves to God, king and country'.[88]

Despite this statement, only a small number of works – for example, 'A discourse between two councillors of state', the text of one play, a précis of another, a reprint of a sermon, and Walter Enos's condemnatory volumes concerning the first Ormond Peace – were directly aimed to produce 'propaganda'.

Similarly, there were few news publications. In one attempt to circulate English news in Ireland *A Brief Relation of the most Remarkable Feats and Passages* (Waterford, 1644) tells us of 'what his most gracious majesty's commanders have done in England against the rebels'. This pamphlet regaled audiences with royalist successes in England throughout 1643 and the summer of 1644. Strangely, there was no attempt to locate their relevance to the Irish experience. For example, there is no reference to the cessation of arms of September 1643. Like confederate attempts to demonise 'puritans', this tract railed against the king's parliamentary enemies and contained a familiar line from Matthew's gospel, 'render unto Caesar the things which are Caesar's', a frequent refrain from royalists. It appears that the *Brief Relation* regurgitated information that already appeared from printing presses in Oxford without tailoring it to an Irish audience or context.[89] It could be said, therefore, that despite Bourke's lofty rhetoric the confederates did not attempt to engage with the wider population via print with the same intensity as witnessed in England in the 1640s.

What is clear from a brief investigation of confederate print in Ireland and on the continent is that a small number of their more important publications were carefully crafted to appeal to different audiences.[90] The prioritisation of secular over religious grievances in their first English-language publications is inverted in confederate print on the continent. Two of their earliest publications, 'A discourse between two councillors of state' and the *Remonstrance of Grievances*, outlined the range of their demands to English-speaking audiences. They were highly critical of more recent plantation schemes in Leinster and Connacht and the implementation of anti-Catholic legislation that eroded the privileges of Catholic elites. Despite public protestations that confederate actions were a defence of the Catholic faith, these publications did not call for any settlement for the Catholic Church.[91] In 1645 *A persuasive letter exhorting the natives of Ireland to stand in defence of their faith, king, and country* identified the English Parliament as the true enemy of Catholicism, but remained silent on the issue of religious toleration.[92] It was not until the negotiations over a further cessation of arms with Charles I took place in the autumn of 1644 that the demands of the Catholic clergy were finally voiced and in May 1645 this issue became a key bone of contention in the general assembly.[93] In contrast, continental publications in French, Spanish and Latin printed within months of the rebellion claimed that the desire for liberty of conscience and the free exercise of the Catholic faith in a similar religious settlement to that enjoyed by the Scots was a key reason for their recourse to arms.[94] For the most part, the press in Ireland was controlled by a more conservative element among the confederates and it was only for a short period of time that the clerical party exercised control. As their printed outputs became increasingly embarrassing to conservative Catholic elites who were eager to reach an agreement with the Stuart monarchy quickly, the press was forcibly removed from their custody.⁹⁵ Thus, unlike the situation in England in the 1640s, print did not facilitate debates about politics in Ireland; however, the press itself was harnessed as a tool of statecraft and of politicking between the competing political factions.

Evidence suggests that these divisions were also visible in wider Irish society. Regulation of the spoken word by the Supreme Council amounted to little more than a failed attempt to paper over the cracks of Irish Catholic politics. By the mid-1640s, it was an open secret and a hot topic of conversation that the supreme council was eager to negotiate a settlement with Charles I. Two proclamations were issued in 1645 and 1646, urging 'disturbers of the public peace' not to engage in discussions about any proposed religious concessions, as this would cause a 'breach of our union' – a clear attempt by the 'peace party' to control negotiations and manage expectations at a popular level.⁹⁶ These tensions that blighted Irish Catholic politics erupted after the announcement of the first Ormond Peace. This settlement proved highly unsatisfactory to the clerical party and its supporters for it provided a poor return after five years of fighting. What is perhaps most intriguing about the first Ormond Peace, however, are the actions taken by Nicholas French on the day of its proclamation. French at this time was in Waterford, where the clerical party had gathered to organise opposition to the peace. He was part of the 'middle party' within the confederation that sought to bridge the divide between the clerical and peace parties. French appealed for calm and reminded his audience of the need for unity. In his name a proclamation for the 'avoiding of unnatural distinction between the old Irish and the old and new English, between septs and families', advised:

> There is not one province distinction between the Irish and English, as those of *Leinster* may truly say of *Ulster* (and so for the rest of the provinces) as *Adam* said to *Eve, this now is bone of my bones, and flesh of my flesh*, Genesis 2. 23. Nemo enim umquam carnem suam odio habuit [For no man ever hated his own flesh] Eph 5. 29. If the blood of the Leinster men run in the veins of the Ulster man, doth not the one effuse his own blood, while he effuses the blood of the other?⁹⁷

French's evocation of the confederate commonwealth was a vain attempt to promote political unity at a tense time. In a matter of weeks, popular protests prevented the proclamation of the peace, which led to its eventual repudiation by the confederates. The attempts of elites to foster a collective outlook (Hiberni unanimes or Irishmen united) based on political pragmatism failed in this instance, which provides another pertinent reminder of the need to integrate popular politics into the high political narratives of the 1640s, particularly at key moments such as these. It also suggests that more work needs to be done on the role of ethnicity and provincialism in shaping contemporary politics, which goes beyond the remit of this chapter.

In conclusion, it must be reiterated that this is an initial foray into a relatively unexplored topic and it is hoped that when more studies have been conducted a more complete picture will emerge. This chapter tentatively suggests that confederate elites sporadically attempted to shape the political views of those outside the corridors of power. From a purely practical viewpoint, the Catholic confederates of Ireland were heavily reliant on the participation of ordinary people in order to exercise de facto authority. Numerous avenues need to be explored in order to understand the complexities of popular politics, most notably the interplay between what prevented and what facilitated political communication; the role of cultural brokers in shaping and disseminating political views; as well the hotly contested nature of Irish Catholic politics. After the initial violence that characterised the early stages of the rebellion subsided, Catholic elites were eager to distance themselves from these alleged atrocities and to justify the recourse to arms with a veneer of political legitimacy – a veneer acceptable to conservative Catholics, a beleaguered Charles I and some of his Irish Protestant subjects. With this in mind, attempts were made to moderate wider aims and expectations of the war and to bind more radical elements within Irish Catholicism into a more moderate vision that relegated the demands of the Catholic Church in any final settlement with the king. This proved difficult, as evidenced by repeated attempts to suppress conversations about any proposed settlement with Charles I and the relative ease through which the Catholic clergy rallied people to reject the first Ormond Peace in 1646 because it failed to deliver any firm guarantees for the Catholic Church.

The use of a range of media – from prophecies, to proclamations, to print – used to 'speak' to ordinary people, via cultural brokers and bilingual interpreters, allowed wide participation in confederate governance. Crucially, these media offered a platform for non-elites to lobby, promote and (in the case of the first Ormond Peace) reject prevailing political trends, suggesting that at times there were real and public debates about contemporary politics. While the highly contested nature of political debates witnessed in English print, particularly around London, was not replicated in Ireland, there was a clear struggle to control the output of the confederate media – in every sense of the word in its early modern context. The question remains, however: to what extent did these factors shape political participation and local and national debates about politics both before, during and after the turmoil of the mid-seventeenth century? This may help us not only to determine what 'really happened' in Ireland in the 1640s but also to understand the contribution of ordinary people to early modern Irish politics and politicking.

NOTES

1 G.D. Burtchaell and T.U. Sadleir, *Alumni Dublinenses* (Dublin, 1935), p. 84. E. Borlase, *The History of the Execrable Irish Rebellion* (1680), p. 115; Temple, *Irish Rebellion*, p. 91; for a broader discussion of the historiography of the 1641 rebellion see J. Gibney, *The Shadow of a Year: the 1641 Rebellion in Irish history and memory* (Wisconsin, 2013).

2 There are fourteen examinations from Fermanagh residents contained within the Dublin volumes (see TCD, MS 809) all of which predate April 1642 with one deposition dated 15 February 1642.

3 H. Jones, *Remonstrance of Divers Remarkeable passages concerning the church and kingdome of Ireland* (1642).

4 J. Cope, 'Fashioning victims: Dr Henry Jones and the plight of Irish Protestants, 1642', *Hist. Res.* 74 (2001), pp. 370–91, at pp. 384–5; E. Darcy, *The Irish Rebellion of 1641 and the Wars of the Three Kingdoms* (Woodbridge, Suffolk, 2013), pp. 85–91.

5 TCD, MS 835, fos 238–9v: deposition of Riccard Bourke; modern Irish rendering from D. Ó hÓgáin, 'Gearóid Iarla agus an Draíocht', in *Scriobh* 4 (1979), pp. 234–59, at p. 246.

6 E. Shagan, *Popular Politics and the English Reformation* (Cambridge, 2002), p. 19.

7 See Armstrong, *Protestant War*; Lenihan, *Confederate Catholics at War*; Ó hAnnracháin, *Rinuccini*; Ó Siochrú, *Confederate Ireland*.

8 L. Bowen, 'Information, language and political culture in early modern Wales', *Past and Present* 228 (2015), pp. 125–58; J. Peacey, *Politicians and Pamphleteers: propaganda during the English Civil Wars and Interregnum* (Aldershot, 2004); P. Lake and S. Pincus, 'Rethinking the public sphere in early modern England', *Journal of British Studies* 45 (2006), pp. 270–92; J. Raymond, *Pamphlets and Pamphleteering in Early Modern Britain* (Cambridge, 2003); D. Zaret, *Origins of Democratic Culture: printing, petitions, and the public sphere in early modern England* (Princeton, 2000).

9 R. Gillespie, 'Negotiating order in early-seventeenth century Ireland', in M. Braddick and J. Walter (eds), *Negotiating Power in Early Modern Society: order, hierarchy, and subordination in Britain and Ireland* (Cambridge, 2001), pp. 188–205; R. Gillespie, 'Political ideas and their social contexts in seventeenth century Ireland', in Jane Ohlmeyer (ed.), *Political Thought in Seventeenth Century Ireland: kingdom or colony* (Cambridge, 2010), pp. 107–30; C. Tait, 'Broken heads and trampled hats: rioting in Limerick in 1599', in L. Irwin and G. Ó Tuathaigh (eds), *Limerick: history and society* (Dublin, 2009), pp. 91–111; C. Tait, 'Riots, Rescues and "Grene Bowes": Catholics and protest in Ireland', in R. Armstrong and T. Ó hAnnracháin (eds) *Insular Christianity: alternative models of the church in Britain and Ireland, 1550–1700* (Manchester, 2012), pp. 67–87; C. Tait, 'Urban riots and popular protest in Ireland, 1570–1640', in M. Cronin and W. Sheehan (eds), *Riotous Assemblies: rebels, riots and revolts in Ireland* (Cork, 2011), pp. 22–49.

10 B. Kane, 'Popular politics and the legitimacy of power in early modern Ireland', in E. Fitzpatrick and A. Horning (eds), *Becoming and Belonging in Ireland, 1200–1600: essays on identity and cultural practice* (Cork, 2018), pp. 328–43, at p. 331.

I am grateful to Dr Kane for sending me a copy of this chapter in advance of its publication.
11 Richard Cobb, *The Police and the People: French popular protest, 1789-1820* (Oxford, 1970).
12 Kane, 'Popular politics', p. 329.
13 P. Palmer, *Language and Conquest in early modern Ireland: English Renaissance Literature and Elizabethan Imperial Expansion* (Cambridge, 2001); P. Palmer, 'Interpreters and the politics of translation and traduction in sixteenth-century Ireland', *IHS* 33 (2003), pp. 257-77.
14 For a brief introduction see: M. Braddick and J. Walter, 'Introduction', in Braddick and Walter (eds), *Negotiating Power*, pp. 1-42.
15 Kane, 'Popular Politics', pp. 332-3.
16 T. Barnard, '"Parlour entertainment in an evening?" Histories of the 1640s', in M. Ó Siochrú (ed.), *Kingdoms in Crisis: Ireland in the 1640s* (Dublin, 2001), pp. 20-43; Darcy, *Irish Rebellion*, pp. 132-67; Gilbert, *Irish Confederation*, i. 34-43.
17 Gilbert, *Irish Confederation*, i. 72-84.
18 A. Clarke, 'A Discourse between Two Councillors of State, the One of England, and the Other of Ireland (1642) from B.M., Egerton MS 917', *Analecta Hibernica* 26 (1970), pp. 170-7.
19 Gilbert, *Irish Confederation*, i. 248; Ó Siochrú, *Confederate Ireland*, p. 38.
20 Gilbert, *Irish Confederation*, ii. 90-1.
21 Ibid., ii. 78.
22 Ibid., ii. 94.
23 Kane, 'Popular Politics', pp. 331-2.
24 Ó Siochrú, *Confederate Ireland*, pp. 49-50, 83-4.
25 J. McHugh, '"For our owne defence": Catholic insurrection in Wexford, 1641-2', in B. Mac Cuarta (ed.), *Reshaping Ireland, 1550-1700: colonization and its consequences* (Dublin, 2011), pp. 214-40; J. Morrill, 'An Irish protestation? Oaths and the Confederation of Kilkenny', in M. Braddick and P. Whithington (eds), *Popular Culture and Political Agency in Early Modern England and Ireland* (Woodbridge, Suffolk, 2017), pp. 243-66, at pp. 260-2; I am grateful to Professor Morrill for sending me a copy of this in advance of publication.
26 Darcy, *Irish Rebellion*, pp. 53-4.
27 Drawing on a point made by Kane, 'Popular politics', p. 340.
28 Ó Siochrú, *Confederate Ireland*, pp. 15-17 argues that 'ethnicity appears to have been less important than social status in determining an individual's political outlook'; nonetheless, it is important to remember that contemporaries conflated ethnic terms with, and used as labels to describe, divergent political outlooks.
29 *Orders Establisht in the Popish Generall Assembly* (1643), p. 8.
30 Ibid., p. 9.
31 Gilbert, *Irish Confederation*, ii. 84.
32 See for example: Gilbert, *Irish Confederation*, i. 368, 403, ii. 100, 102, 103.
33 Lake and Pincus, 'Public Sphere', pp. 279-81.
34 Bowen, 'Information, language and political culture', pp. 125-58.
35 A. Doyle, *A History of the Irish Language: from the Norman Invasion to*

Independence (Oxford, 2015), pp. 66–8; W.J. Smyth, *Map-making, Landscapes and Memory: a geography of colonial and early modern Ireland, c.1530–1750* (Cork, 2006), pp. 403–4.
36 E. Darcy, 'Political participation in early Stuart Ireland', *Journal of British Studies* 56 (2017), pp. 773–96; Gillespie, 'Negotiating Order', pp. 188–205.
37 Palmer, *Language and Conquest*; ibid., 'Interpreters and the Politics of Translation'.
38 Darcy, *Irish Rebellion*, p. 43.
39 TCD, MS 809, fos 52–3, 58–9v, 97–8v, 103–4v, 120–1v, 124, 144–5v, 146–7v.
40 TCD, MS 809, fos 77–8v: examination of Brian Odire.
41 TCD, MS 813, fos 76–83v; A. Clarke, 'Bedell, William', in *DIB*.
42 TCD, MS 833, fos 105–6v, fo. 105v: deposition of Ambrose Bedell.
43 TCD, MS 817, fo. 272: examination of William McCarmacke; ibid., MS 817, fos 330–1v: examination of Katherine Murry.
44 TCD, MS 815, fos 154–5v: deposition of John Winsmore.
45 D. Cregan, 'The Confederate Catholics of Ireland: the personnel of the Confederation, 1642–9', *IHS* 29 (1995), pp. 490–512, at p. 494.
46 J. Tuchet, *The Memoirs of James, Lord Audley, Earl of Castlehaven* (1680), p. 23; J. Tuchet, *The Memoires of James Lord Audley Earl of Castlehaven* (1681), p. 23; J. Tuchet, *The Earl of Castlehaven's Review, or, his Memoirs of his engagement and carriage in the Irish Wars* (1684), pp. 58–62; M. Ó Siochrú, 'Tuchet, James', in *DIB*.
47 B. McGrath, 'Parliament men and the Confederate Association', in Ó Siochrú (ed.), *Kingdoms in Crisis*, pp. 90–105.
48 Gilbert, *Contemporary History*, i, p. 1, p. 69.
49 N. Williams, *Pairlement Chloinne Tomáis* (Dublin, 1981), pp. 97–8.
50 Gilbert, *Irish Confederation*, vi. 117.
51 Darcy, *Irish Rebellion*, pp. 51, 53, 61–2.
52 TCD, MS 809, fos 13–14v: examination of Owen Connolly; Darcy, 'Political participation in early Stuart Ireland', p. 783.
53 TCD, MS 836, fos 82–6v: deposition of William Fitzgerald; *CSP Ire.* 1633–47, p. 342.
54 TCD, MS 835, fos 133–4v: deposition of Grace Lovett.
55 Gilbert, *Irish Confederation*, ii. 85.
56 John Spurr, 'A profane history of early modern oaths', in *Transactions of the Royal Historical Society*, 6th series 9 (2001), pp. 37–63.
57 Gilbert, *Contemporary History*, i, p. 1, pp. 357–8; R. Puttock, *An Abstract of Certain Depositions* (1642), pp. 1–2.
58 Gilbert, *Contemporary History*, i, p. 1, p. 14; This is corroborated by TCD, MS 833, fos 127–33v: deposition of Arthur Culme.
59 Gilbert, *Contemporary History*, i, p. 1, p. 16.
60 J. McHugh, 'The North Wexford gentry and the Rebellion of 1641', in *The Past: the Organ of the Uí Cinsealaigh Historical Society* 24 (2003), pp. 28–42, at p. 35.
61 Gilbert, *Contemporary History*, i, p. 2, p. 405.
62 *Clanricarde Memoirs*, pp. 101–2.
63 Gilbert, *Contemporary History*, i, p. 1, p. 37; Jane Ohlmeyer, *Making Ireland English*, p. 269.

64 *Clanricarde Memoirs*, pp. 81–2; Ó Siochrú, *Confederate Ireland*, pp. 29–30.
65 Gilbert, *Contemporary History*, i, p. 1, p. 225.
66 Gilbert, *Irish Confederation*, vi. 71–2, 96; Ó Siochrú, *Confederate Ireland*, pp. 89–91.
67 Morrill, 'Irish Protestation', p. 252.
68 Ibid.; C. Russell, 'The British Problem and the English Civil War', *History* 72 (1987), pp. 395–415.
69 Cambridge, MS 4352 fo. 43v: 'Dr Walter Enos Reffleccons vppon the Peace, 1646'.
70 'Manifeste et Articles que les Catholiques Confederez D'Hibernie Demandent ...', in Gilbert (ed.), *Irish Confederation*, iii. 336–9.
71 Real Academia de Historia, Madrid M-RAH, 9/3663(48), fo. 406: Humilde peticion de los Chatholicos confederados al rey Carlos, 1642 (The humble petition of the Catholic Confederates before King Charles); *Manifiesto de los Catolicos Confederados* (Seville, 1642); *The coppy of a letter sent by the rebells in Ireland to the Lord Dillon, to declare to his Maiestie the cause of their taking up of armes* (1641); E. Darcy, 'The Spanish-language "Manifesto" of the Catholic Confederation of Ireland, 1642', *Archivium Hibernicum* 67 (2014), pp. 25–34.
72 I. Fennessy, 'Printed items among the Wadding papers', *Collectanea Hibernica* 39/40 (1998), pp. 32–95, at pp. 78–9.
73 *CSP Ire.* 1633–47, p. 404: proclamation by the general assembly of the Catholic Confederates, 4 July 1645.
74 Gilbert, *Irish Confederation*, vi. 71–2, 96; Ó Siochrú, *Confederate Ireland*, pp. 89–91.
75 *By The Generall Assembly of the Confederate Catholiqves of Ireland Mett at the Cittie of Kilkenny The Tenth Day of Ianvary Anno Domini 1646* (Kilkenny, 1647).
76 M. Caball, *Poets and Politics: continuity and reaction in Irish poetry, 1558–1625* (Cork, 1998), pp. 107–9; R. Gillespie, *Devoted People: belief and religion in early modern Ireland* (Manchester, 1997), p. 140; B. Ó Buachalla, 'Aodh Eanghach and the Irish King-Hero', in D. Ó Corráin, L. Breatnach and K. McCone (eds), *Sages, Saints and Storytellers: Celtic studies in honour of Professor James Carney* (Maynooth, 1989), pp. 216–7; K. Murray, '"Ticfa didiu rí aili forae": prophecy, sovereignty narratives and medieval Irish historiography', in P. Gaffney and J.M. Picard (eds), *The Medieval Imagination: mirabile dictu; essays in honour of Yolande de Pontfarcy Sexton* (Dublin, 2012), pp. 111–22; K. Thomas, *Religion and the Decline of Magic: studies in popular beliefs in sixteenth- and seventeenth-century England* (Harmondsworth, 1978), pp. 470–1.
77 Gilbert, *Irish Confederation*, i. 80–1.
78 Gilbert, *Contemporary History*, i, p. 1, p. 30.
79 Gilbert, *Irish Confederation*, i. 45.
80 Darcy, *Irish Rebellion*, pp. 58–9.
81 D. Beresford and A. Mac Shamhráin, 'Fitzgerald, Gerald fitz Maurice ("Gearóid Iarla")', in *DIB*; Dáithí Ó hÓgáin, 'Gearóid Iarla agus an Draíocht', pp. 246–7; Dáithí Ó hÓgáin, '"An é an tam, fós é?": Staidéar ar fhinscéal Barbarossa (Móitif D1960.2) in Éirinn', in *Béaloideas*, pp. 213–308, at pp. 252–3.
82 J. O'Donovan (ed.), *Annala Rioghachta Eireann* (7 vols, Dublin, 1848–51), v, p. 1796 fn. [i]; B. Ó Buachalla, 'An Mheisiasacht agus An Aisling', in P. De Brún, S. Ó Coileáin and P. Ó Riain (eds), *Folia Gadelica* (Cork, 1983), pp. 77–78;

Ó hÓgáin, 'Gearóid Iarla agus an Draíocht', p. 246; Ó hÓgáin, '"An é an tam, fós é?"', p. 213; N. O'Kearney, *The Prophecies of Ss. Columbkille, Maeltamlacht, Ultan, Seadhna, Coireall, Bearcan, Malachy* (London, 1856), pp. 126–7, 205; K. Simms, 'The Geraldines and Gaelic culture', in P. Crooks and S. Duffy (eds), *The Geraldines and Medieval Ireland: the making of myth* (Dublin, 2016), pp. 264–74, at pp. 272–3.

83 P. Mayerne, *The Patterne of all Pious Prayer, and the Epitomie of all Christian Catholique Beliefe being a patheticall and paraphrastical meeter vpon the Pater Noster, Ave Maria, and Credo in Deum* (Douai, 1636); Gillespie, *Devoted People*, p. 69.

84 Ó Siochrú, *Confederate Ireland*, pp. 60–1.

85 Bowen, 'Information, language and political culture in early modern Wales', pp. 135–7; A. Fox, *Oral and Literate Culture in England, 1500–1700* (Oxford, 2000), pp. 364–7.

86 R. Gillespie, *Reading Ireland: print, reading and social change in early modern Ireland* (Manchester, 2005).

87 E.R. McClintlock Dix, 'Printing in the city of Kilkenny in the seventeenth century' and 'Printing in the city of Waterford in the seventeenth century', in *Proceedings of the Royal Irish Academy* 32 (Dublin, 1914–16), pp. 125–37, 333–44.

88 P. Comerford, *The Inqvisition of a Sermon* (Waterford, 1644), 'The printer to the gentle reader'.

89 *A Briefe Relation of the most Remarkeable Feates and Passages* (Waterford, 1644).

90 H. Morgan, 'News from Ireland: Catalan, Portuguese and Castilian pamphlets on the confederate war in Ireland', in M. Ó Siochrú and J. Ohlmeyer (eds), *Ireland, 1641: Contexts and Reactions* (Manchester, 2013), pp. 115–33.

91 *A Remonstrance of Grievances Presented to his most Excellent Majestie, in the behalfe of the Catholicks of Ireland* (Waterford, 1643); Clarke, 'A Discourse Between Two Councillors of State', pp. 159–75; Darcy, 'Spanish-language "Manifesto" of the Catholic Confederation', pp. 24–33.

92 Clarke, 'A Discourse Between Two Councillors of State', pp. 159–75; *A Remonstrance of Grievances presented to his most excellent Majesty* (Waterford, 1643); *Admonitions by the Svpreame Covncell of the Confederat Catholicks of Ireand* [sic] (Waterford, 1643); *A Persvasive Letter Exhorting the Natives of Ireland to Stand in Defence of their Faith, King, and Countrey* (Waterford, 1645).

93 T. Ó hAnnracháin, 'Conflicting loyalties, conflicted Rebels: political and religious allegiance among the Confederate Catholics of Ireland', *EHR* 119 (2004), pp. 851–72, at p. 855; Ó Siochrú, *Confederate Ireland*, pp. 88–90.

94 'Darcy, 'Spanish-language "Manifiesto"', pp. 24–33, quotation from p. 30.

95 *The Decree of Excommunication by John Baptist Rinvccini* (Waterford, 1646); oath for the confederates, 1646 (Gilbert, *Irish Confederation*, vi. 96); W. Enos, *A Survey of the Articles of the Late Rejected Peace* (Waterford, 1646); W. Enos, *The Part of the Survey of the Articles of the Late Rejected Peace* (Waterford, 1646); E.R. McClintlock Dix, 'Printing in the city of Kilkenny in the seventeenth century', *Proceedings of the Royal Irish Academy* 32 (1914–16), pp. 125–37, at pp. 135–7; see also Ó Siochrú, *Confederate Ireland*, p. 40.

96 Gilbert (ed.), *Irish Confederation*, iv. 323–5 contains the order dated to July 1645; *By the Generall Assembly of the Confederate Catholicks of Ireland* (Kilkenny, 1646) in Bodl. Carte MS 18, fo. 8; Ó Siochrú, *Confederate Ireland*, p. 93.
97 RIA, 3 D 1/24: *By the Ecclesiasticall Congregation of the Clergi of Ireland. For avoyding of unnaturall distinction betweene the old Irish and the old and new English* (Waterford, 1646).

10

Oliver Cromwell, priestcraft and the 'deluded and seduced' people of Ireland

JOHN MORRILL

Sometime in January or February 1650 Oliver Cromwell wrote or released for publication a document that was subtitled:

> A DECLARATION OF THE LORD LIEUTENANT OF IRELAND, *for the undeceiving of deluded and seduced people, which will be satisfactory to fall that doe not wilfully shut their eyes against the light. In Answer to certaine declarations and Acts framed by the Irish Popish Prelates and Clergie in a late Conventicle at* CLONMAC'NOISE, *the fourth of December last.*[1]

It is by far the longest text of his that survives – almost 6,000 words in length – and it appears to offer us the clearest statement he ever made about his intentions as lord lieutenant of Ireland and indeed about many other matters. In form it is a systematic answer in neo-classical form, selectively quoting from and challenging a series of acts and declarations drawn up and published by an 'ecclesiasticall congregation' of senior Catholic clergy and addressed to the Catholic people of Ireland.[2] It is a haughty denial of their claim that he had come to 'extirpate the Catholique Religion', and to bring about 'the destruction of the lives of the Inhabitants of this nation' by setting out to 'massacre, destroy and banish' all Catholics. Cromwell accuses the bishops and clergy of being responsible (in the 1640s) for 'the most unheard of & barbarous massacre (without respect of sexe or age) that ever the Sun beheld', and in the last part of his *Declaration* he lays out his plans for a just settlement. This is how S.R. Gardiner summarised it in 1903: 'not to meddle with any man's conscience, but to prescribe the worship that confirmed and strengthened it; to put to death all who resisted him in this enterprise, but to treat non-combatants with moderation in the hope that they would become like Englishmen'.[3]

This is an important document but it has received no close scrutiny, except perhaps by Gardiner, who devoted four pages to it. Most of the other specialist histories of the period devote a single paragraph to it;[4] and none of the major biographies refer to in much more than passing.[5] All the commentators rely on a version of the text published, at least according to the title page, in London on 21 March '1650'.[6] None have noticed that this was a reprint derived, but differing in small but significant ways, from two earlier Irish printings, and so it is with the authority of the text itself that we need to start.

No holograph version of the *Declaration* has survived but there are three different editions printed in 1650, and one undated early manuscript version that survives in the Carte manuscripts in the Bodleian Library (and hence presumably a version made for the king's lord lieutenant, the marquess of Ormond).[7] This is most likely a copy of one of the Irish printings, but it is just possible that it is a copy acquired from a manuscript.[8] This raises the question of whether Cromwell himself wrote it or just lent his name to it. We can only return to this once we have considered the content. But it is a legitimate question never previously asked.

The two Irish printings, from Cork[9] and Dublin,[10] include both the *Actes and Declarations made by the Ecclesiastical Congregation ... met at Clonmacnoise* and *A Declaration of the Lord Lieutenant of Ireland*. The London printing and the Carte manuscript contain only the latter. The Cork printing is dated 'the 25. of February in the yeare of our Lord 1649'[=1650 new style].[11] The Dublin printing is undated but clearly later than the Cork printing since its title page says so.[12] The title page of the London edition states clearly that the *Declaration* was first printed in Cork and now in London, and makes no reference to a Dublin printing. Although there are many differences between the Cork and London editions, where Cork and Dublin differ, London always follows Cork. The London printer was Edward Griffin, a printer occasionally used by the government but who, since the late 1630s, had had a broad commercial portfolio with a special focus on the publication of mainstream Protestant sermons and Bible commentaries.[13] He was never used as a printer for government-sponsored publications, so the choice of Griffin to publish Cromwell's *Declaration* is not easy to explain, especially since the Clonmacnoise decrees sent by Cromwell to Speaker Lenthall had been printed by the most usual 'state' printer of the time, Robert Ibbitson, on 31 January 1650).[14] On the other hand, the title page of Cromwell's *Declaration* does claim to have been licensed by the secretary of the army, John Rushworth. There is no record in the *Commons Journals* or in the papers of the commonwealth's council of state that Cromwell ever submitted it to Parliament. Why not?

There is a lesser puzzle: we know that Cromwell had a copy of the *Actes and Declarations* no later than 16 January, the date on which wrote to the Speaker enclosing a copy of them.[15] His letter and its enclosure were sent by the House of Commons to the Council of State the day they received them, on 29 January,[16] and the Council of State ordered its immediate publication, and it appeared two days later, both in a newspaper and as a separate.[17] So there is at least a six-week gap between his letter to the Speaker on 16 January and the publication of his response on 25 February. Why the delay? He was still in winter quarters at Youghal (31 miles from Cork) two weeks after his letter to the Speaker on 16 January, and that is surely the time when he would have written it, before a gruelling seven-week campaign across counties Kilkenny and Tipperary concluding with a siege of the city of Kilkenny on 23 March. Did he only find out how far the clergy's claims had stiffened resistance once he was on campaign? Was there a delay in the production process? The obvious reason for his forwarding the Catholic clergy's claims to London was to show their recalcitrance and the scale of the opposition he was facing as a way of encouraging Parliament to maintain the supply of men, money and munitions.

Let us for the moment take it that the *Declaration* was written by Cromwell himself. Why delay publication? Why not send a copy to the Speaker of the Commons or to the Council of State as with all his other Irish writings that found their way into print? What precisely was its purpose, and who was its target audience?

The situation Cromwell faced as he authorised the publication of his *Declaration* was both easier and more complicated than when he had arrived in Ireland in August 1649. In August, there were Catholics and Protestants on both sides. Ormond had assembled a rainbow coalition, but at least four major Catholic peers had entered into agreements, or at least truces, with Cromwell. The Scottish Protestants were sufficiently royalist to fight against the English commonwealth, but not realistic enough to join Ormond's coalition. Indeed, in early August 1649 Owen Roe O'Neill was fighting alongside Sir Charles Coote and confronting Robert Monro's Scottish brigade. But by January 1650 ethnic and religious polarities were becoming clearer.[18] In the months before his arrival, Cromwell had moved to neutralise as many Catholics as possible by private deals. This was most obvious in Ulster, where he had bought off the marquess of Antrim[19] and had colluded in a truce with Owen Roe O'Neill.[20] And although O'Neill had finally been reconciled to Ormond, firmly holding his nose as he did so, he was a dying man. By the time of his arrival in August, Cromwell also had hopes of detaching the Protestants of Munster, comprising Old English and Elizabethan/early Stuart planter families that had remained royalist throughout the 1640s, but he had still to realise his hopes.[21]

Despite all this, the fact remains that areas loyal to the English commonwealth were largely confined to the Pale around Dublin and small pockets elsewhere, most importantly around Derry. Cromwell had to defeat and disband tens of thousands of soldiers opposed to him and to capture and occupy or make indefensible well over one hundred walled towns, castles and strongholds of various kinds. Most Protestants in Ireland were loyal to Ormond and the royalists, or, as with almost all the Scots of Ulster, loyal to the crown if not to its representatives.[22] On that royalist side, the tensions between Ormond and his Old English Protestant and Catholic allies and the leadership of the wholly Catholic Confederation of Kilkenny had simply grown exponentially since the second Ormond Peace of January 1649. And of course the deep wounds caused by the feuding between those Catholics who supported the first Ormond Peace of 1646 (and who had been as a result excommunicated by Rinuccini, the papal nuncio) and those who had opposed that peace, still festered.[23] Ormond had succeeded, in that peace signed in January 1649, in bringing most of the Catholics of Leinster and Munster (but not of Connacht and Ulster) on board. To do so he had had to make significant concessions that seemed to guarantee that Catholics would dominate any future Irish Parliament and that they would have a significant share of office and power in any future royal government in Ireland. In return, he had exacted new promises of loyalty to the house of Stuart. But his repeated military defeats, all too credibly attributable to his own strategic incompetence (but also to a desperate shortage of supplies occasioning rock-bottom morale), weakened support for his leadership of the coalition.[24]

So Cromwell came into a situation where he had few supporters he could count on; his opponents controlled most of Ireland, and, with the departure of the nuncio in disgust following the second Ormond Peace, had for most part stopped fighting one another, but they were much less well-resourced and much more ill-disciplined than Cromwell's men. What kept them together, of course, was the realisation that Cromwell was coming not only to incorporate Ireland into an enlarged English state but to avenge the 'massacres' of the winter of 1641–42, when thousands of Protestants had been killed or had died from cold and hunger.[25] Even more specifically, he had come to honour the Long Parliament's pledge in the *Act for the speedy and effectual reducing of the Rebels, in His Majesty's Kingdom of Ireland, to their due Obedience* (1642) to seize 2.5 million acres of productive Irish land to compensate those who adventured money to pay for the British armies sent to crush the rebellion.[26]

By early December, the situation had already changed significantly. Cromwell had gained control of the eastern seaboard of Ireland – all the eastern and southern towns having surrendered to him, except for Waterford – and Ormond's marching army had been largely destroyed. The towns of co. Cork, controlled by Protestant colonists, had for the most part revolted and thrown in their lot with him. Cromwell's subordinates had made major gains in eastern Ulster. Although the need to garrison the towns he had taken, greatly supplemented by the effects of plague and dysentery, had reduced the number of men Cromwell had at his disposal for the work ahead, he had been able to recruit significant numbers of Protestant soldiers who had surrendered when the towns they were defending had fallen into his hands. What the Ormondists had failed to take into account were two weapons at his disposal: the availability of heavy artillery and a willingness to use extreme violence against those who refused to surrender. Cromwell brought with him cannon that could demolish thick medieval walls such as previous commanders in Ireland had never had. Of course, they were hell to move around with the condition of Irish roads, and this is not the least reason why Cromwell concentrated on an amphibious operation along the east coast towns until the end of 1649. But he also brought with him a clear and ruthless strategy. He would summons a town and offer generous terms, with the threat that if those terms were rejected he would make full use of the clearly understood laws of war: the lives of all who continued to resist him would be at his mercy.

It was crucial to this strategy that he honoured any terms that were offered. Those terms always included allowing the garrison to march away immediately with their arms and ammunition, with their drums beating and colours showing (i.e. their honour intact).[27] They often included an opportunity for the civilian population over a much longer period to move away with all their movable possessions, sometimes with an English military escort;[28] and they always included guarantees that 'the Inhabitants of the said Towne shall be protected their lives and Estates from all plunder and violence of the Souldiery'.[29] On occasion the terms also included a more general promise that they 'shall have the same right liberty and proteccion as other subjects under the Authoritie of the Parliamt. of England have or ought to have & injoy within the Dominion of Ireland'.[30] Despite the provocations, Cromwell was adamant (and he was thinking about all the towns, not least Limerick and Galway, still to be taken) that the terms must be honoured. And he stuck by his promises even when he found he had been double-crossed, as in Clonmel.[31] But it was also crucial that those who saw their walls crumbling under his bombardment knew that if he stormed their town the lives of all those in authority and many ordinary soldiers would be taken in hot or in cold blood. Cromwell knew that he had finite resources and also recognised that the political will of the Rump Parliament to pour resources into this Irish campaign would dribble away. This had to be a quick campaign. The massacres of Drogheda and Wexford[32] would, as he himself made clear, 'tend to prevent the effusion of blood for the future'[33] and would need to be balanced against the fairly generous terms he was willing to give to prevent that effusion of blood.

Let us go back for one moment to the Clonmel articles: that the inhabitants 'shall have the same right liberty and proteccion as other subjects under the Authoritie of the Parliamt. of England have or ought to have & injoy within the Dominion of Ireland'.[34] The grammar here is unclear. Were the right[s], the liberty and the protection that the people of Clonmel were to enjoy the same as those of the people of England or as those devised in

England for people in the dominion of Ireland? On a strict reading, it should mean those that the people of England enjoyed. And that would make them safe from plunder and abuse in the short time, and from mass expropriation of their property in the aftermath of conquest. Those guilty of participation in the initial rebellion or in war crimes could expect no mercy under existing legislation, but others would be liable to the same moderate penalties as English royalists. This would be good news for Clonmel's Protestants but not so much for Clonmel's Catholics. This is important when we turn to examine *A Declaration*. And it must be said, those rights and liberties did not include a right or liberty to freedom of religion. Wherever we have details of the terms asked for by the military or civil leaders of Irish towns, they always included some rights to practise their religion. Cromwell's words to Lucas Taaff at New Ross when the latter asked for 'liberty of conscience to such as stay'[35] is explored later in this chapter. But in all other cases, nothing is ever included in the articles of surrender for or against the rights of Catholics. For *or* against.

Most of the clerical leaders of the Catholic Church gathered in Clonmacnoise at the beginning of December 1649. Over ten days of meetings, those present agreed to and promulgated two sets of acts and declarations. The first document was signed on 4 December by the four archbishops of Armagh, Dublin, Cashel and Tuam, sixteen bishops and a further six vicars apostolic and provincials of regular orders. The other, signed on 13 December bore the signatures of the same twenty bishops but of rather more others. The choice of Clonmacnoise for their meeting was almost certainly not accidental. Sitting on a high ridge looking down over a sweeping bend in the River Shannon, it is at the very heart of Ireland – as far from the north as from the south, from the east as from the west, the gaunt ruin of a once mighty abbey founded by St Ciaran in 544, predating the monasteries founded by Columba.[36] Here in this place, at once a symbol of Ireland's proud Catholic history and of the desolation wrought by the English, these leading men of the Irish church met to contemplate what they believed to be a planned extermination of their faith and of their flocks.

At the heart of their dilemma was the decade-long tension represented by the oath they had all administered and taken at the creation of the Catholic Confederation of Kilkenny: *pro deo, rege et patria, Hiberni unanimes*. How far could they compromise a yearning for a Catholic Ireland by signing up to a Stuart Ireland? However much worse a conquered puritan and republican Ireland, unqualified support for Charles II in return for uncertain and to-be-determined religious rights stuck in many craws. In January 1649, they had gritted their teeth and embraced the second Ormond Peace. The experience of the following ten months had been uniformly demoralising. Ormond had been a disastrous leader. He had consistently favoured Protestants over Catholics for key positions. A large proportion of the Protestants whom he had relied on, especially across Munster, had deserted when it was opportune to do so. When towns surrendered, Protestants in the garrisons had changed sides. Some Protestant town councillors had refused to accept Catholic military governors and vice versa. Those Catholics who were not willing to give largely unconditional support to the Stuarts had largely fallen back into line. In early November this had even included an ailing Owen Roe O'Neill, who had made his peace in late October but had died on 6 November, but the fact remains that the conflict had ceased to be so much Irish, Old English and Scottish royalists against the English commonwealth and much more a conflict between Catholics versus Protestants. The Catholic clergy thought the time was right to make an unapologetical appeal to the Catholic people of Ireland outside the terms of the Ormond Peace.

The fruit of the meeting at Clonmacnoise was a six-page pamphlet printed in Kilkenny[37] in time for a copy to be sent to London on 16 January 1650 and reprinted there on 31 January.[38] It was also printed, almost certainly from the Kilkenny print version, together with Cromwell's response in Cork on 25 February and in Dublin after that.[39] The Clonmacnoise document is in three parts. It begins with a declaration written at the end of their meeting and dated 13 December; this is followed first by four acts agreed earlier on 4 December and then by a declaration related to the four acts. Each of these parts is separately attested by twenty archbishops and bishops and by a fluctuating number of other vicars apostolic and superiors of religious orders.

The declaration dated 13 December opens with a frank admission of frailty in the 'late difference of opinion [that] happened amongst the Prelats and Laitie' and called for a new unity and union. We have resolved all our differences, they say, and now

> stand all of us as one entire body for the interest and immunities of the Church, and of every Prelats and Bishops thereof; and for the honour, dignitie, estate, right, and possessions of all and every of the said Archbishops. Bishops and other Prelats. And we will as one entire and united body forward by our counsailes, action and devices the advancement of his Majesties right and the good of this nation in general.

This was to be promulgated and printed in every *parish* (i.e. it was for Catholics only). And it was specifically in the language and priorities of the dissolved Confederation of Kilkenny, and indeed of the clerical party at the time when they disowned the first Ormond peace of 1646.

Nine days earlier, they produced not just an exhortation to unity but a specifically Catholic programme. First they ordered and decreed 'as an Act of this congregation' that all (arch)bishops 'enjoyne publicke prayers, fastings, general confession and receiving [of holy communion] and other works of piety … to withdraw Gods anger, and to render them capable of his mercies'.

Catholics must dissociate themselves from Protestants to have any hope of gaining God's favour and any chance of victory. Second, they would issue decrees to show 'how vaine it is for them to expect ... from Cromwell ... an[y] assurance of their Religion, lives, or fortunes'. No surrender, they might as well have said – never, never, never. Third, all pastors and preachers were to teach and preach that only amity among all Catholics would 'preserve the nation against the extirpation and the destruction of their religion and fortune'. And they repeated words from the articles of association of the Confederation of Kilkenny of 1642 on how national distinctions must not weaken the amity of Catholics. Fourth, as a threat to that unity, all 'highway Robbers, commonly called Idle Boyes [or Tories]' as well as those who harboured them, were to be excommunicated and any clergy who defied this order were to be suspended by their superiors.

Cromwell ignored the four acts and focused his reply principally on the third section, the declaration accompanying these articles of 4 December. So we offer a transcription of the part that he is to assault:

> many of our flock are mislead by a vaine opinion of hopes, that the Commander in chiefe of the Rebells forces (commonly called the Parliamentaries) would affoord them good conditions; and that relying thereon, they suffer utter distruction of Religion, lives, and fortunes, if not prevented. To undeceive them in that their ungrounded expectation, we doe hereby declare as a most certaine truth, that the enemyes resolution is to extirpate the Catholique Religion out of all his Maiesties Dominions, as by their severall Covenants doth appeare, and the practice wherever their power doth extend; as is manifest by Cromwells letter of the 19. of October 1649. to the then Governor of Rosse. His words, are For that which you mention concerning libertie of Religion, I meddle not with any mans Conscience; but if by liberty of conscience you meane a liberty to exercise the Masse, I iudge it best to use plaine dealing, and to let you know; where the Parliament of England have power That will not be allowed of. This tyrannicall resolution they have put in execution in Wexford, Droghedah, Rosse, & elsewhere. And it is notoriously known, that by acts of Parliament called the Acts of subscription, the estates of the inhabitants of this Kingdom are sold; so as there re-raineth now no more but to put the purchasors in possession, by the power of forces drawn out of England. And for the common sort of people, towards whome they shew any more moderate usage at the present, that is to no other end but to their private advantage and for the better support of their Army; intending at the close of their conquest (if they can effect the same, as God forbid) to roote out the commons also, and to plant this land with Colonies to be brought hither out of England, as witnesse the number they have already sent hence for the Tobacco Ilands, and put enemyes in their places. And in effect, this banishment or other destructions of the common people must follow the resolution or extirpating the Catholique Religion, which is not to be effected without the Massacring or banishment of the Catholique Inhabitants. Wee cannot therefore in our duty to God, and in discharge of the care we are obliged to have for the preser-

vation of our flocks, but admonish them not to delude and loose themselves with the vaine expectation of conditions to be had from that mercilesse enemy.[40]

Cromwell received his copy no later than 16 January 1650, the day he sent it to the Speaker of the Rump Parliament with the instructive comment that: 'this inclosed Booke was the result of one of their late Conventions. The Warre thus stated will have good harmony with Montrosse and all his participants. I hope all honest mens eyes will be opened.'[41] Cromwell was of course keen to stress the severity of the opposition he faced: he did after all have an uphill struggle to keep the Rump focused on providing him with enough men, money and supplies. It had the desired effect.[42]

And so at last to Cromwell's *Declaration*. This is a 5,800-word response to the 1,800 document produced by the congregation at Clonmacnoise, and more particularly to the 500-word statement quoted. Early on he attacked the status of their meeting, terming it (not without irony given his own background) a 'conventicle' and challenging them to confirm whether the interest they advocate is that of 'the King of Scotland', Charles II, or that of the king of France or more particularly Spain ('for **you** have some of **you** lately been harping … upon his Majestie of Spaine to be your Protector').

'You'. It is a word he used 137 times in the declaration, a constant jab in the ribs or a poke in the eye of the clergy. Although his audience is not that 'you' of clergy who had gathered at Clonmacnoise but the people they addressed, his aim is to crush with scorn and contempt those who deluded and seduced those in their charge. The pamphlet is vitriolically anti-clerical rather than anti-Irish. The extent to which it is anti-Catholic remains to be examined.

From the start Cromwell launches into an assault on clerical presumption: that they had claimed to meet *proprio motu* – at their own instigation. He attacks their presumption that they are the masters not the servants of the people of God and that as clergy they are set apart from the people of God – *clergy* 'a tearme unknowne to any save to the Antichristian Church'. In your pride and in your love of 'filthy lucre', he tells them, you sought to 'bridle, saddle & ride the [people] at your pleasure … your covenant is with death and hell, your union is like that of Simeon and Levi. Associate your selves and you shall be broken in peeces; take counsel together and you shall come to nought.' He is drawing on Isaiah 8, Genesis 35, Genesis 49 and Isaiah 28. This is classic Cromwell. And it anticipates closely what Cromwell says to the commissioners of the Scottish Kirk nine months later: 'There may be a Covenant made with Death and Hell (I will not say yours was so)' which precedes an exegesis of Isaiah 28, vv.5–15, which immediately precedes the verses quoted to the Irish.[43] This is both compelling evidence that Cromwell is the author of *A Declaration* as he certainly was in his letter to the Kirk, and it reminds us of the depths of Cromwell's anti-clericalism, his loathing of priestcraft Catholic or Protestant. He accused Presbyterian ministers of a 'carnal confidence' which can become 'spirituall drunkennesse' – of claiming a monopoly on the breaking of the Word of God, of preaching;[44] he accused Catholic priests of worse: 'you cannot feed them, you poyson them with your false abhominable & Antichristian doctrine and practices; You keep the Word of God from them, and instead thereof give them your sencelesse Orders and Traditions'.

This priestly love of tyrannising over their 'flocks' extends to a love of working with tyrants. Publicly they supported the first Ormond Peace, but privately they had colluded with the earl of Glamorgan and George Lord Digby and they 'had warrant to agree with the Pope himselfe at Rome, in favour of the Irish Catholiques'. But, he assures them, 'men begin to weary of [arbitrary power] in Kings and Church-men; their juggle betweene them, mutually to uphold Civill and Ecclesiasticall Tyranny'.

This contempt for clerical presumption is, however, fuelled by something more: 'How dare you assume to call these men your Flocks, whom you have plunged into so horrid a Rebellion by which you have made both them & the Countrey almost a ruinous heape, and whom you have fleeced and pold and peeld hitherto, and make it your businesse to doe so still[?]'. Altogether more than 2,200 of the 5,800 words (38 per cent) of his words are directly aimed at the pretensions and wickedness of the clergy as clergy. But the greatest of all the charges is that they were responsible for the Irish rebellion of 1641. Having spoken, with apparent conviction, of the way that the English had come and settled 'peaceably and honestly' in Ireland, bringing 'equall benefit and protection of England with them; And equall Justice from the Lawes', he went on to accuse 'you' the clergy. 'You broke this union, you unprovoked, put the English to the most unheard of & most barbarous massacre (without respect of sexe or age) that ever Sun beheld'. Was not 'this unheard of villany perpetrated by *your* instigation?'

So the common people of Ireland were deluded and seduced. To that extent their responsibility was limited and when Cromwell turned from his assault on the clergy to look at what his victory would mean for the people of Ireland, he follows through on this.

The hinge in *A Declaration*, as it moves from the assault on the clergy to the appeal to the people, is to meet head on the clergy's analysis of Cromwell's own words to Lucas Taaff, governor of New Ross, who had asked Cromwell for 'a liberty of conscience to such as shall stay after the town's surrender'. Cromwell had retorted to Taaff:

> for that which you mention concerning Liberty of Religion, I meddle not with any mans Conscience. But if by libertie of Conscience, you meane a libertie to exercise the Masse, I judge it best to use plain dealing; and to let you know where the Parliament of England have power, that will not be allowed of.

As we have seen, from Clonmacnoise the clergy linked this specifically to the massacres at 'Wexford, Drogheda, Rosse & elsewhere' (there were of course no massacres except at Drogheda and Wexford between September and December 1649), and they linked it specifically to the Acts of Subscription (i.e. the Adventurers' Acts) and to a plan for mass transportation of the Commons to 'the Tobacco Ilands' and to put enemyes in their places. It is this that Cromwell spent the second half of *A Declaration* rebutting in three parts: 'first ... the designe to extirpate the Catholique Religion ... second ... the destruction of the lives of the inhabitants of this Nation ...Thirdly .., the ruin of their fortunes in the Act of Subscription.'

'I meddle not with any man's conscience', Cromwell had told Taaff, and he interrogates what he had meant by that in the same breath as he said that he would not suffer 'the exercise the Masse'. He says that there was no such liberty between the Irish Reformation and the rebellion of 1641.[45] So he tells them that he was only seeking to extirpate something they had 'intruded' into Ireland, since 'the Ominous encreasing with the Woolves [i.e. clergy]' in the 1640s. And then, in an important qualification of his words to Taaff, he refers to banning the '*publique* Exercises of your Masse', implying a distinction from private exercise, and he also speaks of hunting down all priests (but only those priests?) 'where I find them seducing the People'. (Does this imply that some of them were not doing so?) His aim, he repeats, is 'to reduce things to their former state on this behalfe'. Even more importantly he says he will not force anyone's conscience, certainly not requiring them to attend Protestant services. He is very precise in his words:

> As for the People what thoughts they have in matters of Religion in their owne breasts I cannot reach; but thinke it my duty, if they walke honestly and peaceably, not to cause them in the least to suffer for the same, but shall endeavour to walke patiently and in love towards them to see if at any time it shall please God to give them another or a better minde. And all men under the power of England within this Dominion, are hereby required and enjoyned strictly and Religiously to doe the same.

Catholics were to be free to worship together, but without the Mass and with few, if any, priests. From a Catholic point of view this was of course an empty or meaningless offer. From Cromwell's point of view it was consistent with all he stood for. Throughout his life as a public figure he saw all forms of persecution as counter-productive. He allowed freedom of assembly and worship, but supported limits on freedom to evangelise untruth. He would compel no one to act against conscience. What complicated his view of the Catholic Church in Ireland was his conviction that the clergy had organised and spearheaded the rebellion and massacres of 1641–42. Fed, we can be confident, on Dr Henry Jones's *Remonstrance*[46] and Sir John Temple's *The*

Irish Rebellion,[47] which both sought, by tendentious selections from the 1641 depositions, taken from survivors of the 'massacres', to make the case for this being a 'General Massacre' directed by the Catholic clergy under instructions from Rome.[48]

The second part of Cromwell's rebuttal relates to his alleged plan to 'massacre, destroy and banish' the Catholics in general, there being no other way to 'extirpate the Catholique religion' than by extirpating the Catholic population. He began by saying that the common people are barely Catholic, for 'the generality of the Inhabitants are ... ignorant of the grounds of the Catholique religion', and are held to it by force and fear. So there is a better and easier way to extirpate popery: 'to wit the Word of God, which is able to convert ... togeather with humanitie, good life, equall and honest dealing with men of a different opinion which we desire to exercise towards this poore people'. Furthermore, he says, there can be no evidence of any intention to 'massacre, destroy and banish', for those killed are only those in arms, and those banished are only men in arms who had failed to surrender on terms and whose lives were therefore at his mercy: 'I shall not willingly take or suffer to be taken away the life of any man not in Armes, but by Triall to which the People of this Nation are subject by Law, for offences against the same.' As far as deaths in hot blood are concerned, this is economical with the truth; as far as deaths in cold blood and as far as the banishments before and after *A Declaration*, and as far as the terms of all the surrender articles he granted, all go, this is correct.[49] And even the Act for the settling of Ireland of 1652, which he thought too harsh, protected most of the Irish commons from any penalties. Article nine of the Act, guaranteed pardon 'for life and estate' for all those 'having no real estate in Ireland, nor personal estate to the value of ten pounds' who lay down their arms and promised obedience to the 'Commonwealth of England, as the same is now established'.[50]

And so to the third and final section of his response to the charges levelled at him: to 'that of the ruine of their fortunes in the act of Subscription', which would lead to the 'estates of the inhabitants of this nation [being] sold' and 'intending to roote out the Commons also, and to plant the Land with Collonies'. The English army has not just come, he admitted, at some five to six million pounds of expense, to secure the interest of the adventurers who only invested a quarter of a million pounds. 'We come to ask an account of the innocent blood that hath bin shed ... We come to breake the power of a Company of lawlesse Rebells ... We come to hold forth and maintaine the lustre & glory of English liberty'. So he distinguished, as the Act for the settling of Ireland[51] was to do, between those engaged in rebellion and massacre in the winter of 1641–42 and those who later joined the Confederation of Kilkenny in and after the autumn of 1642, from those who laid down their arms and those who continued to fight. He also distinguishes the leaders who would be made examples of from those 'private soldiers as lay downe their Armes and shal live peaceably & honestly in their homes [and] shall be permitted to do so'. He is insistent that he will treat all but those convicted for taking part in the massacres in the same way as English royalists have been treated. Nobility, gentry, commons who were not actors in the original rebellion 'may expect the Protection in their Goods, Liberties and Lives that the Law gives them ... equal justice shall be done them with the English'. And he repeats his promise (which he maintained in practice) that 'if the souldiery bee insolent upon them, upon complaint and proof, it shall be punished with the utmost severity'. Where the clergy of Clonmacnoise wanted to say *all* Catholics were under threat, Cromwell wanted to make very sharp distinctions, the kind of distinctions to be found in the articles he gave to the thirty and more towns that surrendered to him on terms.[52]

There is no direct evidence of the sincerity of what Cromwell wrote in *A Declaration*. Some parts of it – his virulent anti-clericalism – are clearly characteristic. And other parts of it do seem to be supported by his actions towards Ireland and the Irish during and after his time in Ireland. He *did* make great efforts to discipline his men and to punish very publicly those who terrorised the native population.[53] He offered generous terms to those who surrendered just as he made examples of the first two towns to force him to overwhelm them by a military storm.[54] When he left Ireland, he was winning the war but his successors were left with problems that he did not have to face, above all the problem of the Tories or 'woodkerne', large bands of disbanded Irish troops living off the land as brigands, highwaymen, with a natural preference for robbing and killing Englishmen.[55] It was this problem which led Cromwell's successors to plan a settlement at odds with one envisaged in *A Declaration*.

By the spring of 1652, Irish resistance was sufficiently broken for the English state to plan the post-conquest settlement. The military leaders and civil commissioners still had a massive Tory problem and they had many soldiers clamouring for their arrears, and no longer had any English assets (crown or church lands) that could be liquidated to pay them off. The soldiers had their lobbyists in London too, and the adventurers – especially the powerful money men, to whom the Rump still needed to advance credit to keep the commonwealth afloat – wanted their Irish acres. All this required action that went far beyond what Cromwell had envisaged in *A Declaration*. He would not have had any difficulty with the four categories exempt from all pardon, who were to forfeit their lives and all their property. He would have been troubled at the level of severity for those who were to lose one-third or two-thirds of their land and to the mandatory banishment of many who had not been rebels in 1641–42. But he was especially offended and alarmed by, and opposed to, the decision that whatever land any Catholic retained was to be forfeited and replaced by land 'to be assigned in such places in Ireland as the Parliament

... shall think fit', especially since this provision was explicitly to apply to those otherwise protected by 'any articles granted unto them, or agreed upon between them and any commander of the Parliament's forces'. Cromwell's opposition led to his removal as lord lieutenant in May 1652 and to a failed attempt to rush through the Act while he was sent on a pointless journey to Kent to inspect the fleet.[56]

There thus seems plenty of evidence that Cromwell himself wrote and meant what is contained in *A Declaration*. He came to punish rebels, to destroy politically malevolent clergy and to destroy Irish royalism, but he did not come to extirpate the Catholic religion or the Irish people. If we blame Cromwell personally for the catastrophic Cromwellian settlement in Ireland, we let a lot more people, almost all of them English, off the hook.

NOTES

1 The complicated print history is discussed later in this chapter.
2 *Certain Acts and Declarations made by the Ecclesiasticall Congregation of the Arch-bishops. Bishops and other Prelates. Met at Clonmacnoise the fourth day of December 1649. And since concluded. Kilkenny Printed in the Year of our Lord. 1649. And reprinted at London by Robert Ibbitson* (ESTC: R173639); it was also printed in *Severall Proceeedings in Parliament from Friday the 25 to Thursday the 31 January. 1649* [=1650], pp. 133–9 (Nelson and Seccombe 599.018).
3 S.R. Gardiner, *History of the Commonwealth and Protectorate* (4 vols, London, 1903), i. 149.
4 D. Murphy, *Cromwell in Ireland* (Dublin, 1902), p. 248; *NHI*, pp. 344–5; J. Scott-Wheeler, *Cromwell in Ireland* (Dublin, 1999), p. 123; M. Ó Siochrú, *God's Executioner: Oliver Cromwell and the conquest of Ireland* (London, 2008), p. 117.
5 Among the most widely praised of the many biographies some comment in a few sentences without indexing it; these include C. Hill, *God's Englishman: Oliver Cromwell and the English Revolution* (London, 1970), B. Coward, *Oliver Cromwell* (Harlow, 1991) and I. Gentles, *Oliver Cromwell* (Basingstoke, 2011). Others, including C.H. Firth, *Oliver Cromwell and the Rule of the Puritans in England* (1900), P. Gaunt, *Oliver Cromwell* (Oxford, 1996), and J.C. Davis, *Oliver Cromwell* (London, 2001), pass over it in silence; the best-selling and longest biography of modern times, Antonia Fraser's *Cromwell Our Chief of Men* (London, 1973) which weighs in at 772 pages, offers a nine-page account of the taking of Drogheda but a single paragraph, mostly a patchwork of quotations from the unnamed and misdated *Declaration*.
6 The London printing is ESTC R15772 and R37928, Both ESTC and *Early English Books Online* assume that the dating is old style and therefore the date is March 1651 new style; catastrophically they then assume that the author was Henry Ireton. This cannot be right, because Cromwell remained lord lieutenant until May 1652 and in March 1651 Ireton was lord deputy not lord lieutenant. And *A Declaration* is expressly a response to the *Certain Actes and Declarations* of December 1649, and

in the Irish printings the two are published together. Because the Irish were using the Gregorian Calendar, the English in Ireland, when addressing them, frequently used new style (year beginning in 1 January not 25 March) to prevent confusion.
7   Bodl. Carte MS 26, fos 590–6v.
8   Where the Cork and Dublin pamphlets differ, it always follows the Cork edition, and it is clearly not derived from the London version. Might Ormond have had a copy of a manuscript version? It seems unlikely; and since the differences between it and the Cork edition are so small, it probably does not matter except to suggest that perhaps there were manuscript copies in circulation earlier than 25 February.
9   There was a printer in Cork before Cromwell arrived, and that printer quickly made himself available to the lord lieutenant and published several things for him; see E.R. McClintock Dix, 'List of all pamphlets, books &c printed in Cork during the seventeenth century' *Proceedings of the Royal Irish Academy, Section C* 36 (1921), pp. 10–15; less accurate, but still useful, is W.K. Sessions, *First Printers in Waterford, Cork and Kilkenny, Pre-1700* (York, 1990), pp. 93–8.
10 The Dublin printer, William Bladen, was a Protestant Englishman, who had been operating in Dublin for twenty years: see T. Clavin, 'Bladen, William', *DIB*.
11 It is not found in ESTC or *EEBO*; it is noticed by T. Sweeney, *Ireland and the Printed Word: a short descriptive catalogue of early books … relating to Ireland, 1475–1700* (Dublin, 1997), p. 164, item 1079 (and photograph of the title page at p. 257); the only known copy was owned by Tony Sweeney and consisted of pp. 1–22: the remaining six pages are missing; the version used here uses the Cork printing for pp. 1–22 and the Dublin printing (almost identical) for pp. 23–8.
12 'Printed at Cork the 25. of February 1649. and reprinted at Dublin by W[illiam] B[laden]' (ESTC: R171136); although this time [see n. 6] the ESTC editors get the date correct, they continue to misattribute it to Ireton, who was not even lord deputy, let alone lord lieutenant in February 1650; although it is in ESTC, it was not digitally imaged for *EEBO*, and the most accessible (i.e. online) copy is from the Beinecke Library at Yale University, British Tracts 1650, C287.
13 I am grateful to Jason Peacey for his advice on the career of Edward Griffin.
14 *Certain Acts and Declarations made by the ecclesiasticall congregation of the arch-bishops, bishops, and other prelates. Met at Clonmacnoise the fourth day of December 1649. and since concluded* (ESTC: R173639); a first edition, date unknown, was produced at Kilkenny by the printer responsible for much official material issued by the General Assembly of the Confederation of Kilkenny between 1646 and 1649. No copy of the Irish printing is known to have survived.
15 *Severall Proceeedings in Parliament from Friday the 25 to Thursday the 31 January. 1649* [=1650], pp. 131–2 (Nelson and Seccombe 599.018).
16 *CJ*, vi. 352 (29 Jan. 1650).
17 See above, notes 15 and 16.
18 Gardiner, *Commonwealth and Protectorate*, i. chapters 4–6 remains an excellent narrative; more recently, Scott-Wheeler, *Cromwell in Ireland*, and more particularly Ó Siochrú, *God's Executioner*, while paying little attention to *A Declaration* offer excellent accounts; the following section relies principally on these three secondary sources.

19 J. Ohlmeyer, 'MacDonnell, Randall', *DIB*.
20 J. Casway, 'O'Neill, Owen Roe', *ODNB*.
21 P. Little, *Lord Broghill and the Cromwellian Union with Ireland and Scotland* (Woodbridge, 2004), pp. 59–64.
22 D. Stevenson, *Scottish Covenanters and Irish Confederates* (Belfast, 1981), pp. 271–9.
23 Well summarised from his much fuller work by T. Ó hAnnracháin, 'Rinuccini, Giovanni Battista [Gianbattista]', *ODNB*.
24 Ormond's failings, set in the context of his near-impossible position, is well analysed by Ó Siochrú, *God's Executioner*, p. 56 and passim.
25 For the best single study see A. Clarke, 'The "1641 Massacres"', in M. Ó Siochrú and J. Ohlmeyer (eds), *Ireland 1641: contexts and reactions* (Manchester, 2013), pp. 37–51.
26 For the Act, see K.S. Bottigheimer, *English Money and Irish Land: the 'Adventurers' in the Cromwellian conquest of Ireland* (Oxford, 1971).
27 Good examples include the terms accepted at New Ross (19 Oct. 1649), Kilkenny (27 Mar. 1650) and Clonmel (18 May 1650); particularly interesting are the Kilkenny articles: the garrison can leave fully armed (with 'Drums beating, Colours flying, Matches lighted, and [musket] Ball') for the first two miles, but then had to surrender them all up to Cromwell's nominated officers, 'excepting one hundred muskets and one hundred pikes, allowed them for their defence against the Tories'; they were granted passes that would last as long as it took them to reach a friendly garrison, so long as they covered a minimum of ten miles a day; see J. Morrill (ed.) *Letters, Writings and Speeches of Oliver Cromwell* (Oxford, forthcoming), document 1650 03 27.
28 E.g. the New Ross articles: 'and a convoy sent with them to secure them on their journey', Morrill (ed.), *Letters, Writings and Speeches*, document 1649 10 19.
29 These precise words are from the Clonmel articles, as in Morrill (ed.), *Letters, Writings and Speeches*, document 1650 05 18a.
30 Morrill (ed.), *Letters, Writings and Speeches*, document 1650 05 18a.
31 The best modern account is in Scott-Wheeler, *Cromwell in Ireland*, pp. 151–8; Cromwell had lost at least 2,000 men in the course of the siege and the failed attempt to storm the town; and then offered generous terms without being told that the governor, Hugh Dubh O'Neill and all his Ulster fighters had slipped away in the middle of the night. Cromwell was livid but stuck by his word.
32 His words, of course, come from a letter justifying what happened at Drogheda (see note 34). The sack of Wexford had the same effect, but it was not a controlled use of terror. He lost control of his troops after there was an unexpected opportunity to get into the town via the citadel. See O Siochru, *God's Executioner*, pp. 97–8.
33 From Cromwell's letter to the Speaker of the House of Commons after the sack of Drogheda (Morrill (ed.), *Letters, Writings and Speeches*, document 1649 09 17); and cf. his comment in his separate letter, perhaps to John Bradshaw, the previous day: 'The Enemy were filled upon this with much Terror, and truely I believe this bitter-ness will save much effusion of Blood, through the Goodness of God' (ibid., document 1649 09 16).
34 Ibid., document 1650 05 18a.

35 Ibid., document 1649 10 19.
36 J. Ryan, *Clonmacnoise: a historical summary* (Dublin, 1976).
37 See note 14.
38 See note 2.
39 See notes 10–11.
40 *Certain Acts and Declarations made by the Ecclesiasticall Congregation*, pp. 4–5.
41 Morrill (ed.), *Letters, Speeches and Writings*, document 1650 01 16a, from the copy of Cromwell's letter published in *Severall Proceedings in Parliament. From Friday the 25 day of January, to Thursday the 31 day of January 1649*. Number 18.
42 The House of Commons received three letters, including the letter of 16 January, on 29 January and immediately after 'Ordered, That it be specially referred to the Council of State, to consider of the several Letters from the Lord Lieutenant of Ireland, and of the Particulars therein; and what Supply of Ships are fit to be sent thither for the better Carrying on of the Service; and to give present Order for the same. Ordered, That it be also referred to the Council of State, to consider likewise of the Proposition in the Letter, concerning the Supplies of Victuals, Stores, Tackle, and other Necessaries for Ships, that are there to be made in those Harbours; and what Ships are fit to be so furnished there; and how the same may be best done for the Advantage of the State, and promoting the Service; and to report their Opinions therein to the House' (*CJ*, vi. 352).
43 Morrill (ed.), *Letters, Speeches and Writings*, document 1650 08 03a.
44 Ibid.
45 This is of course disingenuous: the Irish Acts of 1560 certainly prohibited all worship other than that of the Irish Book of Common Prayer, but only spasmodic attempts had been made to prevent 'illegal' Masses.
46 H. Jones, *A remonstrance of divers remarkeable passages concerning the church and kingdome of Ireland, recommended by letters from the Right Honourable the Lords Justices, and Counsell of Ireland* (1642) (ESTC: R202636).
47 J. Temple, *The Irish Rebellion: or, An history of the beginnings and first progress of the general rebellion raised within the kingdom of Ireland, upon the three and twentieth day of October, in the year 1641. Together with the barbarous cruelties and bloody massacres which ensued thereupon* (1646) (ESTC: R203774).
48 Clarke, 'The "1641 Massacres"', pp. 37–51.
49 This is not agreed by all historians, but see my position argued at length in J. Morrill, 'The Drogheda Massacre in Cromwellian Context', in D. Edwards, P. Lenihan and C. Tait (eds), *Age of Atrocity: violence and political conflict in Early Modern Ireland* (Dublin, 2007), pp. 242–65.
50 S.R. Gardiner (ed.), *Constitutional Documents of the Puritan Revolution 1625–1660* (3rd edn, Oxford 1906), document 94; for Cromwell's opposition to the severity of this Act, see J. Morrill, 'Cromwell, Parliament, Ireland and a Commonwealth in Crisis: 1652 revisited', *Parliamentary History* 30 (2011), pp. 193–214.
51 Gardiner, *Constitutional Documents*, introduction and articles 1, 4–8.
52 This can most easily be traced through the narrative account in Gardiner, *Commonwealth and Protectorate*, i. chapters 5–6.
53 For Cromwell's actions to prevent any looting or 'depredations' by his men, see

Wheeler, *Cromwell in Ireland*, pp. 81–3 and for an example of his hanging of his own men when they broke his proclamation, see ibid., p. 92. And for remarkable evidence of the toughness of the courts martial he set up in the public severe punishment of English troops (although the records are for the period after his departure), see H. Maclean, I. Gentles and M. Ó Siochrú (eds), 'Minutes of courts martial held in Dublin in the years 1651–3', *Archivium Hibernicum* 64 (2011) pp. 56–164.

54 See note 33.

55 For Tories and Woodkerne, see E. Ó Ciardha, 'Tories and moss-troopers in Scotland and Ireland in the Interregnum: a political dimension', in J.R.Young (ed.), *Celtic Dimensions of the British Civil Wars* (Edinburgh, 1997), pp. 141–63; for their impact in frustrating the English army and administration in Ireland, see Ó Siochrú, *God's Executioner*, pp. 193–9, 210–13, 228–36.

56 Morrill, 'Cromwell, Parliament, Ireland and a Commonwealth in Crisis', pp. 199–200.

Index

Abbot, George, archbishop of Canterbury 151
adventurers for Irish land 1, 43–4, 47, 50, 54, 56, 80–2, 84, 86–7, 89, 90, 91, 204
   Adventurers' Act 13, 44, 47, 56, 110, 133
   Committee for, at Grocers' Hall 44, 50, 80–3, 86–7, 88–91, 95n.11
   protest against John Davies 91–2
   see also Sea Adventure
Alexander, Jerome 82, 83
Andrewes, Thomas 80
Annesley, Arthur 86
Annesley, Francis, Lord Mountnorris 51
Antrim, town 160
Ardfert, bishop of see Fuller, Thomas
Arglass, earl of see Cromwell, Thomas
Armstrong, Thomas 123, 128, 131
Ashe, Henry 126
Ashe, Richard 126
Ashe, Thomas 122, 124, 126, 128
Ashley, Captain 49–50, 53
Athleague, co. Galway 68, 69
Athlone, co. Westmeath 63
Avery, Samuel 89

Badnedge, Thomas 86
Baillie, Robert, minister 155–6
Baillie, William, bishop of Clonfert 117n.43, 140, 150
Ball, Robert 126
Ball, William 122, 126, 127
Ballyeen Castle, co. Waterford 32, 35
Ballyshannon, co. Donegal 87

Baltimore, co. Cork 53
Bandon, co. Cork 22, 23, 45, 51, 52
Barbary Company 46, 48
Barnwall, Nicholas 134
Barnwall, Patrick 125
Barnwall, Peter 122, 125
Barrington, Francis 123, 128
Barry, David, earl of Barrymore 31, 34, 37
Barry family 24
Barry, John, colonel 2
Barry, Richard 126
Barrymore, earl of see Barry, David
Bateman, Serjeant 30
Batten, Richard 124, 128
Beale, William, colonel 86
Bedell, Ambrose 177
Bedell, William, bishop of Kilmore 177
Beecher, Henry 45
Beecher, Phane junior 45, 51
Beecher, Phane senior 45
Belfast, co. Antrim 79, 87, 160, 163, 166
Bellagare Castle, co. Galway 69
Bellings, Richard 119, 182
Benburb, co, Tyrone, battle of (1646) 147, 165
Beresford, Michael 96n.42
Bernard, Nicholas, dean of Ardagh 141, 151
Bettesworth, Thomas 85
Blake, Richard 9
Bolton, Sir Richard, lord chancellor 107
Bond, Dennis 83
Borlase, Sir John, lord justice 105, 114, 126, 132, 134, 174

Bourke, Miles, Viscount Mayo 11
Bourke, Richard, minister 172–3, 175, 182
Bourke, Richard, 4th earl of Clanricarde 66
Bourke, Thomas, printer 183
Bourke, Thomas, Viscount Clanmorris 180
Bourke, Ulick, 5th earl and 1st marquess of Clanricarde 61–74, 129, 162, 165
   Catholicism 62, 65, 180
   Confederates and 66–73
   Galway 49–50, 53–6, 64, 180
   historical assessment 2, 3, 4, 6, 61, 70–1, 72–3
   honour and reputation 61, 63, 64–6, 67–9, 70–4
   Ormond and 64–5, 67, 68, 70–1, 72–3, 164
   Parliament 106–7
   presidency of Connacht 7, 8, 63–5, 74
Boyle, Francis 23, 46
Boyle, Hannah 45
Boyle, Lewis, Viscount Kinalmeaky 23, 26, 34, 37, 52
Boyle, Richard, earl of Cork 4, 8, 20–37, 86
   Catholic Church, attitude towards 25–6
   financial position 28–9
   Irish Adventure and 43–4, 45–6, 48, 49, 51, 53, 55
   Irish employed by 23–4, 27–8, 36, 40n.53
   relations with Sir William St Leger 24–6, 34
   tenant army of 21–3, 27, 30–2
Boyle, Sir Richard, Viscount Dungarvan 23, 26, 27, 30, 32, 33, 34
Boyle, Robert 23
Boyle, Roger, Lord Broghill 2, 23, 26, 28, 29, 30, 33, 34, 85, 86, 88, 93, 96n.42, 117n.35
Bramhall, John, bishop of Derry 112, 139
Brereton, Roger 127
Brice, Worsley 124, 125
Briskett, Anthony 46
Broadrip, Captain 30
Broghill, Lord see Boyle, Roger
Brooke, Lord see Greville, Robert
Browne, Geoffrey 119
Browne, John 82
Bulkeley, Lancelot, archbishop of Dublin 117n.43, 143, 145, 149
Bunce, James, alderman 82, 89
Burke, John 11
Burke, Richard, captain 68
Burrows, Alexander 122, 124, 128
Burrows, Erasmus 30, 123, 124, 126, 127, 128, 130
Butler, Sir Francis 121, 125
Butler, James, marquess of Ormond, lord lieutenant
   authority as lord lieutenant 6–10, 14, 84, 155–7, 158, 159–61, 164–6, 194–5, 198–9
   church appointments 5, 138, 140–7, 149–50
   Clanricarde and 64–5, 67, 68, 70–1, 72–3, 164–5
   Confederate Catholics, negotiations 5, 7, 9, 62, 69, 71, 130, 144–9
   English Parliament 2, 5, 9, 71, 84–5, 89
   historical assessment 2–3, 5, 6, 14–15, 151
   Irish Parliament 4, 105, 113–14, 125, 128–31, 132
   Montgomery of the Ards and 155, 159, 161–3, 164–6, 167n.15
   Ulster Scots 3, 7, 9, 13, 141–2, 146–8, 150, 157, 159–60, 161–2, 165–6
Butler, Richard, Viscount Mountgarrett 28, 120
Butler, Richard of Kilcash, lieutenant general 28
Bysse, John 120, 126–7
Bysse, Robert 120, 124, 126–7

Cadogan, William 122
Canterbury, archbishop see Abbot, George
Cappoquin, co. Waterford 28, 32, 33, 35
Carew, Roger 32
Carey, Henry, Viscount Falkland, lord deputy 125
Caribbean islands 45–6, 48, 51, 52, 56
Carlingford, co. Louth 161, 163
Carlisle, earl of see Hay, James
Carpenter, Joshua 123, 125, 128, 133
Carr, George 133
Carrickfergus, co. Antrim 48, 82, 87–8, 90, 161, 163–4, 166
Carrick-on-Suir, co. Tipperary 163
Carter, Thomas 30, 36
Cashel, co. Tipperary 25, 28
Casteel, Michael 82
Castle Forbes, co. Longford 48
Castlehaven, co. Cork 52
Castlehaven, earl of see Tuchet, James
Castletown, co. Cork 51
Castleyons, co. Cork 32, 33, 34, 35

INDEX   213

Cavan, earl of *see* Lambart, Charles
Cessation of Arms (1643) 21, 35, 61, 62, 67,
    69, 79, 85, 113–14, 128–9, 145
Chamberlain, Abraham 48
Chambre, Walter 122, 126, 128
Charlemont, co. Armagh 164
Charles I, King 6, 8, 11, 13, 43, 49, 70, 113,
    141, 147, 157, 181, 186
  appointments by 63–5
  authority of 6–15, 47, 53
  church policy of 138–9, 140–1, 143–5
  loyalty to 61, 73–4, 130
  see also royalism
Charles II, King 9, 106, 155–6, 157–9, 161,
    162, 163–5, 166, 198, 201
Cheston, John 89
Chichester, Sir Arthur 45
Chichester, Arthur, colonel 79
Chichester, Arthur, Viscount Chichester
    158
Church, Catholic
  authority of 6, 11–12, 15, 198–200
  bishops 6, 11, 139, 164, 198–200
  clergy 25–6, 142, 172, 184, 195, 199, 205
  religious war 173, 179, 183
  synods 12, 193, 198–9, 201, 205
  violence and 172–3, 180
  see also Rinuccini; Scarampi
Church of England 138–9
Church of Ireland 6, 138
  appointment of bishops 5, 7, 138–47, 149
  bishops in House of Lords 108, 114
  Book of Common Prayer 148, 150,
    209n.45
  Catholics and 140, 144–5, 172–4
  Covenant and 141–2, 143–4
  factions 138–9, 143–4, 147, 149, 151
  Ulster and (1649) 158–60
  see also Ussher, James
Church, Presbyterian 161
  declarations 159, 161, 165
  ministers 5, 12, 155, 158, 162
  Scottish Kirk 161, 163, 165, 201–2
  Ulster Presbytery 156, 157, 158–9, 161, 162,
    165–6, 167n.15, 171n.87
  see also Covenant; Ulster Scots
Clanbrassil, earl of *see* Hamilton, James
Clanmorris, Viscount *see* Bourke, Thomas
Clanricarde, marquess of *see* Bourke, Ulick
Clarke, Robert 49
Clarke, Thomas 123
Clement, Gregory 48

Clobery, Oliver 93
Clogher, bishop of *see* Jones, Henry;
    MacMahon, Heber
Clonakilty, co. Cork 51, 52
Clonfert, bishop of *see* Baillie, William
Clongowes Wood, co. Kildare 177
Clonmacnoise, King's County 12, 193,
    198–9, 201
Clonmel, co. Tipperary 26, 164, 197–8,
    208n.27
Clonoulty, co. Tipperary 25
Clotworthy, Sir John 3, 4, 79–93, 127
  English Parliament and 79–80, 83, 84,
    85–7, 90, 93
  Scots, opposition to 79–80
  war in Ulster 80, 82, 87, 90–1, 92
Cloyne, bishop of *see* Synge, George
Cole, Sir William 12, 86, 96n.42
Coleraine, co. Londonderry 160, 163, 166
Colley, William 123, 128
Collins, William 82
Condon, Maurice 23
Confederation of Kilkenny 160, 196, 199
  constitutional status 10–11, 174–6, 183–4
  ethnicity and 175–6, 183, 188n.28
  factions 69–70, 147, 180, 184–5
  General Assembly 9, 10, 105–6, 120, 133,
    174–5, 178, 179, 181
  Glamorgan negotiations (1645) 146
  military campaigns 21, 32, 34, 36, 66, 68,
    70–1, 145
  oath of association 10, 11, 173, 175,
    179–82, 198
  print 5, 183–5
  Supreme Council 10, 11, 14, 175, 178, 183,
    185
  see also Cessation of Arms (1943);
    peace treaties; popular politics;
Connelly, Owen 179
Conway, Edward, colonel 158, 160
Coote, Sir Charles, the elder 53, 54
Coote, Sir Charles, the younger 4, 8, 11, 68,
    71, 86, 88, 93, 96n.42, 96n.57, 142,
    158–60, 161, 163, 164, 165, 168n.23,
    195
Coote, Chidley 86
Coote, Thomas 123, 128
Corbet, Miles 85
Cork, 1st earl of *see* Boyle, Richard
Cork, city 8, 13, 26, 28, 34, 35, 45, 194–5,
    207n.8
Cossens, Edmund 126

Cottington, Francis, Lord Cottington 61, 66
Council of State, English 195-5
Covenant, Solemn League and 12-13, 15, 79, 86, 114, 133, 141-2, 148-9, 157-9, 160-1, 165, 201
Crawford, Lawrence 122, 124, 126, 130, 133
Crisp, Sir Nicholas 48
Croker, Hugh 22, 26, 28, 30
Croker family 23
Cromwell, Oliver, lord lieutenant 14-15, 50
  Catholics and 6, 11, 12, 193, 198, 201-3, 205
  Declaration (1650) 193-5, 198, 201-6, 206n.6
  military campaigns 3, 10, 163, 195-7
  Scots and 12, 13, 160, 201-2
  terms of surrender 196-7, 204, 208n.27
Cromwell, Thomas, earl of Ardglass 162
Crufty, co. Meath 179
Cunningham, Thomas 51
Cusack, Robert 123, 127
Cusack, Walter 112

Darcy, Patrick 68, 69, 113, 119
Davies, John 6, 87-9, 92-4, 96n.42, 96n.57, 97n.59
  Clotworthy and 87, 89, 90
  supply of goods 4, 82, 85, 87, 88-92, 93-4, 97n.67
Davies, Sir Paul 89
Derry, bishop of *see* Bramhall, John
Derry, city 88, 98n.93, 158-9, 160, 162, 165, 166, 195
Desmond, earl of *see* Fitzgerald, Gearóid Iarla
Devereux, Robert, earl of Essex 46, 50, 61, 69, 79
Digby, George, Lord Digby 64, 65, 72, 141, 143, 145, 148, 202
Dillon, James, 3rd earl of Roscommon 106, 121
Dillon, Sir Lucas 67
Dillon, Robert, 2nd earl of Roscommon 121
Dillon, Thomas, Viscount Dillon of Costello-Gallen 8, 63-4, 69, 120
Dixon, Robert 123, 126, 133, 134
Dobbins, William, commissary 82, 83, 86
Donelaine, Mleaghlin 68
Donnellan, James, justice 64, 65, 66
Down and Connor, bishop of *see* Leslie, Henry

Downing, Robert 29, 30
Drimoleague, co. Cork 51, 52
Drogheda, co. Louth 124, 163, 165, 200, 203, 208n.32
Drogheda, earl of *see* Moore, Henry
Dromana, co. Waterford 32, 35
Dromore, co. Down 163
Dublin 88, 178
  archbishop of *see* Bulkeley, Lancelot
  cathedrals and churches 139, 140, 143, 149
  inhabitants 107, 112, 177
  printing in 194, 207n.8
  St Anne's Guild 120, 123, 126, 127, 133
  surrender of (1647) 89, 149-50
  Trinity College 2, 7, 126, 139
Dublin Articles (1647) 150
Duggan, Michael Ignatius, bookseller 102
Duhallow, co. Cork 182
Duncannon Fort, co. Wexford 53, 86, 163
Dundalk, co. Louth 79, 159, 160, 161, 163
Dundrum, co. Down 161
Dungarvan, co. Waterford 28, 29, 32, 33, 34
Dunsany, Lord *see* Plunkett, Patrick
Dyke, John 51

East India Company 48
Edgeworth, Francis 123
Eglish, King's County 179
Elphin, bishop of *see* Tilson, Henry
Elphin, co. Roscommon 145
Enniskillen, co. Fermanagh 158, 160, 163, 164, 172
Enos, Walter 181, 183
Erle, Thomas 82
Erle, Sir Walter 79
Essex, earl of *see* Devereux, Robert
Eustace, Sir Maurice 89, 120, 127, 131
Eustace, Thomas 123, 131

Fairfax, Sir Thomas, lord general 92
Fennell, Edmund 32, 36
Fenton, Sir William 27
Fermanagh, depositions in 172-3, 178, 187n.2
Fermoy, co. Cork 23, 27
Ferns, bishop of *see* French, Nicholas
Ffoulk, Francis 30
Fiennes, William, Viscount Saye and Sele 43, 50
Finch, James 27, 28
Finglas, co. Dublin 160
Fitzgerald family 24

Fitzgerald, Garret 30
Fitzgerald, Gearóid Iarla, earl of Desmond 182
Fitzgerald, George, earl of Kildare 117n.43
Fitzgerald, Gerald 178
Fitzgerald, John 125, 134
Fitzgerald, Richard 88, 130
Fitzwilliam, Thomas, Viscount Merrion 106, 107, 117n.43
Flower, William 122, 126, 128, 131
Foot, Thomas 89
Forbes, Alexander, Lord Forbes 13, 47–8, 52, 53–4, 55
Ford, Mathew 123, 127, 134
Ford, Nicholas 127
Forster, Charles 122, 126, 130, 133
Fossan, Thomas 82
Foster, Daniel 123
French, Nicholas, bishop of Ferns 185
Fuller or Fulwar, Thomas, bishop of Ardfert 143, 146

Galbraith, Humphrey, archdeacon of Clogher 144, 146, 158, 159, 160, 168n.22
Galway, city 13, 49–50, 52, 53–5, 64, 67, 69, 180, 197
    St Augustine's Fort 49, 53, 62
Gauden, Denis 89
'gentlemen of Ireland' 4, 81, 85–7, 89, 93
Gethin, Richard 89
Gilbert, Henry 123, 128
Glamorgan, earl of see Somerset, Edward
Golborne, William, bishop of Kildare 117n.43, 139, 140, 146, 149, 150
Golden, co. Tipperary 25
Gonne, George 177
Goodwyn, Benjamin 82
Goodwyn, John 80, 82, 91
Goodwyn, Robert 90
Gookin, Daniel 45
Gookin, Sir Vincent 51
Gormanston, Viscount see Preston, Nicholas
Gough, John 24
Grace, James 123, 125, 131, 133
Graham, George 122, 126
Graham, James, earl of Montrose 201
Greville, Robert, Lord Brooke 43, 50
Griffin, Edward, printer 194
Guinea Company 48
Gustavus Adolphus, king of Sweden 47

Hale, William 82
Hamilton, Sir Francis 84, 86
Hamilton, James, earl of Clanbrassil 162, 164
Harding, Walter 122, 126, 128, 130
Hardwick, Ralph 82, 83
Harford, Christmas 22, 23
Harrison, John 123, 130
Hatch, John 122, 124, 128
Hawkins, William 50, 80, 89
Hay, James, earl of Carlisle 45
Henrietta Maria, Queen 179
Herbert, Philip, earl of Pembroke 50
Hertford, marchioness of see Seymour, Frances
Hetherington, William 112
Hill, Arthur, colonel 85
Hilton, William, baron of exchequer 141
Holland, earl of see Rich, Henry
Holles, Denzil 85, 90
Hope, Alexander 125
Hoyte, John 123
Huetson, Christopher 122, 126, 133
Hull, Sir William 51–2
Hunt, Raphael 121, 123, 124, 128

Ibbitson, Robert, printer 194
Inchiquin, co. Cork 22
Inchiquin, Lord see O'Brien, Murrough
Ingram, Sir Arthur 51
Ireton, Henry, lord deputy 206n.6
Irish language 173
    bilingualism 5, 176–9, 181

Jennings, William 82, 83
Jephson, William, colonel 82, 84, 86, 90
Jerome, Stephen, minister 139, 140
Johnson, Thomas 113, 132
Joliffe, Richard 22, 27, 28, 30, 32
Jones, Arthur, Viscount Ranelagh 63, 69
Jones, Bryan 126
Jones, Henry, bishop of Clogher 5, 141, 143–4, 145–6, 149, 150–1, 203
Jones, Henry, MP 123, 130
Jones, Lewis, bishop of Killaloe 144, 149
Jones, Michael, colonel 14, 84, 123, 127, 134, 159, 162
Jones, Sir Theophilus 145

Kavanagh, Dermot 182
Keating, Edmund 122
Kelly, Mary 102

Kelly, Thomas 24, 35
Kelly, William 102
Kendrick, John 82, 89
Kennedy, Richard 106, 123, 126, 127, 128
Kennedy, Robert 123, 124, 125, 126
Kennedy, Sylvester 122, 127
Kenny, Henry 123, 130, 134
Kettleby, Thomas 52, 55
Kildare, bishop of *see* Golborne, William
Kildare, earl of *see* Fitzgerald, George
Kilkenny, city 9, 195, 208n.27
Killala, bishop of *see* Maxwell, John
Killaloe, bishops of *see* Jones, Lewis and Parry, Edward
Kilmore, bishop of *see* Bedell, William *and* Maxwell, Robert
King, Sir Robert 86
Kinsale, co. Cork 26, 28, 29, 35, 51-2, 55
Knockmoan Castle, co. Waterford 7, 32, 33
Kyrle, Sir John 86

'Laggan' army 3, 158, 160, 162
Lambart, Charles, earl of Cavan 101
Lambart or Lambert, Richard 123, 127, 130
Lambert, Laurence, provost marshal 113
Lane, George 123, 128, 130
Laughlin, James 122
Leicester, earl of *see* Sidney, Robert
Leigh, Charles 123
Leigh, Thomas 122
Lenthall, William, Speaker 14, 194-5
Leslie, Alexander, general 92
Leslie, Henry, bishop of Down and Connor 117n.43, 140
Leslie, John, bishop of Raphoe 158
Levant Company 48
Lewis, John 123, 128
Limerick, bishop of *see* Sibthorpe, Robert
Limerick City 7-8, 54, 55, 173, 197
Liscarroll, co. Cork, battle of (1642) 21, 34-5
Lisfinny Castle, co. Waterford 23, 33, 36
Lisle, Viscount *see* Sidney, Philip
Lismore, co. Waterford 22, 24, 25, 28, 32, 33, 34, 35, 36
Lisnagarvey (Lisburn), co. Antrim 79, 145, 159, 160, 163, 164
Lisnastrain, co. Antrim, battle of (1649) 155, 164, 166
Llewellyn, William 31
Lodge, John, deputy keeper of records 102, 121-2, 124

Loftus, Sir Adam 85, 88, 129, 134
Loftus, Sir Arthur 85, 96n.42, 124
Loftus, Dr Dudley 124, 127, 128
Loftus, Nicholas 126, 130
Loftus, Walter, lieutenant colonel 96n.42
Louth, county, election in 124
Lovell, Jacob 122
Lowther, Sir Gerald 89
Lucas, Sir Thomas 122, 125, 126, 128
Luttrell, Simon 123, 124

Mac Amhlaoibh, Maol Sheachlainn Óg 182
McAdam, John 85
MacCarthy family 24, 53
McDonnell, Alexander, colonel 160
McDonnell, Randall, earl and marquess of Antrim 1, 65-6, 72, 74, 81, 195
MacGill, Captain 86
McGrath, Terence 123, 124, 125, 133
MacMahon, Heber, bishop of Clogher 172-3
Magavelin, co. Donegal 144
Magrath, Mulmory 30
Maguire, Colonel 160
Maguire, Conor, baron of Enniskillen 178
Maguire, Rory 120
Mallett, Sir John 85
Manchester, earl of *see* Montagu, Edward
Mapother, Thomas 123, 131
Margetson, James, dean of Christ Church, Dublin 145
Martin, Anthony, bishop of Meath 146
Martin, Richard 68
Maryland colony 48
Massachusetts Bay Company 48, 49
Matthews, Edmund, lieutenant colonel 79
Maxwell, John, archbishop of Tuam 140, 141-3, 149
Maxwell, Robert, bishop of Kilmore 140
Mayerne, Patrick 182
Mayo, Viscount *see* Bourke, Miles
Meath, bishop of *see* Martin, Anthony 146
Meath, county, elections in 124, 126
Meredith, Sir Robert 85, 129, 134
Merrion, Viscount *see* Fitzwilliam, Thomas
Mervyn, Audley, colonel 124, 126, 131, 133, 158, 160
Milner, Tempest 89
Mitchelstown, co. Cork 27
Mocollop, co. Waterford 32, 33, 36
Mollineux, Adam 100
Molloy, Cosny 123, 133

Monck, George, colonel 158, 159, 160, 161
Monro, Sir George 5, 9, 160, 161, 162–3, 164, 165–6, 167n.31, 169n.42
Monro, Robert, major general 79, 195
Montagu, Edward, earl of Manchester 82
Montgomery, Hugh, Viscount Montgomery of the Ards 3, 155, 158–66
    military career 160–4, 165, 167n.15, 169n.42
    Presbyterians ministers and 5, 12, 155, 159, 161, 165–6, 171n.87
    royal authority and 159, 160, 161, 163, 166, 168n.31
Montgomery, Sir James 88, 143
Montrose, earl of *see* Graham, James
Moore, Francis 121, 122, 123, 124, 127, 128, 131
Moore, Gerard or Garrett 123, 124, 127, 128, 131
Moore, Henry, earl of Drogheda 100, 121
Moore, Roger 122
Morgan, Lieutenant 30
Mountmellick, Queen's County 177
Mountnorris, Lord *see* Annesley, Francis
Murry, Katherine 177

Naylor, Robert, dean of Limerick 33, 36
New Ross, co. Wexford 163, 198, 200, 202–3, 208n.27
Newcomen, John 123, 125
Newman, John 122, 127
Newry, co. Down 79, 161, 163
Newtownards, co. Down 162, 165
Nicholas, Sir Edward, secretary of state 146
Northumberland, earl of *see* Percy, Algernon
Nugent, James 139
Nugent, Richard, earl of Westmeath 106–7

O'Brien, Barnaby, 6th earl of Thomond 55
O'Brien, Donough, 4th earl of Thomond 66, 76n.40
O'Brien, Murrough, Lord Inchiquin 8, 9, 34, 86, 88, 90, 160, 161, 162
O'Connors of Sligo 11
O'Dowan, John 36
O'Driscoll family 53
O'Farnane, John 30
O'Flynn, Thomas 24
O'Hagherin, Morris Oge 23
O'Leighy family 37

O'Mahony, Conor 10, 183
O'Neill, Daniel 158
O'Neill, Hugh Dubh 208n.31
O'Neill, Owen Roe, general 1, 12, 71, 72, 147, 160–2, 163, 165, 195, 199
O'Neill, Sir Phelim 10, 120, 178
O'Norrowne, John 30, 32
O'Reilly, Philip 120
O'Rowerty, Teige 24
O'Shaughnessy, Lady 52
O'Shaughnessy, Sir Roger 52
Odire, Brian 177
Ormond, marquess of *see* Butler, James
Osborne, Sir Richard 7, 26, 30, 33
Ossory, bishop of *see* Williams, Griffith

Parliament, English 101, 109, 125, 157
    Committees
        Accounts 92, 93
        Both Kingdoms 80–1, 83–4, 85, 86, 87, 89, 90, 93
        Examinations 86
        Irish affairs 13, 47, 50, 80, 81–2, 84, 86, 90, 93
        Prisoners 85
        Scottish affairs 80, 82, 90
        Sequestrations 84
    constitutional relationship with Ireland 6, 8, 13–14, 46–7, 110, 132, 196, 204
    Cromwell and 50, 194–5, 209n.42
    factions 79–80, 90, 93
    interventions in Ireland 27, 34, 85–6, 90, 93–4, 148–50
    Protestant supporters in Ireland 62–3, 68, 71, 85–6, 114, 128, 157, 195
    see also adventurers for Irish land; 'gentlemen of Ireland'; Ulster British
Parliament, Irish 6, 100–37, 196
    constituencies 122–3
    dissolution of (1649) 4, 9, 103
    expulsions 120–1, 125, 128
    fees 117n.35
    Journals 101, 102, 107, 112, 121, 123
    legislation 102–3, 109–11, 113, 114–15, 119, 132
    location 111, 119
    membership and attendance 101, 103–8, 114, 120–1, 131–2
    oath of supremacy 105, 120
    peace treaties and 4, 7, 10, 114, 115, 129–30, 132–3

Parliament, Irish (*cont.*)
  petitions to 111–13
  political role 108, 113, 114–15, 128–31, 132–4
  Poynings' Law 101, 109, 110–11, 114, 120
  privilege 113, 122
  proxies 105
  recruiter MPs
    elections and returns 123–5, 131
    ethnicity 128–9
    identity of 4, 114, 121–3
    networks 125–7
    social status 127–8
Parry, Edward, bishop of Killaloe 143, 146, 149–50, 151
Parry, Robert, dean of Lismore 149
Parsons, John or James 85
Parsons, William, captain 84, 137n.45
Parsons, Sir William, lord justice 84, 85, 88, 105, 114, 129, 134, 174
Payne, Thomas 51
peace treaties
  first Ormond Peace (1646) 5, 7, 11–12, 15, 71–2, 114, 128–30, 141–2, 147, 178, 180–1, 183, 185–6, 196, 199
  second Ormond Peace (1649) 9, 10, 15, 114, 158, 159, 196, 198
  see also Cessation of Arms (1643)
Peisley, Francis 125, 128
Peisley, George 122, 125
Peisley, William 25–6, 123, 125, 128, 131
Pembroke, earl of *see* Herbert, Philip
Pennoyer, William 45, 48, 51, 52, 80, 82, 83
Percivalle or Percival, Sir Philip 30, 85, 86, 88, 96n.58
Percy, Algernon, earl of Northumberland 48
Peter, Benjamin 47, 58n.44
Peter, Hugh 43, 47, 49, 53, 54, 55
Petitt, Edward 125
Pilltown, co. Waterford 32
Pindar, Sir Paul 82
Plunkett, Patrick, Lord Dunsany 112
Plunkett, Walter 123, 127, 128
popular politics 5, 10–11, 134, 173–85, 199
  elite reactions 174–5, 183–4
  oaths 179–82
  prophecy 173, 182–3
Portland, earl of *see* Weston, Jerome
Portumna, co. Galway 62, 71
Povey, Thomas 45
Power family 24

Power, Roger of Ballygarran 30
Presidency system 8, 63–5, 86
Preston, Nicholas, Viscount Gormanston 120
Preston, Thomas, general 12, 68, 70, 71, 72, 73
Privy Council, Irish 7, 8, 9, 65, 71, 110, 132, 146
Providence Island Company 43, 46, 51
Prynne, William 93
Pym, John 43, 46, 50, 83
Pyne, Charles 30

Radcliffe, Sir George 141
Rainsborough, Thomas 48, 55
Rainsborough, William 48
Rainsborough family 46
Raleigh, Sir Walter 22, 24
Ranelagh, Viscount *see* Jones, Arthur
Raphoe, bishop of *see* Leslie, John
Rathmines, co. Dublin, battle of (1649) 162
Rawdon, George, major 158, 160
Rawson, Gilbert 123, 128
Reade, John, colonel 80
Reynolds, Robert 80, 82, 84, 85, 86, 90, 91
Rice, Sir Stephen, chief baron of exchequer 102
Rich, Henry, earl of Holland 50
Rich, Robert, earl of Warwick, 43, 46, 47, 49, 50, 51, 55, 56
Ridgeway, MacWilliam, captain 84
Rinuccini, Giovanni Battista, Archbishop of Fermo 2, 11–12, 70, 72, 181, 196
Roberts, Dr William, Ulster king of arms 7–8, 117n.35, 178
Roche, Maurice 36
Rodbard, Thomas 89
Roscommon, earl of *see* Dillon, James and Dillon, Robert
Roscommon, town 145, 160
Rossington, Henry 30
Rostrevor, co. Down 161
royalism
  in Connacht 63–5, 68, 70, 71, 73–4
  in Ulster 155–6
  see also Bourke, Ulick; Butler, James
Rupert of the Rhine, Prince 160, 165
Rushworth, John, secretary 194
Russell, Edward 22, 30
Ryan or O'Mulryan, Philip 25
Ryan, William of Sologhed 25
Ryves, Charles 123, 128

Ryves, James 30
Ryves, Sir William 107, 177

Sacheverell, William 123, 131
St Leger, lieutenant colonel 91
St Leger, Sir William 4, 8, 21, 24–6, 27–9, 34, 36, 86
Sandes, William, clerk of Commons 123
Saye and Sele, Viscount *see* Fiennes, William
Scarampi, Pietro Francesco, papal agent 11
Schout, Theodore 122, 127
Sea Adventure 13, 43–56, 91
  co. Cork 51–3
  co. Galway 53–5
  mercantile networks 4, 45, 48–9
  religious motives 47–8
Seymour, Frances, marchioness of Hertford 65, 73
Seymour, Henry 163–4
Sherlock, Christopher 122
Sherlock, John 36
Sherlock, Sir John 122
ships 58n.44
  Blessing of London 49
  Charity 48
  Elizabeth of London 48
  Employment 49, 50
  Hopewell of London 91
  Ruth 49, 50
  Swallow 26
Sibbald, Dr James 141–3, 153n.33
Sibthorpe, Robert, bishop of Limerick 117n.43, 140
Sidney, Philip, Viscount Lisle, lord lieutenant 2, 13–14, 84, 93, 122, 124, 125–6, 127, 128, 130
Sidney, Sir Philip 126
Sidney, Robert, earl of Leicester, lord lieutenant 49, 125
Singland, co. Limerick 182
Slany, Humphrey 48
Sligo, town 70, 160
Smith, Francis 83
Smith, John of Ballinascarty, co. Cork 23
Smith, Sir Percy 30, 86
Smith, Robert 30
Soames, Sir Thomas 91
Somerset, Edward, earl of Glamorgan 8, 146, 153n.53, 202
Speene, Francis 96n.42
Stewart, Sir Alexander 158, 162

Stewart, Sir Robert 131, 158, 160, 162–3, 168n.31, 169n.42
Stewart, Sir William 85, 158
Stoughton, John 123, 130
Stradling, Sir Henry 49
Strafford, earl of *see* Wentworth, Sir Thomas
Strangford, co. Down 87
Strode, William 83
Strongman, John 22
Synge, George, bishop of Cloyne 144, 146, 149

Taaff, Lucas 198, 202–3
Taaffe, Francis 160
Taaffe, Theobald, Viscount Taaffe 63, 65, 69, 144–5
Tallant, Patrick 123, 124–5, 133
Tallow, co. Waterford 22, 29, 35
Temple, Sir John, master of the rolls 85, 122, 124–9, 132, 134, 203
Temple, William 126
Thomond, earl of *see* O'Brien, Barnaby *and* O'Brien, Donough
Thompson, Edward 46
Thompson, George 46, 48, 59n.79, 80
Thompson, Maurice 43, 45, 46, 47–9, 50–1, 55, 80–2, 83, 91
Thompson, William 48, 58n.44
Thornbury, Isaac 28
Thurles, co. Tipperary 177
Tichbourne, Sir Henry 124
Tilson, Henry, bishop of Elphin 117n.43, 144–5
Timoleague, co. Cork 52
Tories 205
Townley, Charles 158
Towse, John 80
Trafford, Thomas 123, 131
Trail, James 86
Travers or Trevor, Joseph, minister 139, 140
Trevor, Arthur 8
Trevor, Edward 123, 124, 128
Trevor, Marcus 124, 158, 161, 163, 164
Trevor, Sir Thomas 82, 88
Trim, co. Meath 163
Troughton, John 82
Tuam, archbishop of *see* Maxwell, John
Tuchet, James, earl of Castlehaven 7, 52, 68, 178
Tucker, William 45, 80

Tuite, Edward, sheriff of Meath 123
Tully Castle, co. Fermanagh 172
Turner, Richard 89
Tynt, Sir Robert 22, 29, 30, 41n.68
Tynt, Robert junior 23
Tynt, William 30
Tyrell, Henry 30
Tyrrell, Sir Thomas 141

Ulster British
  royalism 142–4, 145, 147, 150, 158–60, 162–4, 196
  supplies to 79–81, 82, 83–4, 86, 87, 90, 92
Ulster Scots 3, 7, 8, 12–13, 51, 54, 82, 90, 146–8, 150, 155–66, 195–6
  Connacht, threat to 68–9, 71
  see also Church, Presbyterian; Covenant
Usher, Robert 126, 131
Ussher, James, archbishop of Armagh 5, 138–47, 150–1
  patronage of 139–41, 150
  relationship with Ormond 140–1, 142, 150–1, 154n.78

Vallett, Thomas 45
Vane, Sir Henry 80
Vassall, Samuel 48, 49, 80, 91
Veele, Sir John 122, 125, 128, 134
Venables, Robert, colonel 163, 164
Virginia colony 45, 46, 48, 51, 57n.19

Wakefield, Thomas 123, 128
Waller, Sir Hardress 86, 130
Waller, Sir William 79
Walley, John 28, 29, 32, 35
Wallis, Ralph 122, 124, 128, 131
Walsh, Oliver 106, 123, 125, 131
Wandesford, Sir Christopher, lord deputy 51

Ward, Robert 158, 161
Warner, John 80
Warner, Sir Thomas 45
Warren, Henry 122, 124
Warwick, earl of *see* Rich, Robert
Waterford, city 26, 33, 163, 183, 185, 196
Watkins, Sir David 80, 82
Weldon, Christopher 112
Wentworth, Sir George 120, 121, 125, 133
Wentworth, Sir Thomas, earl of Strafford, lord lieutenant 4, 25, 51, 80, 100, 112, 121, 125, 126
Westmeath, county, elections in 123–4
Westmeath, earl of *see* Nugent, Richard
Weston, Jerome, earl of Portland 8
Wexford, town 51, 163, 165, 200, 203, 208n.32
Wheeler, Oliver 106, 123, 125, 130, 131
Whetcombe, Benjamin 49
White, James 122, 126
White, Nicholas 130
White, Walter 126
Whyte, Arthur 123, 125
Whyte, John 123
Whyte, Thomas 123
Whyte, William 122
Williams, Griffith, bishop of Ossory 153n.33
Williams, John, archbishop of York 139
Willoughby, Anthony 49, 50
Willoughby, William 48
Wilmot, Henry, Viscount Wilmot 8, 63
Wingfield, Richard 96n.42
Winsmore, John 177
Wollaston, Richard 89
Wood, John 48
Wybrants, Peter 123, 127, 130

Youghal, co. Cork 26, 28, 29, 32, 33, 34, 35, 88, 195

EU authorised representative for GPSR:
Easy Access System Europe, Mustamäe tee 50,
10621 Tallinn, Estonia
gpsr.requests@easproject.com

www.ingramcontent.com/pod-product-compliance
Lightning Source LLC
Chambersburg PA
CBHW051611230426
43668CB00013B/2067